INDIVIDUAL PSYCHOLOGICAL THERAPIES IN FORENSIC SETTINGS

From the 'nothing works' maxim of the 1970s to evidence-based interventions to challenge recidivism and promote pro-social behaviour, psychological therapy has played an important role in rehabilitation and risk reduction within forensic settings in recent years. And yet the typical group therapy model isn't always the appropriate path to take.

In this important new book, the aims and effectiveness of individual therapies within forensic settings, both old and new, are assessed and discussed. Including contributions from authors based in the UK, North America, Europe, Australia and New Zealand, a broad range of therapies are covered, including Cognitive Behavioural Therapy, Mentalisation Based Therapy, Schema Therapy, Acceptance and Commitment Therapy and Compassion Focused Therapy.

Each chapter provides:

- an assessment of the evidence base for effectiveness;
- the adaptations required in a forensic setting;
- whether the therapy is aimed at recidivism or psychological change;
- the client or patient characteristics it is aimed at;
- and a case study of the therapy in action.

The final section of the book looks at ethical issues, the relationship between individual and group-based treatment, therapist supervision and deciding which therapies and therapists to select.

This is essential reading for probation staff, psychologists, criminal justice and liaison workers and specialist treatment staff. It will also be a valuable resource for any student of forensic or clinical psychology.

Jason Davies is Professor of Forensic and Clinical Psychology at Swansea University, UK and a Consultant Forensic and Clinical Psychologist with ABMU Health Board in South Wales. He has worked in high, medium and low secure mental health settings, and is the author of *Supervision for Forensic Practitioners* (Routledge 2015).

Dr Claire Nagi is a Chartered Psychologist and Registered Forensic Psychologist with ABMU Health Board in South Wales, UK. She is Associate Clinical Tutor at the Department of Applied Psychology, Cardiff Metropolitan University, Wales, UK. She has worked in prison, forensic mental health and community NHS services.

INDIVIDUAL PSYCHOLOGICAL THERAPIES IN FORENSIC SETTINGS

Research and Practice

Edited by Jason Davies and Claire Nagi

LONDON AND NEW YORK

First published 2017
by Routledge
2 Park Square, Milton Park, Abingdon, Oxon OX14 4RN

and by Routledge
711 Third Avenue, New York, NY 10017

Routledge is an imprint of the Taylor & Francis Group, an informa business

© 2017 selection and editorial matter, Jason Davies and Claire Nagi; individual chapters, the contributors

The right of the editor to be identified as the author of the editorial material, and of the authors for their individual chapters, has been asserted in accordance with sections 77 and 78 of the Copyright, Designs and Patents Act 1988.

All rights reserved. No part of this book may be reprinted or reproduced or utilised in any form or by any electronic, mechanical, or other means, now known or hereafter invented, including photocopying and recording, or in any information storage or retrieval system, without permission in writing from the publishers.

Trademark notice: Product or corporate names may be trademarks or registered trademarks, and are used only for identification and explanation without intent to infringe.

British Library Cataloguing in Publication Data
A catalogue record for this book is available from the British Library

Library of Congress Cataloguing in Publication Data
A catalog record for this title has been requested.

ISBN: 978-1-138-95571-4 (hbk)
ISBN: 978-1-138-95572-1 (pbk)
ISBN: 978-1-315-66613-6 (ebk)

Typeset in Bembo
by Out of House Publishing

JD: For Susie, Bryn and Freya
CN: For my late parents, Norman and Miranda

CONTENTS

List of contributors ix

1 Introduction 1
  Claire Nagi and Jason Davies

PART I
Individual therapies 9

2 Acceptance and Commitment Therapy 11
  David Brillhart

3 Cognitive-Behavioural Therapy 28
  Andrew Day

4 Cognitive Analytic Therapy 41
  Karen Shannon and Philip Pollock

5 Exploring Compassion Focused Therapy in forensic settings:
  an evolutionary and social-contextual approach 59
  Paul Gilbert

6 Eye Movement Desensitisation and Reprocessing with
  sexual offenders 85
  Ronald J. Ricci and Cheryl A. Clayton

7	Mentalisation based treatment *Gill McGauley*	100
8	Personal construct psychotherapy *Adrian Needs and Lawrence Jones*	121
9	Psychodynamic psychotherapy *Nigel Beail*	142
10	Schema Therapy *Marije Keulen-de Vos and David P. Bernstein*	157
11	Sensorimotor psychotherapy *Naomi Murphy*	180

PART II
Key issues associated with individual therapies 195

12	Individual psychological therapy with associated groupwork *Claire Nagi and Jason Davies*	197
13	Ethical issues in the treatment of offenders *Tony Ward*	213
14	Supervising the therapists *Jason Davies and Claire Nagi*	228
15	Selecting therapies and therapists *Jason Davies and Claire Nagi*	243
16	Conclusions and future directions *Jason Davies and Claire Nagi*	257

Subject index *265*
Author index *272*

CONTRIBUTORS

Nigel Beail is Professor of Psychology at the Clinical Psychology Unit, Department of Psychology at the University of Sheffield, UK. In addition, he is Consultant Clinical Psychologist and Professional Lead for Psychological Services for South West Yorkshire Partnership NHS Foundation Trust. He has published extensively on practice-based research from his clinical work.

David P. Bernstein, PhD is Professor of Forensic Psychotherapy, an endowed chair sponsored by Maastricht University and Forensic Psychiatric Center de Rooyse Wissel. He received his doctoral degree in Clinical Psychology from New York University in 1990, and joined the faculty of Maastricht University in 2004. He has published extensively on personality disorders, psychological trauma and forensic psychology. He is an internationally known expert on Schema Therapy, an integrative therapy for personality disorders. He has served as Vice-President of the International Society for Schema Therapy, and President of the Association for Research in Personality Disorders.

David Brillhart, PsyD is a licensed psychologist specialising in Acceptance and Commitment Therapy (ACT) with high-risk and special needs violent offenders in correctional and forensic settings. He developed his *ACT Behind Bars* workshop based on his ACT forensic work and outcome measures of his 20-month pilot study using ACT with Sexually Violent Persons (SVP). He has also presented and facilitated workshops nationally and internationally for correctional and forensic-based clinicians using ACT. Working with this difficult population gives him the opportunity to help non-forensic clients navigate life's 'roadblocks' at his private practice, ACT II Psychology. For more information, visit http://actiipsychology.com

Cheryl A. Clayton is a Licensed Clinical Social Worker and a Virginia Certified Sex Offender Treatment Provider. She is the Director of Specialised Treatment Services of Virginia for Resources for Human Development, Inc. Her clinical expertise is in the areas of assessing and treating youths and adults who have committed sexual offences. She has specialised in the treatment of sexual offenders and their families since 1994. She is a Board Member of the Virginia Sex Offender Treatment Association. Her area of specialisation is the research and treatment of sex offenders, with a particular interest in trauma effects and EMDR which she has presented nationally.

Andrew Day is a Professor in the Australian Aboriginal and Torres Strait Islander Centre at James Cook University in Queensland, Australia. Before joining academia he was employed as a clinical psychologist in South Australia and the UK, having gained his Doctorate in Clinical Psychology from the University of Birmingham and his Masters in Applied Criminological Psychology from the University of London. He is widely published in many areas of forensic psychology, with a focus on the development of effective and evidence-based approaches to offender rehabilitation.

Paul Gilbert, FBPsS, PhD, OBE was Professor of Clinical Psychology (University of Derby) and Consultant Clinical Psychologist (Derbyshire Healthcare Foundation Trust) until his retirement in 2016. He has researched evolutionary approaches to psychopathology for more than 40 years with a special focus on mood, shame and self-criticism and their treatment – for which Compassion Focused Therapy was developed. He was made a Fellow of the British Psychological Society in 1993; was president of the British Association for Behavioural and Cognitive Psychotherapy in 2003; was a member of the UK Government's NICE guidelines for depression (2002–2004); and was awarded an OBE in 2011. He has written or edited 21 books and more than 200 papers. In 2006 he established the charity Compassionate Mind Foundation (www.compassionatemind.co.uk).

Lawrence Jones trained as a Forensic Psychologist after working with hard-to-place ex-offenders in the community. He worked in and eventually managed a prison-based therapeutic community. He then trained as a Clinical Psychologist at Rampton Hospital where he helped to set up personality disorder services and is now Head of Psychology. He teaches on the clinical psychology courses at Leicester and Sheffield, and the Nottingham and Lincoln forensic psychology courses. He is a former chair of the Division of Forensic Psychology and has published on therapeutic communities, engagement, offence paralleling behaviour, trauma and interventions with 'personality disordered' 'offenders'.

Marije Keulen-de Vos, PhD is a senior researcher at Forensic Psychiatric Center de Rooyse Wissel. She also manages the development and implementation of evidence-based care pathways for psychotic, intellectually disabled and personality disordered offenders. She received her doctorate degree in clinical psychology from the University of Maastricht, the Netherlands. She is an expert on Schema Therapy.

Recently, she has adapted Schema Therapy for offenders with an intellectual disability. Her research focuses on forensic treatment, intellectual disability and sex offenders.

Gill McGauley, MD was Professor of Forensic Psychotherapy and Medical Education, and Head of The Centre for Clinical Education at St George's University of London. She worked clinically in the NHS as a Consultant Psychiatrist in Forensic Psychotherapy using psychodynamic and psychological therapies to treat mentally disordered offenders. She was involved in developing and delivering forensic psychotherapy services to imprisoned women. Her research interests included the relevance of attachment theory to violent offenders and the application of Mentalisation Based Treatment to personality disordered offenders. She published widely in the fields of forensic psychotherapy, forensic mental health, attachment and personality disorder in offenders. Professor McGauley passed away in July 2016, shortly after her chapter was completed.

Dr Naomi Murphy has worked with forensic service users across forensic settings over a 20-year period. She is Clinical Director of the Fens Service for Offenders with Personality Disorder at HMP Whitemoor. The treatment programme offered reflects her understanding of the role that trauma and attachment failure play in the development and maintenance of personality disorder and offending behaviour. This dual interest led her to explore sensorimotor theory and the ways in which developmental somatic experience could be incorporated into treatment. She is co-editor of *Treating Personality Disorder: Creating Robust Services for People with Complex Mental Health Needs* (Routledge).

Dr Adrian Needs worked in HM Prison Service in the UK for 14 years. Work ranged from assessment and treatment of lifers and sex offenders to the management of individuals with personality disorders, from the facilitation of staff teams to the design and delivery of training for staff in specialised units. Non-routine activities included providing negotiation advice in hostage and firearms incidents and post-incident counselling to prison staff. He is currently course leader of the MSc Forensic Psychology course at the University of Portsmouth and earlier played a prominent role in steering the formulation of national standards for postgraduate training in forensic psychology.

Dr Philip Pollock is a Consultant Forensic Clinical Psychologist, Head of Adult Mental Health specialty for a Health and Social Care Trust in Northern Ireland and Clinical Director of FACET Forensic Psychology Services Ltd. He is a consultant and trainer, and provides expert witness and psychological services worldwide. He has published extensively in several areas including personality disorder, sexual offending, forensic psychotherapy and homicide offenders. He is author of *Cognitive Analytic Therapy for Adult Survivors of Childhood Abuse* (Wiley 2001), the editor of *Cognitive Analytic Therapy for Offenders* (Routledge 2006) and is completing a new book on paedophilic killers (Wiley).

Ronald J. Ricci, PhD, LMFT is a Virginia Certified Sex Offender Treatment Provider and Certified EMDR Consultant and Practitioner. He holds a Governor-appointed seat on the Pennsylvania Sex Offender Assessment Board. He served as Clinical Director for Sex Offender Services for Resources For Human Development, Inc. of Philadelphia, PA, and Clinical Director of Virginia SO Services for Specialised Treatment Services of Virginia. He provides clinical consultation for the adolescent Sexual Responsibility Program at Devereux's Kanner Center in West Chester, PA, and for Psychological and Forensic Services, PLLC of Fredericksburg, VA. His area of specialisation is the research and treatment of sex offenders, with a particular interest in trauma effects and EMDR which he has presented nationally and internationally.

Dr Karen Shannon is a Clinical Psychologist, ACAT practitioner, supervisor and trainer, and Trustee for ACAT. She has worked in high, medium and community NHS forensic services for more than 18 years. She has broad experience of the application of CAT in consultation, court, risk assessments and staff management in a variety of forensic, adult mental health and voluntary sector settings. She is director of Dr Karen Shannon Associates and has published in several areas concerning the practical application of CAT, including supervising those working with forensic clients; risk assessment and management; and as a framework for male aggression and violence.

Tony Ward, PhD is a Professor of Clinical Psychology at Victoria University of Wellington, New Zealand, and has previously taught clinical and forensic psychology at Canterbury, Melbourne and Deakin universities. He has more than 390 academic publications and his research interests are offender desistance and rehabilitation, forensic and correctional ethics, and theoretical issues in psychopathology. His books include *Desistance From Sex Offending: Alternatives to Throwing Away the Keys*, co-authored with Richard Laws (Guilford 2010), and *Evolutionary Criminology*, co-authored with Russil Durrant (Academic Press 2015).

About the editors

Jason Davies is Professor of Forensic and Clinical Psychology at Swansea University, UK and a Consultant Forensic and Clinical Psychologist with ABMU Health Board in South Wales. He has worked in high, medium and low secure mental health settings, inpatient and community rehabilitation and prison and probation services. He leads research and evaluation of the Offender Personality Disorder Pathway within Wales. He has published on topics such as service development, interventions, sadistic interest and staff supervision including a recent book *Supervision for Forensic Practitioners* (Routledge). He is also co-editor of *Research in Practice for Forensic Professionals* (Routledge) with Kerry Sheldon and Kevin Howells.

Dr Claire Nagi is a Forensic Psychologist who has worked in medium, low and community forensic services for over ten years. She received her doctorate degree in forensic psychology practice from the University of Birmingham, UK in 2007. She currently works in Low Secure Services with ABMU Health Board, South Wales and is a Clinical Tutor on the Forensic Psychology programmes at Cardiff Metropolitan University, UK. Her research focuses on forensic mental health and offender intervention, which she has presented nationally and internationally.

1
INTRODUCTION

Claire Nagi and Jason Davies

Individual psychological therapies have a long history, although their application within forensic contexts has been eclipsed by group intervention. Over the last three decades there have been numerous meta-analyses published on the efficacy of various Offender Behaviour Programmes which stand as testament to the value and impact that a groupwork format can bring when delivered according to the 'what works' principles. However, individually delivered treatments continue to be provided in some services and settings as the modality of choice, or where groupwork is unfeasible or contra-indicated, to complement or support group treatment or as an 'intervention of last resort'. This chapter will provide the context and rationale for focusing on individually delivered interventions within forensic settings. This chapter concludes with a brief précis of the sections of the book and the chapters contained within them.

Individual therapy in forensic settings

Psychological therapy has played an important role in rehabilitation and risk reduction within forensic settings. Over the last 40 years, the challenge of 'nothing works' widely attributed to Martinson (1974) has been replaced by evidence that some interventions (e.g. psychological, social and occupational) can promote prosocial thinking and behaviour, reduce risk and foster desistance from crime. An important cornerstone has been the recognition and promotion of the Risk Needs Responsivity principles first articulated by Bonta and Andrews (2017) and built upon by many practitioners and academics. Psychologically based interventions have shown themselves to be important in addressing risk factors, with a range of evidence supporting the delivery of such treatment (e.g. see McGuire, 2013, for a review). In large part, psychoeducational group treatment (Day, Kozar, & Davey,

2013) has dominated this arena. The reasons for group treatment being employed might include resource management, perceived cost effectiveness and the addition of a group process element to treatment (see Davies, in press). However, forensic services research that not everyone benefits from group-based interventions, has led some to begin to describe when individual interventions might be selected as the preferred modality (see Polaschek, 2011, 2013; O'Brien, Sullivan, & Daffern, 2016). Thus the task of describing, choosing, delivering and evidencing individual treatment is a timely one moving individually delivered interventions from a somewhat niche position of use only in highly specialist settings to a more mainstream position. Individually delivered treatments are increasingly being employed as the 'first line' approach when working with those with complex needs such as those with mental health needs and those with responsivity issues or idiosyncratic offending. This is in addition to their widespread use as a precursor to group-based intervention (e.g. engagement and preparatory work) and as a secondary 'pragmatic' option (e.g. when group treatment is not feasible such as when there are insufficient individuals to form a group). In recent years there has also been an expansion of intervention packages that use both individual and group-based therapy. Often each modality is used for specific purposes such as the group setting for imparting knowledge and rehearsing skills and individual components for personalisation, maintaining engagement and addressing responsivity issues. These combined modality approaches are discussed more fully in Chapter 12.

Psychological therapies have developed from a single treatment in the form of psychodynamic therapy to a wide range of treatments that vary in length and their underpinning theory. Theories of change and thus therapy have included various grouping and schools such as *Psychoanalytic/dynamic* (e.g. Freud, 1949; Jung, 1966); *Humanistic* (e.g. Maslow, 1943; Rogers, 1951); *Behavioural* (e.g. Watson, 1924; Pavlov, 1927; Skinner, 1953); *Cognitive* (e.g. Beck, 1976; Ellis, 1957); and 'third wave' therapies (e.g. Linehan, 1993; Segal, Williams, & Teasdale, 2002; Hayes, Strosahl, & Wilson, 1999). Each of these has introduced their own unique view on aspects such as the nature of personality, the causes and resolution of psychological difficulties, psychological strengths, emotions, relationships and motivation. Treatment efficacy and effectiveness for such individual therapies in non-forensic settings has been demonstrated through a large number of studies (e.g. Butler, Chapman, Forman, & Beck, 2006; Kahl, Winter, & Schweiger, 2012; Fonagy, 2015). For our purposes at this point, it is sufficient to note that many therapies have been shown to be better than nothing and that there is evidence of a significant effect for many of the treatments presented. For example, reviews of psychodynamic therapy have shown it to be effective for some difficulties but not others when compared to inactive control conditions (e.g. waiting list or treatment as usual) (Fonagy, 2015; Leichsenring & Leibing, 2007). Similarly, Cognitive Behavioural Therapy (CBT) has shown itself to be effective for some problems (e.g. Hofmann et al., 2012) with the evidence for third-wave therapies being mixed (e.g. Piet & Hougaard, 2011; van der Velden et al., 2015; Öst, 2008; Kahl et al., 2012).

These therapies have also had an impact on approaches to working with those who are in correctional or forensic services, for example through direct behaviour modification or in addressing cognitions believed to be associated with certain behaviour. Although there have been studies investigating the impact of individual psychological therapies in forensic settings, by way of comparison, this does not match the level and type of research conducted on this topic within the mental health field to date. Nonetheless, evidence of treatment efficacy within offender populations has been demonstrated (e.g. McGuire, 2013) warranting further exploration of the role of individual psychological therapies within forensic contexts. The chapters in Part I of this book provide a description which will provide the reader with some insight into the distinct features (and in many cases specialist language) associated with each of the interventions included. They also provide the opportunity to consider aspects common to more than one approach. The authors of each therapy chapter in this book present a summary of key evidence from non-forensic and forensic settings, allowing the reader to determine the type and scale of evidence for the intervention presented.

Definitions

For the purpose of this book, the use of terms such as client, individual, offender and patient have been left to the author(s) of each chapter and are intended as interchangeable (unless otherwise stated). However, we note that those within forensic settings often associate with the term prisoner or patient as this recognises their non-voluntary detention. In reference to the context, a forensic setting is defined as any forensic mental health setting (i.e. inpatient or community) and any correctional setting (i.e. prison or probation/parole). It is also important to note that the primary focus of this text is on psychological therapies for adults. Within this, authors have not specifically commented on issues of difference (e.g. gender, ethnicity or diagnostic group) unless there are significant adaptations made to the intervention for specific groups. The one exception is the chapter on psychodynamic therapy which focuses on working with individuals with Intellectual and Developmental Disability (IDD). As a result, this chapter highlights developmental considerations which readers can consider when examining the other approaches contained within this book. Finally, the 'individuals' presented as the case study in each chapter are highly anonymised or are fictitious amalgamations of several individuals that have been constructed to give a clear example of key aspects of the therapy in practice.

Scope and content

Although we have tried to provide a sample of widely used and emerging therapies that can be implemented, it is accepted that this is not an exhaustive, encyclopaedic review of all possible treatments that could be delivered. Although this book contains therapies across a spectrum of approaches, evidently the breadth of individual therapies delivered within forensic settings has meant that therapeutic approaches have been omitted. It is important to emphasise that this book *is not* an endorsement or recommendation of specific therapies – readers should also not infer anything from treatment approaches being included or absent from this book. Nevertheless, this book will provide the reader with a range of different therapies currently used to enable them to consider methods for selecting individual therapy approaches and/or therapists for particular needs or clients. This idea of treatment selection is discussed further in Chapter 15. This book will allow the reader to examine therapies (old and new) as described by those who practise them, providing details of the approach and the therapy evidence base. Many of the therapies included can be or are also delivered in group formats; however, within this book we focus on their application in a one-to-one format. Our desire is to bring together examples of practice from a range of settings, countries and approaches, in order to showcase ten treatments that can be provided individually and set the scene for reasserting the need to actively consider and examine the place for individual therapy in forensic settings. The chapters in this book are written by contributors, many of whom are active practitioner-researchers, with extensive experience from across the globe including the United Kingdom, Europe, America, Australia and New Zealand.

The book is divided into two parts. In the first, ten therapies are described with most of the chapters using a common framework, in which core information about the therapy, its use in forensic settings and the current state of the evidence base for the therapy is presented. In this section, each chapter will also outline the practicalities faced within practice, including therapy adaptations required for offender populations. In Part I, the chapters have been sequenced in alphabetical order. A brief outline of the chapters in Part I is provided next.

The most widely used basis for group-based interventions within correctional settings is the CBT approach. In Chapter 3, Andrew Day highlights the limited guidance available to therapists in relation to the specifics of CBT when used with forensic clients. He considers adaptations that are needed to implement the approach in the forensic setting and explores approaches to assessing the quality and integrity of treatment. As an extension of cognitive approaches, a third-wave therapy, namely Acceptance and Commitment Therapy (ACT), is described by David Brillhart in Chapter 2. ACT is an action-focused cognitive-behavioural/mindfulness therapy that fosters the development of acceptance of those things that cannot be changed while promoting purposeful living through six core processes. This chapter outlines the evidence base for ACT with offender populations and describes therapy adaptations required for ACT when addressing offender risk.

In Chapter 8, Kelly's Personal Construct Therapy (PCT; Kelly, 1955) is presented by Adrian Needs and Lawrence Jones. Despite a long history in forensic settings, the use of PCT has waxed and waned over the years. In this chapter, the authors examine the use of PCT in a prison setting along with the ways the approach lends itself to assessing individual change. In addition to its use as an approach in its own right, PCT has influenced (and has incorporated aspects into) many other therapy approaches. This includes Cognitive Analytic Therapy (CAT) which is presented by Karen Shannon and Philip Pollock in Chapter 4. This therapeutic model integrates aspects of PCT, cognitive therapy and psychoanalytic ideas. From its origins as a brief therapy for use in the UK National Health Service, the theory and application has been broadened to include complex cases such as those of personality disorder and offender populations. Through case examples, Chapter 4 describes use of CAT with 'hard to help' clients and as an explicit framework to inform staff/team/system care and risk management. In Chapter 6, another integrative therapy – Eye Movement Desensitisation and Reprocessing (EMDR) – is presented by Ronald Ricci and Cheryl Clayton. This approach has been widely used outside the forensic arena as a therapy for trauma and anxiety-based disorders (Shapiro, 1989). They describe the application of EMDR within forensic settings with specific attention to its role as part of a wider package of intervention and management. A final integrative approach, schema therapy, is presented by Marije Keulen-de Vos and David Bernstein in Chapter 10. Schema therapy was first described by Jeffrey Young in the 1990s (e.g. Young, 1990) and was originally developed for working with complex individuals. As a result it has been widely adopted in services for individuals with personality disorder and latterly in forensic settings. It has been subject to a number of research studies in forensic settings, some of which are presented by the authors.

The oldest form of psychotherapy – psychodynamic psychotherapy – is described by Nigel Beail in Chapter 9. This approach has been widely used within specialist forensic services for several decades. The chapter provides an introduction to a Kleinian-informed framework and uses a case example drawn from work in forensic IDD services in the community. In Chapter 7, Gill McGauley presents Mentalisation Based Therapy (MBT), which has its roots in psychoanalytic approaches. Originally developed as a treatment for borderline personality disorder, MBT has since been used more widely. The adaptations needed to the original MBT model, to broaden the applicability of the treatment for offender populations, is described in some detail, along with the outline of a UK feasibility study currently being conducted.

There are several emerging therapies being delivered in forensic settings, two of which are considered in this book. In Chapter 5, Paul Gilbert describes the underpinning theory of Compassion Focused Therapy (CFT), developed by himself and colleagues (e.g. Gilbert, 1992, 2000, 2005) for individuals experiencing shame and self-critical and attacking thoughts. The process of applying a compassion model to forensic settings is outlined which provides a challenge to some of the assumptions and 'custom and practice' evident in many forensic services. Delivering an intervention that 'goes beyond' the traditional realms of talking-based psychotherapy is detailed by Naomi Murphy in Chapter 10. Sensorimotor psychotherapy recognises that physical (body) responses might be important in addressing trauma and for reducing future risk. In considering the use of this novel approach in a high secure prison within the UK, this chapter prompts a fresh look at the ways in which treatments are provided and the assumptions about how change takes place. Together, Chapters 5 and 10 provide both an introduction to two therapies and an opportunity to examine current thinking about offending and some of the possible roots to offending.

Part II of this book considers a number of key issues relating to providing individual therapies in forensic settings from various perspectives. In Chapter 12 we examine the use of individual psychological therapy alongside group-based interventions – so-called combined modality approaches. The merits and disadvantages of each modality are discussed along with ways in which combined approaches can be provided. This chapter also highlights the need for high-quality outcome evaluation to determine for whom combined approaches might be most effective and resource efficient.

Ethical issues in the treatment of offenders (regardless of the treatment modality) are examined by Tony Ward in Chapter 13. By exploring clusters of ethical problems and dilemmas he considers how notions of moral and human rights can be employed to guide ethical practice. One avenue for examining ethical treatment is through the supervision provided to those therapists delivering interventions and influencing service design. It is generally agreed that providing competent treatment requires that the therapist is supervised, with many of the interventions described in Part I having guidelines or requirements for this. In Chapter 14 we consider the role and functions of supervision, and some of the competencies required for those undertaking this task.

Perhaps the most perplexing issues in delivering individual therapy are which one(s) to provide and who should deliver it. In Chapter 15 we consider approaches to selecting therapies and therapists and examine the apparent equivalence of many therapies. We consider approaches to therapist accreditation and examine the ideas of common factors. We argue that evaluation should be used routinely to help practitioners identify 'what works' in individual cases and outline some guiding principles for those providing individual therapies in forensic settings. The book concludes by drawing out some general themes that have emerged from the chapters, provides a summary of some of the main issues for individual therapies within forensic settings and describes the challenge of developing an evidence base for individual therapy that researchers and practitioners should combine forces to address.

Conclusion

This book is intended to provide the reader with the knowledge and understanding to make informed decisions regarding individual psychological treatment within their forensic practice. Our hope is that readers will at least consider the role that individual interventions may play, while also being mindful of the many important areas for consideration in order to successfully implement such an approach.

References

Beck, A. T. (1976). *Cognitive therapy and the emotional disorders.* New York: International Universities Press.

Butler, A. C., Chapman, J. E., Forman, E. M., & Beck, A. T. (2006). The empirical status of cognitive-behavioral therapy: A review of meta-analyses. *Clinical Psychology Review, 26*, 17–31.
Bonta, J., & Andrews, D. A. (2017). *The psychology of criminal conduct* (6th edn). New York: Routledge.
Davies, J. (in press). An examination of individual versus group treatment in correctional settings. In Devon Polaschek, Andrew Day and Clive Hollin (Eds), *Handbook of Psychology and Corrections*. Wiley.
Day, A., Kozar, C., & Davey, L. (2013). Treatment approaches and offending behaviour programs: Some critical issues. *Aggression and Violent Behavior, 18*, 630–635. doi:10.1016/j.avb.2013.07.019
Ellis, A. (1957). Rational psychotherapy and individual psychology. *Journal of Individual Psychology, 13*, 38–44.
Fonagy, P. (2015). The effectiveness of psychodynamic psychotherapies: An update. *World Psychiatry, 14*, 137–150.
Freud, S. (1949). *An outline of psychoanalysis*. New York: Norton.
Gilbert, P. (1992). *Depression: The evolution of powerlessness*. Hove: Erlbaum, and New York: Guilford.
Gilbert, P. (2000). Social mentalities: Internal 'social' conflicts and the role of inner warmth and compassion in cognitive therapy. In P. Gilbert & K. G. Bailey (Eds), *Genes on the couch: Explorations in evolutionary psychotherapy* (pp. 118–150). New York: Brunner-Routledge.
Gilbert. P. (2005). *Compassion: Conceptualisations, research and use in psychotherapy*. London: Routledge.
Hayes, S. C., Strosahl, K. D., & Wilson, K. G. (1999). *Acceptance and commitment therapy: An experiential approach to behaviour change*. New York: Guilford Press.
Hofmann, S. G., Asnaani, A., Vonk, I. J. J., Alice, T., Sawyer, A. T., & Fang, A. (2012). The efficacy of cognitive behavioral therapy: A review of meta-analyses. *Cognitive Therapy Research, 36*(5), 427–440. doi:10.1007/s10608-012-9476-1
Jung, C. G. (1966). *The practice of psychotherapy: Essays on the psychology of the transference and other subjects* (Collected Works Vol. 16). Princeton, NJ: Princeton University Press.
Kahl, K. G., Winter, L., & Schweiger, U. (2012). The third wave of cognitive behavioral therapies. *Current Opinion in Psychiatry, 25*(6), 522–528. doi: 10.1097/YCO.0b013e328358e531
Kelly, G. A. (1955). *The psychology of personal constructs*. New York: Norton.
Leichsenring, F., & Leibing, E. (2007). Psychodynamic psychotherapy: A systematic review of techniques, indications and empirical evidence. *Psychology & Psychotherapy: Theory, Research & Practice, 80*, 217–228.
Linehan, M. M. (1993). *Cognitive behavioral therapy of borderline personality disorder*. New York: Guilford Press.
McGuire, J. (2013). 'What works' to Reduce Re-offending: 18 Years On. In Craig, L. A., Dixon, L., and Gannon, T. A. (Eds), *What works in offender rehabilitation: an evidence-based approach to assessment and treatment*. Chichester: Wiley-Blackwell.
Martinson, R. (1974). What Works? – Questions and answers about prison reform. *The Public Interest, 35*, 22–54.
Maslow, A. H. (1943). A theory of human motivation. *Psychological Review, 50*, 370–396.
O'Brien, K., Sullivan, D., & Daffern, M. (2016). Integrating individual and group-based offence-focussed psychological treatments: Towards a model for best Practice. *Psychiatry, Psychology and Law*, 1–19. http://doi.org/10.1080/13218719.2016.1150143
Öst, L. G. (2008). Efficacy of the third wave of behavioral therapies: A systematic review and meta-analysis. *Behaviour Research and Therapy, 46*, 296–321.

Pavlov, I. P. (1927). *Conditioned reflexes: An investigation of the physiological activity of the cerebral cortex.* Oxford: Oxford University Press.

Piet, J., & Hougaard, E. (2011). The effect of mindfulness-based cognitive therapy for prevention of relapse in recurrent major depressive disorder: a systematic review and meta-analysis. *Clinical Psychology Review, 31*(6), 1032–1040. doi: 10.1016/j.cpr.2011.05.002

Polaschek, D. L. L. (2011). Many sizes fit all: A preliminary framework for conceptualizing the development and provision of cognitive-behavioral rehabilitation programs for offenders. *Aggression and Violent Behavior, 16*(1), 20–35. http://doi.org/10.1016/j.avb.2010.10.002

Polaschek, D. L. L. (2013). How to train your dragon: An introduction to the special issue on treatment programmes for high-risk offenders. *Psychology, Crime & Law, 19*(5–6), 409–414. doi: 10.1080/1068316X.2013.758963

Rogers, C. (1951). *Client-centered therapy: Its current practice, implications and theory.* London: Constable.

Segal, Z. V., Williams, J. M. G., & Teasdale, J. D. (2002). *Mindfulness based cognitive therapy for depression: A new approach to preventing relapse.* New York: Guilford.

Shapiro, F. (1989). Efficacy of the eye movement desensitization procedure in the treatment of traumatic memories. *Journal of Traumatic Stress, 2,* 199–223.

Skinner, B. F. (1953). *Science and human behavior.* New York: Macmillan.

van der Velden, A. M., Kuyken, W., Wattar, U., Crane, C., Pallesen, K. J., Dahlgaard, J., Fjorback, L. O., & Piet J. (2015). A systematic review of mechanisms of change in mindfulness-based cognitive therapy in the treatment of recurrent major depressive disorder. *Clinical Psychology Review, 37,* 26–39. doi:10.1016/j.cpr.2015.02.001

Watson, J. B. (1924). *Behaviorism.* New York: People's Institute Publishing Company.

Young, J. E. (1990). *Cognitive therapy for personality disorders: A schema focused approach.* Sarasota, FL: Professional Resource Exchange.

PART I
Individual therapies

2
ACCEPTANCE AND COMMITMENT THERAPY

David Brillhart

The International Centre for Prison Studies (Walmsley, 2013) estimates that more than 10.2 million people worldwide are currently incarcerated. This staggering number – and the disproportionately high rate of individuals diagnosed with mental health disorders in prisons – is a global concern for the mental health community. Clinicians treating these individuals understand the unique therapeutic challenge navigating their clients' deep-seated cognitive distortions and maladaptive coping strategies. While Cognitive-Behavioural Therapy (CBT) is traditionally the treatment of choice in this setting, CBT typically targets symptom reduction and seldom promotes long-term behavioural change through valued living to mitigate risk for reoffence. Utilising mindful awareness and values-guided behavioural change strategies, Acceptance and Commitment Therapy (ACT) is a powerful treatment alternative helping forensic clients understand what they are capable of changing. ACT is an empirically based, cognitive-behavioural/mindfulness therapy. Simply put, ACT follows the guiding principles of the *Serenity Prayer* in accepting and letting go of the things we cannot control – thoughts, feelings, people – and changing the things we can – our reactions *to* these events. This chapter was written for clinicians who may feel limited using CBT to target symptom reduction at the expense of valued living for their forensic clients. It draws from Dr. Brillhart's considerable forensic clinical experience using ACT with multiple populations of high-risk forensic clients, special needs and those with Serious Persistent Mental Illness. The chapter highlights new ways of understanding our clients from a contextual behavioural perspective, and expands on creative ways of helping our clients promote valued living – even in the midst of this most restrictive environment.

Acceptance and Commitment Therapy (ACT) is an empirically based third wave behavioural therapy approaching human suffering through mindful acceptance of uncontrollable events (i.e. symptoms), while actively pursuing valued living.

Symptom reduction is never the goal of ACT; symptoms typically abate when clients act on valued living in the presence of these public or private symptomatic events. This action-focused therapy, like its acronym ('ACT' not 'A-C-T'), is about **A**ccepting – without trying to change – the physical and emotional pain associated with these events, **C**hoosing valued living in spite of these events, and **T**aking action towards valued living in the midst of these events. In short, ACT mirrors the guiding sentiment of the *Serenity Prayer* by focusing on change we can control, accepting – and letting go – the things we cannot, all in active pursuit of our values.

ACT is based on Relational Frame Theory (RFT), and examines the relationship between human language, cognition and the context in which behavioural change occurs through relational responding (Blackledge, 2003). RFT illuminates the role verbal behaviour, language and human suffering plays when people attempt to avoid uncontrollable and negatively perceived public or private events. With ACT, the context and function of behaviour is defined by assisting clients in recognising language traps, making room for the discomfort arising from these traps, clarifying values, and committing action to behavioural change in service of purposeful living.

The goal of ACT is to increase purposeful living through psychological flexibility (i.e. acceptance) by engaging in 'values-based, positive behaviours while experiencing difficult thoughts, emotions, or sensations' (Substance Abuse and Mental Health Services Administration, 2010, p. 1). ACT accomplishes this through mindfulness training and behavioural choices by helping clients change their reaction *to* uncontrollable public or private events (i.e. **T**houghts, **F**eelings, **P**eople – TFPs) rather than the event itself. This is achieved through intervention-specific focus targeting each of the following six core processes:

1. *Contact with the Present Moment*: A willing mindful stance of bringing awareness to the here-and-now moment in an open, receptive and fully engaged stance. In some instances, this may be particularly difficult because present-moment focus may include thoughts and feelings of the past – or worry about the future – and physiological sensations accompanying these in-the-moment events.
2. *Self-as-Context (SAC)*: The continuous perspective-taking part of us that compares and contrasts ever-changing thoughts and feelings from an observing space. In other words, we can safely observe our thoughts and feelings without getting entangled in the content of these events. Think of SAC as a traffic reporter in a helicopter: from this observing perspective, the traffic reporter assesses all the necessary information to inform audience members on the best course of action. In sharp contrast, when we are stuck in the traffic jams of intrusive thoughts and feelings, we often make maladaptive decisions based on our limited view.
3. *Defusion*: The act of distancing ourselves from – and not buying into – the content of judgmental and intrusive thoughts. *Defusion* helps make this distinction between what a thought really is – a thought – and not what it says it is,

through the observation of language. In defusing from judgmental thoughts, 'they have much less impact and influence' (Harris, 2006, p. 6).
4. *Acceptance*: The willing stance of making room for and allowing uncomfortable TFPs in our lives in service of what really matters to us. Simply put, the active stance of acceptance does not mean we 'agree' with TFPs, but that we are powerless to change these events. In essence, acceptance is an active stance of dropping the tug-o-war rope on the uncontrollable TFPs in our lives.
5. *Values*: Identifying what truly counts and what is actually important for our life. Many people – particularly forensic clients – have never identified the person they want to be, or what truly matters in their life. Values clarification can be illuminating because it is a timely reminder of the reason *why* a person lives their life in the direction of what matters most to them.
6. *Committed Action*: Goal-directed behaviour guided by values, 'and taking effective action to achieve them' (Harris, 2006, p. 7).

From a therapeutic perspective, the ACT clinician intervenes when a client is 'stuck' in any one of the six core processes as each are interconnected and affect one another. For example, a client may struggle with uncomfortable feelings arising from intrusive thoughts (e.g. *Defusion*) which, in turn, impedes their ability to actively pursue valued living (e.g. *Committed Action*). As such, the ACT clinician facilitates psychological flexibility – openness and values-guided movement within each core process – through three mindful steps:

1. Bringing awareness to the TFPs showing up in our lives (with *Contact with the Present Moment* and *Self-as-Context*);
2. Letting go of the struggle to control the TFPs in our lives (via *Defusion* and *Acceptance*);
3. Purposeful living in spite of the TFPs in our lives (by means of *Values* and *Committed Action*).

ACT in forensic settings

For forensic clients, the ACT therapeutic stance centres on prosocial behavioural change to mitigate risk for reoffence. This is primarily accomplished through values clarification, acceptance of the uncontrollable TFPs, mindful interventions for unworkable control strategies, and behavioural activation towards valued living.

Controlling the uncontrollable leads to more pain and suffering. ACT clarifies this point with the powerful distinction between 'clean' versus 'dirty' pain (Dalrymple, Fiorentino, Politi, & Posner, 2010) by helping forensic clients distinguish how their avoidance strategies to TFPs lead to more painful TFPs. Pain is painful. 'Clean' pain is unavoidable; 'dirty' pain occurs when trying to avoid, control or eliminate 'clean' pain. Through this largely unworkable strategy, 'dirty' pain facilitates more pain, which, for the forensic client, leads to more avoidance strategies and interferes with risk-mitigating interventions. To illustrate, in working with some sex offender forensic clients, 'clean' pain often materialises in the form of self-loathing, shame or sexual arousal to paraphilic interests, peers or staff. When attempts are made to control the 'clean' pain to these TFPs through sexualised coping, aggression or other rule-violating behaviour, the 'fix' is generally short term and the ensuing 'dirty' pain is longer lasting and leads to more suffering. This is the reason why ACT does not attempt to change a client's symptoms (i.e. 'clean' pain), but their reaction *to* their symptoms in service of valued living. With forensic clients, this can be particularly counterintuitive due to the very nature of acceptance and restrictions associated with incarceration. For this reason alone, a 'what's in it for me' (i.e. *Values*) approach is used to clarify the 'payoff' for their willingness to make room and accept the 'clean' pain in their life.

Many forensic clients have never identified what truly matters to them or how they want to live their life within the confines of incarceration. Through values-clarifying mindfulness exercises, these clients gain a powerful guiding reason – a True North compass point for living – for making prosocial behavioural choices. Values clarification overlaps nicely with the responsivity portion of the *Risk-Needs-Responsivity* rehabilitation model by matching a forensic client's learning style, motivation and abilities (Washington State Department of Corrections, n.d.), with their 'interests, abilities, and aspirations' found in the strength-based focus of the *Good Lives Model* (goodlivesmodel.com, n.d.). The ACT clinician accomplishes this by helping their clients mindfully identify and intervene with their avoidant strategies to TFPs, and assigns S.M.A.R.T. – **S**pecific, **M**easurable, **A**ttainable, **R**ealistic, and **T**imely – Goals (Doran, 1981) to promote prosocial behavioural change guided by their values. ACT can range from time limited sessions (Strosahl, Robinson, & Gustavsson, 2012) to long-term therapy (Harris, 2006).

In July 2010, ACT was given an overall Readiness for Dissemination rating of 4.0 (0.0–4.0) by the Substance Abuse and Mental Health Services Administration (SAMHSA) based on inclusive criteria (e.g. mental health diagnoses; 18–55-plus age range; males and females; diverse ethnicities, settings and geographic locations). This endorsement of ACT is significant insofar as the sample, symptom presentation, setting and age range are well represented in forensic settings where there is a disproportionately high rate of mental health disorders far exceeding the general population (Fazel & Seewald, 2012). Moreover, some prisoners develop mental health problems because of their incarceration (Armour, 2012); others with preexisting mental health illness can experience exacerbated symptomology when incarcerated (US Department of Justice, 2004).

Providing ACT-based interventions

In certain situations, ACT can be successfully administered individually to forensic clients for whom group therapy might otherwise be contra-indicated (e.g. mixing male and female sex offenders in a single group). Otherwise, group-delivered ACT can be particularly effective and supportive based on shared commonalities of incarceration, mental health symptoms and detachment from valued living in this restrictive environment. A substantial part of this equation is the identification of experiential avoidance strategies and the all-consuming costs and futility for forensic clients who avoid, suppress or control internal experiences – all at the expense of behavioural harm to themselves (Levin et al., 2012). In response, ACT teaches group participants to mindfully accept painful thoughts and emotions (i.e. exposure to aversive experiences) for what they are – thoughts and emotions – not for what they *say* they are. Thoughts and feelings do not define who we are as humans; our actions based on our thoughts and feelings do.

The therapeutic benefits of exposure therapy to reduce avoidance are well known (Taylor et al., 2003). The active and mindful stance of acceptance practiced in ACT fosters repeat prosocial behaviours, thereby assisting clients to initiate and reinforce self-directed exposure to 'produce continuing gains' (Clarke, Kingston, James, Bolderston, & Remington, 2014, p. 186). Within this context and setting, ACT ultimately facilitates psychological flexibility through shared experience, accountability and committed action to valued living.

From an ACT view, valued living becomes the primary focus for clients in forensic settings. To illustrate the practical and economic effectiveness of ACT in forensic settings, Clarke et al. (2014) observed treatment-resistant clients – those with multi-diagnostic presentations and histories of relapse (i.e. forensic clients) who were exposed to group-based ACT. Their findings indicated these individuals 'produced substantial improvement' (p. 185), particularly those who had not benefitted from 'previous first-line interventions, including CBT' (p. 186). Moreover, 'participants who received ACT maintained their post-treatment gains on primary outcome measures … at follow-up, whereas those who received TAU-CBT [Treatment as Usual-Cognitive Behavioural Therapy] showed weaker maintenance' (p. 186).

When ACT is delivered as a group-based intervention, the six core processes dovetail with the five overarching goals in forensic groupwork identified by Morgan, Kroner, & Mills (2006):

1. Self-Exploration and Coping Skills
2. Group Relationship Building and Cooperation
3. Substance Abuse
4. Prosocial Behaviour and Healthy Lifestyle
5. Institutional Adjustment (p. 139)

Self-exploration and coping skills are attended to with mindfulness training (e.g. *Contact with the Present Moment, Self-as-Context, Defusion* and *Acceptance*). The role of the ACT group facilitator modelling psychological flexibility is crucial to **Group relationship building and cooperation**. Moreover, increasing a client's psychological flexibility is the key function of the ACT therapeutic relationship.

Due to the symptom presentation variability in forensic settings, and the sensitivity of topics discussed in session, demonstrating ACT-consistent psychological flexibility can be very difficult to achieve due to our personal histories, idiosyncrasies and the way we respond to others interpersonally. As Luoma, Hayes, & Walser

(2007) note, 'it can be useful for the clinician to maintain a general therapeutic stance that tends to instigate and reinforce psychologically flexible responding on the part of the client' (p. 218). In particular, this can be fostered when the ACT therapist is attentively engaged, aware, accepting, values-based and non-judgmental (Pierson & Hayes, 2007).

Creating a strong therapeutic relationship is key for any therapy. For ACT, it is essential given the role of the therapist to model psychological flexibility and values-congruent living, especially where heightened levels of distrust are inherent in forensic settings. Further complicating this scenario is the need to balance a strong therapeutic relationship with the forensic client's criminogenic thinking and manipulation (Peters & Wexler, 2005):

- [It] should be viewed as an outcome of maladaptive coping strategies rather than as a permanent fixture of the offender's personality.
- [It can be addressed by] identifying offenders' primary thinking errors, instructing clients to self-monitor when these errors occur, and providing regular feedback from peers to prevent reversion to criminal behaviour.
- Manipulative coping strategies readily undermine the treatment process unless they are addressed ... by providing regular feedback to the client, usually from peers in a treatment group (pp. 74–75).

There is a delicate balance – and sometimes daily challenge – for the ACT clinician to balance the therapeutic alliance with a client's criminogenic thinking/behaviour. Here, skilful ACT clinicians set healthy boundaries/confront manipulation, all the while motivating clients to manage their behavioural responses to the uncontrollable TFPs in their lives. One of the ways ACT clinicians accomplish this is with judicious self-disclosure.

Knowledge is power in forensic settings. For this reason alone, ACT clinicians should be mindful of self-disclosure as an illustrative point in therapy, versus too much information shared at the expense of the therapist's vulnerability and safety. Some street-savvy forensic clients can be particularly adept at conning information from staff, engaging in staff-splitting tactics (e.g. pitting one staff member against another, akin to a child who is unhappy with one parent's decision and goes to the other parent for permission) and manipulating staff through grooming tactics to compel them to break facility rules. From an ACT stance, clinicians should respectfully address the client's antisocial behaviour when it occurs, identify the reasons that made their behaviour antisocial and then process the event in therapy to identify prosocial behavioural alternatives.

Substance abuse as a co-occurring disorder figures prominently in forensic settings. Forensic clients, more than most, avoid uncomfortable thoughts and feelings. Some turn to drugs to temporarily 'fix' their clean pain. As such, assessing Experiential Avoidance – and how those actions create psychological *in*flexibility – is routinely addressed with *Contact with the Present Moment, Self-as-Context* and

Acceptance mindfulness exercises to identify avoidance strategies; *Defusion* techniques are used to loosen the grip of judgmental thoughts and feelings.

Values clarification is essential in living a **healthy lifestyle**. For many forensic clients, identifying their core values may not be an easy task. After all, many of these individuals have never asked themselves what really matters to them, or what they truly want for their life. Complicating this scenario are those novice clinicians who believe their forensic clients value an antisocial lifestyle. This is rarely the case. However, should a client say they 'value hurting others' (*content*), the ACT clinicians must listen to the *context* of their client's message to better understand the meaning behind their belief and, in turn, ascertain their core values.

Creating a *Values Masterpiece* (Brillhart, 2013) is a powerful way for clinicians to help forensic clients identify their core values. This values clarification exercise is actually an art project involving household magazines, construction paper, safety scissors and glue sticks. At the onset of this ACT assignment, individuals are asked to review the magazines, and cut out/paste on construction paper pictures representing what they truly want for their life. Adequate time should be allotted to allow an explanation of the commonalities with each chosen picture for his or her *Values Masterpiece*. Within this frame, there may be times when clients have difficulty naming their core value(s). In this instance, the ACT clinician should ask the client to identify the common theme of the collage and listen *contextually* to the responses to establish the identified value(s). To illustrate, should a forensic client choose pictures depicting 'wealth' for their *Values Masterpiece*, an ACT response might question why 'wealth' is so important. In listening to the response, their core values can be identified. As a cautionary note, given the restrictive nature and heightened security of forensic settings, the ACT clinician should be aware of possible risk-relevant issues such as the subject matter in the magazines (e.g. pictures of infants and children may spark sexual desire in those with paedophilic interests), the use of sharp tools and keeping track of all art supplies at the end of this values-clarification exercise.

Following this exercise, the ACT clinician should create a *Values Clarification Certificate* (Brillhart, 2013) specifically naming the client's identified core values. This certificate is an important reminder because it focuses attention on the behavioural choices they can make – in spite of the uncontrollable TFPs – in service of what their core values. In this example, ACT clinicians can also assist their clients in promoting **prosocial behavioural** choices by implementing the aforementioned S.M.A.R.T. (Doran, 1981) goals to facilitate risk-mitigating – and life-affirming – change. To illustrate, if a client has identified rebuilding family relationships as their core value, the ACT clinician might focus on S.M.A.R.T. goal activities the client can do to bolster their value.

Public declaration of *Committed Action* in ACT treatment can be a powerful motivator since many male incarcerates strongly believe they are a 'man of my word'; it can also be a strong incentive for peers to support – and challenge – each other when they fall short of their intended goals toward valued living. As Eddins (2014) aptly notes, publicly stated commitments have a greater likelihood of completion. In these instances, forensic clients may verbalise an external locus of control and blame **institutional adjustment** and their perceived lack of control for their inability to meet their goals.

Bringing mindful awareness of what a client can control within a secure forensic setting can be illuminating. *Hands of Control* (Brillhart, 2013) is one identified method to help clients delineate what is within their power to change. Here, clients are asked to identify a particular psychosocial stressor. Opening up their left palm, identify whether the stressor involves futile attempts to control TFPs. These items are outside the realm of a person's control. Opening up their right palm, identify what actions are in their control in spite of the TFPs. While simplistic in nature, forensic clients often display concretised thinking and actions; *Hands of Control* is an ACT-consistent mindfulness tool to bring in-the-moment awareness to forensic clients of what they can control in spite of blame they might place on **institutional adjustment**.

Finally, ACT can be incorporated into the forensic client's treatment plan once their mental health needs have been assessed and level of treatment identified for either individual or group therapy. In addition, specific interventions (e.g. *Hands of Control*) can be written into the treatment plan as prompts for staff to remind the forensic client to practise this mindfulness skill when they are seen ruminating – and acting – on their TFPs.

Therapist training

Professional training is not required for non-mental health professionals who desire to learn ACT. However, for those who work – or aspire to work – in the mental health profession and use ACT, at minimum Bachelors degree-level training in psychology is recommended. Beyond this level of education, ACT training through graduate-level coursework teaching the theory behind this mindfulness-based psychotherapy is becoming increasingly popular. This coursework can be semester-long, or can extend to research-based labs in select universities. Beyond initial ACT-based classroom education, clinicians are able to apply learned skills and can be supervised at ACT-specific graduate-level practicum and internship sites, predoctoral internships and postdoctoral fellowships; requisite training for licensure. For Masters-level graduate students, practicums and internships typically last one year or less, and are part-time; doctoral-level student internships and postdoctoral fellowships are both full-time and each lasts one year.

For those individuals who have completed their educational training, and who want to learn ACT, the best source of information is the Association for Contextual Behavioural Science (ACBS) website, https://contextualscience.org. This site features the most up-to-date information on ACT trainings worldwide. Membership is values-based, and allows access to demonstration videos, research articles, empirically validated treatment protocols, client handouts and contact information for ACT practitioners worldwide.

For clinicians who want practical experience in ACT, there is a wide array of courses from introductory to advanced techniques facilitated by peer-reviewed

ACT trainers. In addition to the educational approaches indicated on the ACBS website, there are other means of honing ACT skills, including the annual ACBS World Conference, ACT regional conferences, ACT peer consultation groups, ACT Special Interest Groups (SIGs), professional ACT listservs and ACT DVDs. For those with travel limitations, New Harbingers Publications produces an array of ACT-specific books ranging from self-help workbooks for the layperson, to in-depth training manuals for professionals.

Client characteristics (indicators/contra-indicators)

ACT has been empirically validated to address a wide range of populations, life difficulties, and psychopathologies. ACT emphasises the normality of human suffering experienced by humankind, and the lengths individuals go to avoid or eliminate (i.e. experiential avoidance) their discomfort associated with intrusive TFPs. ACT accomplishes this by helping clients 'reduce the influence these experiences exert over behaviour without necessarily reducing their intensity or frequency' (McCracken & Vowles, 2014, p. 181).

Forensic clients are no strangers to experiential avoidance. The lack of control they may experience when freedom is taken away from them can lead to a host of unpleasant thoughts and feelings masking anxiety, depression, Post Traumatic Stress Disorder (PTSD), substance abuse, and psychotic symptoms, etc. ACT can be tailored to this population by helping clients: 1) alter the function – not the existence – of uncomfortable TFPs; 2) become more mindfully aware of internal experiences and physical surroundings; and 3) clarify values and guide values-congruent behavioural change.

Values clarification is particularly important for forensic clients because it serves as the guiding force for prosocial living in this restrictive environment. What complicates this scenario is the fact that many forensic clients have either never identified their values or, if they have, they do not know how to pursue valued living. Equally challenging are the highly antisocial clients who espouse antisocial values (e.g. 'I value taking advantage of others'). In these instances, the skilled ACT clinician must listen for the *context* of the expressed value to elicit and distil the true meaning of their value (e.g. 'what is it about taking advantage of others that you value?'). Once the ACT clinician distills values clarification, the next step is to delineate S.M.A.R.T. goals (Doran, 1981) to help the forensic client achieve valued living through realistic workable goals. In the event the forensic client falls short of their goals, this can serve as a powerful process point – regardless of group or individual setting – to reexamine goals that can be accomplished to ensure success.

Accomplished goals should be celebrated as they serve as motivating factors for the client and peers alike. Through this positive reinforcement, similar prosocial behaviour is likely to be repeatable.

While the underpinnings of the ACT therapeutic model remain consistent with both forensic and non-forensic clients, the application of ACT in forensic settings is somewhat altered to accommodate four basic personality types in corrections (Evert, 2011):

1. *The Entitled*: These individuals are narcissistic, express entitlement and believe society owes them something regardless of circumstances.
2. *The Bully*: These people believe they can get what they want out of life through physical or verbal abuse.
3. *The Self-righteous*: These clients believe they are always right and their actions serve to better society. They typically only associate with others who believe the same as they do.
4. *The Sheep*: The persons are desirous of group inclusion. They adopt their peers' wishes – no matter the cost – to be included in the in-group.

Regardless of theoretical orientation applied in forensic settings, all clinicians should be mindful of the reason why the individual came to the forensic facility in the first place: chiefly, criminogenic behaviour. For the ACT clinician, this poses additional challenges of modelling psychological flexibility amidst the need to address and confront criminogenic behaviour in a non-judgmental and accepting way. This is accomplished by addressing the behaviour *contextually* by bringing awareness to the function of the forensic client's behaviour versus the behaviour itself. Think of it as *Lessons From an Iceberg* (Brillhart, 2013); focus on the meaning of the criminogenic behaviour (below the water, i.e. Context) rather than the behaviour itself (above the water, i.e. Content).

Peters and Wexler (2005) recommend approaching forensic clients in therapy with 'sensitivity, understanding, and honesty … paying careful attention to body language, eye contact, and tone of voice' (p. 80). Doing so not only models non-judgmental psychological flexibility to the client, but brings *Contact with the Present Moment* awareness to the client and to the ACT clinician as well. When processing criminogenic behaviour, avoid personalising their behaviour (Peters & Wexler, 2005), and focus instead on the consequence of their actions in terms of their *Values* (e.g. 'Since you value peace of mind, how did your decision to assault a peer impact this important value?'). Once processed, seek alternative – and workable – *Committed Action* behaviour the client is willing to make in light of their identified *Value*. For forensic clients with higher psychopathic traits, *Values* should still be addressed, but from a more concrete perspective by asking them to identify their 'what's in it for me' response when seeking prosocial/*Committed Action* behavioural change.

Criminogenic thinking should be similarly addressed as it bears impact on the way forensic clients respond to these uncontrollable events. To illustrate, sex offender forensic clients often struggle with judgmental thoughts and feelings associated with paraphilic interests and the lengths they go to in order to avoid these private events. In ACT, the therapeutic goal is *Defusion*; to help clients see their thoughts as distinct from who they are as people (e.g. 'You have no control who – or what – you are sexually attracted to; all you can control is what you choose to do when those sexual attractions occur').

Whereas the above ACT approach has been useful with a wide variety of forensic client presentations and settings, there are situations when ACT is contra-indicated:

ACT is not suitable for people whose cognitive functioning is impaired such that they have difficulty comprehending and generating answers to routine assessment questions or virtually no substantive memory of previous conversations. It is not appropriate for individuals who are floridly psychotic, intoxicated, require emergency medical treatment or have organic brain injury. (Smout, 2012, p. 673)

Status of the evidence in forensic settings

In 2010, SAMHSA formally recognised ACT as an evidenced-based practice based on its review of research on coping with obsessive-compulsive disorder symptom severity, depression symptoms, re-hospitalisation of psychotic patients and general mental health. Moreover, Division 12 of the American Psychological Association (APA) declared ACT as an evidenced-based practice with strong research support for chronic pain; modest research support was identified for depression, mixed anxiety, obsessive-compulsive disorder and psychosis (Society of Clinical Psychology, n.d.). By reason of the mounting evidence supporting the efficacy of ACT across a comprehensive range of psychological problems, Hayes, Pistorello & Levin (2012) conclude ACT 'as a unified model of behaviour change' (p. 989).

As of this writing, the National Library of Medicine (NLM) at the National Institutes of Health (NIH) recognises 31 open current clinical studies of ACT addressing a myriad of psychologically distressing events distinct from the evidence-based trials on anxiety, depression, psychosis and trauma. Highlighted studies include adjustment difficulties in neurological conditions; managing childhood asthma care; long-term pain; adolescents with a range of functional somatic symptoms; inflammatory bowel disease; evaluation of return to work rehabilitation; and engaging HIV patients in primary care by promoting acceptance (ClinicalTrials.gov, 2015). In spite of the growing number of randomised control trials (RCT) with ACT, research in forensic populations using this therapy is scant. Three noted exceptions in forensic populations exist within the same research group; each centres on the use of ACT with incarcerated women for drug abuse:

- Lanza & González-Menéndez's (2013) study of 31 incarcerated women with a substance abuse disorder who were given 16 ACT intervention sessions. Participants were assessed at pre- and post-treatment, and with a six-month follow-up. At the conclusion of the 16 weeks, abstinence rates were 27.8%; after six months, 43.8%. In addition, the treatment also yielded increased psychological flexibility, and reductions in the percentages of comorbid psychopathology including anxiety sensitivity.
- Lanza, García, Lamelas, & González-Menéndez's (2014) study compared ACT with CBT for substance abuse with 50 incarcerated women. Participants were given pre- and post- treatment and six-month follow-up assessments. Results indicated ACT was more effective in reducing drug use at the post-treatment assessment, with an overall improvement in mental health.

- González-Menéndez, Fernández, Rodríguez, & Villagrá (2014) examined long-term outcomes of 37 polydrug incarcerated females comparing ACT with CBT with pre- and post-treatment assessments at the 6, 12 and 18-month intervals. Results at the end of the 18-month assessment indicated that ACT was superior to CBT in the maintenance of abstinence. In addition, only the ACT participants experienced a reduction of mental disorders.

Distinct from the above research on ACT in forensic settings, the only other known research using ACT in forensic settings centres on this author's 20-month pilot study (N = 71) using ACT as a CBT treatment alternative to Anger Management with civilly committed Sexually Violent Persons (SVP). Pre- and post-test data comparison indicated an increase in the participants' willingness to engage in mindfulness practice to monitor their reactions to anger. Although participants' experience of anger did not change in terms of this emotion as an uncontrollable TFP, there was a marked increase in awareness in the way participants expressed anger inwardly or outwardly at the conclusion of each 12-week group. Further details of the study can be obtained directly from the author. Insofar as this was a pilot study, the results need to be replicated and compared to CBT-specific Anger Management groups to ascertain the reason *behind* the increased awareness of the expression of anger.

Case study

The following case study is used to illustrate ACT in forensic settings. To ensure anonymity and confidentiality, a pseudonym has been used and client information has been de-identified commensurate with *The De-Identification Standard of Disclosures of Protected Health Information* (US Department of Health and Human Services, 2012).

Jim is a never-married 38-year-old Caucasian male who was adjudicated for the Felony charge of Rape I for his sexual assault against a 29-year-old female and sentenced to 20 years. He has a lengthy criminal history including crossover sexual offences against a prepubescent girl, an adolescent female and violation of a stalking protective order. During childhood, he was exposed to polysubstance abuse, sex (e.g. sexual abuse and incest) and was sexually promiscuous. Upon intake, Jim was classified as a high-risk sex offender, and diagnosed with Paraphilia Not Otherwise Specified (NOS); Polysubstance Dependence; Anxiety Disorder NOS; Antisocial Personality Disorder; and Borderline Intellectual Functioning.

When Jim began the ACT-based Sex Offender treatment more than two years ago, he presented as highly guarded and, from his history of physical, emotional, and sexual abuse as a child, was wary of trust from authority figures. Because of Jim's immediate family history of alcoholism, and his own abuse history as a child, it was important for the ACT clinician to model psychological flexibility and to non-judgmentally address the client's suppression of emotions, criminogenic thinking, antisociality, callousness, and lack of empathy towards victims and peers in session.

A hallmark characteristic of Jim is the 'Happy Mask' (Hall, 2012) he wears in an attempt to experientially avoid uncomfortable reactions to his TFPs. This is an adaptive skill he learned at an early age to keep others at a psychological arms-length distance; this go-to behavioural trait has also interfered with him building prosocial relationships and making values-congruent behavioural change responses.

Early in treatment, Jim struggled to identify his core values and how they might align with his ACT-based Sex Offender treatment. For this reason, *Values Masterpiece* (Brillhart, 2013) was used wherein Jim identified *integrity* – his desire to change the way society reacts to sex offenders – as his core value.

Highlighted below is the ACT model specific to its application with Jim. His verbatim responses illustrate the impact of the psychological flexibility he has attained through ACT:

1. Bringing mindful awareness to the way Jim responds to psychosocial stressors:
   - *Contact with the Present Moment*: 'I get aggravated, because I get frustrated. I notice it in my mouth, my chest. I just want to get to the bottom of it, to the truth, because I want to be doing my treatment and out in the open and not behind closed doors. Because it's not just about helping me, but helping others. You bury secrets too long; it'll eat you alive. It's like a cancer eating you. It'll start out as a small piece of cancer and turn into a big piece of cancer. And it'll come out somehow and it's usually not good.'
   - *Self-as-Context*: Reinforcing Jim's ability to bring total awareness of the uncontrollable past and present events in his life – the TFPs – without getting caught up in these events. Jim was able to notice those times when he was angered, and the depth of perspective afforded him. 'When I was a teenager, I didn't care [about people]. This is me now, not me then ... I watch my surroundings, who to hang around with. I know the people who trigger me and who rile me up. I talk to people and watch my surroundings and what goes on around me ... When I open up my mind and don't act the way as others do, it gives me freedom.'
2. Helping Jim let go of the struggle he has trying to control his TFPs:
   - *Defusion*: Jim's efforts to change his ruminative thoughts proved fruitless: 'I'm no good ... I'm stupid ... I won't amount to anything ... I can't do this [assignment] ... I regret what I did.' Through *defusion* interventions, Jim learned to reduce the impact of his judgmental thinking by changing his responses to the thoughts versus the thoughts alone. To illustrate, Jim was asked to write his top three judgmental thoughts – the thoughts holding the tightest emotional grip – on a dry erase board. Then he was asked to identify his favourite cartoon character and imitate him to the best of his ability. Jim chose the character 'Thor' from the 1960s animated cartoon series. When he was fully invested in the exercise, Jim was asked to read his top three identified judgments in the voice of 'Thor'. Although reluctant at first, Jim soon got into the spirit of the defusion exercise until he

realised the impact of these judgmental thoughts lost its influence when he got into the character of 'Thor'. This defusion exercise proved to be an illuminating experience for Jim who was later seen at the facility repeating the voice of 'Thor' when he became entangled in his judgmental thoughts.
- *Acceptance*: When Jim learned the *Hands of Control* exercise (Brillhart, 2013), it opened up an array of values-guided behavioural response choices by differentiating controllable versus uncontrollable factors in his life. 'They [people] can think whatever they want to think about me, and I can change the way that people can see me … They don't see me as the SO [sex offender] but just as me … I become more approachable when I don't control my [TFPs] … I can't control what other people feel or think about me. That's why I choose who [sic] to associate with. I tell myself I can't change other people … And that's not the person [sex offender] I want to be.'
3. Facilitating prosocial change through purposeful living in spite of Jim's TFPs:
   - *Values*: Integrity is important to Jim who is motivated by the work he does at the institution: 'Through my work, people can see me as something more than a person with sex offences. I don't want people to see me as the old me, the sex offender. I want them to see me as someone who can change. I'm not just doing it for me, but for all SOs. All of us can change if we want to change. We can change that stigma against us.'
   - *Committed Action*: Jim remains clear on what it takes for him to live a values-congruent life: 'I don't use women as sexual objects. I see them as human beings. I talk respectfully towards others … [I also] help my peers when they have problems … When I'm doing groundwork and have the leaf blower, I turn it off when people are walking, because I wouldn't want the blower blowing on me. I don't go and googly eye women … I used to feed on people's fears and tears. I thrived on their fears. It gave me power … I'm trying to change my old behaviours. I just don't want to be that way.' Because of Jim's *Committed Action* to integrity-focused living, he's noticed staff and peers responding more positively to him. In return, he's become a more active group member, and, coincidentally, his anxiety symptoms have abated too.

Key directions for future research

There is clearly a need for additional ACT-specific research in forensic settings. Notwithstanding the three previously referenced studies using ACT with incarcerated females, research needs to extend to male forensic clients who make up 93.3 per cent of the prison and jail population in the United States alone (Federal Bureau of Prisons, 2015). Given ACT's empirically validated reputation of promoting valued living through mindful acceptance of uncontrollable TFPs, this therapy seems tailor-made for forensic clients. To that end, future research endeavours should focus

ACT's effectiveness versus treatment as usual CBT, and on longitudinal studies gauging the maintenance of treatment gains, risk mitigation and recidivism.

Further reading

1. https://contextualscience.org
2. Harris, R. (2009). *ACT made simple: An easy-to-read primer on acceptance and commitment therapy*. Oakland, CA: New Harbinger Publications.
3. Eifert, G., McKay, M., & Forsyth, J. (2006). *ACT on life not on anger: The new acceptance and commitment therapy guide to problem anger*. Oakland, CA: New Harbinger Publications.

References

Armour, C. (2012). Mental health in prisons: a trauma perspective on importation and deprivation. *International Journal of Criminology and Sociological Theory*, 5(2), August 2012, 886–894.

Blackledge, J. (2003). An introduction to relational frame theory: Basics and application. *The Behavior Analyst Today*, 3(4), 421.

Brillhart, D. (2013). *ACT behind bars: A workshop for mindful and values-based change in correctional and forensic settings*. Workshop presentation on 11 July, 2013, at the ACBS World Conference XI in Sydney, Australia.

Clarke, S., Kingston, J., James, K., Bolderston, H., & Remington, B. (2014). Acceptance and commitment therapy group for treatment-resistant participants: A randomized controlled trial. *Journal of Contextual Behavioral Science*, 3, 185–186.

ClinicalTrials.gov (2015). 31 studies found for acceptance and commitment therapy. *ClinicalTrials.gov*, A service of the US National Institute of Health. Retrieved on 27 June, 2015, from https://clinicaltrials.gov/ct2/results?term=acceptance+and+commitment+therapy&recr=Open&no_unk=Y

Dalrymple, K., Fiorentino, L., Politi, M., & Posner, D. (2010). Incorporating principles from acceptance and commitment therapy into cognitive-behavioral therapy for insomnia: A case example. *Journal of Contemporary Psychotherapy*, 40, 209–217.

Doran, G. (1981). There's a S.M.A.R.T. way to write management's goals and objectives. *Management Review*, 70, 35.

Eddins, R. (2014). Acceptance and commitment therapy in group practice. *Houston Group Psychotherapy Society*, an affiliate of American Group Psychotherapy Association (AGPA), Newsletter, Summer 2014.

Evert, B. (2011). The four inmate personality types. *CorrectionsOne.com*, retrieved on 28 March, 2015, from www.correctionsone.com/correctional-psychology/articles/3261117-The-4-inmate-personality-types/

Fazel, S., & Seewald, K. (2012). Severe mental illness in 33,588 prisoners worldwide: Systematic review and metaregression analysis. *The British Journal of Psychiatry*, 200, 364–373. doi: 10.1192/bjp.bp.11.096370

Federal Bureau of Prisons. (2015). Inmate Gender. *Federal Bureau of Prisons*, retrieved on 28 June, 2015, from www.bop.gov/about/statistics/statistics_inmate_gender.jsp

González-Menéndez, A., Fernández, P., Rodríguez, F., & Villagrá, P. (2014). Long-term outcomes of acceptance and commitment therapy in drug-dependent female inmates: A randomized controlled trial. *International Journal of Clinical and Health Psychology*, 14, 18–27.

Good Lives Model. (n.d.). Introduction. The Good Lives Model of Offender Rehabilitation. Retrieved on 13 October, 2015, from www.goodlivesmodel.com/information

Hall, K. (2012). The Emotionally Sensitive Person – Wearing Masks. *Psych Central*. Retrieved on 24 June, 2015, from http://blogs.psychcentral.com/emotionally-sensitive/2012/01/wearing-masks/

Harris, R. (2006). Embracing your demons: An overview of acceptance and commitment therapy. *Psychotherapy in Australia*, *12*(14), August, 6–7.

Hayes, S., Pistorello, J., & Levin, M. (2012). Acceptance and commitment therapy as a unified model of behavior change. *The Counseling Psychologist*, *40*(7), 976–1002, 989.

Lanza, P., & González-Menéndez, A. (2013). Acceptance and commitment therapy for drug abuse in incarcerated women. *Psicothema*, *25*(3), 307–312. doi: 10.7334/psicothema2012.292

Lanza, P., García, P., Lamelas, F., & González-Menéndez, A. (2014). Acceptance and commitment therapy versus cognitive behavioral therapy in the treatment of substance use disorder with incarcerated women. *Journal of Clinical Psychology*, *70*, 644–657. doi: 10.1002/jclp.22060

Levin, M., Lillis, J., Seeley, J., Hayes, S., Pistorello, J., & Biglan, A. (2012). Exploring the Relationship Between Experiential Avoidance, Alcohol Use Disorders and Alcohol-Related Problems Among First-Year College Students. National Institute of Health. *Journal of American College Health*, *60*(6), 443–448, August. doi: 10.1080/07448481.2012.673522

Luoma, J., Hayes, S., & Walser, R. (2007). *Learning ACT: An acceptance and commitment therapy skills-training manual for therapists*. Oakland, CA: New Harbinger Publications, 218.

McCracken, L., & Vowles, K. (2014). Acceptance and commitment therapy and mindfulness for chronic pain. *American Psychologist*, *69*(2), February–March, 181.

Morgan, R., Kroner, D., & Mills, J. (2006). Group psychotherapy in prison: Facilitating change inside the walls. *Journal of Contemporary Psychotherapy*, *36*, 137–144.

Peters, R., & Wexler, H. (2005). Substance abuse treatment for adults in the criminal justice system. *US Department of Health and Human Services, Substance Abuse and Mental Health Services Administration Center for Substance Abuse Treatment*. DHHS Publication No. (SMA) 05-4056, printed 2005, 75 and 80.

Pierson, H., & Hayes, S. C. (2007). *Using acceptance and commitment therapy to empower the therapeutic relationship*. In P. Gilbert & R. Leahy (Eds), *The therapeutic relationship in cognitive behavior therapy* (pp. 205–228). London: Routledge.

Smout, M. (2012). Acceptance and commitment therapy, pathways for general practitioners. *Australian Family Physician*, *41*(9), September, 672–675.

Society of Clinical Psychology. (n.d.). Division 12 of the American Psychological Association (APA) – Psychology Treatments. Retrieved on 28 June, 2015, from www.div12.org/psychological-treatments/treatments/

Strosahl, K., Robinson, P., & Gustavsson, T. (2012). *Brief interventions for radical change: Principles and practice of focused acceptance and commitment therapy*. Oakland, CA: New Harbinger Publications.

Substance Abuse and Mental Health Services Administration. (2014). Acceptance and Commitment Therapy (ACT). SAMSHA's National Registry of Evidenced-based Programs and Practices. *US Department of Health and Human Services*, 1–8.

Taylor, S., Thordarson, D., Maxfield, L., Fedoroff, I., Lovell, K., & Ogrodniczuk, J. (2003). Comparative efficacy, speed, and adverse effects of three PTSD treatments: exposure therapy, EMDR, and relaxation training. *Journal of Consulting and Clinical Psychology*, *71*(2), 330–338.

US Department of Health and Human Services. (2012). Guidance Regarding Methods for De-identification of Protected Health Information in Accordance with the Health

Insurance Portability and Accountability Act (HIPAA) Privacy Rule. 26 November, 2012, *US Department of Health and Human Services*, 6–8.

US Department of Justice. (2004). Effective Prison Mental Health Services. Guidelines to Expand and Improve Treatment, 2004 Edition. US Department of Justice National Institute of Corrections, 320 First St, NW, Washington D.C. 20534, 1–91.

Walmsley, R. (2013). World Prison Population List (tenth edition). International Centre for Prison Studies, Victoria Charity Centre, 11 Belgrave Rd., London SW1V 1RB, United Kingdom, 1–6.

Washington State Department of Corrections. (n.d.). Risk-Need-Responsivity Model. Offender Change for safer communities. Retrieved on 13 October, 2015, from http://offenderchange.org/programs/risk-need-responsivity-model/

3
COGNITIVE-BEHAVIOURAL THERAPY

Andrew Day

It is both a pleasure and a responsibility to write about cognitive-behavioural therapy. The cognitive-behavioural approach is not only the best established therapeutic modality in forensic settings, but also the most evidence-based. It is, without doubt, the treatment method of choice for treating offenders (see Craig, Dixon, and Gannon, 2013; Tafrate and Mitchell, 2014; Taxman, Shepherdson, and Byrne, 2004). And yet there is surprisingly little guidance available to therapists in relation to the specifics of cognitive-behavioural therapy when used with forensic clients, the adaptations that are needed to implement the approach in the forensic setting, or even how to assess both the quality and integrity of treatment. As Marshall and Marshall (in press) have recently argued (in relation to the treatment of sexual offenders), simply describing a treatment programme as cognitive-behavioural says only a little about what is actually being delivered.

An overview of CBT

There are, of course, many different approaches to cognitive-behavioural therapy. These include multimodal therapy (Lazarus); cognitive therapy (Beck); self-instructional training (Meichenbaum); constructivism (Mahoney); rational-emotive behaviour therapy (Ellis); schema-focused therapy (Young); cognitive analytic therapy (Ryle); and strengths-based CBT (Padesky and Mooney) – to name just a few. It is, however, almost impossible to characterise what is commonly delivered in forensic settings in terms of these specific approaches. Rather, current treatments tend to draw on a general model which highlights the links between thoughts, feelings and behaviour. The interventions that follow are often relatively simple and in many ways remind us of the very origins of the cognitive-behavioural approach as articulated in the writings of Ancient Greek stoic philosophers such as the slave

Epictetus (AD c. 55–135). Epictetus talked about the importance of reflecting on our attributions for negative events, the value of self-efficacy, the need to repeatedly practise good behaviour, and why we should remind ourselves of our goals using positive self-talk and journals (see Epictetus, 2008).

The basic idea underpinning the cognitive-behavioural approach – that we can control our behaviour by the way in which we interpret the world – has remained unchanged since this time and is compatible with many of the theories of crime that underpin contemporary offender rehabilitation programmes. These locate the causes of offending as largely within the individual and draw explicitly on social learning theory to guide programme activity. The Personal, Interpersonal, and Community Reinforcement (PIC-R) perspective (Andrews, 2006; Bonta & Andrews, 2003), which provides the foundation for many offender programmes, suggests that human beings have a high level of agency over their behaviour, including the decision to offend. Individual differences, in relation to the levels of self-control that individuals are able to exert over their behaviour, are thus regarded as particularly important. These are, in turn, influenced by the skills with which the individual is equipped (e.g. ability to problem solve, self-monitor and evaluate behaviour, and cope with temptation), and personal standards around behaviour (e.g. attitudes, beliefs, values, rationalisations, identities). Andrews and Dowden (2007) describe this in the following way:

> Human beings are active, conscious, and wilful, and they are goal-oriented. They are also creatures with biological dispositions and habits and conditioning histories whereby repeated associations among stimuli, responses, and behavioural outcomes can produce automatic, non-conscious cognitive regulation of motivation, perception, and behaviour. Their behaviour is under personal control, interpersonal control, and automatic control. (2007, p. 442)

The focus of cognitive-behavioural treatment is often on changing maladaptive cognitions or cognitive distortions, terms which are used to refer to particular beliefs that either allow or facilitate offending. These have been classified as either primary (self-centred attitudes, thoughts and beliefs) or secondary (blaming others, minimising/mislabelling, assuming the worst of others), although the latter can also be understood as post-hoc rationalisations and justifications of offending (see Gibbs, Potter, & Goldstein, 1995). They can be assessed using self-report tools such as the *Psychological Inventory of Criminal Thinking* (PICTS; Walters, 2010). For example, the *Mollification* subscale of the PICTS assesses the tendency to justify one's actions by projecting blame onto the environment, whereas the *Entitlement* subscale measures beliefs about giving oneself permission to violate societal laws. In Tafrate and Mitchell's (2014) comprehensive handbook of cognitive-behavioural treatment in the forensic setting, the chapter by Seeler, Freeman, DiGiuseppe, and Mitchell (2014) provides some specific illustrations of the method in practice. They describe the connection between what cognitive-behavioural therapists refer to as 'automatic thoughts', 'intermediate beliefs', and 'core beliefs' (also referred to

TABLE 3.1 The links between automatic thoughts, intermediate beliefs, implicit theories and criminogenic need (adapted from Seeler et al., 2014)

Criminogenic need	Example statement	Characterised by…	Intermediate belief	Implicit theory
Disregard	*I'm not interested in his life story*	Callousness/lack of concern. Assume others are weak/gullible	*If people are victimised, they deserve it*	Dangerous world (the world is hostile and people are untrustworthy)
Power and control	*You guys need to respect me*	Need for domination over others	*Nobody can tell me what to do*	Entitlement (I am superior, different and deserve special treatment)
Excitement seeking	*Treatment is boring*	Thrill seeking. Lack of tolerance for boredom	*I can't sit at home all night. I need action*	Emotions are dangerous (… and need to be controlled)

as implicit theories or schema) and how these can be directly linked to different areas of criminogenic need. They highlight how the things that forensic clients sometimes say in treatment (e.g. 'this is boring') can be linked to deeper beliefs (e.g. about thrill seeking) and schema (e.g. about emotions being dangerous) that are directly related to the propensity to act antisocially or offend (see Table 3.1). The cognitive-behavioural therapist will listen carefully for such comments and use them to develop a case formulation that explains the offending behaviour and identify treatment targets.

A key component of treatment is then to modify the automatic thought through using the Socratic method to confront and challenge offenders when they make comments that suggest the presence of beliefs that justify, minimise or excuse offending. At other times, the focus might also be on understanding more about the origins of those core beliefs that give rise to the automatic thoughts. Offenders are then encouraged to monitor these types of thoughts closely (often using diaries) to identify their triggers and consequences, carefully examine whether they are justified, and identify alternative ways of thinking that do not facilitate offending (see Table 3.2). They may also be asked to conduct 'experiments' in which they expose themselves to low level triggers to see what happens when they interpret the situations differently. Particular attention is also given to the development of skills in regulating negative emotion, particularly those associated with impulsive behaviour such as anger (see Fernandez, 2014).

One way to understand the actual structure of cognitive-behavioural treatment is in terms of three distinctive phases: A *beginning phase*, which is concerned with setting up the relationship, setting boundaries, and the development of a case

TABLE 3.2 Example of a completed automatic thoughts worksheet (from Seeler et al., 2014)

Situation or event: Being accused of taking magazines from a waiting room

Automatic thought	Evidence against the thought	Alternative belief
Describe the thinking in your mind which automatically occurred in this situation	*Describe any evidence that goes against this thought or reasons why it may not be true*	*Write in the more realistic belief that better reflects the evidence*
You people think that just because I have been in trouble in the past that I am to blame for anything and everything that goes wrong.	I don't get blamed for everything. People in this program seem to be on my side.	Sometimes people are going to accuse me of things. I don't have to over-react.
I was reading the magazine and it must have accidentally stuck in my pocket.	I sometimes take things I want if I think it is no big deal.	I need to be more careful and remember it might be a big deal to somebody else.
But aren't magazines there for people waiting? It is fine for me to take it home.	If everyone took a magazine there wouldn't be any left.	The magazines are not mine to take. They are there for everyone.

formulation which identifies treatment targets and goals; a *mature phase*, where actual learning takes place, as described above, in the context of a relationship that is more established; and a *termination phase*, which focuses on review and reflection and planning for the future. Beck and Beck (2011) offer a basic structure for each session that begins with a mood check and is followed by a discussion which sets the agenda for the session, the agenda of the client, and/or a review of activities identified in previous sessions. The important point here is that every session is goal directed and there is agreement on what will be discussed in each session and the actions that should follow. Given that the offender is expected to undertake a range of between-session activities, such as diary keeping, self-monitoring or practising skills (such as in managing provocation or physiological arousal), it is important that these are routinely reviewed along with periodic reviews of treatment goals and progress.

Adaptations for the forensic setting

The primary goal of cognitive-behavioural therapy for forensic clients is often to reduce the risk of future offending, with improvement in mental health or well-being usually considered secondary. Treatment is often legally mandated, especially for those who are considered to be at high risk of reoffending, as it is this that provides the context for any therapeutic contact and often determines the goals of treatment. As such, a collaborative approach to negotiating therapeutic goals is essential (Dattilio and Hanna, 2012). Given that the therapist will often arrive with a set of goals relating to risk management and community safety which may not be shared by offenders (who do not necessarily see themselves as at risk, or justify, minimise or seek to excuse their offending behaviour), many therapists incorporate elements of motivational interviewing (Miller & Rollnick, 2013), especially in the early sessions.

A second key difference in delivering cognitive-behavioural treatment in the forensic setting is that treatment is typically offered in small group settings, rather than individually. This is intended to provide greater opportunity for other group members (peers) to identify and challenge cognitive distortions, thereby assisting the therapeutic process. It does, however, impact on the way in which therapy is delivered and, in practice, means that it becomes highly structured, with therapists delivering treatment according to fairly prescriptive manuals (see Kozar, 2010). While this is not necessarily a problem, some such as Marshall (2009) have expressed concerns about the potential for this to limit effectiveness. Marshall argues, for example, that manuals restrict therapist flexibility, leading to too much of a focus on specifying treatment targets and procedures to achieve these targets, and restricting innovation and the integration of new knowledge. Day, Kozar, and Davey (2013) have similarly suggested that manuals are often associated with practice that is much less personalised than when treatment is offered individually and that 'programme manuals cannot be expected to offer much beyond general advice, such as that programme material should be delivered in ways that are concrete, active, participatory and experiential' (p. 631).

A third adaptation to the cognitive-behavioural approach has been the introduction of treatment methods that focus not only on offender deficits, but also their strengths. Cognitive-behavioural therapists have, in recent years, become increasingly interested in the now substantial body of research that suggests that positive outcomes across a range of life domains can be achieved by focusing on human cognitive, behavioural and character strengths (see Sheldon, Kashdan, & Steger, 2011), and methods that aim to promote psychological flexibility, self-efficacy, optimism and hope in offenders are increasingly being incorporated into treatment as means to engage forensic clients (see Woldgabreal, Day, & Ward, 2014). Howells (personal communication, 1 November, 2016), for example, presents a strong rationale for the inclusion of mindfulness-based treatment methods to assist with the development of positive psychological states, rather than focusing solely on ameliorating dysphoric emotion. Such methods are thought to be particularly useful for clients who have limited introspective ability and self-awareness, or may be too reactive to apply an alternative behaviour or thought as is expected in cognitive-behavioural treatment (see Fehrer, 2002).

Therapist training

While those who deliver offender treatment will normally have a background in the human services professions, this is not always the case and not all will have received training in cognitive-behavioural therapy. For example, prison sex offender treatment in the UK is often delivered by prison staff who receive specific training in how to deliver the programme rather than in broader therapeutic approaches. While this has enabled the large-scale delivery of treatment to offenders on a scale that would otherwise not have been possible (see Hollin, 2009), questions remain about the quality and integrity of this type of cognitive-behavioural programme, as well as its overall effectiveness. At the same time, Marshall (2005) does suggest that the characteristics of effective therapists are readily trainable through in-service training (see Fernandez, Mann, Yates, & Marshall, 2000). Nonetheless, it seems reasonable to assume that the quality of treatment will increase with higher levels of professional training, and Lipsey's (2009) meta-analysis of the outcomes of juvenile offender programmes shows us those which are implemented with 'high quality' are most effective.

Although it is not easy to describe a typical training pathway in forensic psychology, and even harder to know how much training programmes provide in cognitive-behavioural therapy, specialist post-graduate training to work as a forensic psychologist is available in the United States (see Burl, Shah, Filone, Foster, & DeMatteo, 2012; Zaitchik, Berman, Whitworth, & Platania, 2007), Canada (Helmus, Babchishin, Camilleri, & Olver, 2011), Australia (Day & Tytler, 2012) and the UK (see www.all-about-forensic-psychology.com/uk-forensic-psychology-course.html). In general, these programmes all rely on an 'apprenticeship' model of skill acquisition, supplemented with face-to-face teaching in small group settings. This means that it is supervised work on placements/internships that provides the main opportunity to develop therapeutic skill and, as such, exposure to the cognitive-behavioural approach will be determined largely by the particular placements that are completed. In the UK the British Association for Behavioural and Cognitive Psychotherapies (BABCP) also accredits a number of different level specialist training courses in cognitive-behavioural therapy, as well as offering workshops and other Continuous Professional Development activities.

Client characteristics (indicators/contra-indicators)

Perhaps the most important criteria used to select candidates for treatment is their risk of reoffending, especially in prison and community correctional settings. This is typically assessed using structured risk assessment tools, either actuarial or structured professional judgment, which assess risk according to the presence of characteristics that are known to be associated with reoffending. This practice has developed as a result of what is now a large body of evidence to show that treatment effect sizes are up to six times larger when higher risk offenders are treated and that treating those who are low risk can actually increase the likelihood of reoffending (see Lowenkamp & Latessa, 2004). The important point here, and as alluded to above, is that many forensic clients do not self-select into treatment and are often reluctant to engage, at least initially. A lack of motivation though is not usually regarded as a contra-indication in the forensic setting. Renwick, Black, Ramm, and Novaco

(1997) have noted this in their work, pointing to the resentful, distrustful and even combative style of some forensic clients, and enduring problems of low motivation, treatment resistance, and avoidance. They suggest that this often disrupts therapeutic work, and requires careful management. Polaschek (2015) describes a number of other characteristics of violent offenders that might influence treatment engagement, although she also argues that this should not prevent treatment from being offered:

> High-risk offenders are often angry and irritable, prone to feeling victimised, suspicious of others' motives, antagonistic, aggressive, untrustworthy, egocentric, non-compliant, and uncommitted to change. Crime-reducing therapies are centrally concerned with helping offenders learn new skills, but higher risk offenders make poor 'students'. They do not persist with treatment when they find tasks hard. They lack self-reflection and self-control. Deficient verbal abilities and a range of other neuropsychological impairments, a history of failing at school, and negative attitudes to new learning only makes matters worse. (p. 598)

Status of the evidence in forensic settings

In 2005 Landenberger and Lipsey published a meta-analysis of 58 experimental and quasi-experimental studies of the effects of cognitive-behavioural therapy on the recidivism of adult and juvenile offenders. This research confirmed the findings of a number of previous studies and reviews that showed that cognitive-behavioural programmes do have a positive effect on recidivism. The odds of not reoffending in the 12 months after intervention for individuals in the treatment group were 1.53 times as great as those for individuals in the control group, representing a reduction from the 0.40 mean recidivism rate of the control groups to a mean rate of 0.30 for those who received cognitive-behavioural treatment – a 25% decrease. A number of variables (subject samples, amount and implementation of therapy, and the treatment elements) were significantly correlated with the reduced reoffending, although much of the variation could be explained by a small number of moderator variables. These were the risk level of the participating offenders (see above), how well the treatment was implemented and the presence or absence of a few treatment elements (for example, the inclusion of anger control and interpersonal problem-solving components in the treatment were associated with larger effects; inclusion of victim impact and behaviour modification were associated with smaller effects). In short, then, these studies provide substantial evidence supporting the use of cognitive-behavioural treatment as a means to reduce reoffending. It may not, however, be the treatment of choice for all offenders. There has, for example, been some discussion of the effectiveness of the cognitive-behavioural approach with forensic clients from cultural minority groups, and recent years have seen the publication of a number of practitioner-oriented texts that identify important differences in how social and cultural issues might be incorporated (see Hays & Iwamasa,

2006; Oei, 1998). Others have suggested that more trauma-informed approaches are better suited to the needs of female offenders (e.g. Ball, Karatzias, Mahoney, Ferguson, & Pate, 2013).

Case study

In this hypothetical case, Mr James is a 35-year-old man who has been referred for treatment after being convicted of murder. There were no witnesses to the offence, but he admitted grabbing a female taxi driver from behind, strangling her and then pushing the body out of the car before driving off. Mr James had no previous criminal convictions, but had been involved in a number of fights and altercations with strangers. He was assessed as at 'moderate to high' risk of further violent offending and as in need of treatment to address the causes of his offending and reduce his level of risk. As usual, treatment began by taking a detailed personal history, which was followed by an analysis of the offence itself to identify those psychological factors that might have been relevant to his risk of further offending. This information was then used to develop a case formulation that could guide his subsequent treatment.

Personal history

Mr James had a childhood which was characterised by chronic abuse; sexual, emotional and physical. He described his father as a heavy drinker with a bad temper who was frequently (and seriously) abusive towards both his mother and himself. He described 'growing up in fear' of his father and by the age of ten was wandering the streets by himself. It was at this time that he first became the victim of a childhood sexual assault, perpetrated by a stranger. Although he remembers feeling close to his mother and being able to talk to her about most things, he was unable to disclose the abuse to her for fear that she would tell his father. As a teenager he disclosed that he was sexually assaulted by a family relative, but he did not want to discuss this further although indicated that this had a profound impact.

Mr James described his early school life as being influenced by events in the home. He described one incident where he was punished by a teacher for not paying attention in class, but remembers thinking about problems at home at the time. He subsequently retaliated by returning to the school with a guard dog from his father's workplace and threatening to set the dog on the teacher. This set up a pattern in later life whereby he learned to use violence as a means of defending himself against what he perceived as unwarranted and unjustified abuse. At the age of 12 his parents divorced, and he enrolled in a different school. His time at this school was not, however, successful – he recalled feeling shunned and rejected by his parents and bullied by other students. He began drinking alcohol, and by the age of 13 had started regularly using drugs, notably cocaine and LSD. He was expelled from school after being found drunk at school and fighting with a teacher who asked him to leave the premises.

Offence analysis

When the offence occurred Mr James was alone in a taxi on his way to visit his father's factory where he intended to take money from his father's safe. Mr James reported that the offence was not premeditated, but could give no account of the specific events leading up to it (e.g. conversation with the victim). He claimed little recollection of what was going through his mind, but was resolute in his assertion that he was not feeling angry at the time and, in fact, rarely experienced anger. He did, however, acknowledge being under the influence of cocaine at the time and reported using cocaine fairly regularly (weekly), although he did not see this as problematic. He saw the offence as both accidental and unintended.

Case formulation

The case formulation developed for Mr James understood the index offence in relation to displaced anger against his father, originating from violence in the family and a perceived failure of his father to protect him against childhood sexual abuse. These experiences were hypothesised to have directly led to an inability to regulate emotions, use of substances and a disregard for the social norms. The key beliefs identified as relevant to his treatment centred on the theme of callousness or a lack of concern for other people which resulted in him feeling entitled to take things from other people. Mr James grew up believing that the world was hostile and that no-one would be there to protect him. In many respects the presentation resembles that of the behaviourally over-controlled offender (see Davey, Day, & Howells, 2005), with his inhibitions overcome when intoxicated.

Approach to treatment

Rather than refer Mr James to a standard violent offender treatment group programme, or anger management, the case formulation suggests that a more individualised approach is required to effectively manage his risk. There is, for example, no rationale for referring him to a programme that focuses only on improving control over anger (if anything he over-regulates anger already). In this case, the experience of childhood abuse, both physical and sexual, was identified as important to understanding the serious violence perpetrated by Mr James. He was, however, initially reluctant to talk at length about this and so agreement was reached to begin treatment by building awareness of how his aggressive feelings had developed. Although the case formulation highlighted the importance of feelings of entitlement, this was approached by suggesting to Mr James that he was often overly unassertive in situations involving interpersonal conflict, relying too heavily on avoidance to deal with this. This, it was suggested, potentially led to attempts to re-exert control through aggression or force when he felt he had the right to do so. Mr James was interested in this hypothesis and willing to consider it further in treatment.

In the early stages of treatment he showed disregard to other people, including his victim, claiming that he was not interested in their experiences. He suggested that generally his view was that if people were victimised then they deserved it, showing a level of callousness that supported the identification of these beliefs as important treatment targets. The underlying schema, that the world is a dangerous place and that people are untrustworthy and malicious, was then explored in some detail in terms of how he had come to adopt this view (linking back to abusive childhood experiences), and how these beliefs influenced the way in which he interacted with others. He was encouraged to start monitoring instances of when he felt that other people were untrustworthy and his reactions to situations in which others were victimised or hurt. These were then discussed at length in sessions, and the strength of his conviction in these beliefs assessed over time. A second, but related, set of beliefs were identified which centred around issues of power and control in Mr James' relationships. He often made statements about how people needed to respect him more. These were interpreted in terms of core beliefs about entitlement (e.g. 'nobody can tell me what to do'), and the sense that he saw himself as in some way different or superior to others or as deserving special treatment. As above, these beliefs were carefully monitored and challenged.

The next component of treatment involved improving Mr James' ability to recognise emotion in other people as well as to acknowledge (rather than suppress) angry feelings when they occurred (see Day & Vess, 2013). Initially he was asked to describe the situations in which he experienced conflict and to simply note what was going through his mind at the time. Examples from his self-monitoring were then used to improve his self-awareness using an experiential method, a version of what is commonly referred to as two-chair work. This is a technique originally developed by Gestalt therapists, although it has also been recognised as a useful component of schema therapy (Seager, 2005). In this case, Mr James was asked to take part in an 'experiment' in which he was first asked to develop a dialogue between himself and a person he had experienced conflict with. This helped to identify his attributions about the causes of the behaviour or event that he experienced as provocative. He was then asked to describe the scenario from the perspective of an outside observer before being invited to imagine himself sitting in a different chair having a dialogue with the protagonist about what had happened. Finally he was asked to physically change seats and respond *as if* he was the protagonist. The dialogue was allowed to continue until Mr James understood more about the other person's point of view and the feelings that he experienced at the time. Importantly, he was not allowed to change the protagonist's view in any way during the exercise (e.g. s/he was not allowed to apologise, or promise to make reparation).

Finally, some behavioural tasks were identified and goals set where he would try to act differently in social situations. Mr James developed a list of everyday prison situations in which he would often feel vulnerable and could therefore use to practise more assertive behaviour. These included recreation or association time in the prison and during visits from his family. He was asked to practise self-talk to challenge any automatic thoughts that arose (particularly, those that were indicative of the underlying schema that the world is hostile and that people are essentially untrustworthy) and, subsequently, let people know when he felt disrespected or victimised in a socially appropriate manner. He quickly learned that he was better able to achieve his goals when he acted in this way and, as such, this new behaviour was quickly reinforced (even though it was not always successful). Others in the prison also noticed a change in his behaviour and gave Mr James positive feedback which gave him confidence in persisting. However, it was also clear to Mr James that changing the way he habitually responded to conflict was not only going to take some time, but also require ongoing effort.

Outcome

Mr James had just started a lengthy period of imprisonment making it difficult to assess the impact of treatment. However, over several months there was evidence of change and this was noted by prison staff as well as by Mr James himself. A number of scenarios were identified from the case formulation in which Mr James might have been expected to act aggressively in the prison. These were carefully monitored, and no incidents were noted when these scenarios (or approximations) occurred. As such, there was some confidence that therapeutic gain had been achieved and that this would be likely to reduce his risk of reoffending after release. However, a number of other factors will also impact on his future safety and other interventions, such as to ensure that Mr James does not use illicit substances, will also be offered.

Key directions for future research

Gannon and Ward (2014) have recently suggested that assessment and case management duties have come to dominate forensic practice in recent years and that more attention needs to be given to implementing basic psychological principles in intervention. This chapter, outlining the cognitive-behavioural approach to the treatment of forensic clients, highlights the ways in which working with offenders can be collaborative and constructive, rather than punitive and risk averse. It highlights just how important it is to pay attention to the actual implementation of treatment in forensic settings, and further research should carefully consider the integrity of those treatments that are offered to offenders which describe themselves as cognitive-behavioural. While cognitive-behavioural therapy is the most effective treatment method currently available (at least when the goal is to reduce reoffending), there is also work to be done adapting the approach to make it suitable for use with offenders, as well as in providing practitioners with specialist training to work in forensic settings. The complexity of many forensic clients suggests that individual therapy has a key role to play in achieving these goals.

Further reading

Craig, L. A., Dixon, L., & Gannon, T. A. (Eds) (2013). *What works in offender rehabilitation: An evidenced based approach to assessment and treatment.* Chichester: Wiley-Blackwell.

Fernandez, E. (Ed.) (2014). *Treatments for anger in specific populations: Theory, application, and outcome.* New York: Oxford University Press.

Tafrate, R. C., & Mitchell, D. (Eds) (2014). *Forensic CBT: A practitioner's guide*. Chichester: Wiley-Blackwell.

Taxman, F. S., Shepherdson, E. S., & Byrne, J. M. (2004). *Tools of the trade: A guide to incorporating science into practice*. National Institute of Corrections, US/Department of Justice/Maryland Department of Public Safety and Corrections.

References

Andrews, D. A. (2006). Enhancing adherence to Risk-Need-Responsivity: Making equality a matter of policy. *Criminology and Public Policy, 5*, 595–602.

Andrews, D. A., & Dowden, C. (2007). The Risk-Need-Responsivity model of assessment and human service in prevention and corrections: Crime-prevention jurisprudence. *Canadian Journal of Criminology and Criminal Justice, 49*, 439–464.

Ball, S., Karatzias, T., Mahoney, A., Ferguson, S., & Pate, K. (2013). Interpersonal trauma in female offenders: A new, brief, group intervention delivered in a community based setting. *The Journal of Forensic Psychiatry & Psychology, 24*, 795–802.

Beck, J., & Beck, A. T. (2011). *Cognitive Behavior Therapy, Second Edition: Basics and Beyond*. New York: Guilford.

Bonta, J., & Andrews, D. A. (2003). A Commentary on Ward and Stewart's model of human needs. *Psychology, Crime and Law, 9*, 215–218.

Burl, J., Shah, S., Filone, S., Foster, E., & DeMatteo, D. (2012). A survey of graduate training programs and coursework in forensic psychology. *Teaching of Psychology, 39*, 48–53.

Dattilio, F. M., & Hanna, M. A. (2012). Collaboration in cognitive-behavioral therapy. *Journal of Clinical Psychology: In Session, 68*, 146–158.

Davey, L., Day, A., & Howells, K. (2005). Anger, over-control and violent offending. *Aggression and Violent Behavior, 10*, 624–635.

Day, A., Kozar, C., & Davey, L. (2013). Treatment approaches and offending behaviour programs: some critical issues. *Aggression and Violent Behavior, 18*, 630–635.

Day, A., & Tytler, R. (2012). Professional training in applied psychology: Towards a signature pedagogy for forensic psychology training. *Australian Psychologist, 47*, 183–189.

Day, A., & Vess, J. (2013). Targeting anger in forensic populations. In E. Fernandez (Ed.), *Treatments for anger in specific populations: Theory, application, and outcome* (pp. 158–175). New York: Oxford University Press.

Epictetus. (2008). *Discourses of Epictetus – Books 1–4*. NuVision Publications.

Fehrer, F. C. (2002). *The awareness response: A transpersonal approach to reducing maladaptive emotional reactivity*. Unpublished doctoral dissertation. Institute of Transpersonal Psychology. Palo Alto, California.

Fernandez, Y. M., Mann, R. E., Yates, P., & Marshall, W. L. (2000). *Training manual for therapists treating sexual offenders*. Ontario: Rockwood Psychological Services.

Gannon, T. A., & Ward, T. (2014). Where has all the psychology gone?: A critical review of evidence-based psychological practice in correctional settings. *Aggression and Violent Behavior, 19*, 435, 446.

Gibbs, J. C., Potter, G. B., & Goldstein, A. P. (1995). *The EQUIP program: Teaching youth to think and act responsibly through a peer-helping approach*. Champaign, IL: Research Press.

Hays, P. A., & Iwamasa, G. Y. (Eds) (2006). *Culturally responsive cognitive-behavioral therapy: Assessment, practice, and supervision*. Washington, DC: American Psychological Association.

Helmus, L., Babchishin, K. M., Camilleri, J., & Olver. M. (2011). Forensic psychology opportunities in Canadian graduate programs: An update of Simourd and Wormith's (1995) survey. *Canadian Psychology/Psychology Canadienne, 52*, 122–127.

Hollin, C. R. (2009). Treatment manuals: The good, the bad and the useful. *Journal of Sexual Aggression, 15*, 133–137.

Kozar, C. (2010). Treatment readiness and the therapeutic alliance. In A. Day, S. Casey, T. Ward, K. Howells & J. Vess (Eds), *Transitions to better lives: Offender readiness and rehabilitation* (pp. 247–274). Willan Press, Cullompton.

Landenberger, N. A., & Lipsey, M. W. (2005). The positive effects of cognitive–behavioural programs for offenders: A meta-analysis of factors associated with effective treatment. *Psychology, Public Policy, and Law, 16*, 39–55.

Lipsey, M. W. (2009). The primary factors that characterize effective interventions with juvenile offenders: A meta-analytic overview. *Victims & Offenders, 4*, 124–147.

Lowenkamp, C. T., & Latessa, E. J. (2004). Understanding the risk principle: How and why correctional interventions can harm low-risk offenders. *Topics in Community Corrections – 2004*. Retrieved 23 February, 2015 from www.yourhonor.com/dwi/sentencing/RiskPrinciple.pdf

Marshall, W. L. (2005). Therapist style in sexual offender treatment: Influence on indices of change. Sexual Abuse: A Journal of *Research and Treatment, 7*, 109–116.

Marshall, W. L. (2009). Manualization: A blessing or a curse? *Journal of Sexual Aggression, 15*, 109–120.

Marshall, W. L., & Marshall, L. E. (in press). Core correctional practices: A critical aspect of the responsivity principle.

Miller, W. R., & Rollnick, S. (2013). *Motivational interviewing: Helping people change*. New York: Guilford Press.

Oei, T. (1998). *Behavior therapy and cognitive-behaviour therapy in Asia*. Glebe, NSW: Edumedia.

Polaschek, D. L. L. (2015). Treating the seriously violent: The New Zealand experience. In Day, A., & Fernandez, E. (Eds), *Violence in Australia: Policy, Practice, and Solutions* (pp. 137–152). Annandale, NSW: Federation Press.

Renwick, S. J., Black, L., Ramm, M., & Novaco, R. W. (1997). Anger treatment with forensic hospital patients. *Legal and Criminological Psychology, 2*, 103–16.

Seager, J. A. (2005). Violent men: the importance of impulsivity and cognitive schema. *Criminal Justice and Behavior, 32*, 26–49.

Seeler, L., Freeman, A., DiGiuseppe, R., & Mitchell, D. (2014). Traditional cognitive-behavioral therapy models for antisocial patterns. In R.C. Tafrate & D. Mitchell (Eds), *Forensic CBT: A Practitioner's Guide* (pp. 15–42). Chichester: Wiley-Blackwell.

Sheldon, K. M., Kashdan, T. B., & Steger, M. F. (2011). *Designing positive psychology*. New York: Oxford University Press.

Walters, G. D. (2010). *The psychological inventory of criminal thinking styles professional manual*. Allentown, PA: Centre for Lifestyle Studies.

Woldgabreal, Y., Day, A., & Ward, T. (2014). The community-based supervision of offenders from a positive psychology perspective. *Aggression and Violent Behavior, 19*, 32–41.

Zaitchik, M. C., Berman, G. B., Whitworth, D., & Platania, J. (2007). The time is now: The emerging need for master's-level training in forensic psychology. *Journal of Forensic Psychology Practice, 7*(2), 65–71.

4
COGNITIVE ANALYTIC THERAPY

Karen Shannon and Philip Pollock

Cognitive Analytic Therapy (CAT) as an individually delivered therapy has become increasingly valued across the range of forensic settings, mental disorders and offence types. This has been coupled with the indirect use of CAT-based reformulation within teams and between services. Through case examples, this chapter describes the use of CAT with 'hard to help' clients and as an explicit framework to inform staff/team/system care and risk management. The use of CAT in the management of problems that reduce treatment efficacy is described, including working with ambivalent client engagement, and managing the replaying of earlier unhelpful relationships in the therapeutic alliance. In addition, the chapter will consider enhancing insight of relational patterns, the management of endings, transitions of care and collaborative relational risk assessment. This chapter aims to show how the use of CAT can make complex dynamics explicit, understandable and manageable. Finally, the ways in which CAT can improve staff relational management, foster risk reduction and enhance public protection and client care will be examined.

Overview of the therapy

Cognitive Analytic Therapy (CAT) is an integrated form of psychotherapy that developed from the work of Tony Ryle in the 1970s. CAT integrates key elements of personal construct therapy, activity theory, the work of Vygotsky and Bakhtin, the dialogical approach and a re-definition of object relations, combined with aspects of cognitive therapy practices. Initially it aimed to deliver a time-limited model of therapy with 16–24 sessions with 1–3 follow-ups primarily addressing mental health disorders and personality disorders in healthcare settings. With expansion of interest and practitioners' innovation, CAT has diversified in its application to a broad range of presenting problems, clinical groups, formats and settings with adaptations for cognitive limitations (see Lloyd & Clayton, 2013).

The theoretical underpinnings of CAT have become more complex as the model has developed and CAT has its own language and description of core processes unique to the model itself. The therapy provides an integrative approach that offers a language to conceptualise the relational nature – intra-psychic and interpersonal aspects – of an individual's functioning. In forensic settings, the primary aim is essentially twofold: (i) to facilitate psychological change by targeting underlying self–self and self–other patterns of relating; thinking and behaving that are causal or contributory to the individual's and others' distress and dysfunction; and, (ii) to actively target those relational processes that underlie offending behaviour i.e. the out of awareness or dissociated assumed solutions for managing discomfort and distress (Shannon, Willis, & Potter, 2006).

CAT is a collaborative and relational model that is grounded in a number of core processes and stages of therapy. The core processes of CAT are described here. Reciprocal Roles (RRs) and associated Reciprocal Role Procedures (RRPs), these represent an internalised system of other–self, self–self and self–other relationship patterns originating from the interactions with significant others such as parents and carers. Examples of RRs are 'nurturing and caring to loved and cared for' or 'neglecting to neglected' where both poles of the RRs are internalised and enacted, for example in experiencing feeling loved (other to self), one also learns the role of loving (self to self and self to other). Similarly, experiencing neglect, a child also learns the role of neglecting (to self and others). RRs incorporate a capacity to predict and adapt to the reciprocating acts of the other, e.g. an anticipation that others will be loving or neglecting, based on early experience. The RRPs or patterns enable the re-enactment of the RR. So RRs therefore become the internalised 'template' that defines the self, the developing personality, and influences how we interact with others and with oneself and the world around us.

Healthy development is characterised by seamless transitions between a wide range of flexible, adaptive and positive RRs. In contrast, an unhealthy, distorted, rigid and narrow repertoire of RRs and RRPs reflects the internalised experiences of abuse, trauma and neglect, in the absence of good enough, consistent care. This forms the basis for unhelpful ways of relating to oneself and others, that dictates the nature of interactions that typify relationships and offending behaviour.

To manage the re-enactment of internalised unhealthy RRs and associated enduring core pain, such as loneliness, unworthiness and feeling unlovable, certain relational patterns (RRPs) emerge (out of the client's awareness) described in CAT language as dilemmas, traps and snags. A dilemma (i.e. either/or thinking or a polarised way of relating) is based on the belief that limited possibilities for relating are available (e.g. 'either be close to others and lose one's sense of identity or avoid intimacy and feel needy and lonely'). Traps represent repeating cycles when apparent solutions make things worse and are self-fulfilling (e.g. self-harm or substance misuse as a coping response to depression and anxiety, resulting in an increase of the symptoms initially intended to avoid). Snags are processes that prevent change (e.g. perhaps not achieving change because progress and good feelings feel undeserved). These common patterns are introduced in written and diagrammatic formats using the CAT Psychotherapy File. In therapy the client is supported to complete it, identifying the patterns that they experience(d) with self and others in the past and present. This aims to foster the client's curiosity and enhance their capacity for self-reflection. It forms the focus for collaborative therapy.

The Multiple Self-States Model (MSSM; Ryle, 1997) describes further levels and degrees of damage to the self with the fragmentation of higher-order RRs. Referred to as self-states, RRs are internalised and become separated as persisting 'parts' of the individual's core personality. Memory, action and emotion are distinct in each self-state where the individual's sense of self, perception of others, affect, thought patterns and responses are also state specific. Dissociation or partial dissociation interrupts awareness between self-states resulting in an impoverished or fluctuating self-reflective ability and dynamic, and often abrupt affect and behavioural shifts between fragmented and polarised ways of relating (Shannon & Swarbrick, 2010). In therapy the self-states and their RRPs are explicitly described, and named, facilitating discussion and exploration of their relevance for the focus for therapy.

CAT uses collaboratively developed diagrams, termed Sequential Diagrammatic Reformulation (SDR), during reformulation to convey pictorially with the individual those relational patterns that account for distress, patterns of unhelpful relating, and unwanted or unhelpful behaviours. These diagrams serve as descriptive 'maps' that sequentially account for abrupt changes in affect/mood, perception of self, perceptions of others, and behaviour patterns. Mitzman (2010) defined the diagrams as tools to offer a 'therapeutic vision' and a coherent framework. They enable a joint, shared meaning-making of the individual's relational difficulties, and a clear focus of the problems to be addressed in therapy.

The core phases of CAT consist of three 'R's – Reformulation, Recognition and Revision. Within therapy, a number of specific tools are used within each phase of the therapy. The reformulation phase (history taking, allowing the individual opportunity to provide a narrative of life events, use of the psychotherapy file) is to aid identification of RRPs: dilemmas, traps and snags. Production of a reformulation letter and the SDR bears witness to the origins of the client's damaging developmental experiences. Use of these CAT tools provides a collaboratively understood conceptualisation of the relational processes of the individual in order to facilitate agreement on the target RR – i.e. Target Problems (TPs) and associated RRPs, i.e. Target Problem Procedures (TPPs) – that form the basis of the work to be undertaken.

The recognition phase of therapy entails increasing the individual's recognition and awareness of the RRs, and patterns that are observable in past orcurrent situations with self and others. The client begins to recognise their role in re-enacting early intolerable experiences with self and others and contribution to their own distress. This phase permits the therapist and individual to explore, understand and experiment with options for exiting and changing such patterns; to learn new ways of relating; thinking, feeling and acting. The SDR is used and enhanced throughout this phase.

The revision phase of CAT utilises a range of tools and techniques to facilitate change. In CAT the therapeutic alliance is a key vehicle for corrective experience where the therapist identifies and reflects with the client the re-enactment of RRs and patterns in the therapeutic alliance. An example of an enactment between a therapist and the client is:

> (Therapist) *It seems as if you fear being controlled and overwhelmed in this therapy (like you repeatedly felt as a child) so you attempt to gain control and to silence me. This makes it difficult to reflect anything to you and so we don't make sense of you and your difficulties, so nothing changes. How can we negotiate what, and how, we discuss difficult issues so you feel less controlled and anxious. So that we can make sense of this together, increase our understanding and perhaps move toward change with a view towards discharge?*

Through this collaborative use of reformulation CAT makes explicit the identification of potential ruptures that may re-occur within the therapist-client relationship (i.e. transference and counter-transference) and links this to other repeated, unrevised relationship patterns in the client's life.

This process aims to ensure, where possible, non-reciprocation of unhealthy enactments for both the client and therapist. The therapeutic alliance allows, perhaps for the first time, the client to experience a healthy, caring, supportive, reflective, boundaried and non-collusive relationship with the therapist, which has the potential to be internalised by the client as a healthy way of relating to themselves, and others.

CAT's use of endings ensures endings and transitions are made explicit in the early stages of therapy and are planned to enable space for unresolved feelings regarding historical, painful endings and the ending of therapy to be expressed and actively worked with. The 'goodbye letter' narrates the journey of key moments in the therapy, changes achieved and areas for focus for the future. Importantly, the CAT letter serves as a tool; a transitional object for the client to internalise a reformulated understanding of their difficulties, the therapeutic alliance, and changes made so they can apply these for themselves post-therapy.

Adaptations to cognitive analytic therapy needed for a forensic setting

Zone of Proximal Development (ZPD), engagement and readiness to change

CAT commences at the point where the forensic client currently is, to collaboratively determine the territory of the therapeutic work. CAT's flexible, relational and collaborative nature means that unlike some individual psychotherapies, CAT does not require psychological mindedness, a high level of emotional identification, verbal ability or clear motivation for engagement. Instead, an aim of CAT can be to help a client become more psychologically minded – working within the client's Zone of Proximal Development (ZPD; i.e. just within the individual's zone of what they can achieve with the help of another; see Vygotsky, 1978), where the individual is able to begin to have a dialogue about the possibility of engaging in therapy, change and what is required. CAT emphasises encouraging the client to be curious, bearing witness to damaging early experience, and joint meaning-making with an empathic, reflective other (Ryle & Kerr, 2002).

The Multiple States Model of CAT explicitly focuses our understanding of the centrality of degrees of dissociation. This awareness assists the therapist to understand the client's experience of the self as discontinuous and fragmented, with limited reflective ability and a lack of skills in relating, poor emotional identification and emotional expressiveness skills. Notably, in forensic services these difficulties are potentially associated with poor client insight regarding the nature of the individual's offending behaviour and risk potential (Shannon, 2009). This CAT understanding of damage and deficit to the personality allows provision of time-limited sessions to reflect with the client on their ability and willingness to engage in change and any adaptations required for therapy (referred to as 'pre-CAT work' in Pollock & Shannon, 2013). The client's reciprocal relationship with engagement in therapy or change can be understood and worked with from the outset (Shannon, 2009). For example, the reciprocal role with therapy might be fear of blaming, accusing (staff) to overwhelmed blamed, responsible (client), or controlling, imposing (staff) to imposed and powerless (client). Depending on the nature of the reciprocal role, this might lead to resistance or passive, resentful engagement and poor treatment efficacy. This approach aims to facilitate a curious and collaborative exploration of the client's patterns of relating to self and others, as opposed to a reductive assessment of motivation to engage in therapy, or the traditional confrontational, imposing or coercive approaches, which can be associated with therapy provision in forensic services. McMurran and Ward (2010) also focus on treatment readiness, to allow consideration of the client's social competencies that are required for successful engagement.

In this collaborative process, key use is made of the therapeutic alliance; the empathy and care provided by the therapist can be internalised. Later in the therapy process this self-empathy can be harnessed (within the ZPD of the client) to assist the offender to identify with the role and experience they enacted on their victim, an important aspect of forensic therapy (Pollock & Belshaw, 1998). Attention to the engagement process requires a slower therapeutic pace, which can require a longer therapy than the traditional 16 or 24 CAT sessions provided in adult mental health settings.

Managing threats to the therapeutic alliance

Forensic clients' damaging and abusive developmental experiences result in early relationships where boundaries are violated, inconsistent or absent. The client therefore has difficulty forming and sustaining healthy, stable relationships including the therapeutic relationship (Waldinger & Gunderson, 1984). They reject or are unable to make use of the care that they need or even seek. Hanson et al.'s (2002) research indicates the median number of psychotherapy sessions attended by forensic clients is just three sessions. There is a hypersensitivity and anticipation (perhaps out of awareness) by the client that they will be let down or mistreated – a re-enactment of early experiences repeated throughout their relationships with others, including with professionals and throughout multiple services. This is likely to result in intolerance for actual or assumed (i.e. 'as if') RR enactments in the therapeutic alliance (e.g. judgmental to shamed, or controlling to rebellious) where the client attributes suspicion and unreliability of the therapist potentially irreparably rupturing the therapy (Timmerman & Emmelkamp, 2006).

The client's reformulation (diagrammatic and written) helps the client and therapist to reflect, and to anticipate and plan for re-enactments. Quality relational supervision for the therapist (Davies, 2015) and therapist skill are necessary to recognise enactments within the alliance, to limit ruptures and to develop alternative ways of relating.

Bennett, Parry, and Ryle (2006) emphasise therapists' competence in resolving alliance threats and ruptures as crucial in helping clients towards an efficacious therapeutic outcome. Bennett et al.'s rupture repair model provides principles and stages to work with alliance-threatening events, which can contain the therapist, the therapeutic alliance and the focus for therapy. Enactments and ruptures that occur with the therapist are likely to be repeated with others, including the client's care or management team and multiple agencies. The target problem and procedure (the RR and procedures related to risk and distress) can therefore be understood and incorporated into relational care planning to facilitate responsive and consistent plans (Pollock, Stowell-Smith, & Gopfert, 2006). As reflective therapists and staff teams, it is we who need to be attuned and flexible and to offer different ways of relating to the client, despite powerful pulls to re-enact unhelpful patterns, so that the client can internalise healthier, non-offending reciprocal roles to enact with themselves and others. 'Complexity [therefore] means harder work for the therapist, not the patient' (Leiman, 1994, p. 81).

Appropriate focus of therapy

Much of the focus of intervention in forensic services (prisons, hospitals, community settings) is upon risk assessment and reduction, as opposed to addressing the relational unmet needs of the individual (Shannon, 2009). More recently there has been awareness of the importance of strengths and protective factors as well as risk factors, such as Ward and Laws' (2010) strengths-based rehabilitation theory: Good Lives Model (GLM).

Use of CAT with offending populations aims to reduce the risk of offending and enable other psychological changes to address the unmet needs of the individual. CAT's focus on gaining a relational understanding of the presenting problem and unmet needs, underpinning the offending behaviour, is one of its strengths. For example, the observable *presenting* problem – e.g. violent behaviour – may be the risk management concern for services and perhaps for the individual. However, CAT relationally recasts the presenting problem in terms of the RRs and RRPs underpinning the offending behaviour, i.e. the *target problem (TP)*, which in this example could be *chronically endured feelings of loneliness and relationship instability (due to repeated experiences of abandonment)*. The target problem procedure (TPP) is understood as an unhelpful relational attempt to find a solution for the target problem, which is outside of awareness and therefore unrevised. An example of this TPP (written in the first person) is the following: *seeking care from others, but fearing abandonment (TP), I assume I must be in control to keep my partner near me so she won't leave me. I become increasingly jealous and restrictive and my initial threats eventually spill into violence. Eventually I am arrested. My partner feels hurt, controlled and suffocated and she rejects me. I end up alone, confirming that I am always abandoned.* The pattern repeats. This TPP captures a specific relational understanding of the presenting problem, i.e. the violence. In this example the focus of CAT therapy would be exploration and resolution of the early origins of and subsequent repeated experiences of rejection and abandonment and development of social and conflict management skills. Alternatively, if this historical exploration was too painful and outside of the client's ZPD, or the therapeutic timing was inappropriate – e.g. due to being in an 'unsafe' prison setting – the therapist could focus the therapy on the enactment and revision of patterns in relationships in the here and now with self and others, including the therapist.

Collaborative uncovering of the relational and unrevised nature of the repeating offending patterns, the client's contribution to it and the link with their chronic emotional pain or unmet needs can create an 'aha' moment. The client can recognise their role in their own unmet needs. This can enhance client motivation to change toward non-recidivism, as opposed to solely focusing on symptoms reduction or offending behaviour. CAT's focus on the core TPs and patterns underlying the offending or risky behaviour reduces the likelihood of offence or symptom substitution or time-limited change (Shannon, 2009).

CAT ensures a planned ending or transition must be considered from the outset with all staff and services surrounding the client, not solely within a therapy. Without this, forensic services unknowingly re-enact forensic clients' damaging early experiences (of unpredictable, painful and confusing endings with clients' historical, multiple care givers) with abrupt, unplanned transitions or changes in services, even where this is due to positive progression, e.g. a move to lesser security. This can result in forensic clients' difficulty in forming a healthy therapeutic alliance, and intolerance to 'mini (as if) endings' or perceived loss (e.g. staff lateness, cancellations, holiday and staff leaving the services). Changes to care are, where possible, communicated to the client by the therapist and team to allow feelings of uncertainty, loss and abandonment to be anticipated and worked with. This nurtures a sense of control and completion for the client, allowing achievements as well as difficult emotions to be acknowledged. Without such a focus, we in forensic services can unknowingly contribute to the psychopathology or increased risks, as clients 'up the ante' with clinging, rejecting or contemptuous responses to perceived re-abandonment or neglect.

CAT contribution to risk assessment and collaborative management

Within the client's ZPD, as described, the client and therapist can gain an explicit risk formulation; a relational understanding of the client's psychological functioning. In CAT, the offender-victim relationship qualities are explicitly defined in diagrams, letters and target problem procedures (Pollock et al., 2006). For the client this can increase insight into the intolerable states of mind from which the risk is more likely. This increased awareness enables integration of the offending behaviour from a partially dissociated and unaccountable state (emotions, memories, thoughts, behaviours, motivation) to a recognised and integrated self-state. This allows awareness of both victim and offender poles of the reciprocal role and with associated accountability as opposed to sole identification with self as a victim and not as abuser (Shannon, 2009). Ultimately, this encourages self-management and risk reduction (Pollock et al., 2006).

The CAT formulation allows the therapist and client to recognise the risk-related behaviours or boundary pushing, which will inevitably arise in therapy and general care of the client, as reciprocal role enactments, or Offence Paralleling Behaviours (OPB; Jones, 2011). This can inform boundary maintenance and risk assessment, and decision making regarding relational, procedural and physical levels of security (Crichton, 2009). Additionally, it can aid the development of exits and relapse prevention plans for use by the client and the teams and services surrounding the client (Shannon & Swarbrick, 2010).

Contextual reformulation

CAT's strength is also as a contextual formulation (Ryle & Kerr, 2002) where a CAT SDR provides a description of the relationship between the team and the client as a reflection of the client's ways of relating to others, internalised from childhood (Kerr, Dent-Brown, & Parry, 2007) (i.e. the RRs and RRPs). The formulation makes explicit the more complex staff processes involved in perpetuating and exacerbating an individual's psychopathology (Carradice, 2004) and offers teams informed ways of relating to the client, which do not enact early experiences (Dunn & Parry, 1997). It provides an understanding of the reasons why staff can find themselves powerfully experiencing polarised opposing feelings (e.g. rejecting to rescuing) elicited by the client at different times (Mitzman, 2010) or polarised responses from colleagues. A CAT formulation explains why staff members have different dysfunctional reciprocation to different parts of the client resulting in splits among staff (Ryle & Kerr, 2002) and associated burnout (Kerr et al., 2007).

Without these considerations, services unknowingly re-enact the client's reciprocal role patterns, which keep the client stuck in their unhelpful relational patterns and limit the possibility of change, non-recidivism and development of trusting relationships. As long as staff and systems re-enact clients' early object relations, they contribute to the long-term psychopathology of the clients (Dunn and Parry, 1997). In forensic services, usually those with the most contact with clients have minimum training (Moore, 2012) and they are more likely to slip into re-enacting clients' unhelpful RRs and (unknowingly) undermining positive clinical gains from other professionals. A relational understanding and regular reflective practice for all staff, preferably enhanced by CAT-informed training for staff, is therefore invaluable.

Increasingly, staff, teams and entire services (e.g. Ramm, 2010) are accessing training in CAT to provide CAT as a therapy and a model of consultation, and contextual CAT to provide a formulated understanding of clients for general multidisciplinary teams (e.g. CAT skills case management training). Evaluation of a skills level training, which included six months supervision in CAT formulation, provided a Community Mental Health staff team with a structured, unified approach and led to enhanced communication, improved confidence, increased team morale, containment of anxiety, and hope for change in the management of complex clients (Thompson et al., 2008).

Within forensic services a detailed, collaboratively derived CAT reformulation can provide a relational framework tailored to inform the client's care pathway; including a sequence of offence-focused interventions, to inform approaches such as the Risk Need Responsivity model (RNR) and Good Lives Model (GLM). This enables all multidisciplinary care provision to be provided in such a way as not to re-enact the client's unhelpful patterns of relating and compound their problems.

Given that risk assessment and formulation lie at the very heart of forensic practice (Shannon, 2009; Withers, 2010; Pollock & Shannon, 2013), a value of CAT is its ability to formulate risk and guide management on an individual level and systemic level. CAT risk formulation provides teams and multiple agencies surrounding the forensic client with a non-pathologising, non-collusive shared language to assist with a unified, proportionate response to manage risk and to enable effective communication and multi-agency management (Shannon, 2009).

Therapist training

ACAT distinguishes two forms of training routes, specifically regarding whether they are likely to lead to a 'CAT career' or not: (1) the CAT Therapist/Practitioner (career route) is for those using CAT in one-to-one therapy roles; and (2) the non-career route is focused on CAT Case Management Skills, with a contextual focus and suited to generic workers or practitioners not in therapy roles. CAT would be used to enhance their current role. See www.acat.me.uk for full course details and hosts.

1. CAT Therapist/Practitioner

The term CAT Therapist has been approved by ACAT Trustees in place of Practitioner to reflect the adopted title emerging from the Centre for Workforce Intelligence (CfWI) title Psychological Therapist. Currently both terms are in use in ACAT.

Two Year CAT Therapist/Practitioner: This two-year training aims to develop skills to practice CAT as a one-to-one therapy. It is open to trainees with a core profession (e.g. nursing, psychology, psychiatry, occupational therapy) and relevant experience. It leads to ACAT accreditation as a CAT Therapist/CAT Practitioner, allowing the graduate to practice CAT within their core profession. It consists of eight modules over two years consisting of theory, skills and supervised clinical case work and is assessed through four clinical appraisals every six months: two clinical case studies and two essays. Trainees must complete a 16-session CAT training therapy. Entry to the two-year course is through application, interview and attendance at a CAT introductory workshop (two days) or equivalent. Those completing this level can undertake supervisor training, trainer development/accreditation and further CAT (psychotherapist UKCP) training.

One Year Foundation: This course is equivalent to the Year One of a CAT Therapist/Practitioner course in academic and clinical content and written work requirements. The therapy component is a brief reformulation experience and is setting-specific. This course was designed following an invitation to train IAPT workers. The award is an ACAT Foundation Certificate in CAT Practice (IAPT setting). The foundation course is modular and has been designed for trainees satisfactorily completing the course to opt to do a second year. Other specialties/contexts can be considered on a case by case basis. This foundation training may be adopted by other professional training courses (e.g. some clinical psychology training courses in the UK).

2. CAT skills – non-career route (CAT Case Management)

ACAT also accredits a six-month long CAT skills course as a non-career route (CAT Case Management). These courses are equivalent to two modules and are designed to enable the use of CAT concepts in case management (not therapy). They aim to enhance skills in team working with complex clients, psychologically informed case management and understanding the impact of working within a context, usually with complex clients. The award is an ACAT CAT Contextual Skills Certificate in Case Management. Possible applications include IAPT/SMI-PD case management, MDT team care and CAT-informed care coordination e.g. for complex cases and forensic settings.

Client characteristics (indicators/contra-indicators)

If clients are not ready to engage in therapy – for instance, if they are floridly psychotic or repeatedly heavily under the influence of substances – there are a range of other ways (apart from individual therapy) in which CAT has enhanced clinical and team practices (Kellett, Wilbram, Davis, & Hardy, 2014; Thompson et al., 2008). A reformulation of the client's repeating patterns can inform 'good enough', non-collusive care and service provision by the staff member/team and service provision effect change, until such a time where the client might engage. CAT therefore offers a conceptualisation of forensic complexity with flexible application for one-to-one therapy, a relational framework for offence-focused intervention (e.g. in an offence-focused group), a CAT-informed intervention and/or as a contextual reformulation to aide team(s) and multi-agency working.

Status of the evidence in forensic settings

Applied to forensic settings, early work took the form of case studies as examples and illustrations of the model, method and tools for offenders. These studies have encompassed a range of offences including serial or single homicide, sexual offending, intimate partner violence, and aggression and violence.

In 2006, Pollock et al. produced the most extensive range of clinical case studies to date that has described CAT application for offenders. CAT is now used across the full gamut of security levels and several case studies have advanced the model and practice to different genders, offence types, age ranges, disorders and settings (Shannon, 2009; Mitzman, 2010; Withers, 2010; Annesley & Sheldon, 2012; Kirkland & Baron, 2014). To date, the application of CAT has been confined to case studies and the research has few controlled studies. A review by Knabb, Welsh, & Graham-Howard (2011) of treatment alternatives for mentally disordered offenders identified that CAT had accumulated multiple studies of the therapy's efficacy in forensic populations. Studies to date were noted to have achieved significant reduction in symptoms and relevant target problems and functioning.

The acknowledged weaknesses of CAT are that currently it lacks broader empirical validation in forensic settings. Although, given the positive outcome of randomised control studies of CAT efficacy for emerging personality disorder in adolescents (see Chanen et al., 2008) and personality disorder in adults (see Clarke, Thomas & James, 2013 for a review), it could be argued that CAT is best served for offenders who present with personality problems, and it is a proven therapy model to address severe personality disorders. The ability to formulate, describe and generate a shared working model of severe personal pathology and other complex processes such as dissociation, and explicit attention to forming a collaborative, 'good enough' therapeutic alliance, are distinct strengths of CAT.

Additionally, CAT explicitly psychotic experiences and symptoms as distorted, muddled enactments of developmentally derived reciprocal role procedures are outside of the individual's awareness, i.e. the experiences are internally and externally 'out of dialogue' (Kerr, Birkett, & Channen, 2003). There is therefore growing empirical evidence for CAT in working with other disorders linked to offending (e.g. bipolar disorder (Evans & Kellett, 2014) and psychosis (Taylor, Perry, Hutton, Seddon, & Tan, 2014)).

Case study

Robert is a 31-year-old man who entered CAT because of the interpersonal nature of his offending and identification that he presented with a range of severe personality problems with some dissociation noted. He was serving a prison sentence for a domestic assault on his 28-year-old female partner who was mother to his young child (unborn at the time of the index offence).

The index offence consisted of a prolonged assault, which lasted for several hours with the client physically assaulting his pregnant partner within the family home. He entrapped his victim, strangled, beat, kicked, punched and bit her and burned her skin before pouring an inflammable liquid over her and threatening to set her alight. He emotionally taunted and harangued the victim, repeatedly vacillating between assaulting her and then comforting her and telling her that he loved her. He was not under the influence of any substances at the time of the offence. The victim's account of the relationship indicated that Robert's relationship behaviour was characterised by dependence, neediness, anxious insecurity, jealousy and preoccupation with his partner's fidelity. Robert aggressively controlled his partner's movements, spending, choice of clothing, social contacts and communication. In contrast to this type of conduct, Robert was also described by his partner as a devoted, loving, attentive and kind partner, usually following an instance of aggression towards her. This typical cycling between aggression and contrition is well documented as a pattern of behaviour shown by men who are domestically abusive (Dutton, 1995). Police records corroborated multiple incidents of domestic abuse.

Robert's early history featured significant adversity and neglect. He had endured severe physical and emotional abuse and rejection from both of his parents whilst in their care until aged 13. His parents were abusive to each other and his father introduced him to drug misuse when aged 12 (his father was a substance abuser himself). His parents separated following social services' intervention. Robert then lived with his mother. The level of abuse was extensive and Robert showed psychological disturbance as a child before he was removed from his mother's care, triggered by her decision to enter and favour a new relationship with a man known to be a sexual offender. Robert was subsequently placed into multiple foster care placements. As an adolescent, he was generally unmanageable. From the age of 14, he showed aggression and oppositional conduct, substance misuse, and associated with criminal and drug-using peer groups. In adulthood, Robert experienced intermittent periods of casual employment when in the community, interspersed with periods of imprisonment for a diversity of offending.

In the midst of such adversity, Robert had experienced an idealised mother–child relationship for a period of time when his mother left his father and she appeared to over-indulge Robert in a privileged, worshipping relationship in the absence of his father's influence. The essence of this relationship was internalised as a narcissistic self-state in which Robert yearned for and sought a recapitulation of this type of relationship within his relationships with partners. Robert's betrayal by his mother in favour of her new relationship instilled a hatred for his mother, a feeling he openly disclosed during his later adolescence. The history, as corroborated from records, indicated that Robert was known to have endured experiences which were likely to have caused development of restricted, narrow and damaged models of relating and a damaged sense of self.

Robert was assessed to demonstrate clinical features of borderline personality disorder with some narcissistic characteristics. Robert's case was formulated using the Multiple Self-States Model (MSSM) of CAT, which accounts for many of the features of borderline personality disorder, i.e. the person's experience of oneself and others is unstable, with variable, mercurial, conflicted and confusing self-states. Their underlying RRPs are imbued with levels of dissociation and fragmentation. The self is experienced as inconsistent, volatile and narrow in terms of the range of RRPs enacted. Relationships with others are similarly compromised with capricious changes in the person's perceptions, attitudes and responses towards the same person (e.g. an 'idealised rescuer' morphing to 'withholding punisher').

Robert's SDR is depicted in Figure 4.1. The SDR diagram represents a simplified version of a more complex diagram, the more simplified version condensed to provide the client with a framework to understand his other-self, self-self and

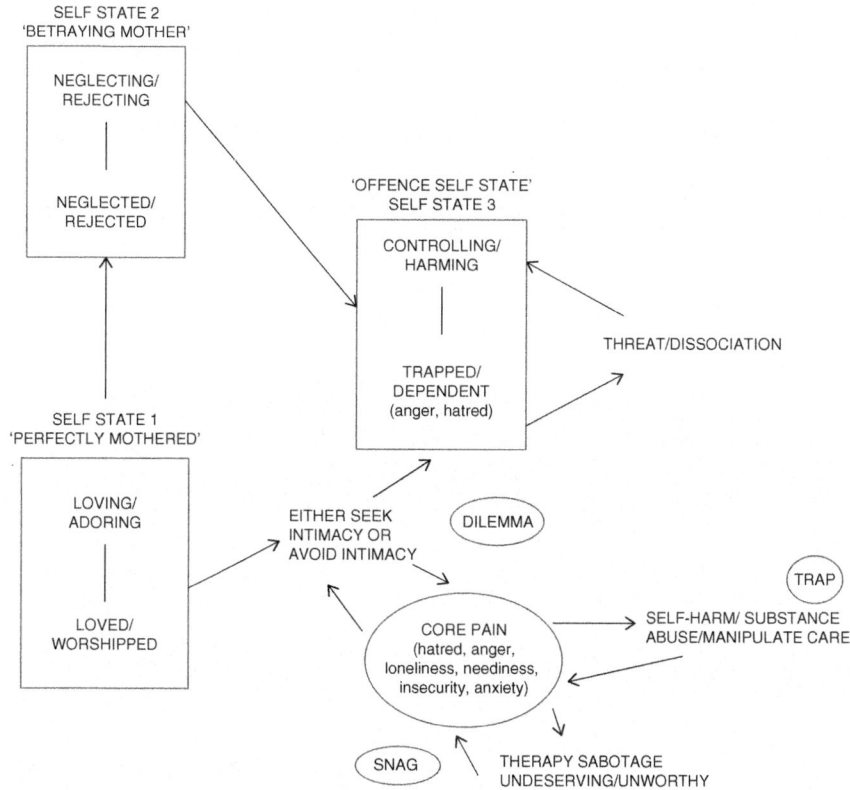

FIGURE 4.1: Robert's Sequential Diagrammatic Reformulation (SDR)

self-other relating and those patterns of relating and behaving that required targeting for change. The elements of Robert's reformulation are detailed here. Robert harboured an unresolved, simmering and intense hatred for his mother because of her betrayal and rejection of him (the 'core pain' state). A degree of dissociation occurred as a feature of this core state as a method of coping with its intense emotional distress (numbness – psychological and/or drug induced, restricted memory, flashbacks to abuse). When Robert experienced this core emotional pain, he often engaged in self-harm, suicide attempts and acts to coerce care. He also misused substances to self-regulate its impact (a 'trap').

In Robert's case, three specific self-states and underlying RRPs were central to his intra-psychic and interpersonal functioning and to the offending itself. Self-state 1 describes the perfect mothering that Robert received from his biological mother following his father's departure. The RRs are 'loving/adoring' to 'loved/worshipped'. This particular self-state highlights his expectations about care from a female and a degree of narcissistic worship and devotion as a fantasised ideal that Robert pursued within relationships. The second self-state described as 'neglecting/rejecting' to 'neglected/rejected' RRs (self-state 2) is defined by the betraying, rejecting mother who induced the core pain of loss, anxiety and extreme neediness. The third self-state defines the dynamics within the offence itself.

In relationships, Robert attempted to cope with the core emotional pain by a pursuit of the care and devotion he sought in the RRs of self-state one. The dilemma he experienced was to either seek intimacy and risk feeling trapped and controlled with further risk of neglect and rejection, or to avoid intimacy and his core pain remained unchanged. Robert was prone to perceive that he was being neglected, anticipating rejection, which activated neediness and behaviours that would result in rejection (controlling his partner's movements, preoccupation about infidelity, etc.). The 'offence RRs' (within self-state 3) emerged when Robert experienced a sense of insecure, anxious dependency, which caused him to perceive that he was somehow trapped and controlled. Furthermore, when in this state, he perceived his partner as betraying and rejecting which triggered him to act violently as a means of changing the 'trapped/controlled – trapping/controlling' threat. This represents an example of projective identification whereby one role is projected onto the other party and the perception of the victim changed dramatically. Robert acknowledged that he would experience a degree of dissociation when experiencing self-state 3 and that he would be amnesic for parts of his violent conduct. He suffered flashback-type, fragmented memories and an out-of-body feeling with emotional numbing during the violence.

In the 'offence self-state' (self-state 3), the RRs within the perpetrator–victim self-state (which were named by the client) are construed as the most significant to predict, target and change. However, it is important to identify that a sequence of changes can precede the entrance to the offence state (e.g. abrupt changes termed state shifts, role reversals, response shifts in experiences of oneself and the other provoked by either actual or perceived external or internal events). This level of analysis permits a degree of prediction of these sequences as a risk management strategy for self-observation and self-management.

A dilemma, trap and snag are highlighted within the Self-States Sequential Diagram (SSSD). For Robert, the dilemma involved either seeking nurturance to obtain the idealised relationship that mirrored what he experienced with his mother at one stage, or avoiding intimate relationships and remaining needy, insecure and alone, which activated the core and enduring emotional pain he felt. This dilemma was unhealthy because Robert's entrance into a relationship featured insecurity, dependency and resentment towards such anxieties with domestically abusive anger occurring. If he chose not to enter a relationship, his neediness was exacerbated. A trap was evident in terms of Robert's engagement in self-harm, substance misuse and crime, which reinforced his sense of being unloved and flawed. The snag noted occurred within the therapy itself, in that Robert believed that progress and positive change should be sabotaged because he was undeserving and unworthy. The TPPs and TPs derived from the reformulation were shared openly with Robert via the reformulation letter and SSSD. A hierarchy of target problems to address was agreed.

CAT anticipates and works with potential ruptures and risks within the therapeutic relationship. The process of therapy with Robert was particularly turbulent with several threats of rupture to the therapeutic relationship itself, Robert voicing his desire to leave therapy when he was challenged or when he felt that therapy was imposing or threatening (i.e. the enactment of the controlling-controlled RRP as transference). The parts of the SDR which showed Robert's risk-related RRPs were disclosed, with Robert's consent, to a selected number of professionals in Robert's care team who were key to his welfare and management within the personality disorder unit of the prison.

Robert's therapy lasted for eight months on a weekly basis. Robert cancelled several sessions on an intermittent basis. These ruptures and challenges were collaboratively understood using the SSSD to contain the therapy and highlight Robert's anxieties and intense feelings of engaging in a 'good enough' therapeutic relationship. The middle phase of therapy concentrated on Robert's narrative sense of himself and others, addressing the most fundamental patterns of relating that occurred within relationships. Within the alliance, options and 'exits' were reflected upon to encourage Robert to learn to relate differently and more adaptively without resorting to narrow, blinkered RRPs derived from past relationships. The CAT reformulation was pivotal to introducing a range of techniques (e.g. compassionate listening to self and others, anger control and emotional self-regulation, learning to communicate his needs, resolution of trauma, exploration of his attitudes to females, victim empathy). A primary focus of the therapy was to address dissociation in two ways. First, to help Robert trace and regulate how he made the transition into self-state 3 and to explore his management of dissociative symptoms. Second, this task aimed to enhance his over-arching ability to observe all of his reactions and responses and to improve his capacity for both self-reflection and self-monitoring and to integrate Robert's sense of self and limit his partial awareness regarding other self-states, which is typical of borderline pathology.

The ending phase and 'goodbye letter' provided to Robert activated strong feelings of neediness and loss, Robert sharing that he felt anger about dependence on others to meet his needs and resentment that relationships had to end. These issues were openly acknowledged and discussed with options for managing loss explored and exits identified.

The outcome measures used were CAT-specific and included a repertory grid technique, symptoms measures and application of a rating scale for borderline personality pathology. Robert self-reported that positive change had been achieved for all target problem procedures addressed. In follow-up, two years post-therapy, Robert had been released into the community on licence conditions and had entered a new relationship. The evidence gathered indicated that Robert had modified his attitudes, responses and conduct within the new relationship and that, during its one-year duration, the partnership had not exhibited any form of relationship abuse.

Key directions for future research

Using CAT as an approach to therapeutic care for complex clients includes, but also goes outside, the therapy room. Multi-professional service provision for forensic clients requires a systemic, formulated, consistent and integrated approach focused upon pathways of care into, within and between multiple health, criminal justice and community services. CAT addresses these needs via a contextual formulation. Varying levels of training for CAT as a therapy and indirect case management are occurring in numerous forensic institutions and community settings in parts of the UK. It would therefore make sense to continue to develop the evidence base for direct therapy, but also regarding CAT informed staff/team trainings (e.g. linked with the Offender PD pathway in the UK) and the impact of this on recidivism and improved client psychological well-being.

Further reading

Pollock, P.H., Stowell-Smith, M., & Gopfert, M. (Eds) (2006). *Cognitive analytic therapy for offenders: A new approach to forensic psychotherapy*. New York: Taylor and Francis.

Ryle, A. & Kerr, I. B. (2002). *Introducing cognitive analytic therapy: Principles and practice*. Chichester: John Wiley & Sons.

Acknowledgement

Thanks to Debby Pickvance, ACAT psychotherapist, trainer and supervisor for her insightful assistance.

References

Annesley, P., & Sheldon, K. (2012). Cognitive analytic therapy (CAT) within the perimeter fence: An exploration of issues clinicians encounter in using CAT within a high secure hospital. *The British Journal of Forensic Practice, 14*(1), 124–137.

Bennett, D., Parry, G., & Ryle, A. (2006). Resolving threats to the therapeutic alliance in cognitive analytic therapy of borderline personality disorder: A task analysis. *Psychology and psychotherapy: Theory, research and practice, 79*, 395–418.

Carradice, A. (2004). Applying cognitive analytic therapy to guide indirect working. *Reformulation, 23*, Autumn, 18–23.

Chanen, A. M., Jackson, H. J., McCutcheon, L. K., Jovev, M., Dudgeon, P., Yuen, H. P., Germano, D., Nistico, H., McDougall, E., Weinstein, C., Clarkson, V., & McGorry P. D. (2008). Early intervention for adolescents with borderline personality disorder using cognitive analytic therapy: Randomised controlled trial. *The British Journal of Psychiatry, 193*, December, 477–484.

Clarke, S., Thomas, P., & James, K. (2013). Cognitive analytic therapy for personality disorder: Randomised controlled trial. *The British Journal of Psychiatry, 202*(2), 129–134.

Crichton, J. H. M. (2009). Defining high, medium, and low security in forensic mental healthcare: The development of the matrix of security in Scotland. *The Journal of Forensic Psychiatry & Psychology, 20*, 3.

Davies, J. (2015). *Supervision for forensic practitioners.* London: Routledge.

Dunn, M., & Parry, G. (1997). A reformulated care plan approach to caring for people with borderline personality disorder in a community mental health service setting. *Clinical Psychology Forum, 104*, 19–22.

Dutton, D. G. (1995). *The domestic assault of women: Psychological and criminal justice perspectives.* Vancouver: UBC Press.

Evans, M., & Kellett, S. (2014). Randomised control trial in CAT and bipolar disorder. *ACAT Annual National Conference 10–12 July, Liverpool.*

Hanson, R. K., Gordon, A., Harris, A. J. R., Marques, J. K., Murphy, W., Quinsey, V. L., & Seto, M. C. (2002). First report of the Collaborative Outcome Data Project on the effectiveness of psychological treatment of sex offenders. *Sexual Abuse: A Journal of Research and Treatment, 14*, 169–194.

Kellett, S., Wilbram, M., Davis, C., & Hardy, G., 2014. Team consultancy using cognitive analytic therapy: A controlled study in assertive outreach. *Journal of Psychiatric and Mental Health Nursing, 21*, 687–697.

Jones, L. (2011). Case formulation for individuals with personality disorder. In Sturmey, P. & McMurran, M. (Eds), *Forensic case formulation.* John Wiley & Sons.

Kerr, I. B., Birkett, P. B. L., & Chanen, A. (2003). Clinical and service implications of a cognitive analytic therapy model of psychosis. *Australian and New Zealand Journal of Psychiatry, 37*, 515–523.

Kerr, I. B., Dent-Brown, K., & Parry, G. D. (2007). Psychotherapy and mental health teams. *International Review of Psychiatry, 19*(1), 63–80.

Kirkland, J., & Baron, E. (2014). Using a cognitive analytic approach to formulate a complex sexual and violent offender to inform multi-agency working: Developing a shared understanding. *Journal of Sexual Aggression*, 1–12.

Knabb, J. J., Welsh, R. K., & Graham-Howard, M. L. (2011). Treatment alternatives for mentally disordered offenders: A literature review. *Psychology, 2*(2), 122–131.

Leiman, M. (1994). The development of cognitive analytic therapy. *International Journal of Short-Term Psychotherapy, 9*, 67–81.

Lloyd, J., & Clayton, P. (2013). *Cognitive analytic therapy for people with intellectual disabilities and their carers.* London: Jessica Kingsley Publishers.

McMurran, M., & Ward, T. (2010). Treatment readiness, treatment engagement and behaviour change. *Criminal Behavioural Mental Health, 20*(2), 75–85.

Mitzman, S. F. (2010). Cognitive analytic therapy and the role of brief assessment and contextual formulation: The jigsaw puzzle of offending. *Reformulation, 34*, Summer, 26–30.

Moore, E. (2012). Personality Disorder: its impact on staff and the role of supervision. *Advances in Psychiatric Treatment, 18*, 1, 44–55.

Pollock, P. & Belshaw, T. (1998). Cognitive analytic therapy for offenders. *Journal of Forensic Psychiatry, 9*(3), 629–642.

Pollock, P., & Shannon, K. (2013). Keynote Address. Cognitive Analytic Therapy (CAT) in Forensic Practice: Reformulation of the Capacity to Harm. *20th Annual ACAT National Conference CAT and Ethical Practice: Maintaining our Professionalism and Humanity.* Reading, Berkshire.

Pollock, P., & Shannon, K. (2013). Keynote Address. Cognitive Analytic Therapy (CAT) in Forensic Practice: Reformulation of the Capacity to Harm. 20th Annual ACAT National Conference CAT and Ethical Practice: Maintaining our Professionalism and Humanity. Reading, Berkshire.

Pollock, P. H., Stowell-Smith, M., & Gopfert, M. (Eds) (2006). *Cognitive analytic therapy for offenders: a new approach to forensic psychotherapy.* Hove: Routledge.

Ramm, M. (2010). Cognitive Analytic Therapy at the Orchard Clinic Medium Secure Unit for mentally disordered offenders. *DCP Scotland Newsletter*, September, Issue 3.

Ryle, A. (1997). The structure and development of borderline personality disorder: A proposed model. *Br J Psychiatry, 170*, 82–7.

Ryle, A., & Kerr, I. B. (2002). *Introducing cognitive analytic therapy: Principles and practice.* Chichester: John Wiley & Sons.

Shannon, K. (2009). Using What We Know: Cognitive Analytic Therapy (CAT) Contribution to Risk Assessment. *Reformulation.* December.

Shannon, K., & Swarbrick, R. (2010). A Cognitive Analytic Therapy (CAT) Framework for Bipolar Disorder. *Reformulation.* June.

Shannon, K. L., Willis. A., & Potter, S. (2006). Fragile states and fixed identities: using CAT to understand aggressive men in relational and societal terms. In Pollock, P. H., Stowell-Smith, M., & Gopfert, M. (Eds). *Cognitive analytic therapy for offenders: a new approach to forensic psychotherapy* (pp. 295–314). London: Routledge.

Taylor, P. J., Perry, A., Hutton, P., Seddon, C., & Tan, R. (2014). Curiosity and the CAT: Considering cognitive analytic therapy as an intervention for psychosis. *Psychosis: Psychological, Social and Integrative Approaches, 7*(3), 276–278.

Thompson, A. R., Donnison, J., Warnock-Parkes, E., Turpin, G., Turner, J., & Kerr, I. B. (2008). Multidisciplinary community mental health team staff's experience of a 'skills level' training course in cognitive analytic therapy. *International Journal of Mental Health Nursing, 17*, 131–137.

Timmerman, I. G., & Emmelkamp, P. M. (2006). The relationship between attachment styles and Cluster B personality disorders in prisoners and forensic inpatients. *Int J Law Psychiatry, 29*(1), Jan–Feb, 48–56.

Vygotsky, L. S. (1978). *Mind in society: The development of higher psychological processes.* Cambridge, MA: Harvard University Press.

Waldinger, R. J., & Gunderson, J. G. (1984). Completed psychotherapies with borderline patients. *American Journal of Psychotherapy, 38*, 190–202.

Ward, T., & Laws, D. R. (2010). Desistance from sex offending: Motivating change, enriching practice. *International Journal of Forensic Mental Health, 9*, 11–23.

Withers, J. (2010). Cognitive analytic therapy (CAT): A treatment approach for treating people with severe personality disorder. Chapter 6, in Tennant, A. & Howells, K. (Eds), *Using time, not doing time: Practitioner perspectives on personality disorder and risk.* Chichester: Wiley-Blackwell.

5
EXPLORING COMPASSION FOCUSED THERAPY IN FORENSIC SETTINGS

An evolutionary and social-contextual approach

Paul Gilbert

Prosocial and antisocial behaviour can be contextualised with an evolutionary approach as strategies linked to survival and reproduction. Whether we harm others or help others relates to many different factors. For example genetic variation impacts on empathic caring and psychopathic traits; social contexts; group identification i.e. whether people are perceived as in the group or outside it (tribal 'wars'); potential personal benefits from harming others (e.g. undermining competitors); and early neglectful or abusive attachment experiences can all impact on the preparedness to be harmful or helpful. This chapter will argue that focusing on compassion seeks to switch the strategic and phenotypic orientation of individuals towards more empathic prosocial outcomes for themselves and others. This means that compassion training links to what we know about its impact on a whole range of (neuro) physiological, psychological and social outcomes. Compassion training seeks to cultivate a particular care-focused motivational system that organises physiological, psychological and social processes.

Compassion Focused Therapy (CFT) is an integrative psychotherapy that is rooted in evolutionary, developmental and biopsychosocial models (Gilbert, 1989/2016, 1998a, 2000a, 2010, 2014, 2015a) and some contemplative, traditional practices (Gilbert & Choden, 2013). It was originally developed for and with people who suffered from high levels of shame and self-criticism, and complex mental health problems and who found it very difficult to change using cognitive-behavioural interventions (Stott, 2007). In addition, they struggled to be open to the helpfulness of others, be self-compassionate or be able to use affiliative emotions for emotion regulation or be compassionate to others (Gilbert, 2000a, 2010, 2014, 2015a). Indeed, when clients were trying to use cognitive coping or 'alternative thinking' approaches to help themselves, the emotional tone to 'these inner thoughts' was often hostile, critical and contemptuous. For example, having coping thoughts, when lying in bed ruminating, such as 'I am feeling depressed, I understand that ruminating makes me feel worse. So if I get out of bed and do some stretches, yoga and gradually focus on doing things, this will help me' can be said with a very understanding, empathic tone or a hostile, contemptuous one. Indeed, you can try reading those statements yourself using different voice tones in your head and see the different impact they have on you. Learning how to stimulate and practise generating friendly, compassionate and affiliative motives and emotional tones to our thoughts was the first step towards CFT. This proved a lot more difficult than was anticipated because of many fears, blocks and resistance (Gilbert, McEwan, Matos, & Rivis, 2011; for a review see Gilbert & Mascaro, in press).

There is considerable evidence now that affiliative emotions, be they directed at self or others, in contrast to hostile, contemptuous and critical ones, facilitate emotion regulation and prosocial behaviour (Gilbert, 2009, in press; Keltner, Kogan, Piff, & Saturn, 2014). Helping clients understand the value of cultivating prosocial motives and emotions and practising prosocial behaviour, for themselves and others, is thus a central aspect of CFT (Gilbert, 2000a, 2009, 2010, 2014).

Although CFT's application to forensic settings is new (da Silva, Rijo, & Salekin, 2014; Laithwaite, O'Hanlon, Collins, & Doyle, 2009; Kolts & Gilbert, in press), CFT has been applied to and developed with a range of mental health problems, including: different types of depression (Gilbert, 2007a); anger problems (Kolts, 2012); post-traumatic stress disorder (Lee & James, 2012); psychosis (Braehler et al., 2013) and acquired brain injury (Ashworth, Gracey, & Gilbert, 2011) with increasing evidence of effectiveness as demonstrated in a recent meta-analysis (Leaviss & Uttley, 2014). Compassion, both giving and receiving, are also important difficulties in people who manifest criminal behaviour, and working with them can be central to the change process (Kolts & Gilbert, in press). The lives of individuals with criminal records often have histories of early childhood trauma, depression, anger/impulse control and shame problems, i.e. lacking in compassionate care. Because of CFT's specific focus on the stimulation and cultivation of care-focused evolved, motivational systems and emotions and their physiological infrastructures (Gilbert, 2014, in press), CFT can be integrated with many other evidence-based interventions and established therapies in forensic settings such as recovery models (Dorkins & Adshead, 2011); the Good Lives Model (Ward, Mann, & Gannon, 2007); and developing a compassion-focused justice system (Shapland, Robinson, & Sorsby, 2011; Wozniak, 2014).

A core element of CFT is similar to the Buddhist concept of bodhichitta, which is to create an inner, compassion-focused, motivational state that will impact on (re) organising emotion, cognition and behavioural patterns (Leighton, 2003; Singer & Bolz, 2012). Individuals train to develop compassionate mindful awareness/ insight into the nature of their own minds (with its multiple evolved dispositions, see below) and adopt a compassion-focused self-identity for patterning the mind (Gilbert, 2000a, 2014; Gilbert & Choden, 2013; da Silva et al., 2014). In contrast to the Buddhist approaches, however, CFT is contextualised in an understanding of how evolution has shaped the human mind for specific motives, emotions and behavioural dispositions (phenotypes) (Gilbert, 1989, 2014) including for criminal behaviour (Buss, 2012; da Silva et al., 2014). In addition, CFT seeks to link evolved strategies with phenotypic development because ultimately therapies need to change the physiological infrastructures from which thoughts, motives and behavioural dispositions arise (Gilbert, 2014).

Antisocial behaviour in historical context: the prevalence of cruelty

One important aspect of CFT is to address the issue of human *cruelty* (Gilbert, 2005, 2015b Gilbert & Gilbert, 2015). Obviously, people working in forensic settings should be prepared to recognise the inherent cruelty in humanity (Abbott, 1993; Taylor, 2009; Zimbardo, 2008). CFT helps people recognise how some of our evolved dispositions for criminal/antisocial acts relate to complex gene environment interactions (Button, Scourfield, Martin, Purcell, & McGuffin, 2005; Moore & Depue, 2016). At a deeper evolutionary level we have different life survival and reproductive-focused strategies that mature different phenotypes, some of which are more conducive to criminality than others. McDonald, Donnellan, and Navarrete, (2012) put it this way:

> Unpredictable environments with high mortality risk tend to produce fast life history strategies in which individuals mature early, produce more offspring, but invest less in each offspring. This strategy is adaptive because it increases the probability of producing at least some surviving offspring. Alternatively, relatively predictable environments with low mortality risk tend to produce slow life history strategies where individuals mature and reproduce at a later age, producing fewer offspring in which they invest heavily. Increased allotment of energy to development may therefore be associated with greater ability to obtain resources, status, and long-term mates. (p. 601)

Criminal behaviour of all kinds, especially criminal behaviour that involves toning down concern for others, is much more likely to emerge in individuals who grow up in threatening environments (Andrews & Bonta, 2010). Indeed, this distinction between prosocial and antisocial behavioural strategies is not specifically human in any way; many primate species can be hostile, aggressive and vengeful to each other and even show inter-group warlike behaviour. The way our brain matures (such as the development of the frontal cortex, emotion regulation, empathic and caring motivation) are significantly influenced by the social relationships and social contexts in which we are embedded and grow. Clearly, if prisons constantly create threatening environments then one is at risk of maintaining or even accentuating what are already antisocial strategies that are operating at deep non-conscious, archetypal levels, rooted in basic reproductive strategies (Huang & Bargh, 2014).

Awareness of these processes are important for clients and professionals to recognise, including: 1) the ease by which we feel threatened and use aggressive defences and justifications, especially when the focus is on a sense of self such as in shame, exclusion and/or down-rank threat; 2) the ease by which we can act out motivations that are based on desires/drives, acquisitions and greed; be highly self-focused on personal desires, and/or wanting and taking what others have, and/or enforcing others to behave as we wish (e.g. sexual exploitation, rape, slavery); 3) the way early life experiences pattern and shape the body and mind as it prepares them for living in certain social niches; 4) the way social contexts create the conditions for moral and immoral behaviour; and 5) the value of, but also the facilitators *and inhibitors* of, prosocial motives, emotions and behaviours (Gilbert & Mascaro, in press; Kolts & Gilbert, in press).

While seeing the obvious importance of assessment of organic issues and serious mental illness, evolution-focused CFT models of human behaviour are cautious of medical, phenomenological approaches to diagnosis because they tend to separate out particular kinds of experience and label them as 'abnormal' rather than as potentially natural and normal phenotypic adaptations. For example, people in forensic settings will have caused harm to others in one way or another. However, although humans can be very prosocial and helpful, they can also be indifferent and neglectful, harmful, cruel and sadistic and often deliberately so. Helping others or hurting/exploiting others is linked to the evolved strategies and phenotypic variations that are often contextually and socially sensitive (Buss, 2012; Cohen, 2001). This is why many individuals who end up in forensic establishments have histories of neglect and abuse rather than love and support (Andrews & Bonta 2010; Mikulincer & Shaver, 2007) and often have PTSDs (Van der Kolk, 2014). But even in the absence of traumatic childhoods, social contexts can easily turn 'good' people 'bad' (Kelman & Hamilton, 1989; Zimbardo, 2008). Tragically, human history is replete with shocking atrocities, tortures, exploitations, slavery and cruelties perpetrated by groups of humans on others. A visit to the Coliseum in Rome, the Tower of London, any preserved torture chamber or the Nazi concentration camps reveals the potentially horrific nature of human cruelty (Abbott, 1993). When nation states murder and use cruelty and torture to protect themselves it is regarded as legitimate and in the national interest; when criminal gangs or individuals do the same to protect *their* interests it is regarded as crime. When cruelties are perpetrated for defensive reasons individuals will argue that they are concerned with protecting the well-being of those they are defending (Taylor, 2009). America was recently shocked to discover the extent of the CIA's recent involvement with torture during the Bush years, resulting in a major congressional report (www.huffingtonpost.com/news/cia-torture-report; 2015). This also led to investigations into how complicit some psychologists had been, as outlined in a damaging independent review commissioned by the American Psychological Association (Hoffman et al., 2015).

Justifications for 'defending one's country' are at the root of this of course but when the sentiment of 'concern for others' and a moral ethic 'in defence' is lost we are extremely vulnerable to our dark sides. We have within us the potential to be a very nasty species indeed and criminality can often be defined as much in terms of its context as its actual behaviours (Gilbert, 1994; 2009; Taylor, 2009). So CFT recruits an *evolutionary functional analysis* as the context and background for understanding criminal behaviour and its therapy – lest we see it as an abnormality or something alien to human potential (Buss, 2012; da Silva et al., 2014).

Social contexts: Although we experience ourselves as having individual minds, we are gene-built biological beings whose physiological systems are coordinated by evolved strategies seeking particular outcomes for survival and reproduction (Buss, 2012; Gilbert, 1989/2016; McDonald et al., 2012). Motives such as power, status and sex are ancient, basic and innate ones that guide animals on their life tasks. Many of these life tasks, such as male sexual reproduction strategies of fighting for status and sexual opportunities within hierarchical groups, do not require consideration of the well-being of others (Garcia, 2015).

What is defined as criminal behaviour is thus highly socially contextualised. Violence to threatening out-groups, including children and families, in war contexts is acceptable, even heroic, but not as in-group behaviour (Kelman & Hamilton, 1989). Paedophilia has been common in many societies and the fact that we now regard it as a 'philia', perversion, a 'pathology' and crime, is very much a modern definition derived from our understanding of child development, its potential harmfulness and empathy for suffering. Empathy for child suffering (because they are children and not mini-adults) is relatively new historically. We don't send young children down mines, into factories or up chimneys either – something completely acceptable 200 years ago, although tragically child labour factories still exist in different parts of the world. And it wasn't so long ago that slavery was completely accepted. Two centuries ago 'people trafficking' was legitimate business. Aristotle was in favour of slavery. In certain passages in the Bible we find that the practice of slavery, and the punishment of slaves, was condoned; slaves were simply property:

> *If a man beats his male or female slave with a rod and the slave dies as a direct result, he must be punished, but he is not to be punished if the slave gets up after a day or two, since the slave is his property.* (Exodus 21: 20–21)

Men's relationship with women has often been poor, with some religious texts and cultural contexts portraying women as subservient to men. The epidemic of domestic sexual violence is yet another tragic demonstration of the ease by which we can behave cruelly and destructively to others. The size of the problem can be seen from a major World Health Organization study in which Garcia-Moreno and her colleagues conducted interviews at 15 sites in ten geographically and culturally diverse countries (Garcia-Moreno et al., 2006). To quote from their own summary of the findings:

> 24,097 women completed interviews, with around 1,500 interviews per site. The reported lifetime prevalence of physical or sexual partner violence, or both, varied from 15% to 71%, with two sites having a prevalence of less than 25%, seven between 25% and 50%, and six between 50% and 75%. Between 4% and 54% of respondents reported physical or sexual partner violence, or both, in the past year. Men who were more controlling were more likely to

be violent against their partners. In all but one setting women were at far greater risk of physical or sexual violence by a partner than from violence by other people (p. 1260).

As the authors point out, violence against women is widespread, has often been ignored, is culturally variant and desperately needs to be addressed *on an international scale*. It also clarifies how arbitrary the boundaries around what is defined as criminality can be.

Antisocial and immoral behaviour, that causes harm to others, is tragically epidemic throughout the business world – from the banks to the oil industries (Bakan, 2005). One of the problems is that as business and political organisations become more powerful there is increasing likelihood that certain personalities, with certain traits, get into positions of power, in particular those represented by what has been labelled the Dark Triad of Machiavellianism, Narcissism and Psychopathy (Furnham, Richards, & Paulhus, 2013). As the recent series of high-profile investigations show, corruption and criminality tend to be more widespread in banks and sport than we would like to think. Social dominance orientation (SDO) is another trait that may incline to immoral and criminal behaviour. SDO is an individual's level of 'basic ruthlessness and a view of the world as a competitive, dog-eat-dog environment of winners and losers' (p. 314) and an in-group's desire to be superior to out-groups (Pratto, Sidanius, Stallworth, & Malle, 1994; Sidanius et. al, 2012).

Natural phenotypes?

There are a range of naturally evolved traits and behaviours that can be classified as psychopathologies or dysfunctions but in fact may represent variations on reproductive strategies and are normal phenotypic variations within populations (Belsky & Pluess, 2009; Buss, 2012; Moore & Depue, 2016). One of the most salient variations in human populations is the degree of prosocial, helpful and caring behaviour conspecifics (members of the same species) show each other, in contrast to aggressive and exploitative behaviour. Human capacities for behaving compassionately and morally, or aggressively and immorally, are related to evolved phenotypes which are shaped and choreographed via the interaction of genetic disposition and environmental priming and shaping (Belsky & Pluess, 2009). Phenotypes, for reproductive strategies, emerged to fit particular social niches (Moore & Depue, 2016). So, for example, in safe and highly investing social niches it is an advantage to develop phenotypes that can exploit that niche by building trusting, supportive relationships and by being relatively altruistic and compassionate to others; having a brain that is motivated for that. In contrast, in low-investing and high-threat environments these phenotypes may be disadvantaged, and more exploitative, self-focused strategies are better reproductive bets (Gilbert, 1998a; Cohen, 2001). Hence, although different alleles of neurotransmitter genes (e.g. short versus long versions) can be associated with increased risk of mental health and antisocial behaviour, there is very good anthropological evidence that men's relationships with each other, with women and with children is very much linked to the ecology in which men grow up. In dangerous ecologies men are much more likely to be competitive and aggressive towards each other, with clear gender divisions in roles and power, and issues of honour and perceived reputation status dominate self-presentation. In contrast, in benevolent ecologies, men are much more likely to regard the control of (especially hostile) emotion and peaceful coexistence and helpfulness as the higher values and more parental (or male) investment in childcare (Gilmore, 1990).

Given this we would anticipate that criminal behaviours and those related to relatively callous actions against others are more common in low-investing and high-threat environments (Buss, 2012). Here the evidence is clear, that early neglect and abuse are very strong risk factors for the development of criminal behaviour (Andrews & Bonta, 2010; Button et al., 2005; Mikulincer & Shaver, 2007), partly, but by no means solely, because of underlying untreated PTSD (Van der Kolk, 2014). Indeed, it is very clear that early backgrounds even shape genetic expressions through a process called methylation (Slavich & Cole, 2013). This can be personalised for clients by inviting them to think about the therapist. For example:

> If I had been kidnapped as a three-day-old baby and raised in a violent drug gang then this (therapist) version of Paul Gilbert would not exist and in its place would be a genetically expressive, psychologically and socially very different individual who may well be in prison, rich or dead. In every individual are multiple possible versions of the self that emerge according to their social niche in which they grow; the self and its strategies are partly socially constructed, played out through brain patterns. The question today is how happy are you with the version of you that has been created *for you* not *by you* and how much would you like to change it and discover and cultivate new versions that may be more conducive to yours and others well-being.

Indeed, this empathic connection, arising from scientific knowledge, to the potential 'criminality' within each of us, is a therapeutic compassionate act and links us to our common humanity. It's an important position for the CFT therapist working with this population. It can be emotionally taxing though, to really empathically connect with some of the darker sides of our clients and hence our own natures.

Compassion as motivation

Competing motives as a social mentality

Compassion is rooted in evolved care-focused motivation (Gilbert, 1989/2016, 2005, 2015; Mayseless, 2016) and contextualised by the fact that the human mind is organised around a number of different and often competing motivational systems (Huang & Bargh, 2014). Although there is no agreed nosology for motivational systems, there are two basic distinctions. The first is the distinction between social and non-social motives. Unlike non-social motives for eating or nest building, social motives are dependent upon complex social interactions where processing systems need to be: 1) motivated to create a certain type of role relationship (e.g. sexual; dominant-subordinate; affiliative-friendly; teacher-learner); 2) able to send the appropriate signals indicating to another their preparedness to enter into that type of relationship (thus stimulate processes 'inside' the other), and elicit the other as a reciprocal partner; thus being able to 3) receive, decode and send social communications from and to other minds that will influence what they subsequently do. So, for example, in animal courting displays, if those signals become mis-attuned then one or both parties may take flight or even attack the other. In the infant–parent caring relationship the parent is attending to the signals of their offspring and provides them protection, rescue, feeding or warmth as required. The infant for their part is physiologically regulated by those inputs.

Social motivations that depend on this complex interplay of moment-by-moment interactions and shifting physiological states have been called social mentalities (Gilbert 1989/2016, 2015b; McEwan, Gilbert, & Duarte, 2012). Social mentalities can be divided into two basic forms: 1) those that are prosocial and focused on the well-being of others; and 2) those that are self-focused, either harm avoidance and/or acquisitive controlling, with little regard to others; they are obviously not mutually exclusive though. These can be subdivided into motivational systems for: a) care seeking; b) care eliciting; c) cooperation and friendship formation; d) competitiveness; and e) sexuality (Buss, 2012; Gilbert 1989/2016, 2014).

Compassion is rooted in both the care-giving and friendship/alliance-building motivational systems with the recognition that evolution has put some constraints around these motives (see Mayseless, 2016 for a review). For example, we tend to be compassionate to those we are (kin) related to, or those we are forming cooperative friendships with, whereas we are much more likely to be competitive, even hostile, to those we don't like or see as out-group enemies. So caring motives versus dominance seeking ones can be in conflict (Tang-Smith, Johnson, & Chen, 2014). This raises the intriguing question of whether or not some individuals are compromised (for genetic or other reasons) in their actual caring motivational capacities and competencies, or whether they tend to classify most individuals as potential threats to them and as out-group members. There are certainly indications that some of the neurophysiological underpinnings of caring behaviours such as polymorphisms of the oxytocin gene and the myelinated parasympathetic system are compromised in some individuals (Mayseless, 2016). In addition, there is neurophysiological evidence that people who have not been able to process their own trauma or emotional pain may lack the capacity to be empathic for the pain they cause others (Shirtcliff et al., 2009)

Compassion has been labelled a social mentality to indicate that it's a socially co-created process in that it is dependent upon attending to social signals, interpreting and then responding to those signals and responding to the respondents' response in a flow of dynamic, ongoing, reciprocal relationship dances. Hence, competitive and sexual behaviour are also social mentalities, dependent upon complex dynamic, reciprocal interactions. So a social mentality is simply a social motive that is textured by the 'social dances' it engages and creates. These dances can also operate inside our heads and in the fantasies we form, e.g. imagining sexual, assertive, fun interactions and being physiologically changed as a result. They can also play out in our own self-to-self relating (e.g. self-criticism can play out dominant/subordinate forms of relating (Gilbert & Irons, 2005)).

Importantly, different social mentalities organise and are organised by different psychological and physiological systems which in turn represent phenotypic strategies (Gilbert 1989/2016, 2015b). So if we are organised and orientated for (say) self-focused competitiveness, or threat and defence, then our whole way of attending, thinking and relating to others will be different than if we are orientated for developing friendships, cooperation or caring. Social mentalities are very sensitive to context. So care-focused and compassion-focused social mentalities will be linked to history of social context and be much more likely to be recruited in affiliative than hostile contexts. This is important because humans have multiple motivational and goal-orientated systems which give rise to conscious and unconscious conflicts as to what will be in control of actual behaviour (Huang & Bargh, 2014). For the most part these are genetically and socially choreographed (using slaves and enjoying the Rome games are clearly socially determined). Hence, as Buddhism has claimed for many centuries, unless one develops a purposeful intention to understand one's mind *and* cultivate certain motives (compassion) at the expense of others (selfishness) our minds can be chaotic and harmful.

Compassion is obviously the opposite motivation to selfishness, threat-based aggression, greed and basic callousness. The point of cultivating this motivational system then is because it has profound effects on a range of psychological and physiological systems and interpersonal behaviours – which stand in complete contrast to threat, greed and self-focused motives (Gilbert, in press; Sappla & Doty, in press).

Like all motives, caring-compassion comes with competencies for its enactment. Although the word compassion comes from the Latin word *compati* meaning 'to suffer with', this is not an accurate *definition* of compassion today. In fact, for over 2,500 years, in the contemplative traditions, and more recently in secular traditions, compassion is related to *motivation*, and defined as 'a sensitivity to suffering in self and others with a commitment to try to alleviate and prevent it' (Gilbert & Choden, 2013; Ricard, 2015). This definition highlights two basic psychologies underpinning compassion. The first relates to the motivation and competencies which allow us to *turn towards suffering* (rather than avoid, dissociate, deny or even enjoy it), and obviously not want to create it for others. It enables us to be moved by, able to tolerate and empathically connect with suffering. It also allows us to begin to see *into the causes of suffering*. The second psychology is focused on the motivation to acquire the wisdom, knowledge, expertise and at times courage *to act and do something about suffering*. So compassion is more than good intentions or spontaneous acts of kindness. In the CFT model of compassion there are six basic characteristics of the first psychology of engagement and six characteristics of the second psychology, acting for alleviation/prevention. These can be depicted in Figure 5.1.

Space only allows a brief exploration of these components but each of them is underpinned by scientific studies (for reviews see Gilbert, 2009, 2015b, in press; Sappla & Doty, in press).

68 Paul Gilbert

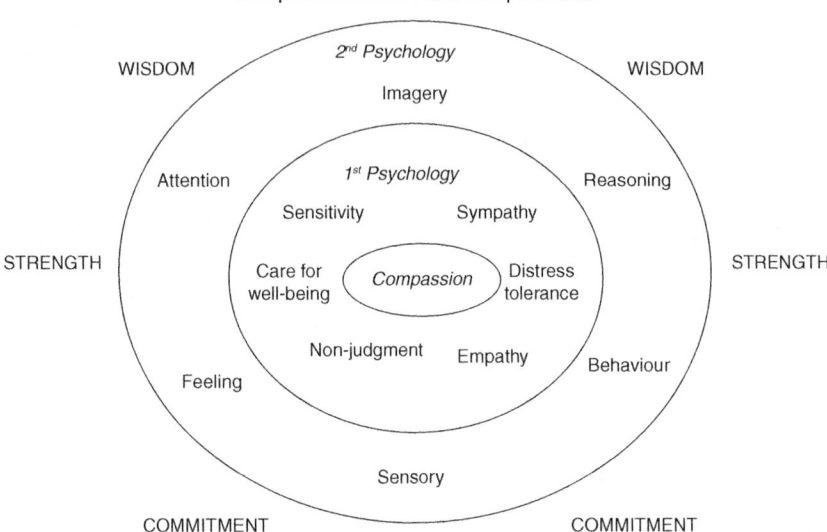

FIGURE 5.1: The two psychologies of compassion: engagement/understanding and alleviation/prevention.

Source: Adapted from Gilbert (2009), *The Compassionate Mind.* With kind permission from Constable Robinson.

Engagement: The inner circle represents the competencies needed for what is sometimes called the first psychology, engagement with suffering. It begins with at least some *motivation to be caring* and, like all motives, it has facilitators and inhibitors (Gilbert & Mascaro, in press). For example, it is easier to be motivated to be compassionate to people we know and like, and who seem to share our values, than people we don't know, dislike or who have dissimilar values (Loewenstein & Small, 2007). With motivation comes the ability to be *attentionally* sensitive. When we attend to suffering, be it in ourselves or others, we can be emotionally moved by it and this links to our capacity for *sympathy*, which is the felt distress we get from being in touch with pain and difficulties (Eisenberg, Van Schyndel, & Hofer, 2015). In fact, *care-focused* distress sensitivity evolved first in the parent–child attachment system. In animals without an attachment system signals of distress simply produce flight and avoidance behaviour (a distress call/signal from another could indicate a predator; a disease and signal an infection). However, in the parent–child relationship distress calls and disease signals produce approach and caring behaviour. In addition, when parents are close to infants they have to be sensitive to the potential damage they could inflict on their infants by careless acts. There is therefore a link between 'distress sensitivity' and the desire not to cause harm, with guilt and harm reparation. These probably first evolved in the mammalian attachment contexts (Gilbert 1989/2016). Indeed, the origins of guilt and shame are very different (Gilbert, 1989/2016, 2007a, 2009). Clearly, however, mechanisms that enable sensitivity to the distress of others, and in particular the distress we might cause others, can be easily turned off in certain contexts. It is understanding the (causes of) lack of responsiveness to distress signals from others, and any sense of guilt or remorse if we have done so, that is particularly important in certain forms of criminal behaviour.

In order to work with the feelings that arise around the experience of suffering, be it in self or others, we have to be able to *tolerate that distress* – and not enjoy it (as in the Roman gladiatorial games!). So a competency for sympathy-based *distress tolerance* is important. If one shuts down to one's own distress, for example from one's own early abusive experiences, then one is more likely to be shut down from the distress one causes others. 'Hurt people hurt people' as the saying goes.

Moving around the circle we come to *empathy* that involves a number of different competencies (Baron-Cohen, 2012; Decety & Cowell, 2014). One is emotional contagion; that is our ability to feel in tune with, and feel similarly to/with, an-other. A second empathy competency is perspective taking which is a more cognitive competency linked to mentalising; we understand not only *what* people are feeling but also (to some degree) *why* (Decety & Cowell, 2014). These competencies allow us to get behind the scenes as it were. So, for example, if somebody is angry we may recognise they are actually fearful or being rejected or hurt. The sixth competency is labelled non-judgment because it's important to be relatively non-critical or condemning of what we are experiencing and not to push it away, avoid or attack it. Condemning or criticising is likely to disturb these care-focused competencies.

These competencies are interdependent. If you lose any one of them compassion can falter. For example, if we lose capacities for mentalising or distress tolerance, or even guilt, compassion is going to struggle. Therefore, building compassion motivation also requires cultivating and developing these competencies. Indeed, different therapies focus on different elements of these competencies such as attention sensitivity or mindfulness, or mentalising or distress tolerance (Fonagy, Gergely, Jurist, & Target, 2002; Linehan, 2015).

Action: The 'second psychology' is focused on developing, learning and practising what we need to do in order to stimulate the motivational system (work it like a muscle) and acquire the wisdom to know how to alleviate and prevent suffering. There will of course be times when suffering and pain cannot be alleviated and it's how we learn to accommodate to it. We will all die one day and can those we love. To some extent the desire to alleviate and prevent suffering also involves taking an interest in the needs of self and others. For example, in order to prevent suffering in one's children one ensures that they flourish; that they have good diets, proper exercise and receive love that stimulates their brains in particular ways. So looking at the second action focused circle in Figure 5.1, we can start with *attention* by focusing on what is helpful. Being able to *imagine* and create images that stimulate our caring and compassion-focused motives and the physiological networks helps to create states of mind conducive to compassion. We can practise these in certain types of imagery practices. Compassion obviously requires rational *thinking* and wisdom; compassion is not stupid. Indeed, sometimes it is important that we use our capacity to reason to override some of our more emotionally driven impulses which may want us to close down compassion (Loewenstein & Small, 2007). So even if we don't *feel* compassion we may logically or rationally be able to understand the value of acting compassionately or helpfully. Indeed, there can be times when clinicians or parents know that they don't *feel* in a compassionate state of mind (perhaps because of fatigue) but still behave compassionately with patients or children because this is part of their self-identity and something they really want to do. The motives for any behaviour can be more important than the feelings.

Compassionate *behaviour* is how we take the actions we need to alleviate suffering and promote flourishing. Those actions sometimes can require courage. For example, an agoraphobic requires the courage to go out and learn to tolerate anxiety. In forensic settings courage may be required to engage with painful traumatic memories or deal with underlying grief and feelings of vulnerability; or to come to terms with harm the clients have caused and the sorrow of guilt. The *feelings* associated with the enacting of compassion can be soothing and may be considered forms of gentle kindness but sometimes they are more active. For example, when running into the burning house to save a baby one is not in a state of soothing, kindly gentleness – but more likely determined anxiety. Sometimes anger at injustice stimulates people to 'fight' for justice for the benefit of others. Indeed, some of the Buddhist bodhisattvas who represent compassion-deity figures can be quite fierce! (Leighton, 2003).

Compassion as flow

As a social mentality compassion can be understood in terms of its interactional dynamics. Hence, there is the compassion we can feel for others but there's also the awareness and responsiveness that we can have to the compassion from others. And thirdly, there is the compassion for self. These are highly interactive but involve these competencies of Figure 5.1. So, for example, compassion *to others* means we have empathy for them whereas compassion *from others* means we are sensitive to the empathy they have for us; and of course self-compassion is having empathy and insight into our own feelings and motives. These emotions are highly interactive and it is a mistake to see CFT as a self-compassion therapy. In a test of social mentality theory, Hermanto et al. (2016) explored the interactions of these processes and found that the combination of high care-seeking and high care-giving predicted the highest level of self-compassion and self-reassurance. However, the combination of low care-seeking and high care-giving was related to the least capacity for self-compassion/reassurance. Another study found that those who had been open to compassion from others significantly moderated the link between self-criticism and depression. Indeed, there is increasing evidence to suggest that the inability to respond to compassion from others plays (maybe because of mistrust or trauma) a salient role in psychopathology, and perhaps more so than self-compassion. Compassion focused therapy helps people with all three orientations.

Revisiting empathy – it's not always pro-moral

Individuals who are a source of suffering to themselves and others are often dissociated from the pain they cause. In a major review, Blair, Mitchell, and Blair (2005) show that people with psychopathic difficulties do not appear to have the care/compassion social mentality accessible. Hence, they are not physiologically responsive to signals of distress. So the problem is more than just empathic failures (Cohen, 2001) and is more likely rooted in motivational systems which would underpin phenotypic strategies. One recent candidate for this has been polymorphism of the oxytocin gene (Mayseless, 2016). Indeed, empathy itself is a set of complex competencies and must be distinguished from the motivational processes that underpin compassion (Gilbert, 2015b). We may not need empathy to behave morally, for example (Decety & Cowell, 2014). Empathy has both an emotional contagion/resonance competency (able to feel what another feels) and a mentalising, perspective-taking competency. Emotional, empathic resonance or contagion without perspective taking may be somewhat overwhelming and directionless while perspective taking without an emotional connectedness can be cold and exploitative.

We may well have emotional empathy for 'a good guy taking revenge on a bad guy', and enjoy that sense of vengeance (indeed the Hollywood movie industry plays on this all the time), but that's unlikely to be regarded as compassionate. The worst torturer to have is an empathic one, and people who are best at marketing and exploiting others are empathic. Indeed, Gilin, Maddux, Carpenter, & Galinsky (2013) have shown that perspective taking (but not necessarily emotional resonance) can be very advantageous in competitive situations. Meffert, Gazzola, den Boer, Bartels, & Keysers (2013) found that people with psychopathic traits, when asked to view video clips of people receiving painful stimuli, did not respond with the empathic neurophysiological profiles that controls did. In other words, empathy circuits seemed to be non-active. But when 'asked to' identify with the person in the video clip then these circuits were activated. People with psychopathic traits might be competent at perspective taking, and can use it when they need or want to, but again lack emotional empathy because they lack *caring motivation* (Blair et al., 2005). In contrast, people with Asperger syndrome appear to have the opposite difficulty in that they can experience emotional reactions (resonance) to emotional pictures but they struggle with perspective taking (Dziobek et al., 2008). So in CFT it's essential to keep clear the distinction between a competency (like empathy) and motivation such as caring.

In addition, there is a question as to whether we need empathy to behave morally – and we may not in all contexts (Decety & Cowell, 2014). Importantly, Zaki (2014) has suggested that empathy can be used in any social context and how it is used is very dependent on the motivation underlining the behaviour and social interaction. Decety & Cowell (2014) suggest that the concept of empathy has become so tricky that '... it may be better to refrain from using the slippery concept of empathy and instead make use of more precise constructs, such as emotional sharing, empathic concern, and perspective taking' (p. 526).

So again there are good reasons to separate out 'caring motivations' from the competencies that fulfil them. People can be very motivated to do things but not very competent/talented, whereas others can be very competent but are not motivated. The take-home message is that if we are going to train people in empathy, mentalising and perspective taking, but not address underlying (caring) *motivation capacities*, we could come unstuck. So in forensic programmes we must distinguish between empathy training and genuine care and compassion training (Kolts & Gilbert, in press). They need each other.

Callousness: What is common to many aspects of criminal behaviour is the *disregard for the feelings and well-being* of others: a certain callousness. There are many sources of callousness, for example to those who are disliked or seen as an enemy, vengeance or sadistic pleasures (the Rome games again), but another is the tendency to dismiss individuals who are perceived as inferior. This is especially associated with certain personality traits (Sidanius et al., 2012). Prosocial motivation is the counterpoint to callousness (Gilbert, 2005, 2014; Penner, Dovidio, Piliavin, & Schroeder, 2005). In fact, some forensic programmes focus on cultivating prosocial behaviour, not only for perpetrators to learn to develop more empathy for others but also the need to experience compassion and empathy themselves, although this aspect can be lacking (Woessner & Schwedler, 2014). It may be difficult for people to be in tune with the harm they cause others if they are dissociated from their own trauma and the harm that was done to them, particularly as children (Van der Kolt, 2014). One reason they are dissociated is because they have unprocessed shame (and grief) which holds them in a self-focused threat orientation to the world (Gilbert & Irons, 2005).

Shame, guilt and compassion

There is now considerable evidence that competencies for shame and guilt are very different in terms of their behavioural and cognitive focus and play out very differently in perpetrators' responses to their harmful acts. For example, shame tends to support tendencies for justification, denial and avoidance, and when repair efforts do occur it's the desire to repair one's reputation in the minds of others or sense of self. In contrast, the emotions of guilt are ones of sorrow, sadness and remorse, empathic engagement with the harm done and genuine desires to help the injured party recover in some way (for reviews see Griffin et al., 2016). Shame does not generally promote moral or prosocial behaviour whereas guilt does (Tangney, Stuewig, & Mashek, 2007).

These models, however, are very cognitively focused whereas CFT highlights the fact that shame and guilt are rooted in very different evolved, motivation, functional systems and have very big differences on aggressive versus prosocial behaviour, and very different physiologies. The human potential for shame is rooted in earlier defensive strategies that evolved within status hierarchies, where subordinates need to show deference and submissiveness to threat from dominant others (Gilbert, 2000b; Gilbert & McGuire, 1998). Shame is linked to what Tang-Smith et al. (2014) refer to as a social dominance system which is part of the social rank system (Gilbert, 2000b). Briefly, shame is related to a focus on the self which can be external (a sense that others look down on the self, seeing the self as inferior, inadequate or bad in some way), and internal (seeing oneself as bad with various forms and degrees of self-criticism). These are basically threat focused and although people can change their behaviour because of shame, and the fear of shame, this is not rooted in any moral or ethical system but mainly fear and avoidance of threats and harms to self; reparation is therefore focused on self, reputation and identity (Gilbert, 1998b, 2007b; Tangney et al., 2007). In contrast, guilt evolved from the caring system (distress recognition) as a harm avoidance system. Once caring and affiliative behaviour evolved there had to be mechanisms for helping individuals track the impact of their own behaviour on others and in particular to avoid causing harm to those they were caring for and to invest in seeing them prosper, with aversive feelings arising if harm was caused (Gilbert, 1989, 2007).

So guilt is linked to recognition of having caused harm/distress to others with motivation for repair to the one harmed. It is typically focused on behaviour rather than a global sense of self – partly because attention is not on the (social or individualised) sense of self, but on the distress caused. From an evolutionary point of view guilt is not about attending to our reputation or evaluating oneself (that's irrelevant) but avoiding causing harm via our actions and repairing it if we do. In contrast, shame is not focused on distress signals particularly – and we can feel shame when the other is laughing at us. Indeed, we often feel shame when people who are more powerful and competent than us look down on us. The emotions that are central to guilt are ones of sorrow, sadness and remorse with a capacity for empathic connection to the distress one has caused. By contrast, with shame the motivation is about self and reputation repair; with guilt the motivation is to repair and *reduce the distress* in the other. Humans can experience many different emotions and motives at the same time. So it is rare, if at all, that individuals will experience pure shame or pure guilt.

This distinction is also important in restorative versus retributive justice (Shapland, Robinson, & Sorsby, 2011; Wozniak, 2014). Restorative justice is about bringing victim and perpetrator together with a focus on facilitating perpetrators *to gain insight into the harm they caused* and to stimulate a sense of sorrow and regret. If one only stimulated shame then that would be self- (not other) focused attention; the focus would be on punishment 'to the self' which would be unhelpful in the long run. This does not mean, however, that CFT is against regulation, punishment and enforcement of regulation. Indeed, it is fairly obvious that regulation is essential for many kinds of prosocial behaviour. For example, inviting people not to smoke in public places was relatively ineffective until regulation came in. Indeed, there are certain parts of the world where you can still go into restaurants and people are quite happy to smoke, completely uncaring that other people around them may not be enjoying their secondhand smoke. Part of CFT is the recognition that the human brain is very tricky and that social regulation is important. This is especially true in large groups because in small groups (where humans evolved) social reputation and awareness would generally be a major inhibitor of antisocial behaviour.

CFT therefore sees fostering prosocial *motivational* states of mind as central for working with people who have behaved harmfully or neglectfully towards others (and self). In essence, their capacities for *caring motivational processing* are often compromised because people can be motivationally more self-focused, threat focused and competitive. In addition, some of the competencies such as distress tolerance, empathy and courage that underpin compassion may be poorly developed (Gilbert, 2014; Shirtcliff et al., 2009). Therapists should be prepared for the fact that as this kind of therapy develops, guilt and negative emotion may increase in their clients, and with them deeper recognition of pain that has been done to themselves (Shirtcliff et al., 2009). At times individuals can become remorseful but also more depressed and even suicidal.

Emotion regulation

Helping people understand, tolerate and regulate their emotions is central to many psychotherapies. CFT helps people understand the functional nature of their emotions by using an evolutionary functional analysis of emotion. This groups emotions in terms of adapted functions. CFT focuses on three basic functions of emotions:

1. To be able to detect and respond appropriately to threats; in the moment but also to avoid them in the future. Typical emotions here are anxiety, anger and disgust.
2. To be able to detect and respond appropriately to signals of resources and rewards conducive to survival and fitness. Typical emotions here are excitement, pleasure and joyfulness.
3. To be able to detect and respond to situations which indicate safeness and facilitate 'rest and digest'. Typical emotions here are calmness, peacefulness and contentment.

These are depicted as three circles that are constantly interacting and from which blends of emotional experience arise.

CFT helps clients think about how these different systems are working for them, their histories and triggers. So, for example, clients may begin to understand that because of early life experiences they are very threat sensitive and rapidly experience activation of anger or anxiety or both – 'the body remembers' (Van der Kolk, 2014) easily activated brain and body states. In terms of drives these can be defensive or highly self-focused and again clients can begin to understand the triggers and nature of the drives. They may distinguish drives to avoid bad things happening from drives to take pleasure from the world. Emotions can also be ones of slowing down, feeling content and safe and where relationships, and our ability to elicit and respond to the care-compassion of others, play key roles (Gilbert, 2014).

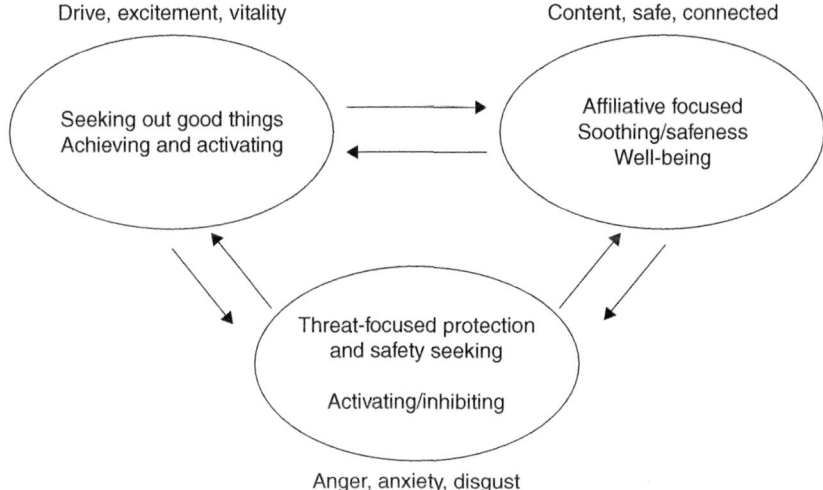

FIGURE 5.2: Three types of evolved functional affect regulation system.
Source: Adapted from Gilbert (2009), *The Compassionate Mind.* With kind permission from Constable Robinson.

For the most part threat and drive systems are 'activating' and involve the sympathetic nervous system, whereas soothing involves the parasympathetic system and in particular the myelinated vagus nerve (though of course in reality it is the complex reciprocal relationship balance between them that's important). The myelinated vagus and its role as a soothing process evolved with attachment (Porges, 2007). In attachment theory, the caring and support of the parent provides a secure base (which provides the supports to go out and explore the world) and a safe haven (which provides a source of comfort and soothing when distressed) (Bowlby, 1969; Mikulincer & Shaver, 2007). Over time, children who experience these physiologically and phenotypically important inputs become able to turn to others when distressed and are also able to be sensitive to the distress of others; indeed, early attachment relationships are linked to subsequent compassion competencies (Gillath, Shaver, & Mikulincer, 2005). Individuals who come from neglectful or abusive backgrounds clearly do not experience these sources for developing a secure base and safe haven and have poorly developed parasympathetic regulation and poor heart rate variability. Indeed, there is now considerable evidence that heart rate variability develops in the context of affiliative caring relationships and orientates people towards creating and maintaining caring relationships (Keltner, Kogan, Piff, & Saturn, 2014; Kogan et al., 2014). These findings must be contextualised in what we've noted before, which is that environments are choreographing different phenotypic, reproductive strategies (McDonald et al., 2012; Moore & Depue, 2016).

Hence, while some therapies focus on cognitive or behavioural change, CFT tries to also work on basic motivational (and hence phenotypic) systems by generating (compassion focused) practices and exercises that have physiological impacts. Indeed, there is considerable evidence that certain kinds of compassion practices are physiologically powerful and may even influence genetic expression (see Gilbert, in press; Sappla & Doty, in press; Singer & Bolz, 2013). Part of the focus is to begin to build a sense of secure base and safe haven (Gilbert, 2014).

There are a number of different compassion focused exercises that seek to do this that include:

1. Learning how to use the body to stimulate or calm the mind. For example, using certain kinds of breathing patterns designed to stimulate the vagal system (e.g. compassion – shoulders back posture with five breaths per minute breathing patterns). In addition we practice using affiliative and friendly facial expressions and voice tones. These are not only be used to stimulate different patterns but also to help people become more body aware – and learn how to ground themselves and refocus attention when stressed. These techniques support becoming more body aware and with that more emotionally sensitive.
2. Reflecting on and imagining what safeness is and would be like. What is the difference between safety (stopping bad things happening) and safeness (the freedom 'to be' and to explore); what would one like to do if one felt safe. Imagining a place may enable a sense of playfulness and open and creative exploration that some clients may never have really felt before.
3. Imagining a safe, compassionate other. Here we explain that just as we can imagine arguments with others or sexual encounters with others, and these will stimulate different physiological systems, so we can practise imagining interactions with compassionate other(s). Part of the practice encourages clients to think about what they would like from a compassionate other and importantly what might their fears, blocks and resistances might be. Again we stress that these practices are partly to help stimulate physiological patterns that enable our minds to be able to operate in different and new ways.
4. Compassionate self practices use acting techniques (amongst other processes) to help people imagine themselves at their compassionate best and then practise compassion competencies. For example, we can help people compare and contrast different patterns of activation within themselves. For example, we might invite them to imagine an argument with somebody they care about and how would they respond if angry self was in control or anxious self. Then we can explore how they would ideally like to be with the strength and courage of compassionate self. This does a number of things including being able to recognise that in any situation like this, there are a range of alternative ways of responding. The key is choosing wisely rather than reactively. All the time fears, blocks and resistances are explored. The therapist may spend some time working on individual competencies of the compassionate self such as empathy, distress tolerance, mindfulness or body awareness and grounding.

Here also the therapist is encouraging a creating, stepping into and becoming sense of a new identity – with a particular motivational focus – rather than just a change of beliefs. Clients are helped to develop their capacities for distress tolerance and empathy for self and to bring the compassionate self (pattern) to particular life problems by using the breath slowing and compassionate attentional focusing. Hence the importance of becoming mindfully aware and choosing as best one can the aspects of self one wants to bring to that situation.

Compassion focused therapy

CFT is a motivation focused therapy that utilises a range of other evidence-based interventions. For example, in this population it will be essential to assess and address problems such as chronic post-traumatic stress disorder, particularly for individuals who have been abused in childhood. The first stage in a therapy might therefore be to develop compassion motivation in order to work with trauma rather than try to develop moral behaviour first.

CFT helps clients develop the motivation and competencies for compassion as outlined in Figure 5.1. Therapy can therefore go through various stages. In addition to the usual process of therapy such as assessment, history taking and creating the conditions for a therapeutic relationship, CFT adds:

1. A psychoeducation component based on the fact that the human brain, which evolved in a rather piecemeal way, is full of inbuilt problems with biases and inherent conflicts making us very vulnerable to antisocial behaviour and also mental health problems. Much of what goes on in our brains is not our design or our intention and in that sense is not our fault, but our behaviours are very much our responsibility. So it may not be our fault that we have genes for obesity and bowel cancer or smoking and lung cancer but if we don't plan how to regulate our behaviour we could end up dying in rather horrible ways. CFT suggests that the more individuals identify with the problems of common humanity and the troubles of the evolved tricky brain, the less personalised and the easier it is to work with shame and take responsibility for change.
2. Formulation is based on the evolutionary model and on helping people to understand that many of their basic phenotypes, which lead to life-strategies for dealing with threats and trying to advance oneself, are very much the consequence of genes interacting with social contexts. Helping individuals understand the unintended and often unhelpful consequences of their safety or acquisition strategies is important. Once again de-shaming is central to this intervention.
3. Part of psychoeducation involves helping individuals begin to understand the nature of their different emotion systems and how they can learn to be more mindfully aware of them and develop body awareness of different emotions. Mindfulness therefore is an important element of CFT, enabling people to be

more attentive to what is going on in their own minds and bodies as it arises. In addition, CFT teaches specific breathing exercises (called soothing rhythm breathing) that are designed to stimulate the parasympathetic system which in turn has an impact on the frontal cortex and capacities for reflective thinking (Lin, Tai, & Fan, 2014). The key focus is on helping the person experience sensations of slowing down and being present and connecting with the sense of self one is trying to become (Gilbert & Choden, 2013).

4. Central to this is building compassion motivation. In CFT this is seen as a core transforming process that arises from insight. There are a range of interventions for building compassion motivation, including the use of compassion imagery, compassionate reflection, compassion-focused empathy, developing a compassionate self-identity, regular practise of compassionate behaviour and keeping compassion diaries (Gilbert, 2010). It's helpful to recognise that sometimes individuals can practise behaving and thinking in compassionate ways long before they start 'feeling' compassion. Indeed, sometimes the emergence of compassion 'emotions' is unpredictable.

Fears, blocks and resistances to compassion

The journey through CFT is rarely straightforward and will meet many fears, blocks and resistances (Gilbert & Mascaro, in press; Gilbert et al., 2011). There are different dimensions and levels to these fears. One can be at the level of meta-cognitive beliefs such as 'compassion is weak and indulgent' or 'is not helpful'. Individuals may believe they don't deserve care or compassion; they may have beliefs that 'if you really knew what went on in my head you wouldn't think I deserve compassion'. This is shame based on the fear of being shamed through certain discoveries and revelations. These can be sexual, aggressive or sometimes fear-based (being seen as weak). It is paradoxical then that as clients begin to reveal more of the dark side of themselves shame can make it even more difficult for them to experience helpful compassion.

In some caring situations, fears may occur automatically (presenting as anxiety). In these cases, a sense of caring, or the need for caring itself, stimulates aversive emotion. This can be rooted in classically conditioned emotional responses. For example, a parent might have been loving in the morning but drunk and abusive at night, creating considerable confusion as to the experience of care (Van der Kolk, 2014). Additionally, evoking and using a 'caring approach' can be used by adults as a way of manipulating a child sexually or to foster guilt. Such 'fears of care and closeness' are very likely in people with disorganised attachment (Liotti, 2010).

Blocks and inhibitions to compassion can also operate at physiological levels. Gillie and Thayer (2014) reviewed the evidence that parasympathetic tone is important for executive control and the integration of frontal cortical systems with deeper brain systems. They describe how both are compromised in people with post-traumatic stress disorder. Austin, Riniolo, and Porges (2007) found that people with borderline difficulties do not differ in terms of sympathetic activation to threat compared to controls, but differ significantly in the parasympathetic responses to potential helpfulness – actually showing a more fight-flight profile in situations of helpfulness. In essence, these individuals find it difficult to use the parasympathetic system as a calming and grounding system. This will have knock-on effects to a whole range of emotion regulation abilities not to mention frontal cortical ones that are linked to moral behaviour, self-reflection and impulse inhibition. CFT recommends attention to these physiological processes.

As clients begin to realise the roots of human interdependence and need for social connectedness and compassion, it is not uncommon for them to also come to recognise an inner grief process which they can (at first) be very avoidant and even contemptuous of. Indeed, facilitating grief for the life they wanted (e.g. to be loved and cared for, especially by parents) and the life they had (abused, neglected and unwanted) can have profound effects. Grieving for the harm that was done to self, and perhaps the loneliness they have felt, can be central to the change process and shifting social mentalities (Gilbert & Irons, 2005).

Criminal behaviour obviously has multiple sources. Some individuals are clearly carrying severe trauma, others may be more genetically inclined, some have Asperger-like syndromes, others complex learning difficulties, others have severe mental health problems, others have difficulties of alexithymia and dissociation, others substance abuse, others may have minimal brain damage possibly due to alcohol foetal syndrome or acquired subsequently during maturation. Any psychological therapy, including CFT, must have very careful assessments to know what is actually presenting to them in the clinic and to focus on. The textures of the therapy will be different according to the nature of the problem. CFT offers new ways of conceptualising and working with this population but is integrated into already established interventions.

Conclusion

CFT considers criminal behaviour within this human context and recognises that to some degree what we call criminality, and the very fact that we need the rule of law, is based on the recognition that humans can behave badly and harmfully when free to do so. Evolutionary strategies for survival, advancement and reproduction don't always follow moral rules. It is easy to think of compassion as something soft and fluffy but in reality it is core to how to approach the problems of the species that we are and the terrible things we are capable of. In addition, we note that some of what we now regard as criminal behaviour, including towards women and children, is partly because we are becoming more sensitive, empathic and indeed compassionate. Law and prevention is focusing more and more on suffering whereas in centuries past laws were more linked to protection of property and wealth.

CFT is an integrative psychotherapy rooted in these evolutionary approaches, helping clients recognise just how much of what goes on in our minds is very tricky, and is not our fault. This seeks to de-shame people (given that shame does not motivate moral behaviour and undermines mental health; Griffin et al., 2016) but also seeks to stimulate responsibility taking, capacities to feel and tolerate guilt and remorse, and preparedness to practise change-focused processes and behaviours. CFT spends some time explaining the genuine nature of compassion (and many clients and indeed even some staff have a poor or even contemptuous understanding of compassion), its roots in both *courage* and *commitment*, along with the practices that develop it.

CFT uses a range of evidence-based practices designed to stimulate particular physiological systems that create the platform for psychological change. In particular, exercises are used that stimulate parasympathetic systems and facilitate better frontal cortical control of emotion. Central to CFT is not only to build and practise the constituent attributes and competencies of compassion, but work with the fears, blocks and resistances, which can be central to the therapy. Sometimes grieving plays a key role as individuals begin to engage with understanding their own suffering and early losses with the recognition of how lonely and uncared for they may have felt. This may be an essential process for people to start to be sensitive to the harm they cause others (Shirtcliff et al., 2009).

As forensics establishments become more scientific in understanding basic human psychology, as opposed to simply using ancient systems of 'good and bad', 'reward and punishment', a biblical approach to wrongdoing – the roles of compassion motivation training and cultivation will become more apparent. Psychological therapies can be rooted in our understanding of the role of affiliative behaviour in preventing not only mental health problems but also in developing more moral and prosocial behaviour to others.

Further reading

Buss, D. M. (2012). The evolutionary psychology of crime. *Journal of Theoretical and Philosophical Criminology*. Special edition, 1, 90–98.

Gilbert, P. (2015b). The evolution and social dynamics of compassion. *Journal of Social & Personality Psychology Compass*, 9, 239–254. doi: 10.1111/spc3.12176

Singer, T., & Bolz, M. (2013). *Compassion: Bridging practice and science*. Max Planck Institute for Human Cognitive and Brain Sciences. www.compassion-training.org/

Zaki, J. (2014). Empathy: A motivated account. *Psychological Bulletin*, 140, 1608–1647. http://dx.doi.org/10.1037/a0037679Prof

References

Abbott, G. (1993). *Rack Rope and Red Hot Pincers: A History of Torture and its Instruments*. London: Headline.

Andrews, D. A., & Bonta, J. (2010). *The Psychology of Criminal Conduct*. New York: Anderson.

Ashworth, F. M., Gracey, F., & Gilbert, P. (2011). Compassion Focused Therapy after traumatic brain injury: Theoretical foundations and a case illustration. *Brain Impairment*, 12, 128–139.

Austin, M. A., Riniolo, T. C., & Porges, S. W. (2007). Borderline personality disorder and emotion regulation: Insights from the Polyvagal Theory. *Brain and Cognition*, 65, 69–76.

Bakan, J. (2005). *The Corporation: The pathological pursuit of profit and power*. London: Constable.

Baron-Cohen, S. (2012). *Zero Degrees of Empathy*. London: Penguin.

Belsky, J., & Pluess, M. (2009). Beyond diathesis stress: Differential susceptibility to environmental influences. *Psychological Bulletin*, 135, 885–908. doi: 10.1037/a0017376

Blair, J., Mitchell, D., & Blair, K. (2005). *The Psychopath: Emotion and the Brain*. London: Wiley-Blackwell.

Bowlby, J. (1969). *Attachment: Attachment and Loss*, Vol. 1. London: Hogarth Press.

Braehler, C., Gumley, A., Harper, J., Wallace, S., Norrie, J., & Gilbert, P. (2013). Exploring change processes in compassion focused therapy in psychosis: Results of a feasibility randomized controlled trial. *British Journal of Clinical Psychology, 52*, 199–214.

Buss, D. M. (2012). The evolutionary psychology of crime. *Journal of Theoretical and Philosophical Criminology*. Special edition, *1*, 90–98.

Button, T. M. M., Scourfield, J., Martin, N., Purcell, S., & McGuffin, P. (2005). Family dysfunction interacts with genes in the causation of antisocial symptoms. *Behavior Genetics, 35*, 115–120.

Cohen, D. (2001). Cultural variation: Considerations and implications. *Psychological Bulletin, 127*, 451–471.

da Silva, D. R., Rijo, D., & Salekin, R. T. (2014). The evolutionary roots of psychopathy. *Aggression and Violent Behavior, 21*, 85–96.

Decety, K., & Cowell, J. M. (2014). Friends or foes: Is empathy necessary for moral behavior? *Perspectives on Psychological Science, 9*, 525–937. doi: 10.1177/1745691614545130

Dorkins, E., & Adshead, G. (2011). Working with offenders: challenges to the recovery agenda. *Advances in Psychiatric Treatment, 17*, 178–187.

Dziobek, I., Rogers, K., Fleck, S., Bahnemann, M., Heekeren, H. R., Wolf, O. T., & Convit, A. (2008). Dissociation of cognitive and emotional empathy in adults with Asperger Syndrome: Using the Multifaceted Empathy Test (MET). *Journal of Autism and Developmental Disorders, 38*, 464–473. doi: 10.1007/s10803-007-0486-x

Eisenberg, N., Van Schyndel, S. K., & Hofer, C. (2015). The association of maternal socialization in childhood and adolescence with adult offsprings' sympathy/caring. *Developmental Psychology, 51*, 7–16. doi: 10.1037/a0038137

Fonagy, P., Gergely, G., Jurist, F. L., & Target, M. (2002). *Affect regulation, mentalization, and the development of the self*. London: Other Press.

Furnham, A., Richards, S. C., & Paulhus, D. L. (2013). The dark triad of personality: A 10 year review. *Social and Personality Psychology Compass, 7*(3), 199–216. doi: 10.1111/spc3.12018

Garcia, H. S. (2015) the Alpha god: The psychology of religious violence and oppression. New York: Prometheus Books.

Garcia-Moreno, C., Jansen, H. A., Ellsberg, M., Heise, L., & Watts, C. H. (2006). Prevalence of intimate partner violence: findings from the WHO multi-country study on women's health and domestic violence (on behalf of the WHO multi-country study on women's health and domestic violence against women study team) *Lancet. 368*(9543), 7–13, October, 1260–1269.

Gilbert, P. (1989/2016). *Human nature and suffering*. Hove: Lawrence Erlbaum Associates.

Gilbert, P. (1994). Male violence: Towards an integration. In J. Archer (Ed.), *Male Violence* (pp. 352–389). London: Routledge and Kegan Paul.

Gilbert, P. (1998a). Evolutionary psychopathology: Why isn't the mind better designed than it is? *British Journal of Medical Psychology, 71*, 353–373.

Gilbert, P. (1998b). What is shame? Some core issues and controversies. In P. Gilbert & B. Andrews (Eds), *Shame: Interpersonal Behavior, Psychopathology and Culture* (pp. 3–36). New York: Oxford University Press.

Gilbert, P. (2000a). Social mentalities: Internal 'social' conflicts and the role of inner warmth and compassion in cognitive therapy. In P. Gilbert & Bailey K.G (Eds), *Genes on the Couch: Explorations in Evolutionary Psychotherapy* (pp.118–150). Hove: Psychology Press.

Gilbert, P. (2000b). Varieties of submissive behaviour: Their evolution and role in depression. In L. Sloman & P. Gilbert (Eds), *Subordination and Defeat. An Evolutionary Approach to Mood Disorders* (pp. 3–46). Hillsdale, NJ: Lawrence Erlbaum.

Gilbert, P. (2005). Compassion and cruelty: A biopsychosocial approach. In P. Gilbert (Ed.), *Compassion: Conceptualisations, research and use in psychotherapy* (pp. 3–74). London: Routledge.

Gilbert, P. (2007). *Psychotherapy and Counselling for Depression (3rd edition)*. London: Sage.
Gilbert, P. (2009). *The compassionate mind: A new approach to the challenge of life*. London: Constable & Robinson.
Gilbert, P. (2010). *Compassion focused therapy: The CBT distinctive features series*. London: Routledge.
Gilbert, P. (2014). The origins and nature of compassion focused therapy. *British Journal of Clinical Psychology, 53*, 6–41. doi:10.1111/bjc.12043
Gilbert, P. (2015a). Affiliative and prosocial motives and emotions in mental health. *Dialogues in Clinical Neuroscience, 17*, 381–389.
Gilbert, P. (2015b). The evolution and social dynamics of compassion. *Journal of Social & Personality Psychology Compass, 9*, 239–254. doi: 10.1111/spc3.12176
Gilbert, P. (in press). *Compassion: Concepts, Research and Applications*. London: Routledge.
Gilbert, P., & Choden (2013). *Mindful Compassion*. London: Constable Robinson.
Gilbert, P., & Gilbert, H. (2015). Cruelty, evolution, and religion: The challenge for the new spiritualities. In T.G. Plante (Ed.), *The Psychology of Compassion and Cruelty: Understanding the Emotional, Spiritual and Religious Influences* (pp. 1–15). Oxford: Praeger.
Gilbert, P., & Irons, C. (2005). Focused therapies and compassionate mind training for shame and self-attacking. In P. Gilbert (Ed.), *Compassion: Conceptualisations, Research and Use in psychotherapy* (pp. 263–325). London: Routledge.
Gilbert, P., & Mascaro, J. (in press). Compassion: Fears, blocks, and resistances: An evolutionary investigation. In E. Sappla & J. Doty (Eds), *Handbook of Compassion*. New York: Oxford University Press.
Gilbert, P., McEwan, K., Matos, M., & Rivis, A. (2011). Fears of Compassion: Development of three self-report measures. *Psychology and Psychotherapy, 84*, 239–255.
Gilbert, P., & McGuire, M. (1998). Shame, status and social roles: The psychobiological continuum from monkeys to humans. In P. Gilbert & B. Andrews (Eds), *Shame: Interpersonal Behavior, Psychopathology and Culture* (pp. 99–125). New York: Oxford University Press.
Gilin, D., Maddux, W. W., Carpenter, J., & Galinsky, A. D. (2013). When to use your head and when to use your heart: The differential value of perspective-taking versus empathy in competitive interactions. *Personality and Social Psychology Bulletin, 39*, 3–16.
Gillath, O., Shaver, P. R., & Mikulincer, M. (2005). An attachment-theoretical approach to compassion and altruism. In P. Gilbert (Ed.), *Compassion: Conceptualisations, research and use in psychotherapy* (pp. 121–147). London: Routledge.
Gillie, B. L., & Thayer, J. F. (2014). Individual differences in resting heart rate variability and cognitive control in post traumatic stress disorder published on line. *Frontiers in Psychology, 15*, 758. doi: 10.3389/fpsyg.2014.00758
Gilmore, D. D. (1990). *Manhood in the making: Cultural concepts of masculinity*. Cambridge, MA: Harvard University Press.
Griffin, B. J., Moloney, J. M., Green, J. D., Worthington, Jr., E. L., Cork, B., Tangney, J. P., Van Tongeren, D. R., Davis, D. E., & Hook, J. N. (2016). Perpetrators' reactions to perceived interpersonal wrongdoing: The associations of guilt and shame with forgiving, punishing, and excusing oneself. *Self and Identity* (advanced publication). doi: 10.1080/15298868.2016.1187669
Hermanto, N., Zuroff, D. C., Kopala-Sibley, D. C., Kelly, A. C., Matos, M., & Gilbert, P. (2016). Ability to receive compassion from others buffers the depressogenic effect of self-criticism: A cross-cultural multi-study analysis. *Personality and Individual Differences, 98*, 324–332. doi.org/10.1016/j.paid.2016.04.055
Hoffman, D. H., Carter, D. J., Viglucci Lopez, C. R., et al. (2015). Report to the special committee of the board of directors of the American Psychological Association: Independent review relating to APA ethics guidelines, national security interrogations, and

torture. Chicago: Sidley Austin. Retrieved from www.apa.org/independent-review/APA-FINAL-Report-7.2.15.pdf, accessed 1 December, 2015.

Huang, J. Y., & Bargh, J. A. (2014). The Selfish Goal: Autonomously operating motivational structures as the proximate cause of human judgement and behavior. *Behavioral and Brain Sciences, 37*(2), 121–135.

Kelman, H. C., & Hamilton, V. L. (1989). *Crimes of Obedience*. New Haven: Yale University Press.

Keltner, D., Kogan, A., Piff, P. K., & Saturn, S. R. (2014). The sociocultural appraisals, values, and emotions (SAVE) framework of prosociality: Core processes from gene to meme. *The Annual Review of Psychology, 65*, 425–460.

Kogan, A., Oveis, C., Carr, E. W., Gruber, J., Mauss, I. B., Shallcross, A., et al. (2014). Vagal activity is quadratically related to prosocial traits, prosocial emotions, and observer perceptions of prosociality. *Journal of Personality and Social Psychology, 107*, 1051–1063.

Kolts, R. (2012). *The Compassionate Mind Approach to Managing Anger using Compassion Focused Therapy*. London: Constable Robinson.

Kolts, R. L., & Gilbert, P. (in press). Understanding and using Compassion Focused Therapy in forensic settings. In A. Beech (Ed.), *The Wiley-Blackwell Handbook of Forensic Neuroscience*. Oxford: Wiley-Blackwell.

Laithwaite, H., O'Hanlon, M, Collins, P, & Doyle, P. (2009). Recovery after Psychosis (RAP): A Compassion Focused Programme for individuals residing in high security. *Behavioural and Cognitive Psychotherapy, 37*(5), 511–526.

Leaviss, J., & Uttley, L. (2014). Psychotherapeutic benefits of compassion focused therapy: An early systematic review. *Psychological Medicine, 45*, 927–945. doi:10.1017/S0033291714002141

Lee, D., & James, S. (2012). *The Compassionate Mind Approach to recovering from trauma using Compassion Focused Therapy*. London: Constable Robinson.

Leighton, T. D. (2003). *Faces of compassion: Classic Bodhisattva archetypes and their modern expression*. Boston, MA: Wisdom.

Lin, I. M., Tai, L. Y., & Fan, S. Y. (2014). Breathing at a rate of 5.5 breaths per minute with equal inhalation-to-exhalation ratio increases heart rate variability. *International Journal of Psychophysiology, 91*, 206–211.

Linehan, M. M. (2015). *DBT Skills Training Manual*. Second Edition. New York: Guilford.

Liotti, G. (2010). Attachment and dissociation. In P. F. Dell & J. A. O'Neil (Eds), *Dissociation and the Dissociative Disorders: DSM-V and Beyond* (pp. 53–66). London: Routledge.

Loewenstein, G., & Small, D. A. (2007). The scarecrow and the tin man: The vicissitudes of human sympathy and caring. *Review of General Psychology, 11*, 112–126. doi: 10.1037/1089-2680.11.2.112

McDonald, M. M., Donnellan, M. B., & Navarrete, C. D. (2012). A life history approach to understanding the Dark Triad. *Personality and Individual Differences, 52*, 601–605.

McEwan, K., Gilbert, P., & Duarte, J. (2012). An exploration of competitiveness and caring in relation to psychopathology. *British Journal of Clinical Psychology, 51*, 19–36. doi:10.1111/j.2044-8260.2011.02010.x

Mayseless, O. (2016). *The caring motivation and integrated theory*. New York: Oxford University Press.

Meffert, H., Gazzola, V., den Boer, J. A., Bartels, A. A. J., & Keysers, C. (2013). Reduced spontaneous but relatively normal deliberate vicarious representations in psychopathy. *Brain, 136*, 2550–2562.

Mikulincer, M., & Shaver, P. R. (2007). *Attachment in adulthood: structure, dynamics, and change*. New York: Guilford.

Moore, S. R., & Depue, R. A. (2016). Neurobehavioral foundation of environmental reactivity. *Psychological bulletin, 142*(2), 107–164. doi: org/10.1037/bul0000028

Penner, L. A., Dovidio, J. F., Piliavin, J. A., & Schroeder, D. A. (2005). Prosocial behavior: Multilevel perspectives. *Annual Review of Psychology, 56*, 1–28. doi: 10.1146/annurev.psych.56.091103.070141

Porges, S. W. (2007). The polyvagal perspective. *Biological Psychology, 74*, 116–143.

Pratto, F., Sidanius, J., Stallworth, L. M., & Malle, B. F. (1994). Social dominance orientation: A personality variable predicting social and political attitudes. *Journal of Personality and Social Psychology, 67*, 741–763. doi:10.1037/0022-3514.67.4.741

Ricard, M. (2015). *Altruism: The power of compassion to change yourself and the world.* London: Atlantic Books.

Sappla, E., & Doty, J. (in press). *Handbook of Compassion.* New York: Oxford University Press.

Shapland, J., Robinson, G., & Sorsby, A. (2011). *Restorative justice in practice: Evaluating what works for victims and offenders.* London: Willan.

Shirtcliff, E. A., Vitacco, M. J., Graf, A. R., Gostisha, A. J., Merz, J. L., & Zahn-Waxler, C. (2009). Neurobiology of empathy and callousness: Implications for the development of antisocial behavior. *Behavioral Science and the Law, 27*, 137–171. doi:10.1002/bsl.862

Sidanius, J., Kteily, N., Sheehy-Skeffington, J., Ho, A. K., Sibley, C., & Duriez, B. (2012). You're inferior and not worth our concern: The interface between empathy and Social Dominance Orientation. *Journal of Personality, 81*, 31–323. doi: 10.1111/jopy.12008

Singer, T., & Bolz, M. (Eds) (2013). Compassion: Bridging practice and science. www.compassion-training.org/

Slavich, G. M., & Cole, S. W. (2013). The emerging field of human social genomics. *Psychological Science.* Advance online publication. doi:10.1177/2167702613478594

Stott, R. (2007). When the head and heart do not agree: A theoretical and clinical analysis of rational-emotional dissociation (RED) in cognitive therapy. *Journal of Cognitive Psychotherapy: An International Quarterly, 21*, 37–50. doi: 10.1891/088983907780493313

Tangney, J. P., Stuewig, J., & Mashek, D. J. (2007). Moral emotions and moral behavior. *Annual Review of Psychology, 58*, 345–372.

Tang-Smith, E., Johnson, S. L., & Chen, S. (2014). The dominance behavioural system: A multidimensional transdiagnostic approach. *Psychology and Psychotherapy: Theory, Research and Practice.* Online advanced publication. doi:10.1111/papt.12050

Taylor, K. (2009). *Cruelty and the human brain.* Oxford: Oxford University Press.

Van der Kolk, B. (2014). *The body keeps the score: Brain, mind, and body in the transformation of trauma.* London: Viking.

Ward, T., Mann, R., & Gannon, T. (2007). The good lives model of offender rehabilitation. Clinical implications. *Aggression and Violent Behaviour, 12*, 87–107.

Woessner, G., & Schwedler, A. (2014). Correctional treatment of sexual and violent offenders: Therapeutic change, prison, climate and recidivism. *Criminal Justice and Behavior, 41*. Originally published online 13 February, 2014.

Wozniak, J. F. (2014). Unlocking the legal system from vengeance, harm, and punitive justice: Toward a compassionate revolution of peace, caring, and unitive justice. *Journal of Theoretical and Philosophical Criminology, 6*, 231–250. Commentary special edition.

Zaki, J. (2014). Empathy: A motivated account. *Psychological Bulletin, 140*, 1608–1647. http://dx.doi.org/10.1037/a0037679

Zimbardo, P. (2008). *The Lucifer Effect: How good people turn evil.* London: Rider.

6
EYE MOVEMENT DESENSITISATION AND REPROCESSING WITH SEXUAL OFFENDERS

Ronald J. Ricci and Cheryl A. Clayton

Evidence shows that individuals with criminal careers have higher levels of adverse childhood experiences than do the general population, with sex offenders having even higher levels of adverse childhood experiences than other criminal populations. Although formerly best practice was to deter sex offenders from examining their abuse histories for fear of excuse making, the Pathways Model, which highlights etiology, opened the door for considering these vulnerability factors as legitimate treatment targets. EMDR is a well-supported treatment model shown by research to be efficient, effective and durable in treating PTSD and other trauma-related conditions. The Adaptive Information Processing model inherent in EMDR offers an explanation for the effective restructuring of distorted implicit cognitions and personal vulnerability factors which drive offending behaviours, a misguided effort to maladaptively meet basic human needs. This chapter provides a brief overview of the evolution of sex offender treatment, and describes the present state of the field which opens the door for trauma resolution as a legitimate treatment method to enhance motivation, restructure distorted offence-supporting beliefs, decrease deviant sexual arousal, and thereby reduce recidivism risk. The chapter explains how to address the *offence drivers*, i.e. those cognitions, vulnerability factors, self-regulation styles and dynamics that drive the individual to cross the line between prosocial and antisocial, or legal and illegal, sexual behaviours. By targeting and resolving the offence drivers, the EMDR therapist has the ability to complement and enhance treatment for forensically involved individuals and thereby to reduce recidivism.

Results from the Sex Offender Treatment Evaluation Project (SOTEP; Marques, Wiederanders, Day, Nelson, & van Ommeren, 2005) called into question Cognitive-Behavioural Therapy – Relapse Prevention for use with sexual offenders, the primary treatment model for sex offenders in use for more than 20 years (Marques, 1982; Pithers, Marques, Gibat, & Marlatt, 1983; Hanson et al., 2002). Around the same time, Ward & Seigert (2002) introduced the Pathways Model of sexual offending which they developed by knitting three well-regarded extant theories in the field. While the Relapse Prevention model focused on high-risk situations that offenders needed to avoid, the Pathways Model considered the idiosyncratic roots of sexual offences which formed the framework for individualised treatment directed at etiological factors. The introduction of this model coincided with the work we were doing on resolving childhood trauma and adversity believed to contribute to these pathways, and hence to sexual offending. Formerly, best practice was to deter sex offenders from examining their abuse histories for fear of excuse making, but the Pathways Model opened the door for considering these vulnerability factors as legitimate treatment targets.

Evidence shows that individuals with criminal careers have higher levels of adverse childhood experiences than do the general population, with sex offenders having even higher levels of adverse childhood experiences than other criminal populations (Reavis, Looman, Franco, & Rojas, 2013; Levenson, Willis, & Prescott, 2014). In addition, the SOTEP researchers found that those participants without histories of childhood physical abuse responded better to treatment (Marques, Day, Nelson, & West, 1994). This supports the notion that addressing and resolving the lasting effects of childhood adversity may be an effective means to enhance treatment benefit and to interrupt chronic patterns of antisocial behaviour. These ideas are compatible with the well-regarded Risk, Needs, Responsivity model (Andrews & Bonta, 2003) which states that scarce treatment resources be allocated based on the offender's estimated level of *risk*; that treatment specifically targets the offender's *needs* or criminogenic factors, and finally that treatment delivery is individualised to ensure accessibility. Criminogenic needs include several facets of antisocial thought patterns, associations and behaviours common in those with forensic histories who, as mentioned previously, have been found to have higher evidence of childhood adversity and trauma.

Perhaps in response, the sex offender treatment field is shifting to a trauma-informed approach that considers trauma effects when implementing treatment interventions. We suggest, as do Greenwald (2002, 2009), D'Orazio (2013) and Carich, Colwick, Cathell, and Moore (2015), that while this is a good start, it fails to adequately address etiological contributors to offending. Our approach to treatment is to look for, examine and *resolve* those early life adverse experiences that set the stage for subsequent antisocial behaviour. This therapeutic framework suggests that therapists listen for the implicit beliefs that stem from childhood events. This includes beliefs about the world in general as well as views of self and others which contribute to criminogenic factors. Therapists then contract with the client to resolve those memories and resultant implicitly held distorted theories and social and psychological deficits. This is of course consistent with the ideas that early life experiences create beliefs, perceptions and implicit theories that guide expectations and future behaviour (Dweck, Chiu & Hong, 1995; Mihailides, Grant & Ward, 2004).

Eye movement desensitisation and reprocessing

Eye movement desensitisation and reprocessing (EMDR) therapy is an eight-phase treatment initially developed to treat emotional trauma (Shapiro, 1989, 1995, 2002). Processing the emotionally traumatic targets includes addressing the memories that set the foundation for current dysfunction, the triggers of current disturbances, and templates for appropriate future functioning. EMDR's eight-phase treatment protocol (Shapiro, 1995, 2001, 2002) accesses and processes this traumatic material, thus facilitating appropriate storage of the memory within integrative memory networks (Siegel, 2002; Stickgold, 2002; van der Kolk, 2002) leading to trauma resolution.

The eight phases of treatment

Phase 1 of treatment involves thorough discussion of the problem that brought the client into therapy, the behaviours stemming from that problem and the symptoms of the problem. This information guides the treatment plan for EMDR therapy. Phase 2 involves explaining the theory and process of EMDR, and what the person can expect during and after treatment. To prepare for disturbance which may arise during processing, clients learn relaxation techniques for calming with the goal of self-induced state-change. Phase 3 involves selecting an image that best represents the target memory, identifying the negative self-belief associated with the memory, picking a positive self-statement that they would rather believe and identifying the negative emotions and physical sensations associated with the target. Phase 4 involves employing some form of bilateral stimulation (BLS) to desensitise and reprocess the traumatic memories. A set of standardised procedures guide the focus of attention as the client is instructed to attend to the different aspects of the memory network identified in Phase 3. Initially, the client concentrates on the disturbing memory, including the accompanying cognitions and emotions. The therapist provides BLS in the form of visual tracking, auditory stimulus or tactile stimulation. Treatment progress is assessed using the Subjective Units of Distress Scale (SUDS; Wolpe, 1982). Phase 5 involves strengthening and installing the client's positive cognition which is measured using the Validity of Cognition (VOC) scale (Shapiro, 1989). Phase 6 involves evaluating any residual tension the client feels in the body and targeting remaining physical sensations for reprocessing. Phase 7 is a Closure phase at the end of each session which ensures that the person leaves the session feeling better than at the beginning. If the processing of the traumatic target event is not complete in a single session, the therapist assists the client in using a variety of self-calming techniques in order to regain a sense of equilibrium. Phase 8 occurs at the beginning of subsequent sessions. The therapist checks to make sure that the positive results (low SUDs, high VOC, no body tension) have been maintained, identifies any new treatment targets and reprocesses them.

Sexual offending, offence drivers and EMDR

EMDR therapy has utility with the forensic population, including sex offenders, in reducing recidivism risk by addressing the contributing and vulnerability factors to the offence. We use the term *Offence Drivers* to represent these idiosyncratic factors. As a background, think about the fact that while many adults may find children sexually appealing not all adults act on that attraction. For instance, it is common for adult heterosexual males to be sexually attracted to post-pubescent individuals of their preferred gender. Similarly, many college-age men admit to ideation about engaging in sex even when they know it is unwanted. Yet some men act on these urges while others do not. We hold that sexual offences are propelled by *offence drivers* which may be implicitly held beliefs, vulnerability factors, maladaptive coping strategies or any combination of the above that contribute to crossing the line between legal and illegal sexual behaviour. In child molesters, for example, Ward and Keenan (1999) identified five such implicit theories, which they found to account for the majority of offence-supportive beliefs articulated by sexual offenders against children. Briefly, these distortions are that: (a) *children are sexual beings* who desire sex and have the knowledge and the capacity to initiate sexual activity in pursuit of pleasure; (b) the *offender is entitled* to seek what he wants at the expense of others because men are of greater importance than children; (c) the *world is a dangerous place* where it is necessary to fight to achieve dominance and control and adults are not as trustworthy as children; (d) the *world is uncontrollable* where emotions, sexual feelings, and events happen to people, none of whom have the ability to exert major personal influence on the world; and (e) *nature of harm* meaning that sex between adults and children is benign assuming the absence of violence or threat. It is easy to imagine how experiencing an adverse, hostile, sexualised, abusive or neglectful environment during one's developmental years might forge these perspectives for the abused individual. Polaschek and Gannon (2004) found implicit theories of men who have raped as follows: a) women are unknowable meaning they are so inherently different from men that men cannot easily understand them; b) women are sex objects, they view their own sexual needs as being primary over other domains and view women as constantly sexually receptive; c) male sex drive is uncontrollable meaning men's sexual energy can be difficult to control and can build to dangerous levels; d) entitlement meaning that one's needs should be met on demand; and e) dangerous world, in which the offender sees the world as hostile and threatening where actors must be constantly on guard against exploitation by others.

The aforementioned Pathways Model to offending considers dysfunctional mechanisms which tend to block the offender from achieving his basic human needs in healthy and legal ways, and can help set a course for inappropriate or illegal sexual behaviour. These pathways are *intimacy deficits* wherein skill deficits or trust/attachment issues prevent essential human bonding, *emotional dysregulation* which simply stated means the individual may rely on sexual ideation or behaviours to regulate his mood states, *distorted sexual scripts* which aligns with implicit beliefs described earlier and *antisocial or criminal attitudes and behaviours* which is akin to the dangerous world theories defined above. The authors of the Pathway Model describe a fifth pathway of *Multiple Mechanisms* that encompasses all four of the former plus deviant sexual interest which is oftentimes related to childhood sexual abuse (CSA). Marshall and Barbaree (1990) define vulnerability factors as deficits in the skills, attitudes, preferences, values and beliefs which, when functioning, serve to avoid the temptation or opportunity towards sexual aggression. The authors were perhaps the first to discuss the idea that these deficits are formed via critical adverse developmental antecedents to sexually offensive behaviours. These deficits, thereby, leave the individual vulnerable to maladaptively attempting to get their basic human needs and wants met. Again, it is evident how these deficiencies can be forged by childhood trauma or adverse childhood experiences including single or multiple incident major trauma such as sexual abuse, or chronic trauma such as repetitive bullying by peers or loved ones. Once the relevant mechanisms are identified by the specialised sex offender treatment provider, the treating EMDR therapist then can guide the selection of relevant target memories and the formulation of negative cognitions and cognitive interweaves which are standard elements of EMDR therapy. Our experience is that properly applied EMDR therapy works rapidly to resolve these issues and full reprocessing and resolution of the *offence drivers* typically occurs within an average of six sessions (Ricci, Clayton, & Shapiro, 2006).

The Adaptive Information Processing (AIP) Model (Shapiro, 1995, 2001) inherent in EMDR therapy provides a framework for understanding the rapid change process noted above. AIP offers an explanation for the negative effects of unresolved experiences, including those involving dysfunctional and deviant behaviour. AIP suggests that the intense affect associated with the initial experience interferes with the brain's ability to process the information to an adaptive resolution. Consequently, perceptual information associated with the traumatic or overwhelming event, including affect, cognitions, images and bodily sensations, becomes dysfunctionally stored and essentially isolated within the memory network. Similar events encountered subsequently serve to trigger this material, thus causing the individual's view of the present to be influenced by affective and cognitive distortions forged in the past. Various kinds of adverse childhood experiences (e.g. related to the desire for love or attention, or sexual arousal) leave offenders with distorted memories of their victimisation creating implicit beliefs that they must have wanted their abuse; there was 'no violence hence no harm' or that they as children invited and were thereby responsible for their own abuse. Others who recognise harm may develop the belief that the world is a dangerous place, that one is entitled to take what one wants or that sex is an uncontrollable urge, as it was in their perpetrator (Ward & Keenan, 1999).

Adaptations for forensic settings

In many ways, EMDR therapy is employed with a forensic population in the same manner as with any client who experienced childhood trauma or adversity. However, there are some primary differences that demand close attention. First, the forensic client has acted out criminally or sexually against someone else, and this must be considered at every step of treatment. Dissimilar to work with trauma victims who internalise their trauma (e.g. depression, anxiety), or externalise their trauma in other ways (e.g. compulsive behaviour, self-abuse), the primary goal with the forensic population needs to remain focused on community safety. This cannot be ignored and warrants special attention to the EMDR preparation (Phase 2) to reduce the risk of relapse. This can take the form of safety contracts or including probation/parole officers or other community accountability partners to ensure maximum support and resources.

Second, somewhat related perhaps, is the close coordination required with other stakeholders. Clinicians who are unfamiliar with working with forensic clients need to remain acutely aware of the legal and ethical considerations of working with this population. Forensic populations are oftentimes served by a management or 'containment' team which might include treatment providers, probation or parole officers and the courts, polygraph examiners and a community support and accountability team. When adding EMDR therapy to treatment, therefore, it is important for the EMDR therapist to become a collaborative member of the larger team. In this way, conceptualisation and implementation of interventions can complement rather than compete.

Third, is that those individuals who are forensically involved are frequently mandated to treatment which can inhibit the client's motivation to form a working therapeutic alliance with the therapist. This can create a non-trusting, even hostile, attitude towards treatment and requires special attention to trust and rapport building. One way to achieve this is to bridge the trusting relationship the client has with the primary sex offender therapist to the intervening EMDR therapist through a unified and collaborative relationship between therapists. This can help the client to more quickly feel safe and thus to better engage with the EMDR therapy.

A fourth, unconventional practice, is the use of BLS with the client's offence as the target memory. Sex offences, often (although not always) have behaviours and dynamics which are isomorphic to an offender's own childhood victimisation. For example, an incestuous sexual offender may have been incestuously offended against, or was perhaps offended by someone that was loved, admired and trusted creating dynamics similar to those in an incestuous offence. In our experience the offender's clarity about the offence(s) perpetrated often follows coming to fully understand (adaptively process and resolve) what happened in the past. Because of this phenomenon, we often employ an uncommon technique of using BLS as the client re-experiences being a perpetrator. This practice surfaces the offender's interpretation, motivation and emotions associated with their own offending and can provide a window into parallel dynamics between their own childhood sexual abuse (CSA) and later perpetration which may have become dysfunctionally stored. Once surfaced, the client can examine, clarify and resolve the essential elements of their own CSA which untangles the maladaptive dynamics which contributed to the perpetrated offence(s) and vice versa. For example, if in processing their perpetrated offence(s) the client verbalises a belief that the victim seemed to be enjoying the attention brought on by the sexual interaction, this becomes an important element to clarify and restructure via AIP as it likely contributed to their motivation to offend. In the case study presented later in this chapter, for example, Del maladaptively stored the idea that a child's sexual compliance with an important adult is associated with love, caring and attention. By omitting verbal and physical violence when molesting his daughter, his behaviour remained ego syntonic.

Finally, when dealing with clients who have sexually offended, one additional departure from the standard EMDR therapy protocol is that the memory target is most often selected by the therapist instead of by the client. In this way, the therapist is more likely to reprocess the memory(ies) theorised to be linked with the *offence drivers*, thereby resolving the maladaptively stored data and dysfunctional dynamics which motivated the client to act out. To restate, forensic clients are typically mandated to treatment and are therefore often resistant. They may also be fearful of self-incrimination, and distrustful of the 'system' altogether. Finally, given our society's vitriolic views of child molesters, their denial tends to be prevalent. These reasons are among those which make it less likely that the client will voluntarily elect the pertinent and relevant target memory(ies) for processing. Where this is the case, the therapist, based on his or her knowledge of the client's offence history and the *offence drivers* identified by the primary sex offender therapist, will identify and suggest memories to be targeted through EMDR.

Therapist training

A clinical background of education and practice in a mental health field is necessary for the effective application of EMDR. Admission to a training programme approved by the Eye Movement Desensitisation and Reprocessing International Association (EMDRIA) requires a master's degree or higher in the mental health field and a licence or certification earned through a state or national board which authorises independent practice. The training provides 40 hours of didactic instruction and experiential practice presented by a certified training instructor. The trainings are typically offered in two separate three-day training episodes, with the expectation that trainees will perform 20 hours of supervised practice using EMDR and receive five hours of supervision by an approved supervisor in between the two training dates. Then, following the second level of training the trainee is expected to continue their practice under five more hours of approved supervision. Training requirements and information are available at www.emdria.org.

Client characteristics (indicators/contra-indicators)

EMDR therapy is identified for use with children, adolescents and adults. It is specifically endorsed for use with American Indian, Alaska Native, Black or African American, Hispanic or Latino and White populations (SAMHSA, 2010). An unfortunate reality is that mental health problems are over-represented in the forensic population; however, this shouldn't automatically preclude clients from EMDR. Two studies have indicated that EMDR therapy has provided positive treatment effects to traumatised psychotic patients (deBont, van Minnen, & de Jongh, 2013; van den Berg & van den Gaag, 2012). A more recent RCT with three arms that included 155 adult patients with lifetime psychotic disorder and current, chronic PTSD showed that those who received prolonged exposure or EMDR for eight weeks had a greater reduction in trauma symptoms and were more likely to achieve a loss of diagnosis compared with wait-listed participants. The study concludes that EMDR protocols are effective and safe for individuals with comorbid psychotic disorders and PTSD symptoms (van den Berg et al., 2015).

There is some evidence (e.g. Diaz, Belena, & Baguena, 1995) that intellectual functioning in the forensic population is lower than in the general population. Five studies showing effectiveness, which have high clinical salience and high external validity, were evaluated with results indicating cautious optimism about use of EMDR therapy with those who have intellectual and developmental disabilities (Gilderthorp, 2015).

Status of the evidence in forensic settings

Since its introduction, EMDR has garnered a great deal of attention from scientists and professionals alike. Randomised studies of EMDR have prompted mental health agencies around the world to recommend EMDR in the treatment of trauma (Bleich, Kotler, Kutz, & Shalev, 2002; Clinical Resource Efficiency Support Team, 2003; Department of Veterans' Affairs & Department of Defense, 2004; Dutch National Steering Committee, 2003; French National Institute of Health and Medical Research (INSERM), 2004; National Institute for Clinical Excellence, 2005). Notably, the American Psychiatric Association (2004) identified EMDR as one of the most highly regarded treatments for post-traumatic stress disorder (PTSD). A number of studies have compared EMDR with Cognitive-Behavioural Therapy or Exposure Therapy with results favouring EMDR in almost all cases for efficacy, efficiency or both (Arabia, Manca, & Solomon, 2011; Graca, Palmer, & Occhietti, 2014; Ironson, Freund, Strauss, & Williams, 2002; Karatzias et al., 2007; Lee, Gavriel, Drummond, Richards, & Greenwald, 2002; Nijdam, Gersons, Reitsma, de Jongh, & Olff, 2012; Power et al., 2002; Rothbaum, Astin, & Marsteller, 2005; Taylor et al., 2003).

An RCT published in 2004 showed EMDR to be equally effective but more efficient than CBT with sexually abused girls (Jaberghaderi, Greenwald, Rubin, Zand, & Dolatabadim, 2004). The first published study applying EMDR treatment to victims of the 9/11 attacks reported successful outcomes. In 2007, EMDR was designated as an efficacious treatment for PTSD in the Cochrane Review (Bisson & Andrew, 2007), and the first study comparing EMDR to pharmacological treatment for PTSD showed EMDR to be more successful in sustaining reduced symptomatology (van der Kolk et al., 2007). In 2010, the US Department of Health and Human Services agency, the Substance Abuse and Mental Health Services Administration's (SAMHSA) National Registry of Evidence-based Programs and Practices endorsed EMDR therapy as a treatment modality for PTSD symptoms, anxiety symptoms, depression symptoms and global mental health functioning. In 2013 the World Health Organization (WHO) named trauma-focused CBT and EMDR as the only psychotherapies recommended for children, adolescents and adults with PTSD. Similar to CBT with a trauma focus, EMDR aims to reduce subjective distress and strengthen adaptive cognitions related to the traumatic event. However, EMDR does not require: (a) detailed descriptions of the event; (b) direct challenging of beliefs; (c) extended exposure to the memory; or (d) homework. Further information including meta-analyses, randomised clinical trials and non-randomised studies are available in the Francine Shapiro Library created by Dr Barbara Hensley and maintained by Northern Kentucky University (http://emdria.omeka.net).

To date there is limited research about the use of EMDR therapy with forensic populations. Two of the first known applications of EMDR with the forensic population can be found in Datta and Wallace's (1994, 1996) studies which found an increase in perpetrator empathy subsequent to EMDR treatment, and Finlay's (2002) dissertation in which she found a decrease in justification for perpetrator behaviour. Ricci (2006) illustrates EMDR as a useful trauma treatment with a child molester, as evidenced by increased motivation for treatment. This was found to be a missing factor in the SOTEP study, and was a differentiating factor between those offenders who 'got it' and those who did not, with recidivism rates being notably lower for the former (Marques et al., 2005). Ricci's case study also found increased empathic response by the incest offender post-EMDR treatment. EMDR was again employed with sex offenders and showed significant changes in insight (understanding of offence), deviant thoughts (offence-related impulses), awareness of situational risks (challenges the capacity for self-control), motivation (as for personal change through treatment), victim empathy (emotional impact of sexual offences) and offence disclosure (Ricci & Clayton, 2008), as well as sustained reductions in deviant sexual arousal as measured by penile plethysmography in nine of ten subjects (Ricci, Clayton, & Shapiro, 2006). Of particular note is that deviant arousal to children as measured by the penile plethysmograph was shown to be the strongest indicator of sexual recidivism (Hanson & Bussiere, 1998). Clinical observations support the notion that those sexual offenders with histories of childhood sexual abuse may be left with aberrant sexual arousal, which is one of the major pathways to sexual offending along with antisociality. The adaptive information processing model offers an explanation of the sustained decrease in deviant arousal observed in this study. This preliminary evidence supports a call for further research into this phenomenon.

Case study

Forty-one-year-old Del's sex offender therapist identified that his sexual abuse of his ten-year-old daughter was motivated by *offence drivers* of antisocial attitudes, emotional dysregulation, intimacy deficits and deviant sexual attraction. He carried the implicitly held belief that children are sexually curious beings and that sex without violence causes them no harm. After two years of group sex offender treatment his therapist noted that despite considerable progress there remained an evident rage, a likely route to recidivism if not addressed. Unknown at that time was that Del continued to fantasise about his daughter while masturbating. Del believed he had resolved, via talk therapy, his childhood trauma to the degree possible, and resisted a referral for EMDR. He considered his anger to be frustration from a troublesome childhood and his life situation. In other words, he perceived life and others needed to change, not him. His therapist eventually persuaded him to try EMDR therapy.

For five sessions, Del brought exigent issues which effectively blocked onset of BLS processing. In measured doses he touched on childhood physical, emotional and sexual abuse by his father. Del resisted engaging in BLS. ('If I get into my past I might lose myself, break down. I feel it under the surface. If I cry I know I won't be able to stop. I believe I could kill someone.'). He noted that he had 'glued, chained, taped…wrestled the anger into a metal strongbox which I sealed with barbed wire, chains, padlocks and metal rivets.' Yet Del willingly discussed his daughter's abuse by him which apparently felt safer than addressing his own.

Del eventually revealed that at age eight he caught his father molesting his younger brother, which left him feeling both sexually excited and jealous. His father then included him in the sexual activities. Del agreed to use this target memory with BLS which brought with it physical responses of heart palpitations, hot flashes and a tightened chest. He assigned a SUDS of 8–9, and a negative cognition that he is 'weak' (for participating). During BLS Del acknowledged associated physical and emotional pleasure, noting the sexual attention by his father left him feeling validated, accepted and included. As anger arose, he recognised he had misplaced the anger on self and the world instead of its rightful place on his father. Del was pleased that he was able to tolerate these emotions which, for over thirty years, he believed he could not; a key treatment milestone. Another turning point was the acknowledgement of the parallel between father and self as 'predators', a word that previously triggered rage and inhibited introspection.

In the next session Del revisited the abuse he perpetrated on his daughter and we agreed to use it as a BLS target given that Del sensed there were parallel underlying dynamics. He recalled a sexual incident against his daughter which brought at once anger at self and father. Through BLS he felt embarrassment, shame and regret, but also the physical pleasure associated with the sexual behaviours. Through the affect bridge technique (the client is asked to let his mind float back to earlier memories evoking similar sensations) Del identified similar feelings related to the physical, emotional and sexual abuse by his father. This permitted deeper processing of father's abuse, but this time he placed responsibility with father rather than self. He described the release of a 'huge knot' in his chest and commented that for the first time he felt like his father was not controlling his life anymore.

The following week Del engaged in BLS on this same target without hesitation. The memory travelled to other disturbing incidents of abuse. Cognitive interweaves (thoughts or ideas interjected by the therapist to shift thoughts or feelings when forward movement appears stalled meaning no new information spontaneously emerges after two consecutive sets of BLS) were employed to encourage him to consider the needs of his abused child self. These interweaves were selected as they shifted responsibility and thereby stood to restructure Del's implicitly held belief regarding children as sexual beings. At the end of BLS he smiled and said he was able to successfully 'help the kid', recognising that in reality what the child had wanted from his father was 'attention, love and understanding, not sex'.

The next step was to revisit his disclosure of ongoing fantasies about his daughter. He admitted he understood that this behaviour was problematic in the eyes of others, but that he believed that it was normal and harmless. Yet now for the first time he actually believed (in his view, not the view of others) they were not harmless. This was another major milestone for Del as it was clear the implicit beliefs that forged, drove and sustained his offence patterns, beliefs he HAD to adopt in order to survive emotionally, were beginning to dissipate. For the final time we revisited the target memories of the abuse from his father while using BLS. During BLS Del saw the abuse clearly without the confounding features of 'attention and caring'. He voiced the 'eye-opener' that he had never trusted his own decisions, but now recognised the origins of that false perception. Del's thought processes became stuck and repetitive regarding the negative aspects of his father so a cognitive interweave was again introduced to allow for a broader view. Del quickly began to see positive aspects of his father which had been overshadowed and forgotten for many years, a typical response to dysfunctionally stored information. At the same time he started to see himself in a broader context as well and found previously unrecognised 'evidence' about himself being smart and capable.

In the final two sessions Del voiced his life plans with renewed excitement. He also quit smoking (an unstated goal) and applied for a better job. Del no longer needed his father to make amends as once he let go of the 'hatred' for his father, he no longer felt controlled by him and therefore amends were no longer necessary. Del also recognised that his ex-wife had treated him much like his father had, and he no longer pined for that relationship which he now identified as destructive. Finally, and perhaps most importantly, he stated that while unhealthy sexual thoughts still come into his mind occasionally, he no longer perceives them positively and that they no longer cause sexual arousal (erection).

Key directions for future research

The sex offender and forensic treatment fields have been impacted by the Pathways Model of sexual offending and a focus on targeting criminogenic needs in the forensic population. Results from an analysis of the Adverse Childhood Experiences study (Centers for Disease Control and Prevention, 2014) show that childhood adversity is higher in the offender population than in the general population (Reavis et al., 2013). Results from a few published and unpublished studies showing benefit to resolving those etiological factors discussed herein show promising results, and warrant further research. Two such RCT studies are presently underway. Researchers at Sand Ridge Secure Treatment Center in Wisconsin are implementing a study of civilly committed sexual offenders by examining brain images pre- and post-EMDR trauma treatment. A team is working with the Virginia Center for Behavioural Rehabilitation to study the pre-post EMDR trauma treatment effects on deviant sexual arousal as measured by penile plethysmography, deviant sexual interest as measured by visual reaction time assessment, and criminogenic factors. Treatment of the forensic population is a worthwhile societal goal which warrants these and more research efforts. Given that EMDR is suitable for addressing those overwhelming and dysfunctionally stored experiences, and those experiences are now understood to contribute to antisociality, researching the utility of EMDR with these populations is a natural next step.

Further reading

www.emdr.com/index.php?option=com_content&view=article&id=12&Itemid=18#meta
http://nrepp.samhsa.gov/ViewIntervention.aspx?id=199
https://emdria.omeka.net/ (Francine Shapiro Library)

References

American Psychiatric Association. (2004). *Practice guideline for the treatment of patients with acute stress disorder and posttraumatic stress disorder.* Arlington, VA: American Psychiatric Association Practice Guideline.

Andrews, D., & Bonta, J. (2003). *The psychology of criminal conduct* (3rd edn). Cincinnati, OH: Anderson.

Arabia, E., Manca, M. L., & Solomon, R. M. (2011). EMDR for survivors of life-threatening cardiac events: Results of a pilot study. *Journal of EMDR Practice and Research*, 5, 2–13.

Bisson, J., & Andrew, M. (2007). Psychological treatment of post-traumatic stress disorder (PTSD). *Cochrane Database of Systematic Reviews*. doi: 1002/14651858.CD003388.pub3

Bleich, A., Kotler, M., Kutz, I., & Shalev, A. (2002). *A position paper of the [Israeli] National Council for Mental Health: Guidelines for the assessment and professional intervention with terror victims in the hospital and in the community.* [Israeli] Jerusalem, Israel: National Council for Mental Health.

Carich, M. S., Colwick, R., Cathell, K., & Moore, M. E. (2015). Resolving trauma-related issues in contemporary treatment of offenders: A brief overview. *ATSA Forum Newsletter*, 27(3).

Centers for Disease Control and Prevention. (2014, May). *The adverse childhood experiences study.* Retrieved from www.cdc.gov/violenceprevention/acestudy/

Clinical Resource Efficiency Support Team (CREST). (2003). *The management of post traumatic stress disorder in adults.* Belfast: Northern Ireland Department of Health, Social Services and Public Safety.

Datta, P. C., & Wallace, J. (1994, May). *Treatment of sexual traumas of sex offenders using eye movement desensitization and reprocessing.* Paper presented at the 11th Annual Symposium in Forensic Psychology, San Francisco.

Datta, P. C., & Wallace, J. (1996, November). *Enhancement of victim empathy along with reduction in anxiety and increase of positive cognition of sex offenders after treatment with EMDR.* Paper presented at the annual conference of the EMDR International Association, Denver, CO.

de Bont, P. A., van Minnen, A., & de Jongh, A. (2013). Treating PTSD in patients with psychosis: A within-group controlled feasibility study examining the efficacy and safety of Evidence-based PE and EMDR protocols. *Behavior Therapy, 44*(4), 717–730.

Department of Veterans' Affairs & Department of Defense. (2004). *VA/DoD clinical practice guideline for the management of post-traumatic stress.* Washington, DC: Veterans Health Administration, Department of Veterans Affairs and Health Affairs, Department of Defense. Office of Quality and Performance Publication 10Q-CPG/PTSD-04.

Diaz, A., Belena, A., & Baguena, M. R. (1995). The role of gender in juvenile delinquency: Personality and intelligence. *Personality and Individual Differences, 16*(2), 309–314.

D'Orazio, D. M. (2013). Lessons learned from history and experience: Five simple ways to improve the efficacy of sexual offender treatment. *International Journal of Behavioral Consultation & Therapy, 8*(3–4), 2–7.

Dutch National Steering Committee. (2003). *Guidelines for mental health care: Multidisciplinary guideline anxiety disorders.* Utrecht: Quality Institute Health Care CBO/Trimbos Institute.

Dweck, C. S., Chiu, C., & Hong, Y. (1995). Implicit theories and their role in judgments and reactions: A world from two perspectives. *Psychological Inquiry, 6*(4), 267–285.

Finlay, P. (2002). Eye movement desensitization and reprocessing (EMDR) in the treatment of sex offenders. *Dissertation Abstracts International, 63*(10). UMI No. 3068413.

Gilderthorp, R. C. (2015). Is EMDR an effective treatment for people diagnosed with both intellectual disability and post-traumatic stress disorder? *Journal of Intellectual Disabilities, 19*(1), 58–68. doi:10.1177/1744629514560638

Graca, J. J., Palmer, G. A., & Occhietti, K. E. (2014). Psychotherapeutic interventions for symptom reduction in veterans with PTSD: An observational study in a residential clinical setting. *Journal of Loss and Trauma, 19*(6). doi:10.1080/15325024.2013.810441

Greenwald, R. (2002). The role of trauma in conduct disorder. *Journal of Aggression, Maltreatment, and Trauma, 6,* 5–23.

Greenwald, R. (2009). *Treating problem behaviors: A trauma-informed approach.* New York: Routledge.

Hanson, R. K., & Bussiere, M. T. (1998). Predicting relapse: A meta-analysis of sexual offender recidivism studies. *Journal of Consulting and Clinical Psychology, 66*(2), 348–362.

Hanson, R. K., Gordon, A., Harris, A. J. R., Marques, J. K., Murphy, W., Quinsey, V. L., & Seto, M. C. (2002). First report of the Collaborative Outcome Data Project on the effectiveness of psychological treatment for sexual offenders. *Sexual Abuse: A Journal of Research and Treatment, 14*(2), 169–194.

INSERM. (2004). *Psychotherapy: An evaluation of three approaches.* French National Institute of Health and Medical Research, Paris, France.

Ironson, G. I., Freund, B., Strauss, J. L., & Williams, J. (2002). Comparison of two treatments for traumatic stress: A community-based study of EMDR and prolonged exposure. *Journal of Clinical Psychology, 58,* 113–128.

Jaberghaderi, N., Greenwald, R., Rubin, A., Zand, S. O., & Dolatabadim, S. (2004). A comparison of CBF-BT and EMDR for sexually abused Iranian girls. *Clinical Psychology and Psychotherapy, 11,* 358–368.

Karatzias, A., Power, K., McGoldrick, T., Brown, K., Buchanan, R., Sharp, D., & Swanson, V. (2007). Predicting treatment outcome on three measures for post traumatic stress disorder. *European Archives of Psychiatry and Clinical Neuroscience*, *257*(1), 40–46.

Lee, C., Gavriel, H., Drummond, P., Richards, J., & Greenwald, R. (2002). Treatment of post-traumatic stress disorder: A comparison of stress inoculation training with prolonged exposure and eye movement desensitization and reprocessing. *Journal of Clinical Psychology*, *58*, 1071–1089.

Levenson, J. S., Willis, G., & Prescott, D. (2014). Adverse childhood experiences in the lives of male sex offenders and implications for trauma-informed care. *Sexual Abuse: A Journal of Research and Treatment*. Advance online publication. doi:10.1177/1079063214535819

Marques, J. (1982, March). Relapse Prevention: A self-control model for the treatment of sex offenders. Paper presented at the 7th Annual Forensic Mental Health Conference. Asilomar, CA.

Marques, J. K., Day, D. M., Nelson, C., & West, M. A. (1994). Effects of cognitive behavioral treatment on sex offender recidivism: Preliminary results of a longitudinal study. *Criminal Justice and Behavior*, *21*, 28–54.

Marques, J. K., Wiederanders, M., Day, D. M., Nelson, C., & van Ommeren, A. (2005). Effects of a relapse prevention program on sexual recidivism: Final results from California's sex offender treatment and evaluation project (SOTEP). *Sexual Abuse: A Journal of Research and Treatment*, *17*(1), 79–107.

Marshall, W. L., and Barbaree, H. E. (1990). An integrated theory of the etiology of sexual offending. In W. L. Marshall, D. L. Laws and H. E. Barbaree (Eds), *Handbook of sexual assault: Issues, theories and treatment of the offender* (pp. 257–275). New York: Plenum.

Mihailides, S., Grant, J. D., & Ward, T. (2004). Implicit cognitive distortions and sexual offending. *Sexual Abuse: A Journal of Research and Treatment*, *16*(4), 333–350.

National Institute for Clinical Excellence. (2005). *Post-traumatic stress disorder (PTSD): The management of PTSD in adults and children in primary and secondary care*. London.

Nijdam, M. J., Gersons, B. P. R., Reitsma, J. B., de Jongh, A., & Olff, M. (2012). Brief eclectic psychotherapy v. eye movement desensitisation and reprocessing therapy in the treatment of post-traumatic stress disorder: Randomised controlled trial. *British Journal of Psychiatry*, *200*, 224–231.

Pithers, W. D., Marques, J. K., Gibat, C. C., & Marlatt, G. A. (1983). Relapse prevention: A self-control model of treatment and maintenance of change for sexual aggressives. In J. Greer & I. R. Stuart (Eds), *The sexual aggressor: Current perspective on treatment*. New York: Van Nostrand Reinhold.

Polaschek, D. L. L., & Gannon, T. A. (2004). The implicit theories of rapists: What convicted offenders tell us. *Sexual Abuse: A Journal of Research and Treatment*, *16*(4), 299–314.

Power, K. G., McGoldrick, T., Brown, K., Buchanan, R., Sharp, D., Swanson, V., & Karatzias, A. (2002). A controlled comparison of eye movement desensitisation and reprocessing versus exposure plus cognitive restructuring, versus waiting list in the treatment of posttraumatic stress disorder. *Journal of Clinical Psychology and Psychotherapy*, *9*, 299–318.

Reavis, J. A., Looman, J., Franco, K. A., & Rojas, B. (2013). Adverse childhood experiences and adult criminality: How long must we live before we possess our own lives? *Permanente journal*, *17*(2), 44–48.

Ricci, R. J. (2006). Trauma resolution using eye movement desensitization and reprocessing with an incestuous sex offender: An instrumental case study. *Clinical Case Studies*, *5*, 248–265.

Ricci, R. J., Clayton, C. A., & Shapiro, F. (2006). Some effects of EMDR on previously abused child molesters: Theoretical reviews and preliminary findings. *Journal of Forensic Psychiatry and Psychology*, *17*, 538–562.

Ricci, R. J., & Clayton, C. A. (2008). Trauma resolution treatment as an adjunct to standard treatment for child molesters: A qualitative study. *Journal of EMDR Practice and Research, 2*(1), 41–50.

Rothbaum, B. O., Astin, M. C., & Marsteller, F. (2005). Prolonged exposure versus eye movement desensitization (EMDR) for PTSD rape victims. *Journal of Traumatic Stress, 18,* 607–616.

Substance Abuse and Mental Health Services Administration (SAMHSA). (2010). National Registry of Evidence-based Programs and Practices. Retrieved May 2015 from http://nrepp.samhsa.gov/ViewIntervention.aspx?id=199.

Shapiro, F. (1989). Efficacy of the eye movement desensitization procedure in the treatment of traumatic memories. *Journal of Traumatic Stress Studies, 2*(2), 199–223.

Shapiro, F. (1995). *EMDR: Basic principles, protocols, and procedures.* New York: Guilford Press.

Shapiro, F. (2001). *Eye movement desensitization and reprocessing: Basic principles, protocols and procedures* (2nd edn). New York: Guilford Press.

Shapiro, F. (2002). Paradigms, processing, and personality development. In F. Shapiro (Ed.), *EMDR as an integrative psychotherapy approach: Experts of diverse orientations explore the paradigm prism* (pp. 3–26). Washington, DC: American Psychological Association Press.

Siegel, D. J. (2002). The developing mind and the resolution of trauma: Some ideas about information processing and an interpersonal neurobiology of psychotherapy. In F. Shapiro (Ed.), *EMDR as an integrative psychotherapy approach: Experts of diverse orientations explore the paradigm prism* (pp. 85–122). Washington, DC: American Psychological Association Press.

Stickgold, R. (2002). EMDR: A putative neurobiological mechanism of action. *Journal of Clinical Psychology, 58,* 61–75.

Taylor, S., Thordarson, D., Maxfield, L., Fedoroff, I., Lovell, K., & Ogrodniczuk, J. (2003). Comparative efficacy, speed, and adverse effects of three PTSD treatments: Exposure therapy, EMDR, and relaxation training. *Journal of Consulting and Clinical Psychology, 71,* 330–338.

van den Berg, D. P. G., & van den Gaag, M. (2012). Treating trauma in psychosis with EMDR: A pilot study. *Journal of Behavior Therapy & Experimental Psychiatry, 43,* 664–671.

van den Berg, D. P., deBont, P. A., van der Veiugel, B. M., de Roos, C., de Jongh, A., Van Minnen, A., van der Gaag, M. (2015). Prolonged Exposure vs Eye Movement Desensitization and Reprocessing vs Waiting List for Posttraumatic Stress Disorder in Patients With a Psychotic Disorder: A Randomized Clinical Trial. *Jama Psychiatry, 72*(3), 259–267. doi: 10.1001/jamapsychiatry.2014.2637

van der Kolk, B. A. (2002). Beyond the talking cure: Somatic experience and subcortical imprints in the treatment of trauma. In F. Shapiro (Ed.), *EMDR as an integrative psychotherapy approach: Experts of diverse orientations explore the paradigm prism* (pp. 7–84). Washington, DC: American Psychological Association Press.

van der Kolk, B., Spinazzola, J., Blaustein, M., Hopper, J., Hopper, E., Korn, D., & Simpson, W. (2007). A randomized clinical trial of EMDR, fluoxetine and pill placebo in the treatment of PTSD: Treatment effects and long-term maintenance. *Journal of Clinical Psychiatry, 68,* 37–46.

Ward, T., & Keenan, T. (1999). Child molester's implicit theories. *Journal of Interpersonal Violence, 14,* 821–838.

Ward, T., & Siegert, R. J. (2002). Toward a comprehensive theory of child sexual abuse: A theory knitting perspective. *Psychology, Crime, and Law, 8,* 319–351.

Wolpe, J. (1982). *The practice of behavior therapy.* New York: Pergamon Press.

World Health Organization. (2013). *Guidelines for the management of conditions specifically related to stress.* Geneva: World Health Organization.

7

MENTALISATION BASED TREATMENT

Gill McGauley

Mentalisation based treatment (MBT) is an evidenced-based psychotherapy originally developed to treat Borderline Personality Disorder (BPD) (Bateman & Fonagy, 2004, 2006). Over the last decade its application to other psychiatric and psychological disorders has blossomed, reflective of the fact that the capacity to mentalise is an essential human ability which can be impaired in a wide range of conditions (Bateman & Fonagy, 2012). This chapter will focus primarily on the use of MBT to treat people with a diagnosis of BPD and the emerging evidence base for its effectiveness in treating Antisocial Personality Disorder (ASPD) as these conditions are over-represented in forensic settings. Forensic settings are taken to include prisons, secure psychiatric units and community-based forensic services. I will also discuss how a failure of mentalisation can precipitate some forms of violence and therefore how MBT allows a focus on both psychological change and the drivers behind some offending behaviour.

What is mentalising and how does it develop?

It is a given that mental states influence our behaviour. Mentalisation is 'the process by which we interpret the actions of ourselves and others in terms of those underlying intentional states such as personal desires, needs, feelings, beliefs and reasons' (Bateman & Fonagy, 2006). In other words, mentalisation is the capacity to think about one's own mental state and the mental states of others (Allen, Fonagy, & Bateman, 2008). Mentalisation allows the individual to process experience and to represent and distinguish between mental states of the self and of the other (Fonagy, 2003a; Steele, 2003). It shapes our understanding of others and underpins our interpersonal relationships.

The capacity to mentalise develops within early secure attachment relationships where we experience our internal states being understood by another mind (Koren-Karie et al., 2002; Fonagy, 2003b). Classical attachment theory, as laid down by John Bowlby and Mary Ainsworth, is a body of knowledge concerned with the emotional bonds and affective interactions between human beings and the psychological difficulties and psychopathological consequences which arise when these processes go awry (Bowlby, 1977; Holmes & Farnfield, 2014).

If the child is accurately represented as a thinking and feeling individual in the mind of the attachment figure, then the child's capacity to mentalise will develop smoothly; securely attached children outperform insecure children on mentalising tasks (de Rosnay & Harris, 2002). However, the development of healthy mentalising is thought to depend on more than just a secure attachment relationship with caregivers. The emotional availability of the caretaker is also important. If the parent is able to understand the infant's emotional signals, to reflect on them and to mirror them back then the child will develop the capacity to understand interpersonal behaviour in terms of mental states (Fonagy, Lorenzini, Campbell, & Luyten, 2014). Mirroring must be accurate (contingent) and marked (exaggerated) or slightly distorted as this allows the infant to differentiate the infant's emotional experience from that of the caregiver. The absence of marked, contingent mirroring has been linked to the development of disorganised attachment (Bateman & Fonagy, 2006) while parental mentalising is linked to both secure attachment and the capacity to regulate affect and stress (Oppenheim & Koren-Karie, 2002). Contemporary interest in attachment has grown because it is recognised that early attachment experiences, with mindful parents, equip the child's mind with an intra-psychic mechanism, that of mentalisation, which acts to process experience and allows the person to represent mental states of the self and other and understand the interpersonal world (Fonagy, 2003a, 2003b; Steele, 2003).

Developmental threats to mentalisation

Trauma, maltreatment and exposure to violence, disorganise the attachment system, disrupt the development of mentalisation and compromise affect regulation (Cicchetti & Valentino, 2006). Potential mechanisms for the association between adversity and poor mentalisation include: that the child defensively inhibits their capacity to think about the mind of the abusing attachment figure as to do so would expose the child to the hostility in the abuser's mind directed towards him or her (O'Connor, 2006); that chronic early stress distorts arousal mechanisms and inhibits neural mechanisms that underpin mentalisation; that trauma arouses the attachment system as the child seeks protection. If trauma is at the hands of an attachment figure then the child becomes chronically traumatised as they repeatedly seek proximity to the abuser. Trauma therefore has a dual liability (Allen, Lemma, & Fonagy, 2012) that stems from traumatic childhood attachments which, not only stimulate extreme distress, but also impair the child's capacity to regulate emotional distress, partly through compromising the development of mentalising. These individuals show deficits in empathy and struggle to differentiate their own mental state from that of others. In the face of subsequent trauma, mentalising breaks down.

What happens when mentalisation falters; some theoretical concepts

Before discussing the origins and application of MBT to the treatment of particular personality disorders in forensic settings, the consequences of failures and imbalances in mentalisation are considered as these are theorised to give rise to the core symptoms and phenomenology of BPD and ASPD. According to the MBT model, the breakdown or suppression of mentalisation leads to the emergence of prementalistic modes of thinking (see below) which organise the individual's subjective experience and act as powerful disorganisers of the person's interpersonal relationships. Mentalisation is prone to fail in the context of high emotional arousal, often in the context of attachment relationships. Within MBT, therapists must be alert to the loss of mentalisation as signalled by the emergence of these developmentally earlier modes of thinking. Bateman and Fonagy (2006) describe three modes of subjective experience that predate mentalisation.

In *psychic equivalence*, the individual's inner reality is believed to be the same as outer reality. In other words, what the person thinks is experienced as real or true. The individual has a strong and inappropriate conviction of being right; there is no room for alternative perspectives, doubt or curiosity. For example, 'if I think you hate me then you do hate me'. In this state of mind frightening thoughts are felt to be real and the subjective experience for the individual can be terrifying (such as in flashbacks). Clinicians sometimes refer to this non-mentalising state as 'concrete thinking'.

In *teleological mode*, the only way the individual can work out the intentions of the other is by their physical behaviour and observable actions as the individual cannot fathom the mind of the other. For example, 'if you really cared for me you would have held my hand; let me phone you; given me a birthday card.' For the patient, the professional's motivation to help has to be demonstrated by increasingly heroic acts. If the therapist accepts these teleological invitations there is a risk of boundary transgressions. Self-harm, suicide attempts and other dramatic actions, often directed towards an attachment figure, are conceptualised as teleological driven attempts to alter the behaviour of the other as this may be the only way the patient can experience being cared about.

In *pretend mode*, ideas form no bridge between inner and outer reality and emotional experience can become dissociated from thoughts. This often leads to feelings of emptiness. In this state of mind, patients can talk about their experiences; however, the narrative is cut off from any meaningful link to his or her internal experience and, at the extreme, may have a dissociative quality; it can often sound inauthentic to the listener – that the patient is 'talking the talk'. In an attempt to find a connection to his or her feelings the patient may talk extensively but the link often seems random or confusing to the listener and further exploration fails to clarify. For example, a patient who is separated from her children begins to talk about how she misses them but her narrative lacks emotion and she quickly jumps to talk about how the trees she can see through the window are like those in the woods she used to walk in (ten years ago) and provides the listener with a detailed description of these walks as if she was talking about the recent past. The therapist needs to avoid getting caught up in these convoluted, non-mentalising discussions about the patient's internal experiences which ultimately lead nowhere.

In addition to recognising these states of mind, MBT therapists need to appreciate that mentalising is a multidimensional construct and that patients may have different degrees of mentalising ability on each dimension. According to Luyten (Luyten, Fonagy, Lowyck, & Vermote, 2012), mentalisation has four dimensions or polarities that are underpinned by relatively distinct neural mechanisms. These are: 1) automatic-controlled; 2) internally focused – externally focused; 3) self-orientated – other-orientated; and 4) cognitive-affective. In good mentalising each dimension is best conceptualised as a balanced seesaw; for example, with affective mentalising being in balance with cognitive mentalising. It follows that a dysfunction in one part of the complementary pair tips the seesaw so that the other part is much more evident. For example, a dysfunction in cognitive mentalisation may be manifested as excessively focused emotional mentalisation, unbalanced by cognitive consideration.

Automatic (implicit) – controlled (explicit) mentalising; most of the time mentalising is implicit and happens automatically out of conscious awareness. Explicit mentalisation kicks in when we get an unexpected response or cannot fathom another's behaviour. For example, when listening to a conference speaker mentalisation would be automatic but if the speaker suddenly stopped for no apparent reason the listener might begin to think 'what is going on for him? Is he anxious?'. Explicit mentalisation requires reflection and effort, and needs to connect meaningfully with the patient's emotional experience.

Internally focused – externally focused mentalisation; denotes mental processes that arise from a focus on one's own or another's internal states, i.e. thoughts and feeling. External mentalisation relates to mental processes that arise from observations of the visible, physical features or actions of one's self or others such as posture or facial expression. For example, 'when she looked at me like that she was disrespecting me, so I went for her.' The internal-external dimension of mentalising may be focused on either the self or the other.

Self-orientated – other-orientated mentalisation; refers to impairments and imbalances in the capacity to reflect about the self and others. Imbalance in this dimension can lead to excessive rumination and inferences about the mental states of others or the self which far exceed observable behaviour and is described as hypermentalising. For example, 'after she said hello to me on the phone she sounded angry with me. It must be because she is upset with me for not inviting her to my party last year. Come to think about it she has always been quick to take offence.'

Cognitive – affective mentalising; refers to the balance and integration of cognitive aspects of mentalising such as reasoning and perspective taking with other more affectively driven components related to empathy. For example, patients with ASPD can often describe highly emotionally charged interpersonal interactions in a 'matter of fact' way that is cut off from the appropriate affect – 'well I stabbed him because I wanted to try out my new knife' – whereas individuals with BPD are often overwhelmed with affect indicating that the cognitive dimension of their mentalising has failed.

The relevance of the mentalisation model for BPD, ASPD and violence

BPD

Bateman and Fonagy see the failure of mentalisation, within an attachment context, as the core pathology of BPD (Bateman & Fonagy, 2004, 2006). Childhood abuse and neglect are over-represented in the early lives of these individuals (Baird, Veague, & Rabbitt, 2005) as are levels of insecure attachment. These factors threaten the child's developing capacity to mentalise and later disrupt mentalisation in adult attachment relationships.

People with BPD may be able to mentalise reasonably except in the context of attachment relationships. The model proposes (Luyten & Fonagy, 2014) that the attachment systems of people with BPD are hyper-activated, as a result of interpersonal experiences of childhood trauma. As a consequence they actively need to be in relationships but, in this context, minor experiences of loss or small emotional upsets may cause an intense activation of the system. At this level of arousal explicit mentalisation fails and implicit mentalisation dominates. People with BPD have difficulty understanding the minds of others based on internal features but often quickly infer mental states from behaviour (unbalanced internal-external dimension) and, with a hyper-activated attachment system, this can result in emotional dysregulation. For example, a partner's slightly late return from work precipitates a highly distressed state in an individual with BPD as she believes that her partner no longer loves her. Individuals with BPD are prone to hypermentalising about the self or the other and can become caught in endlessly going through internally constructed scenarios about the mind of the other based on very little real-life data. For example, 'When she paused on the phone I thought she wanted to hang up and that she was upset with me. I think it was because of what I said in my letter last month. I should have said it differently. If I had said it like this instead of like that then she wouldn't have been upset but then she might have thought…'. Individuals with BPD are often overwhelmed by automatic, affectively driven mentalisation which is untempered by cognitive understanding.

With the inhibition of mentalisation, prementalistic modes of experiencing reality predominate and lead to impulsiveness, emotional dysregulation and problems in interpersonal relating. The rigid views that characterise psychic equivalence make the person with BPD vulnerable to affect dysregulation and impulsive acts. In psychic equivalence mode, negative thoughts about the self can become overwhelming and self-harm or suicide is an attempt at trying to regain some sense of self cohesion; suicide can also occur when pretend mode and dissociation are the ascendant mental states. From a forensic perspective, impulsive acts of violence in BPD, particularly interpersonal violence, can occur when psychic equivalence and teleological states of mind predominate and are often precipitated by the individual feeling humiliated which induces overwhelming shame.

Case study

In psychic equivalence, a young woman 'knows' that when her partner doesn't return her text quickly enough that he 'doesn't love her'. Her inability to have an alternative perspective heightens her sense of humiliation and shame. Later in their local pub, she sees him cast a glance at the barmaid's cleavage. In teleological mode, his action triggered huge feelings of humiliation and intense anger. Despite the young man's attempts to say that he really does love her, she lashed out and attacked him; she later set a fire in his flat.

As Bateman and Fonagy stress (Bateman & Fonagy, 2006), in teleological mode it is not the action itself that carries the most meaning but the deviation from expected actions which are contingent with the person's wishes. In other words, it was not the look in itself but the fact that, in her mind, his look was a deviation from her rigid view that he should only have eyes for her. Her violence can be conceptualised as an attempt to stabilise the massive affect dysregulation she then experienced by externalisation. In teleological mode actions do speak louder than words.

ASPD

Within MBT, ASPD is conceptualised as arising from an interaction between a genetically determined predisposition and an adverse early environment which results in abnormal personality development; particularly in the areas of affect regulation, impulse control, violent acting out and the ability to mentalise. The early life of individuals with ASPD is characterised by threats to the developing attachment system in terms of losses, neglect and abuse (Luntz & Widom, 1994; Pert, Ferriter, & Saul, 2004). Insecure attachment, particularly dismissing attachment, is overrepresented in forensic populations many of whom have ASPD (Frodi, Dernevik, Sepa, Philipson, & Bragesjo, 2001; van IJzendoorn et al., 1997) and poor mentalisation (Levinson & Fonagy, 2004). Being dismissive and devaluing of attachment relationships can be understood as a protective attempt to limit the affective pain of abusive attachment experiences. Meta-analyses have linked attachment insecurity to sexual and violent offending (Ogilvie, Newman, Todd, & Peck, 2014).

People with ASPD can explicitly mentalise but they fail to connect this with emotional experience in the self or other. For example, a patient may be able to work out that his victim would have felt terrified of him but fails to feel any sorrow for the suffering of the other. Individuals with ASPD have difficulty reading fearful emotional expressions (an aspect of external mentalisation) (Marsh & Blair, 2008) but can often accurately read the internal states of other (self-other mentalisation). However, without an emotional connection this capacity to mentalise the mind of the other can be misused to coerce or dominate others. Other individuals with ASPD may excessively focus on their own internal states but in a narcissistic fashion – working out what others need to do to meet their desires or needs (Bateman & Fonagy, 2016). ASPD individuals may be able to cognitively understand mental states in the self and other but these remain unlinked to the affective component of self or other experience.

In individuals with ASPD, prementalistic modes of thinking frequently predominate. Psychic equivalence states of mind result in inflexible views about how relationships should be organised which are often along hierarchical lines with 'respect for the other' being a key organiser. People with ASPD often find the rigid hierarchy of gangs and the capacity to control and denigrate a partner stabilising of their often inflated, and therefore fragile, sense of self-worth (Yakeley, 2013). Teleological mental states result people with ASPD basing their understanding of the mind of the other on their actions. If the other 'steps out of line' or challenges the inflexibility of psychic equivalence, this constitutes a threat and triggers emotional arousal; for example, a young son or daughter who's crying does not subside despite the efforts of the ASPD parent.

In their developmental model of violence (Fonagy, 2003b; Levinson & Fonagy, 2004), the capacity to mentalise is thought to be a crucial inhibitory factor for interpersonal violence. Poor mentalising means that ASPD individuals frequently mis-read the minds and actions of others, 'seeing' slights, insults and markers of disrespect all too easily. The feelings of shame and humiliation generated are unbearable. Poor mentalisation means that these cannot be processed and contained by normal mental representational mechanisms; they are experienced concretely as feelings or sensations that need to be expelled through violence. Psychic equivalence may gain a greater hold so that the person cannot differentiate between their own internal experience and external reality and is unable to see the other as having a different mental state from him/her. Indeed the aggressor may so mis-identify the mental state of the other as to be convinced that his victim is as angry and aroused as s/he is and, consequently, feel under threat and attack (Yakeley, 2013; McGauley, Yakeley, Williams, & Bateman, 2011).

Pretend mode, where the person is cut off from the affective component of mentalising, can compound this situation and increase the risk of violence as the person with ASPD cannot empathise with how their impending violence will result in suffering for the other. In the highly dissociative states of pretend mode the violent act can seem unreal; 'I don't know what happened. I looked down and there was a knife in my hand and blood on the floor'.

ASPD patients may show some enhanced areas of mentalisation (Bateman & Fonagy, 2006) in their ability to deceive and exploit others, which necessitates an ability to understand the mind of the other and to predict what s/he will and will not believe. These individuals often fall into the small subgroup of ASPD patients who have pronounced psychopathic traits and they exhibit a partial, but fundamental, impairment of mentalising, what Baron-Cohen (2005) called 'mindreading without empathising'.

The origins of MBT and its relevance to forensic settings

MBT is a modified psychodynamic treatment originally designed for the treatment of BPD in non-forensic populations. The original Randomised Control Trials (RCTs) (Bateman & Fonagy, 1999, 2001) were embedded in an 18-month partial hospital programme where MBT was offered in a combination of individual and group sessions. Recipients showed significant improvements in mood states and interpersonal functioning. The benefits, relevant to treatment as usual, were large with the Number Needed to Treat (NNT) of around 2. The NNT offers a measurement of the impact of the therapy by estimating the number of patients that need to be treated for one patient to benefit compared with a control in a clinical trial. These benefits increased during the 18-month follow-up phase in contrast to Dialectical Behavioural Therapy (DBT) treatment where NNT stayed level. Treatment was deemed to be cost effective (Bateman & Fonagy, 2003) and improvements maintained at an eight-year follow-up (Bateman & Fonagy, 2008a). A second variant of MBT for BPD was subsequently developed as an intensive 18-month outpatient programme where patients received one individual session a week and one 90-minute group session.

In contrast to the optimistic treatment landscape for BPD, the treatment of ASPD remains shrouded by therapeutic pessimism and the evidence base for effective treatments is far less robust (Duggan, Huband, Smailagic, Ferriter, & Adams, 2007; National Institute for Health and Clinical Excellence (NICE), 2009; Warren et al., 2003). On the basis of a few trials with offenders, some of whom may not have had ASPD, NICE recommended using cognitive-behavioural interventions to treat individuals with ASPD. A systematic review (Gibbon et al., 2010) of the small number of quality studies confirmed the weak evidence base for the treatment of ASPD. As it is proposed that many of the symptoms and mental states associated with ASPD are underpinned by deficits in mentalisation there has been increasing interest in whether MBT would be an effective treatment (Bateman & Fonagy, 2008b; McGauley et al., 2011; Yakeley & Williams, 2014).

Personality disorder accounts for the majority of psychopathology of individuals in forensic settings, with an estimated prevalence of 70%; ASPD and BPD being among the principal subtypes (Singleton, 1998). Individuals with ASPD are over-represented in the criminal justice system. In their systematic review of 23,000 prisoners across Western countries, including the United States, Fazel and Danesh (2002) found that 65% of male prisoners and 42% of female prisoners had a personality disorder. Forty seven per cent of the male prisoners and 21% of the women prisoners, who had a diagnosis of personality disorder, had ASPD. Overall, it is estimated that the prevalence of ASPD among prisoners is slightly less than 50% (NICE, 2009). ASPD is most likely associated with violence in secure settings as well as with self-directed aggression. It is estimated that around a fifth of women in custody fulfil criteria for BPD (Singleton, Meltzer, Gatward, Coid, & Deasy, 1998), and research suggests that prison may exacerbate BPD (Wolff & Shi, 2009). In women a diagnosis of personality disorder in prison has been associated with fire setting, self-harm and suicide (Coid, Wilkins, & Coid, 1999; Chapman, Specht, & Cellucci, 2005; Gorsuch, 1998). Of course, diagnostic grouping does not cleave as neatly as this and in reality studies of populations with severe levels of personality psychopathology have revealed high levels of comorbidity for mental illness, personality disorder and substance misuse (Coid et al., 1999).

The aims and focus of treatment

MBT is a relational psychotherapy where the primary aim is to create a therapeutic process in which mental states of self and others become the focus of concern. MBT is tailored for patients where specific deficits in mentalisation are core to the disorder.

The overarching aims (adapted from Bateman & Fonagy, 2006) are to:

- Ensure that the person's mind and their relationship with other minds are the focus of therapy;
- increase the patient's understanding about how they feel and think about themself and others;
- help the patient understand how their thoughts and feelings about themself and others influence interpersonal relationships;
- learn how 'errors' in understanding themself and others result in actions in an attempt to stabilise themself and manage confusing or overwhelming feelings;
- and strengthen and extend the patient's capacity to mentalise. For example, especially in the context of attachment relationships for BPD individuals and when there are real or perceived threats to self-esteem for ASPD individuals.

In generic settings, where MBT was first developed, treatment was aimed at improving psychiatric symptomatology such as mood states and interpersonal functioning, decreasing self-harming and suicidal behaviours and helping individuals' process trauma. When working with offenders and forensic patients MBT has the additional aim of reducing the risk of aggressive and violent acts within the forensic setting and decreasing the risk of particular offences; those that involve the impulsive, interpersonal violence that emerges when mentalisation fails (Bateman & Fonagy, 2008b). This mentalisation model of violence allows for offence-related work from a mentalisation perspective. The capacity of MBT to help process trauma is also extremely relevant to forensic populations due to the ubiquity of trauma in the lives of these individuals.

To achieve the therapeutic aims of MBT all that the therapist has to do is to keep a mentalising focus and stimulate the patient's capacity to mentalise. This sounds deceptively simple; however, it requires the therapist to have a firm grasp of the theoretical concepts outlined above as well as clinical concepts, and to be active in applying them:

- Recognising when mentalisation has been lost and prementalistic modes of thinking emerge;
- evaluating and monitoring the individual's mentalising profile in terms of the dimensions of mentalisation;
- recognising narrative markers of poor mentalisation;
- maintaining a particular therapist's stance (the inquisitive stance);
- and delivering a range of mentalising interventions according to the MBT model in order to both re-establish and strengthen the capacity to mentalise.

Key clinical concepts

The sequelae of disruptions in mentalisation, either through temporary loss of mentalisation and the emergence of prementalistic modes of thinking or as a result of an imbalance in the components of mentalisation, are evident in the individual's narrative. The therapist needs to be alert to these markers, such as: expressions of certainty; sweeping generalisations; a focus on external events; blaming; and denial of involvement in a problem. It is important to keep in mind that poor mentalising may be generalised or context specific. Situation-specific breakdown of mentalisation can occur in the context of attachment relationships (including the therapeutic one), when thinking about traumatic experiences or in relation to specific people or situations that generate high arousal; for example, 'My Mum, she does my head in. I can't think once she starts on me.'

One of the characteristics of mentalising, which underpins the therapist's approach, is that all mental states (emotions, thoughts) are opaque; however, we make inferences about them but these inferences are prone to error. As we cannot really 'know' what is in the mind of another person the overarching principle for the therapist is to take a mentalising position, sometimes referred to as the 'inquisitive' stance or 'not-knowing' stance (Bateman & Fonagy, 2006). This requires the therapist to demonstrate an authentic interest in and willingness to find out and explore what is happening in the patient's mind. This is achieved by active questioning, which can also introduce the possibility of alternative perspectives. For example, 'How did that make you feel?'; 'What was happening for you before you felt like hitting her?'; 'I can see why you thought that but maybe she was preoccupied with something else which might explain why you thought she was blanking you.' The therapist needs to suspend any pressure to quickly understand and become 'the expert' offering interpretations and advice.

Key to the inquisitive stance is a focus on the patient's mind rather than on the individual's behaviour (self-harm; drinking; violence) and encouraging the patient to do the same. In particular, the therapist is interested in helping the patient to articulate how they were feeling and to look at the meaning behind the person's behaviour. This can be a challenging task for forensic patients who, all too often, act in an attempt to stabilise a swath of emotions that coalesce into an undifferentiated affective storm; for example, 'I hit her, I lost it. I don't know how I felt. Well it was like someone just stuck a huge needle into me and I just saw red.' The mentalising stance also means that the therapist must accept his or her own mentalising errors and be transparent about his or her own role in any misunderstandings.

Another crucial clinical concept is that interventions need to relate to current mental reality that the patient can recall; the model de-emphasises unconscious concerns. The model also cautions the therapist against making historical causal interpretations that link past and present as these often close down mentalising.

The MBT model describes a clinical pathway aimed at strengthening the patient's capacity to mentalise. The pathway starts with identifying affects and exploring the emotional and interpersonal context in which they arose outside of the session, moving eventually to an exploration of affect and interpersonal interaction between the therapist and patient. To achieve this, the model provides a series of stepwise interventions which increase in complexity and emotional intensity. They begin with supportive and empathic ones, moving through clarification and elaboration, to basic mentalising, interpretative mentalising and mentalising the transference. A key concept is that progression along the pathway and the use of any intervention must be in keeping with the patient's capacity to mentalise at that point. Going beyond the patient's mentalising ability will, at best, result in a failure of mentalisation and, at worst, become iatrogenic.

Throughout this whole process the therapist is alert for the appearance of pre-mentalistic modes of thinking and works to reinstate mentalisation when these emerge. The therapist is also aware of the patient's mentalisation profile and seeks to rebalance the seesaw for each dimension of mentalising. For example, encouraging a patient with BPD, who has become too 'self-focused' in a critical, self-blaming way, to consider the effect on the mind of the other; or to nudge the ASPD patient away from purely cognitive thinking to consider their emotional response.

MBT in forensic settings

Adaptations to the original MBT treatment model, designed for BPD, can be considered to fall into three areas: those adaptations needed to tailor MBT to the treatment of ASPD, the development of mentalisation based art therapy (MBAT) and those adaptations needed to deliver MBT-BPD, MBT-ASPD or MBAT within forensic settings.

Treatment adaptations for ASPD

As MBT was developed for people with BPD, treatment focuses on mentalising deficits, triggered by high emotional arousal, in the context of attachment relationships where the attachment system is hyper-activated. Individuals with ASPD have different mentalising problems which are particularly associated with external mentalising, such as an inability to read fearful emotional expressions, and affective mentalising. Both these aspects have been linked to amygdala dysfunction which manages the processing of fearful expression (Jones, Laurens, Herba, Barker, & Viding, 2009). These neural deficits mean that people with ASPD fail to recognise distress signals in others, resulting in a lack of empathy and failure to curtail aggressive behaviour; normally inhibited by observation and empathic identification of distress in another (affective/other mentalising) (Bateman & Fonagy, 2012). Individuals with ASPD are skilled at reading the internal states of others, and often misuse this aspect of mentalising to dominate and manipulate others, but they have very little understanding of their own affective experiences.

Other features of ASPD which necessitate changes in the emphasis of the MBT model arise because of the nature of the interpersonal relationships in ASPD. Unlike the rapidly oscillating and affectively stormy relationships of the BPD individual, people with ASPD establish inflexible relationships founded upon hierarchical lines in which their own emotional states are highly controlled. The structure of these relationships is maintained by dominating and controlling others. Threats to this hierarchy stimulate arousal in the attachment system which inhibits mentalisation, prementalistic modes of thinking emerge which further distort mentalisation and lead to a fear of losing status. Gilligan (2000) describes the threat of loss of self-esteem as terrifying as it exposes the individual to internal feelings of shame which are felt to be overwhelming (Bateman & Fonagy, 2016)

As in MBT-BPD, groupwork is essential for people with ASPD as they are more likely to be influenced by their peer group than by clinicians who they see as unlikely to understand the socio-cultural context in which they live. Crucially, groupwork stimulates a hierarchical process within the peer group, which can be used in the group by the therapists to explore the individual's sensitivity to authority and their mentalising distortions (Bateman & Fonagy, 2016). In MBT-ASPD the individual sessions are primarily to support the person with ASPD in the group and are provided by the group therapists, rather than a different therapist. This limits the possibility of deception about what happens in the group in the context of the individual session.

In summary, the primary aims of MBT-ASPD are to stimulate mentalising, especially within hierarchical interpersonal interactions, and to decrease the aggressive acting out. To achieve these, therapists help the individual understand emotional cues (external mentalising) and their link to internal states; help the person recognise emotional states in others (affective/other mentalising); focus on the more rigid and inflexible aspects of the mind especially with respect to hierarchy and authority (self/cognitive mentalising); and clarify how failed mentalisation can lead to teleological thinking (self/other mentalising) (Bateman & Fonagy, 2016).

The development of MBAT

MBAT developed in prison settings as this is where BPD women, who have the most impaired capacity to mentalise, can find themselves; these women rely heavily on automatic/implicit mentalising. Art therapy facilitates explicit, reflective mentalising in a way that can be tolerable for highly disturbed minds. If the individual has a fragile capacity to mentalise then thinking about being a victim of the violence of others or of perpetrating violence cannot be sustained. The use of art allows the internal to be expressed externally so that it can be verbalised at a distance, through an alternative medium and from a different perspective (Allen et al., 2008). The art each patient produces allows the group and patient to reflect on aspects of their mind in the presence of other minds. For some women with BPD this is more manageable than directly reflecting internally on themselves in relation to others. As Collier (2015) says, 'if mentalisation collapses, then these expressions of a patient's internal world can be put away, kept safe and brought out again when the patient can mentalise.'

Delivery adaptations

According to the standard model, MBT is delivered as a combination of individual and group sessions. There are variations in frequency of individual sessions. For example, MBT-ASPD in forensic community settings combines weekly group therapy with monthly individual sessions, whilst the original MBT programme for BPD had weekly individual sessions. In general, most MBT programmes start with an introductory MBT group based around the 12-week MBT-I designed for BPD but now adapted for ASPD. These introductory groups are aimed at enhancing engagement and have a strong psychoeducational focus. The length and components of the programme are often adapted depending upon the profile of group members.

Case study

This vignette presents some aspects of a brief four-month individual MBT treatment for Ms A and has been chosen as it illustrates some of the constraints to MBT in prison settings.

Ms A had spent several years in prison as a result of committing a highly violent offence against an attachment figure. One of the difficulties for Ms A was that things had 'gone wrong' for her when she had been released on licence resulting in her recall to prison. When she was referred for MBT her next parole hearing was due in four months. The reason for her referral was an episode of aggressive behaviour towards another prisoner because she had felt she was 'not being listened to'. She had previously completed both a cognitively based Enhanced Thinking Skills and Thinking Skills Programme, which she had found helpful.

Ms A had been given a diagnosis of BPD and had a history of self-harm. There was no collateral information available. Her parents' relationship had been violent and she described becoming the parental child in trying to look after her mother and deal with her father's alcohol-induced rages. She suffered childhood abuse from some of her attachment figures and was eventually taken into care. In adulthood Ms A presented of herself as having few close friends and 'keeping herself to herself'. However, Ms A spoke warmly of relatives who had provided her with shelter and care when she needed to flee the family home as a child. She had kept in contact with them and valued their support.

Ms A and her therapist identified a pattern where she had difficulty in asking for help and, more importantly, when she did ask, something often went awry in her communication so that the other person didn't accurately gauge how much distress she was in or how much help she needed. This pattern seemed to have been present in the interactions with her key worker and probation officer which resulted in her recall. In the here and now of therapy, the therapist noticed an incongruity between how Ms A asked for day-to-day help and her internal affective experience of feeling in need or 'out of her depth'. She often asked 'with a smile on her face' or brushed away the fact that she had asked, quickly reverting to self-sufficiency mode. On further exploration her difficulty in asking for help stemmed from her belief that others would see her as a failure and that she would have let them down. These beliefs meant that she asked for help in a very tentative manner and often only fleetingly, quickly retreating. Ms A placed an over-reliance on mentalising (probably inaccurately) the minds of others and erroneously concluded that others would view her as a failure and as letting them down if she let them know she needed support.

Using the dimensions of mentalising, Ms A began to understand her difficulties as arising from an imbalance in cognitive-affective and the self-other dimensions of mentalising. She was also able to understand how, when upset and aroused, she would fall into a non-mentalising psychic equivalence state of mind; if she thought she had let people down then she had and there was no other perspective. Part of the work in treatment was aimed at helping Ms A mentalise her affective and internal emotional states and the mind of the other more accurately. Ms A frequently brought examples from her interactions with officers on her wing which illustrated how she monitored her own mentalising and applied what she had learnt in therapy to her interpersonal interactions.

Although a brief therapy, it was possible to make some sense of Ms A's original offence from a mentalising perspective. An over-reliance on cognitive, at the expense of emotional, understanding was characteristic of her interpersonal relationship with her victim. Ms A 'fitted in' to what her attachment figure demanded as she dreaded the possibility of feeling abandoned but took little heed of her growing resentment. In the heat of an argument her mentalisation collapsed precipitating her violent attack. Ms A's parole hearing was successful.

Indications and contra-indications for MBT in forensic settings

As described, the main indicators for MBT are individuals whose core problems relate to BPD and ASPD. Individuals are often referred because of behaviours such as self-harm or aggression and a good clinical assessment will clarify the underlying psychological problems and whether MBT is likely to be helpful. Free-standing psychoeducational one-off groups such as 'Understanding Personality Disorder', can be usefully offered as a first step to see if prisoners can engage with any form of treatment. Prison-accredited cognitively based treatment programmes such as

Enhanced Thinking Skills may also help. These programmes will help the cognitive and other dimensions of mentalisation. Our pragmatic experience, within prisons, indicates that treatment interventions are best organised sequentially, unless they are part of an integrated programme. Two consecutively running treatment interventions can place too much of a demand on the individual's capacity to mentalise and attendance at either one or the other often declines. In our experience, assessment for MBT treatment needs to be delayed until the prisoner has completed the acute stages of any detoxification programme; low doses of methadone are not a necessary contra-indication to starting treatment as long as the individual's affective and attentional control is adequate.

A careful assessment of mentalisation is necessary to identify those individuals who, when mentalisation breaks down, revert to psychic equivalence states of prementalistic functioning. In this state of mind, frightening thoughts are felt to be real and catapult the thinker into re-experiencing the traumatic thought as a flashback and can often precipitate self-destructive or aggressive behaviour in an attempt to re-stabilise the concomitant affective dysregulation. Heavy reliance on psychic equivalence thinking may be a relative contra-indication, not only to MBT, but to other psychological interventions. In particular, therapeutic approaches that focus on original trauma, as opposed to helping the patient develop secondary representations of trauma, will be persecutory and iatrogenic for individuals who are stuck in psychic equivalence. Clues that the individual is functioning in this way may be that the person deteriorates after initial assessment. If psychic equivalence thinking emerges during treatment the therapist needs to be pro-active in trying to help the patient re-establish mentalisation.

Those individuals whose mentalising is highly rigid with respect to the self and other, such as in highly narcissistic and paranoid personality disorders, tend to fare poorly with MBT. Additionally, those patients with ASPD, who also have high levels of psychopathic callous, unemotional traits, are unlikely to benefit from MBT or other psychotherapies as they avoid self/affective states and appear unable to develop any real understanding of their own inner world and their motives. The concern with this group is that they misuse their capacity to cognitively mentalise the mind of the other to coerce and manipulate others, often in a sadistic way. Indeed, the initial studies of ASPD excluded patients with scores greater than 30 on the Revised Psychopathy Checklist (Hare, 2003).

Status of the evidence in forensic settings

The UK Offender Personality Disorder Pathway (OPD) is a joint National Offender Management Service (NOMS) and NHS strategy for violent male and female offenders that has driven the development of more joined-up services for PD across the criminal justice system, the NHS and in the community (Joseph & Benefield, 2012). The RCT evidence base for MBT-BPD has led to it being imported into forensic settings and, as far as the author is aware, there have not been any high-quality treatment trials of MBT-BPD in these settings to date. The OPD initiative has resulted in MBT individual and group approaches being embedded in several prison treatment programmes (NOMS, 2015). These programmes are in their infancy and outcome evaluation is awaited.

The evidence base for MBT-ASPD rests on two completed and one ongoing study. The first study was a part of the original series of RCTs of MBT which compared MBT with structured clinical management (SCM) for patients with BPD (Bateman & Fonagy, 2009). A sub-analysis of the data, for a subgroup of patients who had a diagnosis of ASPD and comorbid BPD, showed that MBT had a significant impact on the target symptoms and secondary consequences of aggression and suggested that MBT is an effective treatment for comorbid antisocial patients (Bateman & Fonagy, 2008b). The authors acknowledge the limitations that the study was underpowered to demonstrate real differences between the two groups, and therefore the implications of the findings are restricted to demonstrating feasibility rather than effectiveness; that there is no follow-up data as yet to establish if improvements were maintained; and that primary outcomes beyond self-reported psychiatric symptoms are required.

The second observational study examined whether an 18-month MBT-ASPD treatment programme had positive effects in individuals with a main diagnosis of ASPD and a history of violent offending, who presented to a forensic rather than a generic personality disorder treatment service. The primary objective was to investigate the feasibility of engaging and sustaining a treatment programme with this difficult-to-treat group and obtain preliminary data on the size of change. Results indicated that MBT reduced aggression and violence as measured by the self-report Overt Aggression Scale-Modified (OAS-M) (Coccaro, Harvey, Kupsaw-Lawrence, Herbert, & Bernstein, 1991). The major limitations of the study are the small sample size, that it lacks a control group and that the data are based on self-report patient measures. However, it is the first study to assess MBT with community-based offender patients with ASPD and the results indicate that an MBT approach is both acceptable and feasible for ASPD patients (McGauley, Yakeley, Williams, & Bateman, 2011).

The researchers argue that these constitute a substantial trial platform for a much-needed, large-scale investigation into effective treatments for ASPD in the form of a multi-site, pragmatic randomised controlled superiority trial of MBT-ASPD effectiveness in reducing aggression compared to probation as usual (PAU) (Bateman et al., in press).

In 2013 NHS England commissioned the Portman and Tavistock NHS Trust under the leadership of Jessica Yakeley to implement 13 MBT-ASPD community services for offenders who were under the statutory supervision of the National Probation Service as part of the OPD pathway. The third study is ongoing and comprises a multi-site RCT feasibility study of MBT-ASPD intervention led by Peter Fonagy. The overall aim of the study is to ascertain whether it is feasible to recruit and randomise potential participants in a probation setting; explore how patients experience participation so that the clinical service, recruitment protocols and research protocols can be improved; and how large an effect MBT is likely to have on aggressive and antisocial behaviour in this context. The data gathered from this feasibility RCT will inform the protocol for a larger-scale nationwide multi-centre RCT.

Therapist training

Details of the MBT training programme are described on the Anna Freud website along with the range of MBT trainings available. In order to access current information on training the reader is directed to www.annafreud.org/training-research/mentalisation-based-treatment-training/mbt-training-programme/. Essentially, the MBT training programme is a three-step process which allows the individual to reach MBT Practitioner status, and then progress to MBT Supervisor status and finally to MBT Trainer status. The training programmes are short (3–5 days) but skills need to be embedded through supervised clinical practice with a recognised MBT supervisor before progression to the next stage. The practitioner training does not have prescribed entry criteria. The Quality Manual of Standards for MBT, available to download from the website, provides a useful description of MBT therapist and supervisor competencies.

Key directions for future research

MBT is in its developmental infancy in forensic settings; however, its robust theoretical framework and the translation of this into an evidenced-based treatment for some PDs is a source of optimism. However, more high-quality empirical studies are needed in forensic populations and the multi-site RCT for MBT-ASPD is keenly awaited. Two pressing research questions are whether different components of MBT have differing therapeutic potencies and what the optimum treatment time needed is. The realities of working with offender patients, the constraints of the systems, resources shortages and funding pressures mean that gold-standard MBT programmes where patients receive individual and group interventions for 12–18 months may be increasingly difficult to implement and sustain in forensic settings. Would a six-month MBT group be more or less effective than a 12-month one, and by how much? How much change could brief individual MBT treatment effect? At present we cannot answer these finer-grained questions. Recently a range of mentalisation based treatment approaches have been developed for specific conditions such as for the treatment of trauma, depression, eating disorders and comorbid personality disorder and drug addiction to name a few. Many of these conditions are over-represented in forensic populations and evaluating these MBT approaches would be a welcome direction of travel.

The social environment can interact synergistically with therapy and, indeed, a thoughtful and sensitive social environment can increase prosocial interactions and decrease aggression (Fonagy et al., 2009). Mentalisation is not only at the core of a range of treatment approaches but a mentalisation based approach can provide staff with additional skills to engage offenders, and is already being used in some forensic institutions and services. Embedding a mentalisation based approach offers the possibility of supporting patients, teams, systems and networks and, as such, can help shape the social environment in forensic services and institutions.

Further reading

Anna Freud Centre Website for MBT Training; www.annafreud.org/training-research/mentalization-based-treatment-training/
Anthony W. Bateman & Peter Fonagy (Eds) (2012). *The handbook of mentalizing in mental health practice*. London, and Washington, DC: American Psychiatric Publishing.
Bateman, A., & Fonagy, P. (2016). *Mentalization based treatment for personality disorder: A practical guide*. Oxford: Oxford University Press.

References

Allen, J. G., Fonagy P., Bateman, A. (2008). *Mentalizing in Clinical Practice*. American Psychiatric Press.
Allen, J. G., Lemma, A., & Fonagy, P. (2012). Trauma. In A. W. Bateman, & P. Fonagy (Eds), *Handbook of mentalizing in mental health practice* (pp. 419–444). Washington, DC: American Psychiatric Publishing.
Baird, A. A., Veague, H. B., & Rabbitt, C. E. (2005). Developmental precipitants of borderline personality disorder. *Developmental Psychopathology, 17*, 1031–1049.
Baron-Cohen, S. (2005). The empathizing system: A revision of the 1994 model of the mindreading system. In B. J. Ellis & D. F. Bjorklund (Eds), *Origins of the social mind: Evolutionary psychology and child development* (pp. 468–492). New York: Guilford.
Bateman, A. W., & Fonagy, P. (1999). Effectiveness of partial hospitalization in the treatment of borderline personality disorder: A randomized controlled trial. *The American Journal of Psychiatry, 156*, 1563–1569.
Bateman, A. W., & Fonagy, P. (2001). Treatment of borderline personality disorder with psychoanalytically oriented partial hospitalization: An 18-month follow-up. *The American Journal of Psychiatry, 158*, 36–42.
Bateman, A. W., & Fonagy, P. (2003). Health service utilization costs for borderline personality disorder patients treated with psychoanalytically orientated partial hospitalization versus psychiatric care. *The American Journal of Psychiatry, 160*, 169–171.
Bateman, A. W., & Fonagy, P. (Eds) (2004). Chapter 2: Mentalization-based understanding of borderline personality disorder. In *Psychotherapy for borderline personality disorder: Mentalization-based treatment*. Oxford: Oxford University Press.
Bateman, A. W., & Fonagy, P. (Eds) (2006). The structure of mentalization based treatment. In *Mentalization based treatment for borderline personality disorder* (pp. 37–59). Oxford: Oxford University Press.
Bateman, A. W., & Fonagy, P. (2008a). 8-year follow-up of patients treated for borderline personality disorder: Mentalization-based treatment versus treatment as usual. *American Journal of Psychiatry, 165*, 631–638.
Bateman, A. W., & Fonagy, P. (2008b). Comorbid antisocial and borderline personality disorders: Mentalization-based treatment. *Journal of Clinical Psychology: In Session, 64*(2), 181–194.
Bateman, A., & Fonagy, P. (2009). Randomized controlled trial of outpatient mentalization-based treatment versus structured clinical management for borderline personality disorder. *American Journal of Psychiatry, 166*(12), 1355–1364.

Bateman, A. W., & Fonagy, P. (2012). Chapter 12: Antisocial Personality Disorder. In Anthony W. Bateman, & Peter Fonagy (Eds), *Handbook of Mentalizing in Mental Health Practice*. Washington, DC, and New York: American Psychiatric Publishing.

Bateman, A., & Fonagy, P. (2016). Chapter 13: Antisocial personality disorder; mentalizing, MBT-G, and common clinical problems. In *Mentalization Based Treatment for Personality Disorder: A Practical Guide*. Oxford: Oxford University Press.

Bateman, A., Yakeley, J., McGauley, G., Lorenzini, N., O'Connell, J., Gardner, T., & Fonagy, P. (in press). *A programme of studies to establish the feasibility of a randomised controlled trial for Mentalization-Based Treatment for antisocial personality disorder*.

Bowlby, J. (1977). The making and breaking of affectional bonds. I. Aetiology and psychopathology in the light of attachment theory. An expanded version of the Fiftieth Maudsley Lecture, delivered before the Royal College of Psychiatrists, 19 November, 1976. *British Journal of Psychiatry*, *130*, 201–210.

Chapman, A. L., Specht, M. W., & Cellucci, T. (2005). Factors associated with suicide attempts in female inmates: The hegemony of hopelessness. *Suicide and Life-Threatening Behavior*, *35*(5), 558–569.

Cicchetti, D., & Valentino, K. (2006). An ecological-transactional perspective on child maltreatment: Failure of the average expectable environment and its influence on child development. In D. Cicchetti & D. J. Cohen (Eds), *Developmental Psychopathology*, *3*(2), 129–201. Chichester: John Wiley & Sons.

Coccaro, E. F., Harvey, P. D., Kupsaw-Lawrence, E., Herbert, J. L., & Bernstein, D. P. (1991). Development of neuropharmacologically based behavioral assessments of impulsive aggressive behavior. *Journal of Neuropsychiatry and Clinical Neuroscience*, *3*(2), S44–51.

Coid, J., Kahtan, N., Gault, S., & Jarman, B. (1999). Patients with personality disorder admitted to secure forensic psychiatry services. *British Journal of Psychiatry*, *175*, 528–536.

Coid, J., Wilkins, J., & Coid, B. (1999). Fire setting, pyromania and self-mutilation in female remanded prisoners. *Journal of Forensic Psychiatry*, *10*(1), 119–130.

Collier, J. (2015). 3 man unlock: Out of sight, out of mind. Art psychotherapy with a woman with severe and dangerous personality disorder in prison. *Psychoanalytic Psychotherapy*, *29*, 243–261.

De Rosnay, M., & Harris, P. L. (2002). Individual differences in children's understanding of emotion: The roles of attachment and language. *Attachment and Human Development*, *4*, 39–54.

Duggan, C., Huband, N., Smailagic, N., Ferriter, M., & Adams, C. (2007). Use of psychological treatments for people with personality disorder: A systematic review of randomized controlled trials. *Personality and Mental Health*, *1*, 95–125.

Fazel, S., & Danesh, J. (2002). Serious mental disorder in 23000 prisoners: A systematic review of 62 Surveys. *The Lancet*, *359*, 545–550.

Fonagy, P. (2003a). The interpersonal interpretive mechanism: The confluence of genetics and attachment theory in development. In V. Green (Ed.), *Emotional development in psychoanalysis, attachment and neuroscience: Creating connections* (pp. 107–126). London: Karnac.

Fonagy, P. (2003b). Towards a developmental understanding of violence. *The British Journal of Psychiatry*, *183*, 190–192.

Fonagy, P., Lorenzini, N., Campbell, C., & Luyten, P. (2014). Chapter 2: Why are we interested in attachments? In Paul Holmes, & Steve Farnfield (Eds), *The Routledge handbook of attachment: Theory* (pp. 31–48).

Fonagy, P., Twemlow, S. W., Vernberg, E. M., Nelson, J. M., Dill, E. J., Little, T. D., & Sargent, J. A. (2009). A cluster randomized controlled trial of child-focused psychiatric consultation and a school systems-focused intervention to reduce aggression. *Journal of Child Psychology and Psychiatry*, *50*(5), 607–616.

Frodi, A., Dernevik, M., Sepa, A., Philipson, J., & Bragesjo, M. (2001). Current attachment representations of incarcerated offenders varying in degree of psychopathy. *Attachment and Human Development*, 3(3), 269–283.

Gibbon, S., Duggan, C., Stoffers, J., Huband, N., Völlm, B. A., Ferriter, M., et al. (2010). Psychological interventions for antisocial personality disorder. *Cochrane Database Systematic Review*, 16(6), CD007668.

Gilligan, J. (2000). *Violence: Reflections on our deadliest epidemic*. London: Jessica Kingsley.

Gorsuch, N. (1998). Unmet need among disturbed female prisoners. *The Journal of Forensic Psychiatry*, 9(3), 556–570.

Hare, R. D. (2003). *The Psychopathy Checklist-Revised*. Toronto: Multi-Health Systems.

Holmes, P., & Farnfield, S. (2014). Overview: Attachment theory, assessment and implications. In Paul Holmes, & Steve Farnfield (Eds), *The Routledge handbook of attachment: Theory* (pp. 1–10).

Jones, A. P., Laurens, K. R., Herba, C. M., Barker, G. J., & Viding, E. (2009). Amygdala hypoactivity to fearful faces in boys with conduct problems and callous-unemotional traits. *American Journal of Psychiatry*, 166, 95–102.

Joseph, N., & Benefield, N. (2012). A joint offender personality disorder pathway strategy: An outline summary. *Criminal Behaviour and Mental Health*, 22, 210–17.

Koren-Karie, N., Oppenheim, D., Dolev, S., Sher, E., & Etzion-Carasso, A. (2002). Mothers' insightfulness regarding their infants' internal experience: Relations with maternal sensitivity and infant attachment. *Developmental Psychology*, 38, 534–542.

Levinson, A., & Fonagy, P. (2004). Offending and attachment: the relationship between interpersonal awareness and offending in a prison population with psychiatric disorder. *Canadian Journal of Psychoanalysis*, 12, 225–251.

Luntz, B. K., & Widom, C. S. (1994). Antisocial personality disorder in abused and neglected children grown up. *American Journal of Psychiatry*, 151(5), 670–674.

Luyten, P., & Fonagy, P. (2014). Chapter 6: Mentalising in attachment contexts. In Paul Holmes, & Steve Farnfield (Eds), *The Routledge handbook of attachment: Theory* (pp. 107–126).

Luyten, P., Fonagy, P., Lowyck, B., & Vermote, R. (2012). Chapter 2: Assessment of mentalization. In Anthony W. Bateman, & Peter Fonagy (Eds), *Handbook of mentalizing in mental health practice* (pp. 43–65). Washington, DC, and New York: American Psychiatric Publishing.

McGauley, G., Yakeley, J., Williams, A., & Bateman, A. (2011). Attachment, mentalization and antisocial personality disorder; the possible contribution of mentalization-based treatment. *European Journal of Psychotherapy and Counselling*, 13(4), 1–23.

Marsh, A. A., & Blair, R. J. (2008). Deficits in facial affect recognition among antisocial populations: a meta-analysis. *Neuroscience and Biobehavioral Reviews*, 32, 454–465.

National Institute for Health and Clinical Excellence (NICE). (2009). Borderline Personality Disorder: Recognition and Management. National Clinical Guideline Number 78. National Collaborating Centre for Mental Health, Commissioned by the National Institute for Health & Clinical Excellence.

NOMS. (2015). Brochure of offender personality disorder services for women. www.academyforjusticecommissioning.org.uk/wp-content/uploads/2015/03/Brochure-of-Womens-OPD-services-Feb-2015.pdf

O'Connor, T. (2006). In D. Cicchetti, & D. J. Cohen (Eds), *The persisting effects of early experiences on psychological development in developmental psychopathology*, 2(2) (pp. 202–234). Chichester: John Wiley & Sons.

Ogilvie, C. A., Newman, E., Todd, L., & Peck, D. (2014). Attachment and violent offending: A meta-analysis. *Aggression and violent behavior*, 19(4), 322–339.

Oppenheim, D., & Koren-Karie, N. (2002). Mothers' insightfulness regarding their children's internal worlds: The capacity underlying secure child-mother relationships. *Infant Mental Health Journal, 23,* 593–605.

Pert, L., Ferriter, M., & Saul, C. (2004). Parental loss before the age of 16 years: a comparative study of patients with personality disorder and patients with schizophrenia in a high secure hospital's population, *Psychology and Psychotherapy, 77*(3), 403–407.

Singleton, N., Meltzer, H., Gatward, R., Coid, J., & Deasy, D. (1998). Psychiatric morbidity among prisoners in England and Wales. *Office of National Statistics*. London: Stationery Office.

Steele, M. (2003). Attachment, actual experience and mental representation. In V. Green (Ed.), *Emotional development in psychoanalysis, attachment theory and neuroscience. Creating connections* (pp. 86–106). New York: Brunner-Routledge.

van IJzendoorn, M. H., Feldbrugge, J. T., Derks, F. C., de Ruiter, C., Verhagen, M. F., Philipse, M. W., van der Staak, C. P., & Riksen-Walraven, J. M. (1997). Attachment representations of personality-disordered criminal offenders, *American Journal of Orthopsychiatry, 67*(3), 449–459.

Warren, F., McGauley, G. A., Norton, K., Dolan, B., Preedy-Fayers, K., Pickering, A., and Geddes, J. R. (2003). Review of Treatments for Severe Personality Disorder. Online report 30 March. www.homeoffice.gov.uk/rds/pdfs2/rdsolr3003.pdf. London: Home Office.

Wolff, N., & Shi, J. (2009). Victimisation and feelings of safety among male and female inmates with behavioural health problems. *Journal of Forensic Psychiatry & Psychology, 20,* 56–77.

Yakeley, J. (2013). Chapter 8: Mentalization-based group treatment for antisocial personality disorder. In John Woods, & Andrew Williams (Eds), *Forensic group psychotherapy: The Portman clinic approach* (pp. 151–182). Karnac.

Yakeley, J., & Williams A. (2014). Antisocial personality disorder: new directions. *Advances in Psychiatric Treatment, 20,* 132–143.

8

PERSONAL CONSTRUCT PSYCHOTHERAPY

Adrian Needs and Lawrence Jones

Personal construct theory (PCT) derives its name from its focus on how people construe: behaviour, thought and emotional states are seen as mobilised by systems of connected anticipations, based on past experience, as people attempt to make sense of what they face in life. These systems are heavily permeated by individuals' unique ('personal') experiences. The 'theory' aspect points to its set of formally articulated and testable propositions concerned with the operation, organisation, and evolution of the systems upon which construing depends. Construing PCT's unfamiliar perspectives and intentionally abstract language can at first seem difficult. With this in mind and the widespread availability of more conventional introductions, this chapter begins by outlining some key ideas with an account in the 'Gulliver's Travels' tradition before moving on to considering implications for understanding psychological problems, offending and change. Some of these are sketched with reference, where appropriate, to congruent insights and findings from research outside of PCT. Along the way certain techniques for assessment and intervention (though often one merges into and informs the other) particularly associated with PCT are described. These include self-characterisations, repertory grids, laddering, Fixed Role Therapy and WOMBATs. Opportunities for training in PCT are touched upon. A detailed case study illustrating an application of repertory grid technique with a violent sex offender is presented. The chapter concludes with a brief overview of research on PCT's effectiveness in other contexts and some words on its potential for providing an integrative perspective on processes within more familiar approaches.

Overview

A place for personal construct theory?

Most of us have some recognition that how people act is related to how they make sense of what they encounter. Sometimes the actions and perspectives of others are difficult for us to make sense of; they can appear alien, confused, limiting or self-defeating. As professionals we can bring to bear our own perspective of concepts, theories and procedures, confident that we are part of a tradition of objectivity and able to deliver the best bet in terms of what empirical science, based for the most part on probability, controlled conditions and differences between large groups, can offer. Thus armed we can also meet the expectations of official systems.

Some clients embrace our efforts as a means of reducing distress, breaking with the past or fulfilling their own obligations in relation to official systems. On the other hand, the sense-making and views of the world of some forensic clients is notoriously refractory. It is not unknown for the efforts of psychologists to be met with suspicion or disillusionment (Maruna, 2011), for effectiveness of standardised programmes to all but disappear when current contexts intrude (Hough, 2010) or for clients to reject what they feel they may become as a result of our efforts (Kirchner, Kennedy, & Draguns, 1979; Winter, 1992a). Standardised approaches sometimes appear remote from personal concerns (Ross, Polaschek & Ward, 2008) and complex personal experiences might be perceived as reduced to labels and manifestations of needs or deficits (cf. Polaschek, 2012).

There are many practitioners who are very skilled in the exercise of empathy and motivational work. Nonetheless, it is suggested in this chapter that benefits can be gained from an integrative approach centred upon making sense of sense-making. Personal Construct Theory (PCT: Kelly, 1955) is concerned with exploring personal perspectives and fostering renewed development in the individual. The word 'construct' derives from the verb 'to construe' or interpret. As the term 'personal construct' implies, the focus is on the interpretations of the client since it is in terms of these that the client acts, thinks and feels.

There are several excellent accounts of PCT and its clinical applications, including in work with offenders (e.g. Houston, 1998; Winter, 1992b). However, one reason why PCT has not been used more widely in recent years may be that its intentionally abstract terminology can appear rather complex and unfamiliar. Another reason is the mistaken assumption that it is subsumed by more familiar cognitive-behavioural approaches. With this and the availability of more formal accounts in mind, this chapter starts by offering a brief 'Gulliver's Travels' style construction of some central premises in order to provide a context for understanding personal construct psychotherapy. Suspending disbelief to consider from the vantage point of 'as if' is an established technique that has influenced and found applications within PCT (Watts, Peluso, & Lewis, 2005).

Some central premises

Imagine a land where people engage with the world through anticipation. In this land it is not only scientists who act on hypotheses derived from underlying 'theories' of the world. The ordinary inhabitants learn to depend upon discriminations or 'constructs' that imply other discriminations and hence provide a basis for expectations or predictions. For example, one inhabitant, when starting a new job and being introduced to a series of unfamiliar people, discriminated between those that 'seemed friendly' and those that 'only seemed interested in themselves'. This discrimination in turn carried the implications (therefore enabling the anticipations) that the 'friendly' people would be 'helpful' as opposed to 'can't be bothered' and that they would have a 'sense of humour' as opposed to 'being stuck up'.

Anticipations (expectations or predictions) that seem relevant in any given instance come from awareness of apparently recurring patterns. Those that lead to outcomes that match anticipations (in other words, those that have proved their predictive value) are likely to be used again, though as life progresses they usually need to be revised considerably. Some commentators have suggested that behaviour can be seen as like an experiment that tests a hypothesis with discrepant results leading to the modification of underlying theories. In the situation referred to above the inhabitant ventured a joke, in effect testing the possibility of a particularly friendly individual having a sense of humour. However, it became apparent that this inhabitant would have to be a little more careful in future about the type of jokes used.

This appears to be a useful way of operating. The inhabitants would not be able to function if they had not learned to make discriminations, since these enable them to anticipate and anticipations provide a guide to future action. This presupposes organisation and retention of perceived patterns; otherwise experience would be fragmented and learning would evaporate. Organisation is achieved efficiently by subsystems of connected discriminations at different levels of generality (for example, 'dog' is more general than 'Labrador'). Some inhabitants have developed very detailed and organised ways of making sense in some areas of their lives but not in others. This often appears to relate to amount of practice and familiarity in an area and whether they see it as important to how they think about themselves.

Such systems are individual affairs in that, for example, what appears to be the same situation can have quite different meanings for different people. One inhabitant reported enjoying socialising at a party, whereas another who had been at the same event reported being convinced that nobody would be interested in her. These differing perspectives influenced the ways each behaved and hence the outcomes they experienced (including apparent confirmation of their initial anticipations). There can be convergence amongst inhabitants though, informed by common reference points in culture, circumstances and daily interactions. Inhabitants with similar ways of anticipating and understanding areas important to them tend to get on better with each other than those with very different outlooks. Similarity makes for easier communication whilst increasing inhabitants' confidence that their outlooks are viable and accurate. Anticipating the anticipations of other inhabitants is regarded as important in social interaction. The inhabitants most able to do this are those who have wide, detailed but well-organised sets or 'systems' of discriminations/anticipations that enable them to apprehend a range of possibilities. Having available a range of options enables a degree of flexibility and a foundation for continued development.

Problems in living

Unfortunately, variations on these processes can contribute to problems. This is rather like the way that biological evolution, whilst having many advantages, can also confer vulnerability to certain illnesses in the presence of certain environmental conditions. Psychological systems that evolve in interaction with the environment are vulnerable to the system and environment becoming out of step.

What is adaptive in one setting or time period may not be in another. For example, some inhabitants learn at an early age that anticipating the worse from people can be protective; however, this can be limiting in relationships if carried into later life. Such anticipations can also prompt experimenting with related strategies such as putting up a false front or attempting to secure control over others. These may develop at the expense of learning to anticipate more flexibly, or considering the perspectives of other people more deeply. Indeed, these latter options are likely to have had little relevance in the environments where these inhabitants learned that responsiveness to their own needs cannot be relied upon. In addition, current difficulties may resonate with earlier themes in their experience.

Another variation is that some inhabitants appear to have learned anticipations that were effective in a particular context (such as military service) but to have difficulty in learning anew when circumstances change (such as the transition to civilian life). When life gets complicated (for example, during and after dissolution of a relationship), some experience difficulty in developing new ways and try instead to preserve existing understanding. Events outside of the ability to anticipate tend to evoke anxiety, whilst the experience that the ways that have been relied on previously are no longer relevant or viable is often psychologically threatening. Change involves living with unpredictability and the setting aside of what has been invested in. Inhabitants who have most difficulty with this appear to be those who have evolved narrow and inflexible systems for anticipating. This often accompanies limited awareness of other people's perspectives.

Inhabitants who try to force others to comply with their anticipations are especially troublesome. Those who do not share their views may have to be 'taught a lesson', especially if it is inferred that such dissent is intentional and malicious. It can, in certain circumstances, be necessary to test others, though it is important to be selective in evaluating the evidence when the purpose is to confirm rather than revise understanding. One cynical inhabitant suggested that some 'real' scientists do something rather similar when threatened by alternative perspectives.

Inhabitants may also seek to maintain predictability and control in life by being selective in their contacts with other people and involvements. Associating only with like-minded people can be a way for these inhabitants to avoid subjecting what they are trying to rely on to wider testing. Then there are those who become so narrowed in their anticipations and action that their contacts with others are restricted altogether. Some inhabitants caught in ever decreasing circles avoid awareness of wider issues by recourse to intoxicating substances though this can further exacerbate narrowing of anticipations. Blaming others can provide a ready explanation for difficulties and a focus for one's attention. Fantasy can provide a 'safe' way of exploring new hypotheses, though ultimately it can be unsatisfying and require real tests involving precipitating new, intense situations and extending anticipations regarding the self on one's own terms. These processes seem to have much in common with 'symptoms' that provide meaning and structure when life threatens chaos and alternatives seem unavailable, though the majority of inhabitants who struggle to make sense in their lives do so largely in ways that do not involve harm to others.

Freeing an inhabitant for new cycles of development involves helping them find new ways of navigating life. The following account leaves behind the 'as if' in a foreign land account. From a PCT perspective, the land described above is the world we all inhabit.

A PCT perspective on helping people with problems in living

To help clients find new ways of navigating their lives, PCT has techniques for helping clients explore their present ways. These include approaches such as 'self-characterisation' (see Fransella, 1981; Horley, 2006). Here a client is asked to produce a written sketch describing him or herself as it might be written by a hypothetical friend. Writing from a different perspective to their own encourages insight and conveys how life is experienced by the client. There is also a more familiar body of procedures referred to as 'repertory grid' techniques (see Jankowicz, 2004, and the case study below). Potential applications of grids include exploring how an individual is making sense of self and others, situations, relationships, roles, locations, emotional states or objects.

The first step in a grid is to identify a representative sample of things in the domain of interest. In PCT these are referred to as 'elements'. The next step is systematic inquiry, usually centred upon comparisons, regarding the constructs (aspects of meaning or ways of anticipating the world) that a client uses to discriminate amongst the elements. A typical routine is to present elements, each written on a card, in sets of three followed by a question along the lines of 'In what way are two of these alike that makes them different from the third?'. Procedures used at this stage are adaptable and often include the use of additional questioning strategies (e.g. 'Why might that be important to you?'). The client is then asked to evaluate, usually through rating or rank ordering, each element in terms of each construct. Analysis of the resulting matrix (hence 'grid') by computer represents the information from the evaluation task in terms of mathematical relationships.

From these the therapist can infer psychological relationships between constructs, between elements and between constructs and elements.

As with self-characterisations, grids provide signposts for exploring and clarifying the client's personal meanings. There is no clear line between assessment and intervention. Even the process of assessment tends to promote reflection, insight and a collaborative focus. These continue to be harnessed as therapy moves more explicitly into the realms of possible change. Here, too, specialised techniques are available. There is a focus on helping the client to 'elaborate' or think through more clearly the implications, contradictions, consequences and often the origins of his or her construing so that new pathways come into view (Fransella & Dalton, 1999; Winter, 1992b). As indicated below, this is not just a matter of talking. The stance of forming, testing, reviewing and revising new hypotheses becomes increasingly prominent. The therapist's role edges into something akin to a research supervisor as the client is helped with designing and carrying out experiments (with his or her own behaviour as the independent variable) and the results are formulated in terms of implications for future steps. At times the therapist will step into the role of 'coach', perhaps modelling the use of particular skills, encouraging imaginary try-outs or acting the role of a target person.

This ethos also pervades 'Fixed Role Therapy' (see Horley, 2006), in which the client is encouraged, for a limited period, to act the part of an imaginary character. Whilst helping to elaborate construing and choice through a focus on action, it can also demonstrate to the client that change is possible and that the ways that led them to 'paint themselves into a corner' (in Kelly's words) may have outlived their usefulness. As with other techniques, the process is optimised if conducted with a clear understanding of PCT and its research base. Many practitioners find that PCT's perspective, techniques and findings can enhance their practice in areas such as more conventional interviewing and interventions.

Adaptations for forensic settings

Consistent with its philosophical position of 'constructive alternativism' (the idea that 'all of our present interpretations of the universe are subject to revision or replacement': Kelly, 1955, cited in Winter, 1992b, p. 4), PCT is very open to creative application. Kelly (1955) expected his theory to be developed beyond recognition and saw it as based on, and subject to, the same processes as other systems for construing. It should be emphasised that PCT should not be construed as presenting a mentalistic, solipsistic, 'in the head' view of human functioning. People are not bundles of constructs (like repertory grids on legs); they *construe*, and construing, like other forms of action, always takes place in a context. In this sense PCT is perfectly consistent with views of 'mind' that locate it in a wider system that incorporates both person and environment, including other people (see Echterhoff, Higgins, & Levine, 2009; Barrett, Mesquita, & Smith, 2010; Ward, 2009). A major implication of this is that, in addressing many issues with forensic clients, the context in which people attempt to anticipate, such as a custodial setting, is likely to be more than just background.

Aspects such as subcultural norms, intimidation, distrust, loss of agency and an uncertain future are often prominent in the daily currency of secure environments and institutional life. They influence anticipations and do little to foster openness and engagement in therapy (Butler, 2008; Horley, 2006; Ross, Polaschek, & Ward, 2008). They should be taken into account in therapy (indeed, related problems may well be part of its focus) and make establishing a therapeutic alliance all the more essential. The 'credulous approach' (trying to see the world through the client's eyes) and values associated with PCT such as being non-judgmental (whilst encouraging responsibility for choices) can be helpful here (Winter, 2003a). None of this should be taken as implying that 'anything goes'. Healthy functioning includes the client attempting to understand and respect the perspectives of others (Winter, 2003b), although it might be suggested that this develops best if they have some personal experience as recipients of this to relate to. This is part of the rationale for attempting to improve the psychosocial environment of secure settings more generally (Akerman, Needs & Bainbridge, in press). Otherwise there can be a default tendency for custodial environments both to reflect and to perpetuate the anticipations and world views of those within them (Needs, 2016). Limited construing at the organisational level may contribute to outcomes such as the 'lowered self-respect and lowered aspirations' found by Norris (1977, p. 135) in a PCT-based study of a detention centre for young offenders.

In both penal environments and community services the dominant official agenda has come to focus on assessment and reduction of 'risk'. Due largely to prevailing research designs and a pre-emptive tendency to construe risk as a property of the individual, attention to contextual processes is as under-developed in most protocols for risk assessment as it is in most programmes for risk reduction. With few exceptions, research into proximal life events, for example, remains neglected in relation to crime despite its established contribution within the field of mental health (Needs, 2015). Even the detailed analysis of index offences can be relatively sidelined outside of a more individualised 'case formulation' approach (Hart, Sturmey, Logan, & McMurran, 2011; Needs & Towl, 1997; West & Greenall, 2011).

A noteworthy way in which case formulation regarding offences can be enhanced is by employing a version of the PCT technique of 'laddering'. Needs (1988a) outlined how a sample of 'elements' based on stages of an offence, proximal events and key aspects of a client's past can be compared to elicit constructs. The elements are derived from interview and written on small cards. The client is then asked to sort these cards into sets where all have something in common. A pair of cards from within a set is then separated from the rest and the client is asked to explain how they are similar. They are then asked to put into words what the contrast to this might be. This yields a bipolar construct. This method is easier for most clients when comparing situations than the more familiar presenting elements in threes and asking 'In what way are two of these alike that makes them different from the third?'. The client is then asked which pole describes how they prefer things to be. For each construct the client is then asked why the preferred pole might have been important to them; when an answer is given, the question is asked again in relation to preferred pole of the new answer and so on, climbing up the ladder of increasingly core values until a final abstraction is reached. After this, a new pair of cards is selected from the same set and the process repeated. When all cards in a set have been covered, the process is repeated using cards within the next set and so on, perhaps also exploring comparisons across sets. This results in a number of 'ladders' of progressively core concerns and, as with all construct elicitation, clients tend to develop a greater facility with this process as familiarity increases. Ladders can be cross-referenced, in that apparently similar concerns from different ladders can be compared or contrasted to aid further exploration and check interpretation.

This form of inquiry enables formulation of hypotheses concerning meanings that were invoked or challenged. The intensity and unfamiliarity of this, especially for those accustomed to standard protocols and giving scripted replies to scripted interviews, elevate the importance of issues of informed consent, sensitivity and support in order to ensure the well-being of the client. However, many clients have welcomed the chance to explore their sense-making and views of the world as a means of facilitating growth of adaptive meaning (Park, 2010). It can also help formulate a monitoring strategy where parallels are anticipated between sequences of current and offence-related behaviour (Jones, 2004). Of special relevance to risk assessment, what Mischel (1973) termed 'idiographic stimulus and response equivalences', a major influence on the continuity of behaviour, become amenable to examination in relation to future contexts. Readers interested in developing this area should consult the recent review and suggestions regarding laddering more generally by Korenini (2014).

Other adaptations of PCT techniques for forensic clients include the incorporation of elements in repertory grids such as victims, people representing categories of interest (such as women or children, those who are admired or have ostensibly similar problems to oneself) and the self at different points in time such as at the time of the offence and in the future (a similar adaptation can be used with self-characterisations). These can of course be used alongside more conventional elements such as parent figures, ideal and feared selves (see Houston, 1998). Grids (and/or laddering) can also be used to explore what is at stake for a person in situations relevant to, for example, anger or difficulties in social interaction.

It should not be overlooked that meanings are affected at a fundamental level by an individual's sense of connectedness to others (Lambert et al., 2013; Williams, 2007), an area in which many offenders have a constellation of difficulties (Ansbro, 2008; Fonagy, 2004). Though therapists need to balance connectedness versus separateness in working with clients (Leitner, 1988), therapy that does not engage this area is unlikely to be successful. Doing so is relevant even to clients who see themselves as inhabiting a world where the only security lies in 'looking after Number One'. An emphasis on 'relational context' as a means of fostering agency through greater awareness of the perspectives of others has gained ground in the criminological literature on desistance from offending (Weaver, 2012). Allied notions of the need for desistance to be supported by development of a non-offending identity and an accompanying personal 'narrative' (or integrating, guiding story that re-defines an individual's place in the world) have also been formulated (Maruna & Ramsden, 2004; McNeill, 2012; Vaughan, 2007). Such aspects are highly congruent with PCT and other 'constructivist' approaches (Neimeyer, 2009), even extending to particular techniques such as self-characterisation (Androutsopoulou, 2001). So too is the influential 'cognitive transformation' model of desistance proposed by Giordano, Cernkovich and Rudolph (2002) that refers to fostering openness to change, exposure to new experience, seeing new possibilities for the self and finally, re-construing from a standpoint that is incompatible with continued offending. Environments such as therapeutic communities can be helpful in engaging these processes (Needs, Salmann, & Kiddle, 2011).

One technique that embodies some of these aspects is the WOMBAT (Needs, 1988b, 1995). This stands for 'Way Of Me Behaving And Thinking'. An adaptation of Kelly's (1955) Fixed Role Therapy, it also draws upon research into perspective-taking and cognitive elaboration of roles to facilitate change and new processing (Radley, 1974) and the idea of possible selves (Markus & Nurius, 1986). It includes an emphasis on clarifying connotations of personal change (Tschudi, 1977) and shares a focus on working collaboratively with an individual to formulate and render personal goals attainable in prosocial ways with the Good Lives Model (GLM: e.g. Ward & Stewart, 2003). A central idea is that major personal change is facilitated when actions and sense-making are integrated explicitly within potential core roles rather than regarded as discrete 'skills'. These roles (WOMBATs) are identified and formulated by the client with assistance from the therapist, with reference to relevant goals, situations and current construing. For example, one volatile client, near the start of the process came to entertain the possibility that 'keeping his head screwed on *vs.* always dances to their tune' allowed more choice than the previously dominant 'wild versus soft'. As this new possibility had a powerful personal resonance, we were able to elaborate what keeping his head screwed on would involve. Beyond this, therapy proceeds in much the same way as Fixed Role Therapy (Horley, 2006; Winter, 1992b) with the use of experiments and coaching as appropriate and detailed consideration of contextual issues. Handling processes such as dislodgement from existing core roles and tightening versus loosening of construing is best undertaken from the vantage points of PCT and, as the acronym might imply, the use of humour is not forbidden.

Therapist training

Practitioners of PCT psychotherapy (actually, these days it is common to talk of PCP or 'Personal Construct Psychology') will have initial professional qualifications as psychologists, psychotherapists, psychiatrists or similar. Many have started with workshops (e.g. on repertory grid networks), supervision from experienced practitioners and using PCT in research. Within the UK, the University of Hertfordshire runs a part-time Master's degree in PCP (www.constructivistpsych.org/archives/3560) and its clinical doctorate has a constructivist slant (unsurprisingly, with Professor David Winter at the helm!). A recent venture is the

UK Personal Construct Psychology Association (www.personalconstructuk.org), a member of the Constructivist and Existential College of the UK Council for Psychotherapy that keeps a register of qualified PCP therapists in the UK. For information about the international scene the reader is also referred to the Personal Construct Gateway (www.personal-construct.net).

Client characteristics (indicators/contra-indicators)

In its own terminology, PCT has a wide 'range of convenience'. It has been applied to a broad range of mental health concerns, difficulties in living and problematic choices including offending (Walker & Winter, 2007). PCT does entail a degree of ability in verbalising and reflection. On the other hand it lends itself to creative application even when language has to be kept simple and direct (see, for example, Spindler Barton, Walton, & Rowe, 1976). Most individuals will engage with making comparisons and contrasts, exploring examples or dilemmas, taking implications to extremes and pondering alternatives, especially if they feel that what they say is being listened to more than just a sign of something else. Where grid methods are used, cognitive load can be reduced by presenting cards representing elements in pairs rather than the more familiar threes and asking for similarities/differences and contrasts (this can also be used more generally for complex elements such as situations). Constructs identified from interviews can supplement (or if necessary replace) this step and some clients find rank ordering (starting with 'Which of these is the most ....?') easier to do than rating.

It should be recognised that some clients prefer an emphasis on 'doing' rather than 'talking' (Winter, Caine, & Wijesinghe, 1981). This should be borne in mind but PCT is notable for the degree to which its unifying perspective allows it to be 'technically eclectic' (Winter, 2003b) beyond the distinctive methods outlined above. As with any approach, cooperation is needed and, as indicated, in a custodial environment there is often much to be overcome in terms of distrust and pessimism. Caution is needed with clients who have very 'tight' construing related to themselves and other people – where their construing may have become dominated by limited concerns such as 'for me versus against me'. Such clients can be difficult to engage and dislodgement from their stance can face them with the possibility of chaos. However, clients who have been labelled as personality disordered are far from being outside of PCT's range of convenience (Houston, 2003). It is necessary for any therapist to be aware of the challenges of working with the idiosyncratically defensive (even retaliatory) world views of some clients (Needs, 1992). This does not mean having to be inattentive to genuine distress and confusion or to the possibility that these might extend to the client's offending (Adshead, Ferrito, & Bose, 2015; Winter, 2003a).

Studies of the evidence in forensic settings

The central tenets of PCT have been reflected in a great range of published research with a variety of target populations; much of this has been based on repertory grid data (Walker & Winter, 2007). Studies of offenders have elaborated our awareness of possible processes and issues, highlighting the relevance of, for example, biased, rigid or polarised views of other people, having difficulty in apprehending others' perspectives, a tendency to see oneself as different and the testing of idiosyncratic views of the self in perplexing 'experiments' (such as self as powerful, or spontaneous and unfettered by convention, or as a righteous avenger (Houston, 1998, 2003; Needs, 1988a; Youngs & Canter, 2012).

Insights can also be gained from PCT research with other groups. At first sight, Fransella's (1972) work with stutterers might not seem very applicable to work with offenders. However, the finding that, after therapy focused on construing fluent rather than problematic speech, fluency increased alongside a measurable growth in connections between constructs related to the non-stutterer 'role' may hold more general lessons concerning personal change; lasting behavioural change can only occur when it is supported by the development of new ways of predicting and understanding the world that supersede those that supported problematic behaviour. Behavioural change is likely to endure only when new ways of sense-making become integrated within the sense of self (Stein & Markus, 1996) and are sufficiently detailed and organised to permit consonant understanding and action within relevant domains (see Coleman, 1975). These ideas have parallels with the view of desistance from offending as involving the development, consolidation and active use of new ways adumbrated by Giordano et al. (2002), mentioned above. Indications of persistent limitations in sense-making and prediction that may be associated with continued offending can also be found in research from other theoretical starting points, including studies of the 'implicit theories' regarding victims held by sexual offenders (Ward, 2000), sexual murderers (Beech, Fisher, & Ward, 2005), perpetrators of intimate partner violence (Weldon & Gilchrist, 2012) and the beliefs about self, other people and the world constructed by personality disordered individuals (e.g. Beck et al., 2001).

Successive grids can be compared on a variety of measures to identify changes in construing in response to therapy (Houston, 1998; Winter, 1985). Despite 'the obscure meanings of some grid measures and the absence of normative data' (Watson & Winter, 2005, p. 345) several studies suggest that some at least can predict therapeutic outcomes and that successful therapy is associated with reconstruction (Walker & Winter, 2007). Research into outcomes of PCT-based psychotherapy comes largely from single case studies or small groups (Winter, 2003b). One reason for this is the lack of programmes based specifically on PCT (Horley & Bennett, 2003). Nonetheless, the detailed study of NHS clients by Watson and Winter (2005) indicated that experiences in cognitive therapy and a PCT-based approach could be differentiated and that the latter was at least as effective as the former. Furthermore, meta-analyses of (largely non-forensic) outcome studies, that met criteria such as use of a comparison group, produced effect sizes that indicated advantages after completion of PCT psychotherapy over no treatment, waiting list controls and other interventions. However, although a moderate effect size over no treatment and waiting list controls was maintained in the few studies that included a follow-up, the superiority of PCT over other approaches disappeared (Viney, Metcalfe,

& Winter, 2005). Overall, it was concluded by the latter authors that their meta-analyses and preceding systematic review provided 'encouraging evidence of the effectiveness of personal construct psychotherapy' (p. 363).

Case study

James was a 30-year-old man serving an eight-year sentence for a violent assault and rape of a woman.

James described repeated trauma in his childhood. He reported that his parents were heavy drinkers and neglected him to drink and spend time in the pub. He described his father as violent to him and to his mother, and that on occasion he feared that he was going to be killed. He would spend much of his time trying to avoid being assaulted – particularly when his father returned from the pub drunk and aggressive. He reported that he had been anally raped on several occasions by a relative of his mother with whom he was sent to stay (a source of flashbacks) and that his parents' response on being told was to punish him severely for making up stories. Feeling betrayed and unloved, he went on to harbour urges to take revenge both on his family and on people he saw as representing a social order that had colluded with, and not protected him from, abuse. He also described not being able to forgive himself for 'letting it happen' and not going back and avenging himself on the perpetrator as an adult. These feelings were reflected later in life in protracted periods of self-harm and self-sabotage in the context of therapy. In addition, he reported being forced to have oral sex with a female baby sitter at the age of nine. For much of his life prior to therapy he had construed the latter as a good experience and he became preoccupied in his sexual fantasies with having oral sex with people in a coercive manner.

Against a background of a period of heavy substance misuse which followed the break-up of a relationship, he would intimidate vulnerable (often drunken) women in the street and steal their bags. In his index offence he followed the victim from a nightclub and asked her if he could 'walk her home'; she did not agree to this but he accompanied her anyway. When she arrived at the housing estate where she lived he followed her into a lift area, forced her to have oral sex with him and vaginally and anally raped her. The depositions described him as switching between being violent and coercive and asking the victim if she 'enjoyed' what he was doing to her. At the end of the assault he asked her for her number so that he could meet with her again. He described feeling surprised and shocked when the police came to arrest him. He had beliefs about women enjoying violent sexual behaviour and reported that he thought that his victim had fitted the image he had of an individual who enjoyed this.

Repertory grid assessment

The grid assessment was tailored to focus on his construal of his offending and how this linked with his construal of adverse developmental experiences; for serious offenders a history of sexual abuse in childhood can be linked with risk of reconviction (e.g. Levenson & Socia, 2015).

Elements

The elements James identified collaboratively are shown in Table 8.1.

Constructs

Constructs were elicited by comparing elements three at a time in terms of ways two were alike that made them different from the third. The constructs are shown in Table 8.2.

TABLE 8.1 Elements used by James

Self elements:	Family elements:
Me as victim 1 (self as victim of babysitter)	Mum
	Mum not believing
Me as victim 2 (self as victim of abuse by mother's relative)	Dad
	Granny
As I'd like to be	John (brother)
Me offending	
Me now	
Victim elements:	**Significant other elements:**
Victim of the offence	Jane (ex-girlfriend)
Mother's friend who abused me	Pete (staff member)
Babysitter who abused me	Andrew (friend)

TABLE 8.2 Constructs used by James

Lazy, didn't want to help	–	Wanted to be a provider
Bully, rebel	–	Understands and cares
Dismissing	–	Respects you
Always wanting revenge	–	Happy, wants a laugh
Not able to change	–	Learn by looking
Coward runs away	–	Stands up to people
Hates everyone	–	A person who likes people
Open-minded about sex	–	Frightened of sex
Upbeat, straightforward, confident	–	Not confident, scared of sex
No cares	–	Full of shame
Concerned about others	–	Doesn't care, dangerous, self-centred
Very contented	–	Terrified, easily taken advantage of
No love, live in terror, unhappy	–	Genuinely loving
Will try anything	–	Sexually inhibited
Lost innocence wanting to be rescued	–	Doing childish things happily
Outward going, giving, helps people	–	Very wicked and not worried about this
Helps people, concerned about others	–	A brute trying to hurt people
Strong and fearless	–	Extremely frightened

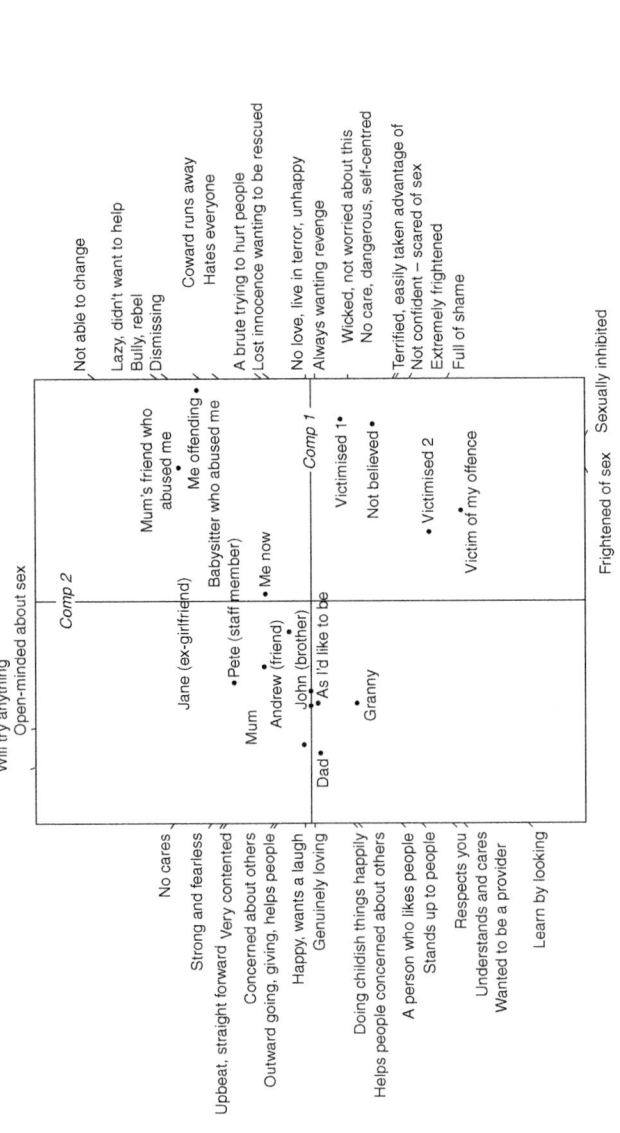

FIGURE 8.1: Principal component analysis of construing of self and other people, incorporating aspects relevant to offending and experiences of abuse.

Analysis

The next step was to obtain ratings for each of the elements on a scale of 1 to 7 using each bipolar construct to anchor the scale. This resulted in a construct by element matrix of ratings. This matrix was then analysed using principal component analysis (PCA) in order to attempt to identify underlying factors in the way the person is construing the elements. Principal component analysis by the Idiogrid programme gave a starting point for exploration (see Figure 8.1).

This plot shows elements plotted in construct space as represented by the PCA. Constructs are represented by lines running across the mapping with a pole at each side of the plot. Constructs close to each other are correlated, e.g. 'Happy, wants a laugh' vs 'Always wanting revenge' is correlated with 'Genuinely loving' vs 'No love, live in terror, unhappy'. Elements are placed in the plot according to how they are rated on each of the constructs, e.g. 'Dad', 'Mum', 'Brother' and 'As I'd like to be' are all close to each other and towards the 'Happy, wants a laugh' and 'Genuinely loving' ends of these constructs. The resulting plot can be used to explore the way the individual construes themselves and their social world.

Exploration included the following areas:

1. *How he construed sexual 'openness'*

    He had engaged in a number of different sexual acts in the course of his offence and the grid suggests that he saw himself offending [me offending] as 'open-minded about sex' whereas he saw his victim [victim of my offence] as being 'sexually inhibited'; he also construed himself as a victim [victimised 2] in this way. Exploration identified how he had justified his offending to himself as being about 'helping' his victim to experience new things. He had attempted to explain his own abuse [mum's friend who abused me] in this way to himself also. The grid helped him to acknowledge how frightening sexual abuse was for him and for his victim and that this was not about not being 'open-minded'.

2. *Links between his own victim experiences and his offending*

    Exploration of states of terror, shame, wanting to be rescued and wanting revenge as part of his own victim experience helped him to think about how he had impacted on his own victim. He clearly used the same constructs to make sense of what happened to his victim [victim of my offence] as he did to think about what had happened to him [victimised 1 and victimised 2]. It became clear that his numbing and cutting off of emotion linked with his own abuse.

    He explored the way that abuse-linked self-states were associated with wanting revenge, not caring and becoming dangerous and callous ('wicked and not caring about it'). He acknowledged the way in which he was compensating for trauma-related extreme states of vulnerability by becoming emotionally cut off and interested in hurting others in a vengeful manner. He explored the way in which he had made his victim have the feelings that he experienced when abused. For example, when anally raped he had been asked if he 'liked' this and he replicated this with his own victim.

3. *Identifying where he wanted to be in the future*
   Where his ideal self was placed in the grid helped him identify ways of being that were important to him. He saw his mother and father as loving. He discussed this in terms of idealising them despite their abusive behaviour. This facilitated an elaboration of his concept of 'loving'. He acknowledged that he might at times want an idealised version of being 'loved' in a relationship. He also looked at healthy and unhealthy versions of being 'strong and fearless'. He saw that being strong did not mean being violent in the way his father had been.

Outcome

For some individuals it can be useful to re-administer the same grid post-therapy, preferably after making predictions about how the second analysis would turn out if the therapy had been successful. In James' case, however, the change was more about recognising the links between his own abuse and the offences that he had committed. This insight was evidenced in the way he talked about his offending. In addition, his self-report reflected his changes in view about what constitutes 'love' which in turn was reflected in his later work on concerns about whether he would be able to get into a long-term relationship in the future. Similarly, his new understanding and perspectives on his need to be 'strong and fearless' allowed him to explore different ways of achieving status that did not involve hurting or deprecating others.

Key directions for future research

At its inception PCT was ahead of its time, prefiguring and influencing many developments in psychology; since, it has both endured and continued to develop (Walker & Winter, 2007). It still has many advantages, such as providing a detailed, explicit and testable body of theoretical principles and methods. In its clinical applications these centre upon understanding 'where clients are coming from', 'what they face' and how they can be helped in finding new ways of 'navigating and engaging the world'. These issues are no less relevant to more mainstream approaches that have given less overt attention to the role of personal meanings in psychological problems and change. PCT's willingness to embrace techniques from other approaches due to its ability to conceptualise them within a unifying perspective (Winter, 2003b) enhances its potential to be an integrating force in therapeutic work with forensic clients.

It might, for example, enable improvements to be made in the area of 'Responsivity' to clients in group-based programmes targeting offending behaviour within the rubric of 'Risk – Need – Responsivity' (RNR: Andrews & Bonta, 2010). Feeling that uniquely personal concerns, sources of confusion and dilemmas are recognised and amenable to exploration in a non-judgmental fashion may encourage greater engagement, a sense of support and hope. As such it may enable processes of change to be harnessed and managed more effectively than, according to critics of RNR (e.g. McNeill, 2012), is often the case at present. The compatibility of PCT with the collaborative, strengths-based orientation of the Good Lives Model and with the emphasis in desistance-based approaches on aspects such as identity, narrative and contexts has been noted. In addition to possibilities for direct integration, it is worth considering that PCT might provide a conceptual medium for the fusion of these with the elements of RNR. It is encouraging that there continue to be reminders of how personal construct theory and its methods can provide new perspectives, compatible with other approaches, on a range of issues including denial in sex offenders (Blagden, Winder, Gregson, & Thorne, 2014), anger in young offenders (Yorke & Dallos, 2015) and terrorists' understanding of themselves and their roles (Canter, Sarangi, & Youngs, 2014). Such a footing for exploration might also help provide a basis for clinical acumen that goes beyond adherence to manuals (cf. Gannon & Ward, 2014) and is consistent with arguments for integrating principles, components and knowledge of moderators and mediators across therapies (Laurenceau, Hayes, & Feldman, 2007).

In psychotherapy research there have been calls for moving beyond a narrow focus on *whether* change occurs to exploration of *how* it occurs, for greater awareness of discontinuous and nonlinear patterns and attention to individual differences and contextual factors (Hayes, Hope, & Hayes, 2007; Laurenceau et al., 2007). These arguments parallel those in favour of evaluation of initiatives in all areas of interest to psychologists being 'realistic' and not simply a matter of aggregated data from group or pre-post comparisons (see Davies, Jones, & Howells, 2010; Pawson & Tilley, 1997). Such an endeavour is an invitation for psychologists to continue to reflect critically upon their own sense-making and views of the world as professionals.

Further reading

Houston, J. (1998). *Making sense with offenders: Personal constructs, therapy and change.* Chichester: Wiley.

Jankowicz, D. (2004). *The easy guide to repertory grids.* Chichester: Wiley.

Winter, D. A. (1992). *Personal construct psychology in clinical practice: Theory, research and applications.* London: Routledge.

Winter, D. A., & Reed, N. (Eds) (2015). *The Wiley handbook of personal construct psychology.* Chichester: Wiley-Blackwell.

References

Adshead, G., Ferrito, M., & Bose, S. (2015). Recovery after homicide: Narrative shifts in therapy with homicide perpetrators. *Criminal Justice and Behavior, 42*(1), 70–81.

Akerman, G., Needs, A., & Bainbridge, C. (Eds) (in press). *Transforming environments in offender rehabilitation.* London: Routledge.

Andrews, D. A., & Bonta, J. (2010). *The psychology of criminal conduct* (5th edn). Abingdon, UK: Routledge.

Androutsopoulou, A. (2001). The self-characterisation as a narrative tool: Applications in therapy with individuals and families. *Family Process, 40*(1), 79–94.

Ansbro, M. (2008). Using attachment theory with offenders. *Probation Journal, 55*(3), 231–244.

Barrett, L. F., Mesquita, B., & Smith, E.R. (2010). The context principle. In B. Mesquita, L. R. Barrett, & E. R. Smith (Eds) *The mind in context*. New York: Guilford Press.

Beck, A.T., Butler, A. C., Brown, G. K., Dahlsgard, K. K., Newman, C. F., & Beck, J. S. (2001). Dysfunctional beliefs discriminate personality disorders. *Behavior Research & Therapy*, *39*(10), 1213–1225.

Beech, A. R., Fisher, D., & Ward, T. (2005). Sexual murderers' implicit theories. *Journal of Interpersonal Violence*, *20*, 1336–1389.

Blagden, N., Winder, B., Gregson, M., & Thorne, K. (2014). Making sense of denial in sex offenders: A qualitative phenomenological and repertory grid analysis. *Journal of Interpersonal Violence*, *29*(9), 1698–1731.

Butler, M. (2008). What are you looking at? Prisoner confrontations and the search for respect. *British Journal of Criminology*, *48*, 856–873.

Canter, D., Sarangi, S., & Youngs, D. (2014). Terrorists' personal constructs and their roles: A comparison of the three Islamic terrorists. *Legal and Criminological Psychology*, *19*, 160–178.

Coleman, P. G. (1975). Interest in personal activities and degree of perceived implications between personal constructs. *British Journal of Social and Clinical Psychology*, *14*(1), 93–95.

Davies, J., Jones, L., & Howells, K. (2010). Evaluating individual change in forensic settings. In M. Daffern, L. F. Jones, & J. Shine (Eds), *Offence Paralleling Behaviour: A case formulation approach to offender assessment and intervention*. Chichester: Wiley-Blackwell.

Echterhoff, G., Higgins, E. T., & Levine, J. M. (2009). Shared reality: Experiencing commonality with others' inner states about the world. *Perspectives on Psychological Science*, *4*, 496–521.

Fonagy, P. (2004). The developmental roots of violence in the failure of mentalization. In F. Pfafflin & G. Adshead (Eds) *A matter of security: The application of attachment theory to forensic psychiatry and psychotherapy*. London: Jessica Kingsley.

Fransella, F. (1972). *Personal change and reconstruction*. London: Academic Press.

Fransella, F. (1981). Nature babbling to herself: The self-characterisation as a therapeutic tool. In H. Bonarius, R. Holland & S. Rosenberg (Eds), *Personal construct psychology: Recent advances in theory and practice*. London: Macmillan.

Fransella, F., & Dalton, P. (1999). *Personal construct counselling in action* (2nd edn). London: Sage.

Gannon, T. A., & Ward, T. (2014). Where has all the psychology gone?: A critical review of evidence-based psychological practice in correctional settings. Aggression and violent behavior, 19(4), 435–446.

Giordano, P. C., Cernkovich, S. A., & Rudolph, J. L. (2002). Gender, crime and desistance: Toward a theory of cognitive transformation. *American Journal of Sociology*, *107*, 990–1064.

Hart, S. D., Sturmey, P., Logan, C., & McMurran, M. (2011). Forensic case formulation. *International Journal of Forensic Mental Health Services*, *10*, 118–126.

Hayes, A., Hope, D. A., & Hayes, S. (2007). Towards an understanding of the processes and mechanisms of change in cognitive behavioural therapy: Linking innovative methodology with fundamental questions. *Clinical Psychology Review*, *27*(6), 679–681.

Horley, J. (2006). Personal construct psychotherapy: Fixed role therapy with forensic clients. *Journal of Sexual Aggression*, *12*(1), 53–61.

Horley J., & Bennett, J. (2003). Psychological treatment of offenders in institutions. In J. Horley (Ed.), *Personal construct perspectives on forensic psychology*. London: Brunner-Routledge.

Hough, M. (2010). Gold standard or fool's gold? The pursuit of certainty in experimental criminology. *Criminology and Criminal Justice*, *10*(1), 11–22.

Houston, J. (1998). *Making sense with offenders: personal constructs, therapy and change*. Chichester: Wiley.

Jones, L. (2004). Offence Paralleling Behaviour (OPB) as a framework for assessment and interventions with offenders. In A. Needs & G. Towl (Eds), *Applying psychology to forensic practice*. Oxford: BPS Blackwell.

Jankowicz, D. (2004). *The easy guide to repertory grids*. Chichester: Wiley.

Kelly, G. (1955). *The psychology of personal constructs*. New York: WW Norton.

Kirchner, E., Kennedy, R., & Draguns, J. (1979). Assertion and aggression in adult offenders. *Behavior Therapy, 10*(4), 452–471.

Korenini, B. (2014). Consistent laddering: A new approach to laddering technique. *Journal of Constructivist Psychology, 27*(4), 317–328.

Lambert, N. M., Stillman, T. F., Hicks, J. A., Kamble, S., Baumeister, R. F., & Fincham, F. D. (2013). To belong is to matter: Sense of belonging enhances meaning in life. *Personality and Social Psychology Bulletin, 39*(11), 1418–1427.

Laurenceau, J. P., Hayes, A. M., & Feldman, G. C. (2007). Statistical and methodological issues in the study of change in psychotherapy. *Clinical Psychology Review, 27*(6), 715–723.

Leitner, L. M. (1988). Terror, risk, and reverence: Experiential personal construct psychotherapy. *International Journal of Personal Construct Psychology, 1*, 261–272.

Levenson, J. S., & Socia, K. M. (2015). Adverse childhood experiences and arrest patterns in a sample of sexual offenders. *Journal of Interpersonal Violence*, 1–29.

Markus, H., & Nurius, P. (1986). Possible selves. *American Psychologist, 41*, 954–969.

Maruna, S. (2011). Why do they hate us? Making peace between prisoners and psychology. *International Journal of Offender Therapy and Comparative Criminology, 55*(5), 671–675.

Maruna, S., & Ramsden, D. (2004). Living to tell the tale: Redemption narratives, shame management and offender rehabilitation. In A. Lieblich, D. P. McAdams, & J. Josselson (Eds), *Healing plots: The narrative basis of psychotherapy. The narrative study of lives*. Washington, DC: American Psychological Association.

McNeill, F. (2012). Four forms of 'offender' rehabilitation: Towards an interdisciplinary perspective. *Legal and Criminological Psychology, 17*, 1–19.

Mischel, W. (1973). Toward a cognitive social learning reconceptualization of personality. *Psychological Review, 80*, 252–283.

Needs, A. (1988a). Psychological investigation of offending behaviour. In F. Fransella & L. Thomas (Eds), *Experimenting with personal construct psychology*. London: Routledge.

Needs, A. (1988b). *The subjective context of social difficulty*. Unpub. D.Phil thesis, University of York.

Needs, A. (1992). *Working with personality disorders: Some points for special unit staff*. Unpub. Training manual, H. M. Prison Service.

Needs, A. (1995). Social skills training. In G. Towl (Ed.), *Groupwork in prisons. Issues in Criminological and Legal Psychology* No. 23. Leicester: The British Psychological Society.

Needs, A. (2015). 'Outrageous Fortune': Transitions and related concerns in the genesis of violence. Paper presented at the Conference of the International Academy for Law and Mental Health, Vienna.

Needs, A. (2016). Rehabilitation-writing a new story. The Psychologist, 29(3), 192–195.

Needs, A., Salmann, L., & Kiddle, R. (2011). Personality characteristics, change and attitudes to bullying in a therapeutic community. Paper presented at the Conference of the Division of Forensic Psychology, Portsmouth.

Needs, A., & Towl, G. (1997). Reflections on clinical risk assessment with lifers. *Prison Service Journal, 113*, 14–17.

Neimeyer, R. A. (2009). *Constructivist psychotherapy: Distinctive features*. London: Routledge.

Norris, M. (1977). Construing in a detention centre. In D. Bannister (Ed.), *New perspectives in personal construct theory*. London: Academic Press.

Park, C. L. (2010). Making sense of the meaning literature: An integrative review of meaning making and its effects on adjustment to stressful life events. *Psychological Bulletin, 136,* 257–301.

Pawson, R., & Tilley, N. (1997). *Realistic evaluation.* London: Sage.

Polaschek, D. L. L. (2012). An appraisal of the risk–need–responsivity (RNR) model of offender rehabilitation and its application in correctional treatment. *Legal and Criminological Psychology, 17*(1), 1–17.

Radley, A. R. (1974). The effect of role enactment upon construed alternatives. *British Journal of Medical Psychology, 47,* 313–320.

Ross, E. C., Polaschek, D. L. L., & Ward, T. (2008). The therapeutic alliance: a theoretical revision for offender rehabilitation. *Aggression and Violent Behavior, 14,* 462–480.

Spindler Barton, E., Walton, T., & Rowe, D. (1976). Using grid technique with the mentally handicapped. In P. Slater (Ed.), *The measurement of intrapersonal space by grid technique.* Vol. 1. Explorations of intrapersonal space. London: Wiley.

Stein, K. F., & Markus, H. R. (1996). The role of the self in behavioral change. Journal of Psychotherapy Integration, 6(4), 349–384.

Tschudi, F. (1977). Loaded and honest questions: A construct theory view of symptoms and therapy. In D. Bannister (Ed.), *New perspectives in personal construct theory.* London: Academic Press.

Vaughan, B. (2007). The internal narrative of desistance. *British Journal of Criminology, 47,* 390–404.

Viney, L. L., Metcalfe, C., & Winter, D. A. (2005). The effectiveness of personal construct psychotherapy: A systematic review and meta-analysis. In D. A. Winter & L. L. Viney (Eds), *Personal construct psychotherapy: Advances in theory, practice and research* (pp. 347–364). London: Whurr.

Walker, B. M., & Winter, D. A. (2007). The elaboration of personal construct psychology. *Annual Review of Psychology, 58,* 453–477.

Ward, T. (2000). Sexual offenders' cognitive distortions as implicit theories. *Aggression and Violent Behavior, 5,* 491–507.

Ward, T. (2009). The extended mind theory of cognitive distortions in sex offenders. *Journal of Sexual Aggression, 15*(3), 247–259.

Ward, T., & Stewart, C. A. (2003). The relationship between human needs and criminogenic needs. *Psychology, Crime, & Law, 9,* 219–224.

Watson, S., & Winter, D. A. (2005). A process and outcome study of personal construct psychotherapy. In D. A. Winter & L. L. Viney (Eds), *Personal construct psychotherapy: Advances in theory, practice and research* (pp. 335–346). London: Whurr.

Watts, R. E., Peluso, P. R., & Lewis, T. F. (2005). Expanding the acting as if technique: An Adlerian/constructive integration. *The Journal of Individual Psychology, 61*(4), 380–387.

Weaver, B. (2012). The relational context of desistance: Some implications and opportunities for social policy. *Social Policy and Administration, 46*(4), 395–412.

Weldon, S., & Gilchrist, E. (2012). Implicit theories in intimate partner violence offenders. *Journal of Family Violence, 27*(8), 761–772.

West, A. G., & Greenall, P. V. (2011). Incorporating Index Offence Analysis into Forensic Clinical Assessment. *Legal and Criminological Psychology, 16*(1), 144–159.

Williams, K. (2007). Ostracism. *Annual Review of Psychology, 58,* 425–452.

Winter, D. A. (1985). Neurotic disorders: The curse of certainty. In E. Button (Ed.), *Personal construct theory and mental health.* London: Croom Helm.

Winter, D. A. (1992a). A personal construct view of social skills training. In P. Maitland & D. Brennan (Eds), *Personal construct theory, deviancy and social work (2nd edn)*. Inner London Probation Service/Centre for Personal Construct Psychology.

Winter, D. A. (1992b). *Personal construct psychology in clinical practice: theory, research and applications*. London: Routledge.

Winter, D. A. (2003a). A credulous approach to violence and homicide. In J. Horley (Ed.), *Personal construct perspectives on forensic psychology*. Hove: Brunner-Routledge.

Winter, D.A. (2003b). The evidence base for personal construct psychotherapy. In F. Fransella (Ed.). *International handbook of personal construct psychology*. Chichester: Wiley.

Winter, D.A., Caine, T., & Wijesinghe, S. (1981). *Personal styles in neurosis: Implications for small group psychotherapy and behaviour therapy*. London: Routledge and Kegan Paul.

Yorke, L., & Dallos, R. (2015). An interpretative phenomenological analysis and repertory grid exploration of anger in young offenders. *Journal of Constructivist Psychology, 8*(2), 126–138.

Youngs, D., & Canter, D. (2012). Narrative roles in criminal action: An integrative framework for differentiating offenders. *Legal and Criminological Psychology, 17*, 233–249.

9
PSYCHODYNAMIC PSYCHOTHERAPY

Nigel Beail

Psychodynamic psychotherapy has been provided as a treatment option for offenders since the 1930s when the Portman clinic was founded (Cordess, 1992). It then spread to other outpatient and secure offender settings with the development of the National Health Service in the UK. This chapter will consider the provision of individual psychodynamic psychotherapy for offenders with a specific focus on those who have intellectual and developmental disabilities (IDD) reflecting the specialism of the author. Most people who have IDD live in the community like anyone else, and some commit offences and come into contact with the criminal justice system. In recent years there has been a move away from incarcerating people who have IDD due to their vulnerability in prison. Courts, where possible, seek to look at alternatives such as community-based treatment or secure accommodation provided for people who have IDD. However, psychodynamic psychotherapy has only been part of service provision for people who have IDD for the last 30 years (Jackson & Beail, 2013).

Psychodynamic psychotherapy: an overview

Freud's psychological theories, which lay at the foundation of his treatment approach, psychoanalysis, were first formed in the latter part of the nineteenth century (Freud, 1940). Freud revised his theory over his lifetime and his followers developed other ideas which have resulted in different psychoanalytic models and schools of thought that exist today. Psychodynamic psychotherapy has been one of those many developments. Whereas psychoanalysis involves sessions lasting 50 minutes, five times a week, for a few years, psychodynamic psychotherapy is less frequent and briefer. It has become much more widely available and less costly to provide.

Blagys and Hilsenroth (2000) identified seven features that characterise psychodynamic psychotherapy: (1) a focus on the relationship between client and therapist, (2) a focus on interpersonal relations, (3) a focus on affect and expression of emotions and (4) the exploration of fantasy life. The therapist (5) explores attempts to avoid distressing thoughts and feelings (the defences), (6) identifies recurring themes and patterns and (7) recognises that past experience affects our relation to, and experience of, the present. In psychodynamic psychotherapy, the therapist is concerned with the way the person represents or sees themselves in the world. The therapist seeks to develop a relationship with the client through empathic, warm and genuine engagement. Together, the therapist and client seek to identify the origin and meaning of these representations, and to seek resolution of difficult feelings and inappropriate behaviours in doing so.

When treatment is being provided as an alternative to incarceration, whether in a secure service or in the community, the primary concern of the criminal justice system, policy makers and the public is the extent that the intervention will reduce reoffending. Thus this must be the primary outcome for any intervention including psychodynamic psychotherapy. However, in addition to specific target symptom reduction (e.g. in forensic settings, reducing offending behaviour), the goals of psychodynamic psychotherapy are also to foster the development of psychological capacities and resources; in particular the development of more positive and fulfilling relationships, to tolerate difficult feelings and emotions, to develop and maintain self-esteem and understand themselves and others better. The therapy promotes the assimilation of painful and warded-off experiences. The work entails making links between past life experiences and how these experiences influence unconscious and conscious expectations of relationships in the present day.

Therapists pursue three central activities in psychodynamic psychotherapy therapy sessions: the gathering of information; the recontextualisation/formulation of the material; and the communication of potential meaning to the person. Typically, psychodynamic therapy begins by providing the client with space to free associate. The therapist will be interested in anything that the client says. Most clients seem to start talking about current issues and concerns, but the therapist will also explore past relationships, dreams, fantasies and so on. The therapist resists giving the client information about them; by doing this they try to offer themself as a type of screen on to which the client can project their imagined perceptions of the therapist or transfer their way of being with others outside of therapy now and in the past, into the relationship with the therapist.

There are a number of methods that the therapist uses to help the client tell their story, to explore it further and then formulate an understanding or meaning aimed at helping the client to access and make sense of unconscious content. Advice and instruction are not usually within the remit of the psychodynamic model. The therapist will be carefully listening to the client's verbal communications, and attends not only to what the person says in terms of the factual content and the words used but also to what is not said. The therapist also observes the client's mood, as communicated through what they say, the way they say it and how they behave. The client may talk about a range of things and the therapist does not interrupt. At various times when the client is telling their story, the therapist may reflect back, paraphrase or précis what the client has been telling them or acting out. The therapist may also use exploratory and information-seeking responses to attempt to draw out more information from the client. Freud found the therapist's own feelings, fantasies and reactions in response to the client's material to be an interference to the therapeutic endeavour. However, since the late 1950s this view has been challenged, and now these feelings and reactions are accepted as meaningful elements in the communications between client and therapist and are referred to as the counter-transference. Basically, the therapist's response could be reflecting those of others outside of therapy, and developing awareness of these with the client may aid the process of resolving relationship difficulties with others.

Psychodynamic therapists recontextualise the conscious content of the client's verbal and behavioural communications as transference (Smith, 1987). Freud (1912) described transference as occurring when psychological experiences are revived and instead of being located in the past are applied to dealings with a person in the present. This allows the therapist to identify interpersonal issues which present in their relationship with their client as not unique to them but contain information about current and past relationships. So the process of transference allows past difficulties in relationships, traumatic experiences and empathic failures on the part of parents and other caregivers to be re-experienced in the safety of the relationship with the therapist. This is explored and hopefully, through understanding, giving meaning to and interpretation, conflicts within the self and with others can be worked through to bring about an improvement in psychological well-being. In this process the psychodynamic psychotherapist uses a number of methods that are more interventionist. They may use confrontation to draw the client's attention to what they are doing or avoiding, apparently unaware. These interventions are generated from hypotheses – not only about what is actually said, but also about what the client may not be saying in words but hinting at through behaviour or tone of voice. The therapist also makes responses that link words and/or actions together as a tentative interpretation to try and understand the nature of the client's anxiety in the session. These responses differ from the others in that they aim to elucidate unconscious feelings and ideas.

In psychodynamic psychotherapy, the main approach to intervention is through the provision of interpretations. One process of interpretation is through the application of the framework provided by Malan's two triangles (Malan, 2010) (see Figure 9.1). The first of these triangles represents a framework for understanding conflict between hidden feelings (which are unconscious) and anxiety about their expression and the defences used to prevent their expression. This is based on Freud's structural model (1940).

Freud (1940) described a psychical apparatus or model of the mind consisting of three parts; the id, the ego and the super-ego. It is the ego that functions as an intermediary between the id (which contains the unconscious life and death drives), and the real world. In Freud's theory, the ego has the task of self-preservation and

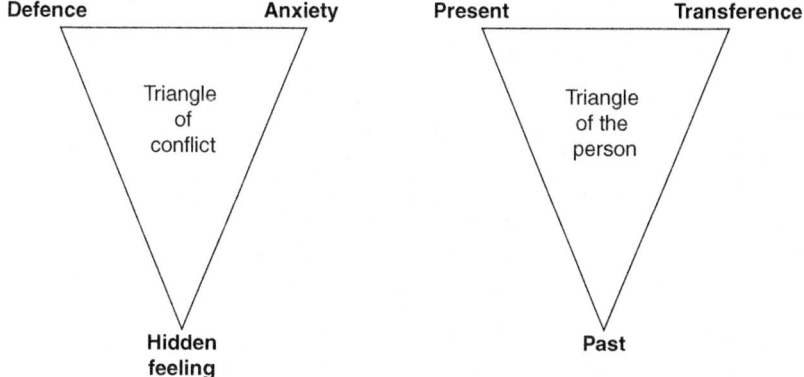

FIGURE 9.1: Malan's triangles of conflict and person (2010).

performs such tasks as becoming aware of stimuli and building memories. The ego also takes action in the service of self-preservation in the form of helping the person to avoid or adapt to situations, or through activity to bring about advantageous changes through the use of defence mechanisms (for example, denial and repression). Thus the ego uses a range of mechanisms to enable the person to put things out of mind, which makes them unconscious or in Malan's triangle – Hidden. The ego simultaneously gains control over the internal drives which may manifest as feelings of hate or anger. Thus the ego is the location of feelings of tension created by the conflict between the internal drives; the defended-against unconscious material and the real world. When tension is raised the person experiences feelings of anxiety. It is the role of the therapist to identify the defences used by the client, draw attention to these and link them to the feelings of anxiety as part of a process of trying to help the client access the hidden unconscious material.

The second triangle represents the person and their life stages. There are a range of psychodynamic theories relating to development, which the therapist may also employ to understand the origins or development of the client's difficulties and conflicts, as well as coping styles. Freud (1940) also described a further internal agency called the super-ego into which we take representations of the parents and the parental influence. This will include those aspects of our parents we idealise and look up to, as well as their moral code and values; building conscience. Thus the ego has to manage the tensions that arise between the internal world of the unconscious drives and unconscious material, reality, and the super-ego. The definition of the ego has also changed over time. Jung (1963) described the ego as an agglomeration of highly toned contents which can form into separate complexes or little personalities of their own. He described these as taking on different characters such as traumatic, painful or highly toned. His ideas predate the views of Klein and others regarding the splitting of the ego or self into parts; initially good and bad. Freud's followers in the Ego Psychology School have described the ego as containing the functions of thought, perception, language, learning, memory and rational planning

(Hartmann, 1964). In Freud's lifetime psychoanalysis was adapted and developed for use with children by his daughter Anna Freud and Melanie Klein. In addition to the development of the super-ego, Klein also laid the foundation for the theoretical model of object relationships; i.e. the introjection or taking in as an internal mental representation, of other people over the course of one's lifetime (Klein, 1975). This includes good objects such as a caring and nurturing parent or a good teacher but also bad objects such as an abusive parent or teacher. Klein (1975) focused on the early nature of the person's relationships, then later Bowlby developed attachment theory (Bowlby, 1988). It is the experience that we have of people (objects) inside ourselves that give us a sense of existence and identity. The struggle to attain a secure and stable good internal world inside ourselves is seen as the core of a stable personality that can weather emotional disturbance. To achieve this, the self (ego) has to form an integration of the various part objects and of the parts of the self. It is the psychodynamic hypothesis that people who need psychological help may have had significant difficulties in this integration.

Klein (1975) also extended the range of defences to more primitive levels such as splitting and projective identification. These terms have become important for staff working with offenders, especially those who have mental health concerns. Projective identification involves one person unconsciously splitting off an unacceptable and disturbing part of their ego or self and projecting it outside of themself and then onto or into another person. This then leads to them perceiving the other person as containing or being like the projected part. Thus, if they project a violent part of their self they will perceive the other person as now being potentially violent. This disrupts the relationship with the other person as they will now act towards them as a potential threat or danger. This may lead to the emergence of fight or flight feelings. For the receiver of the projection they may feel pressure to think, feel and act in a way congruent with the projected part of the other person. This can be a very powerful influence in interpersonal relationships in services for offenders. Staff need support to enable them to identify that this process is occurring in those they support so that they can contain these feelings and not act on them. A relevant issue for people who have intellectual disabilities is the dysynchrony between emotional, cognitive and physical development, including sexual development. This lack of synchrony may be a factor in the presentation of inappropriate sexual behaviour in adults who have IDD.

In situations where the client's original parenting or caring relationships were deficient, abusive or overprotective, the therapist provides a reparative or replenishing parental relationship or action (Clarkson, 1993). For example, the client's past experience of strong negative reaction to what they say becomes an expectation in other relationships, and then with the therapist. However, with the therapist the expectation is not realised. The therapist may feel the same strong reaction (counter-transference) as those in the client's other current or past relationships, but they remain calm and draw attention to what the client is doing, and how others might feel when they do that. As therapy progresses the people or person to whom the feelings originate should emerge and can be worked through.

Whilst psychodynamic therapy as described above can be used when working with individuals with IDD, several adaptations are commonly found. In their review of psychodynamic practice with people who have IDD, Jackson and Beail (2013) found that therapists tended to work according to the traditional frame, in terms of frequency (once weekly), location (a private room), and context (1:1) of the therapy. However, Beail & Newman (2005) suggest a need for flexibility for clients with IDD around the duration of sessions. They assert that the typical 50 minutes should be reduced to accommodate people with low tolerance for the full duration. Jackson and Beail (2013) also found that some therapists described involving staff and family members in the process of assessment and therapy, with the client's agreement. Further, whereas free association is often used in the early stages of therapy, in work with people who have IDD, therapists typically prefer to focus on the reason why they have been referred; thus taking a more problem-focused approach.

In summary, the therapist attempts to help the client identify the hidden (unconscious) feelings which lead to the ego employing defence mechanisms to keep them out of consciousness. In the sessions, the therapist notices defences and identifies anxieties and interprets potential meanings by triangulation of the information available (linking information together). This process involves making links between Malan's triangles: the stages of conflict and the person's life stages. The diagram thus depicts the entire picture: the origin of the information, the setting in therapy (the transference), the person's present living environment and the person's past (usually with parents).

Adaptations for forensic and/or IDD clients

The term offender can be broadly used to refer to a person who has committed a (criminal) offence, and been found guilty and convicted by a court. This would certainly characterise the majority of those in prison or secure facilities. However, some behaviour that would be seen as criminal in the general population is not treated as such when the person committing them has IDD. For example, although behaviour such as hitting others or destroying property constitute an offence, when the person engaging in the behaviour has IDD, this may not be viewed as a crime. This is because in many jurisdictions the person also has to have a guilty state of mind in relation to the behaviour. Thus, when the person has an IDD they are often described as engaging in problematic behaviour or behaviours that challenge although they may still become the recipients of services for offenders who have IDD. Therefore, this chapter concerns alleged offenders, those at risk of offending and those who have been convicted. It is also important to note that most offences committed by people who have ID concern aggression (verbal and physical), property damage and sexual offences; with theft and alcohol/substance abuse-related offences being relatively rare (Lindsay et al., 2010).

As offenders come from all walks of life, many will be typically developing and should be able to use psychodynamic psychotherapy in the same way as anyone else. However, surveys of prison populations have found large numbers with borderline or extremely low levels of intelligence. When an intelligence quotient of 70 or below is used, estimates vary widely from seven per cent in adult prisons to 23 per cent in young offender facilities. When the IQ level is raised to 80 the figures rise to 32% and 56% respectively. Importantly, these figures were derived from administrations of the Wechsler Adult Intelligence Scale and the Wechsler Abbreviated Intelligence Scale. Thus we can have some confidence in these data as these scales are recognised as the gold standard for clinical and research applications in IQ measurement (Beail, 2010). When working with people who have lower levels of intelligence or IDD, adaptations need to be made to the clinical approach (whether in a forensic or other setting). People who have IDD have poor or delayed language development and so the therapist has to work within the client's communication abilities. Therefore, the therapist must pay careful attention to the words used and attempt to identify problems from non-verbal communications, or accept some acting out within the session as a means of communication. This can be problematic with offenders as there is a chance that offending behaviours could be acted out within the session. Thus the therapist needs to have a good understanding of the client's offences and what they could potentially act out. Where appropriate, the therapist may introduce a therapeutic contract concerning what is acceptable and not acceptable behaviour in the session and what would happen if such behaviour occurred.

Clients who have IDD may need some help in sessions to enable them to communicate. The therapist may need to suggest words for actions or feelings and/or use alternative means of communication such as drawing or using objects. To avoid confusion or misunderstandings, the therapist needs to allow time for the client to tell their story, listen carefully and check that they have a shared understanding of the characters and event being described. When dreams are reported or elicited, the therapist needs to be aware that people with IDD may believe that those in their dreams share their dreams (Krose, Cushway, & Hubbard, 1998). Hence, therapists wishing to explore dreams with clients should be aware that they may conceptualise them differently. Additionally, the communication of interpretations should be done in manageable parts using short sentences. Ann Alvarez has developed thinking around interpretation, and suggests that the therapist may need to consider different levels of interpretation when working with children, people who have autism spectrum disorder or are developmentally delayed (Alvarez, 2012). Consider, for instance, a client with IDD who is referred for the offence of assault and who has problems managing anger. In the session the therapist will need to explore these difficulties and their origins; however, the client may start to act in an angry manner because of the perception that others are angry with them. Typically, the therapist might extend a reflective comment 'you feel angry …' into an interpretation – 'you feel angry because…'. However, in the case of the person with IDD, an interpretation with this location, i.e. 'you', may feel accusative and intolerable. This may be heard as 'all of you', or 'you are nothing but angry'. Thus they may defend themselves against the internal distress caused by this interpretation by acting out these feelings of anger toward the therapist. So, it may be better to use a more developmentally appropriate level of interpretation and say 'part of you feels angry'. This too may fail to be accepted and, in this case, Alvarez suggests using the ideas of Winnicott, and locating the feeling, behaviour or issue in others. Hence the therapist may say something like 'isn't it annoying when people get angry?'

One of the objections to working psychodynamically with people who have IDD is the higher risk that they may act out. Acting out has been a long established contra-indication for suitability for this approach for adults. However, this was never the case for work with children. In acting out situations, the therapist's interpretation may have to be put on hold whilst the therapist brings the client back into the reality of the relationship with the therapist, rather than the transferred one (the person they really feel angry towards) they are acting into. Here, Alvarez (2012) suggests methods of gaining the client's attention, such as saying 'hey', or saying the person's name clearly and firmly (Beail and Newman, 2005).

Therapist training

Currently there are different professional groups providing psychodynamic psychotherapy. The training that people undertake also varies around the world. However, in most areas those providing psychotherapy have a health or social work professional qualification and undertake further training through university programmes or internships. People can undergo accredited training programmes in psychodynamic psychotherapy and then practice on completion. However, some psychiatrists and clinical and forensic psychologists also may undertake some training in this approach during their core training, and then continue training when they qualify as members of their profession. In the field of IDD, the National Association for the Dually Diagnosed promotes training and provision in the United States (Fletcher, 2011) and members of the Institute for Psychotherapy and Disability in the UK include psychodynamic psychotherapists, and psychiatrists and clinical psychologists who practice psychodynamic psychotherapy. A new training in disability psychotherapy has also been established (Frankish, 2016).

Client characteristics

The psychotherapeutic literature contains various selection criteria concerning suitability for psychodynamic treatment. These include factors such as the 'ability to enter an intensive treatment relationship', possessing psychological mindedness, motivation and adequate ego strength. Some even suggest that the person should be of at least average intelligence (Brown & Pedder, 1979). Motivation includes the degree to which the offender experiences their behaviour as ego-dystonic, i.e. their behaviour causes them some degree of psychological distress. Those for who their (offending) activities are ego-syntonic might be viewed as 'careerists' and will be less amenable to treatment (Welldon, 2015). Traditionally, some crimes, e.g. violent and sexual offending, would be viewed by providers of psychodynamic psychotherapy as acting out behaviour and thus a contra-indication for this treatment.

This is reflected in the 'unsuitability criteria' in suitability scales (see, for example, Laaksonen et al., 2012). However, this view is not shared by those who work with children and people with IDD.

Evidence emerging with respect of other talking therapies – notably Cognitive-Behaviour Therapy (CBT), including for those offenders who have ID (Lindsay, 2009; SOTSEC-ID, 2010) – suggests that potential recipients of CBT need to be ready (Willner, 2006), including having an awareness of the problem they have. Unfortunately, not all offenders referred for treatment present in such a state of readiness. However, the exploratory approach of psychodynamic psychotherapy has been shown to be effective in enabling assimilation of problems (Newman & Beail, 2005). Thus a key application of this approach is for offenders who are in denial providing they are willing to accept therapy. This is illustrated through the later case study.

Client characteristics (indicators/contra-indicators)

Clinical judgment is required for each individual case, but common contra-indications include where a person is abusing drugs or alcohol, and where the person is experiencing an acute psychotic episode. In the case of a psychotic episode, therapy can begin once the acute phase of psychosis has passed. It is good practice to make such a decision in conjunction with both the client and, where involved, a psychiatrist. People often also find it difficult to engage in therapy when the rest of their life is in chaos. In such circumstances, action may be necessary so that the individual has some stability or structure prior to therapy. Where the therapist anticipates that the individual might act out, therapy should be offered in settings that are equipped to manage the risk of violence. Clients also need to have some motivation to change, although for some their apparent change motivation may disguise a goal to reduce the level of security or supervision they experience in order to access possible victims. There are a number of specific considerations in relation to those with IDD. People who have ID have had a number of myths associated with them. One has been that people who have ID are at a higher risk of offending, and another is that IDD is a contra-indication for psychodynamic psychotherapy. Lindsay (2009) has reviewed the relationship between IDD and offending and concluded that there is no evidence to support the link. Conversely, he reports that research shows offenders with IDD commit fewer offences than other offenders, and have lower rates of recidivism. The application of some of the criteria described above, would exclude people with intellectual disabilities from treatment. However, the application of psychodynamic therapy with adults who have intellectual disabilities has shown that factors such as IQ level may not be as relevant as claimed. As with all talking therapy, those entering psychodynamic psychotherapy require sufficient verbal understanding and expressive abilities to have a dialogue with the therapist. However, most offenders who have IDD do. Psychodynamic therapy was adapted and developed for use with children by Anna Freud and Melanie Klein. It is these developments along with the ideas of Bowlby and Winnicott, amongst others, that have influenced the development of the adaptations that enable an age-appropriate treatment approach for people who have ID.

Status of the evidence in forensic settings

Evidence for psychodynamic psychotherapy indicates that it is effective for a range of psychological problems (Abbass, Hancock, Henderson, & Kisely, 2006; Shedler, 2010). Despite provision, over many years, of individual and group psychodynamic psychotherapy for people who offend in the general population, quality research is non-existent. The only review of treatment outcome for offenders in the Cochrane Library concerns sex offenders (Dennis et al., 2012). This only identified one study of group therapy based on a psychodynamic approach, with equivocal findings (Romero & Williams, 1985). However, the reviewers state that the study did not meet their strict criteria for a psychodynamic intervention. Recent special editions on forensic psychotherapy in the journals *Psychoanalytic Psychotherapy* (McGauley, 2015) and the *International Journal of Applied Psychoanalytic Studies* (Gilligan, 2015) only included anecdotal and case report evidence for psychodynamic psychotherapy. This may be, in part, due to the objection by many psychodynamic psychotherapists to placing evaluative frameworks around treatment. They argue that this interferes with the therapeutic relationship. It may also reflect difficulties with doing evaluative research in prison and secure settings. However, this has not deterred behavioural and cognitive-behaviour research being undertaken.

The main body of literature on the application of psychodynamic psychotherapy with people who have ID is comprised of case studies (see Jackson & Beail, 2013, for a review, and Curren, 2009 for case examples of psychodynamic work with offenders). James and Stacey (2013) reviewed the outcome research on psychodynamic psychotherapy for people who have ID. Although the volume of literature was small and limited to case series and open trials, they conclude that the reviewed studies offer some preliminary support for the use of psychodynamic psychotherapy with people who have IDD. Only one study focused on work with offenders. Beail (2001) reported a study on the outcomes of psychodynamic psychotherapy for 18 offenders who have ID who were diverted for assessment for treatment from the criminal justice system. All 18 men were offered treatment following assessment, but five chose to continue their journey through the criminal justice system rather than enter treatment. Of the 13 who engaged with and completed therapy, all but two men remained offence-free at the end of therapy and at four years follow-up. The five men who refused treatment were all referred again as they had all re-offended within two years.

Case study

Daniel represents many offenders who have IDD that are referred to services for assessment and treatment. Daniel was initially referred by the Court Diversion Service for assessment following being arrested for allegations of a sexual offence against a child. The Court Diversion team had assessed Daniel at the police station and felt that he may have IDD. Daniel was 18 years old but not known to the local services and there was no information on him. He was brought to the outpatient clinic so that an assessment of his intellectual and social functioning could be made. This found that he met the diagnostic criteria for IDD in that his IQ was below 70 and he had concurrent deficits in his adaptive behaviour. Daniel had also attended a school for children with special educational needs. As a result, the Court Diversion team asked for an assessment of his risk of future offending and suitability for treatment.

Daniel's risk of offending was assessed according to the guidelines of the British Psychological Society (O'Rourke and Bailes, 2005) and specific research on risk assessment of offenders who have IDD (Lindsay, 2009). During assessment, Daniel denied the offence and claimed he was somewhere else at the time it was alleged to have occurred. The risk assessment identified many factors associated with poor outcome and that if Daniel had committed the alleged offence, then the conclusion was that he was at medium to high risk of reoffending. In view of his immaturity and vulnerability, prison would not be a suitable place for him and so it was recommended that if he was found guilty, he should receive a period of treatment in a low secure facility.

At Court Daniel pleaded guilty and was given a probation order with a condition of treatment. He was referred for treatment and so he was reassessed. The first session focused on the reason why he was referred and he talked about the offence that he was accused of. However, despite pleading guilty in Court he made no admission of guilt. When put to him that he had pleaded guilty to the offence he said he did this because his lawyer had advised him to do so to avoid going to prison. During the rest of the assessment he denied the offence. However, he also said that he had agreed to the treatment order and said he wanted to comply with it. This seemed largely because he did not want to go to prison. This places the therapist in an ethical dilemma. If the therapist accepts he is telling the truth and is innocent, then there are no grounds for treatment to be offered. Daniel would simply be attending weekly sessions in order to keep out of prison, but at the same time be taking up a limited resource. However, the refusal of treatment would mean a return to Court, and having pleaded guilty he would most likely be detained and incarcerated. On the other hand if his presentation in therapy was conceptualised as denial – a defence to ward off thoughts and feelings he finds distressing, unacceptable or frightening – along with his willingness to attend, then psychological work could proceed. We also have to weigh the evidence for the effectiveness of going to prison against the evidence for psychological intervention. The current evidence for the effectiveness of incarceration suggests a poor outcome in comparison with psychological interventions (Taylor and Lindsay, 2007). Therapy was therefore offered on the basis that previous research has shown that psychodynamic psychotherapy can facilitate change from denial to acceptance (Beail & Newman, 2005).

Using the framework of the Assimilation Model (Stiles et al., 1990), Daniel presented for treatment at the lowest level of assimilation of his problem; 'warded off'.

The aim of therapy would be to move him through the next stages of 'unwanted thoughts' prior to 'vague awareness' and then to 'problem statement'. At that point, treatment of his offending behaviour would be possible and we would hope to move further up the model to 'understanding/insight' of his difficulties, 'working through' them, 'problem solving' and 'mastery' over them.

In sessions with Daniel, the therapist acted in a warm, empathic way to develop a relationship with him, focused on him and what happens between them. The aim was to help Daniel accept parts of himself that he could not. The psychodynamic model supposes that these unacceptable aspects (offence-related) are kept from conscious thought through a range of defence mechanisms such as, in Daniel's case, denial (it wasn't me, I wasn't in the area).

In his sessions, Daniel would sit in silence or talk about topics such as playing computer games. The therapist asked questions to obtain information about him, and posed exploratory statements; these were generated from hypotheses about what Daniel may not be saying in words but may be hinting at through behaviour or tone of voice. It was clear in sessions with Daniel that he would not mention the reason why he was attending. Thus the therapist reflected back that he was either silent, or talking about computer games. Following this the therapist re-focused on the problem, i.e. the reason why he was attending; 'Daniel could I get back to the reason why you are here, a child said you had sex with them.' The therapist also reflected Daniel's attempts to ignore the focus on this. A return by Daniel to the subject of computer games might result in a response from the therapist; 'when I raise why you are here you change the subject to computer games.' Psychodynamic psychotherapists will also confront the client to help them attend to their feelings; 'when I asked you about what the child said, how did you feel?' Here the therapist is drawing attention to Daniel's defensive inhibition and trying to get him to connect to the difficult feelings he is trying to avoid. The therapist then used more interpretative responses by linking the defence of denial to the anxiety; drawing attention to his repeated avoidance or changing of the subject and commenting that this was due to the anxiety he was feeling. At this stage of Daniel's therapy there was a lot of reflecting back and gentle confrontation with attempts to help him focus on his feelings.

Daniel's behaviour in the session was re-contextualised as transference; reflecting how he was with others. Thus the therapist put to him that he was keeping any mention of his offence hidden in his relationship with the therapist and that he was doing this in his relationships outside of therapy. This gave rise to further anxieties for Daniel and he expressed concern of what others would do to him if they knew about the allegations. In Daniel's sessions the focus was on the triangle of conflict, that is on his anxiety (fear of what he had done and what that means) and the defences (denial, splitting off and disowning) he uses to avoid that anxiety and keep the offending part of him out of his conscious thoughts, i.e. hidden.

For Daniel the therapy was an exploratory process which began with a focus on why he was there, and the role of the therapist was to maintain that focus. Daniel continued to deny any wrongdoing, but his story started to change over time. He stopped denying being in the location. His story developed to being in the location and perhaps being seen going to the toilet by the child, rather than doing anything sexual with the child. This suggests a shift towards 'unwanted thoughts'. The exploratory process looked at his past and his sexual development. In assessment and the early stages of therapy he denied any sexual feeling or experience. However, he did admit that he masturbated which facilitated a focus on his sexual fantasies when masturbating. However, Daniel would try and avoid such issues and move the conversation to safer topics (playing computer games). The same methods of reflection, problem focus and gentle confrontation continued. By focusing on the physical sensation he was able to talk about the pleasurable aspect of sex and then towards what he found stimulating. When focusing on the sexual act he had pleaded guilty to he started to talk about how awful such a thing would be for the victim, but still denied he had done this. This was a significant development as he had not talked about the sexual act he pleaded guilty to this way before. But also he was now describing the act that he denied doing. The detail suggested a real shift towards 'vague awareness'. After a year of exploratory psychodynamic psychotherapy Daniel moved to being able to talk about what he did with the child. This was consistent with the child's account given in their statement to the police. Thus Daniel had reached 'problem statement' and therapy could now embark upon understanding his problem and working through the issues. Thus he was now at a stage in the assimilation model where he would be seen as prepared to work to change. At this stage Daniel would be ready to join an offender treatment programme based on CBT and we explored this for him. Unfortunately, no groups were running and so he chose to continue to work with his current therapist. Progress was small and slow but Daniel completed the agreed two years with his therapist. Two years after discharge he was still in touch with the local IDD service and had not reoffended.

Key directions for future research

In the field of IDD services there are few specialist forensic services. Most offenders with IDD are supported and treated through specialist health and social care IDD services such as community teams. This chapter has been based on the provision of psychodynamic psychotherapy in this context. In such settings, psychodynamic psychotherapy can be provided in service pathways as long as there is a clinician competent to provide it (Jackson & Beail, 2016). However, the approach is also used with those placed in secure facilities and may facilitate access to and improve outcomes in treatment programmes.

Further reading

Blagys, M. D., & Hilsenroth, M. J. (2000). Distinctive activities of short-term psychodynamic-interpersonal psychotherapy: A review of the comparative psychotherapy process literature. *Clinical Psychology: Science and Practice.* 7, 167–188.

Curren, R. (2009). Can they see the door? Issues in the assessment and treatment of sex offenders who have intellectual disabilities. In T. Cottis (Ed.), *Intellectual disability, trauma and psychotherapy.* London: Routledge.

Jackson, T., & Beail, N. (2013). The practice of individual psychodynamic psychotherapy with people who have intellectual disabilities. *Psychoanalytic psychotherapy*, 27, 108–123.

References

Abbass, A. A., Hancock, J. T., Henderson, J., & Kisely, S. (2006). Short-term psychodynamic psychotherapies for common mental disorders. *Cochrane Database of Systematic reviews*, 4, Article No. CD004687.
Alvarez, A. (2012). *The thinking heart: Three levels of psychoanalytic therapy with disturbed children.* London: Routledge.
Beail, N. (2001). Recidivism following psychodynamic psychotherapy amongst offenders with intellectual disabilities. *The British Journal of Forensic Practice*, 3, 33–37.
Beail, N. (2010). Prisoners' voices: experiences of the criminal justice system by prisoners with learning disabilities. *Tizard learning Disability Review*, 15, 42–45.
Beail, N., & Newman, D. (2005). Psychodynamic counselling and psychotherapy for mood disorders. In P. Sturmey (Ed.), *Mood disorders in people with mental retardation*. New York: NADD Press.
Blagys, M. D., & Hilsenroth, M. J. (2000). Distinctive activities of short-term psychodynamic-interpersonal psychotherapy: A review of the comparative psychotherapy process literature. *Clinical Psychology: Science and Practice*, 7, 167–188.
Bowlby, J. (1988). *A secure base: Clinical applications of attachment theory.* London: Routledge.
Brown, D., & Pedder, J. (1979). *Introduction to psychotherapy.* London: Routledge.
Clarkson, P. (1993). *On psychotherapy.* London: Whurr Publishers.
Cordess, C. (1992). Pioneers in forensic psychiatry. Edward Glover (1888–1972): Psychoanalysis and crime – a fragile legacy. *Journal of Forensic Psychiatry*, 3, 509–530.
Curren, R. (2009). Can they see the door? Issues in the assessment and treatment of sex offenders who have intellectual disabilities. In T. Cottis (Ed.), *Intellectual disability, trauma and psychotherapy.* London: Routledge.
Dennis, J. A., Khan, O., Ferriter, M., Huband, N., Powney, M. J., & Duggan, C. (2012). Psychological interventions for adults who have sexually offended or are at risk of offending. *Cochrane Library.* doi:10.1002/14651858CD007507.pub.2.
Fletcher, R. J. (Ed.). (2011). Psychotherapy for individuals with intellectual disability. NADD.
Frankish, P. (2016). *Disability psychotherapy: An innovative approach to trauma-informed care.* London: Karnac.
Gilligan, J. (Ed.) (2015). Forensic psychotherapy: Applying psychoanalysis to the treatment of violent offenders. *International Journal of Applied Psychoanalytic Studies*, 12, 89–188.
Freud, S. (1912). The dynamics of transference. *The standard edition of the complete psychological works of Sigmund Freud*, Vol. 12, 97–108. London: Hogarth.
Freud, S. (1940). An outline of psychoanalysis. *The standard edition of the complete psychological works of Sigmund Freud*, Vol. 23. London: Hogarth.
Hartmann, H. (1964). *Essays in ego psychology: Selected problems in psychoanalytic theory.* New York: International Universities Press.
Houston, J. C. (2003). Mentally disordered offenders. In J. Horley (Ed.) *Personal construct perspectives on forensic psychology.* London: Routledge.
Jackson, T., & Beail, N. (2013). The practice of individual psychodynamic psychotherapy with people who have intellectual disabilities. *Psychoanalytic psychotherapy*, 27, 108–123.
Jackson, T, & Beail, N. (2016). Accessibility, efficiency and effectiveness in psychological services for adults with learning disabilities. *Psychological therapies and people who have intellectual disabilities.* Leicester: The British Psychological Society.

James, C. W., & Stacey, J. M. (2013). The effectiveness of psychodynamic interventions for people with learning disabilities: a systematic review. *Tizard Learning Disability Review*, *19*, 17–24.

Jung, C. G. (1963). *Memories, dreams and reflections*. London: Routledge.

Klein, M. (1975). *The writings of Melanie Klein*, Volume 3. London: Hogarth Press.

Krose, B. S., Cushway, D., & Hubbard, C. (1998). The conceptualisation of dreams by people with learning disabilities. *Journal of Applied Research in Intellectual disabilities*, *11*, 146–155.

Laaksonen, M. A., Lindors, O., Knekt, P., & Aalberg, V. (2012). Suitability for psychotherapy scale (SPS) and its reliability, validity, and prediction. *British Journal of Clinical Psychology*, *51*, 351–357.

Lindsay, W. R. (2009). *The treatment of sex offenders with developmental disabilities*. Chichester: Wiley-Blackwell.

Lindsay, W. R., O'Brien, G., Carson, D. R., Holland, A. J., Taylor J. L., Wheeler, J. R., Middleton, C., Price, K., Steptoe, L., & Johnston, S. (2010). Pathways into services for offenders with intellectual disabilities: Childhood experiences, diagnostic information and offence related variables. *Criminal Justice and Behaviour*, *37*, 678–94.

McGauley, G. (Ed.) (2015). Forensic psychotherapy. *Psychoanalytic Psychotherapy*, *29*, 205–310.

Malan, D. H. (2010). *Individual psychotherapy and the science of psychodynamics*. London: Butterworth.

Newman, D. W., & Beail, N. (2005). An analysis of assimilation during psychotherapy with people who have mental retardation. *American Journal on Mental Retardation*, *110*, 359–365.

O'Rourke, M., & Bailes, G. (2005). *Risk Assessment and Management*. Leicester: The British Psychological Society Faculty for Forensic Clinical Psychology.

Romero, D., & Williams, L. M. (1985). Recidivism among convicted sex offenders: a ten year follow-up study. *Federal Probation*, *49*, 58–64.

Shedler, J. (2010). The efficacy of psychodynamic psychotherapy. *American Psychologist*, *65*, 98–109.

Smith, D. (1987). Formulating and evaluating hypotheses in psychoanalytic psychotherapy. *British Journal of Medical Psychology*, *60*, 313–316.

SOTSEC-ID. (2010). Effectiveness of group cognitive-behavioural therapy for men with ID at risk of sexual offending. *Journal of Applied Research in Intellectual Disabilities*, *23*, 537–551.

Stiles, W. B., Elliott, R., Llewelyn, S. P., Firth-Cozens, J. A., Margison, F. R., Shapiro, D. A., & Hardy, G. E. (1990). Assimilation of problematic experiences by clients in psychotherapy. *Psychotherapy*, *27*, 411–420.

Taylor, J. L., & Lindsay, W. R. (2007). Developments in the treatment and management of offenders with intellectual disabilities. *Issues in Forensic Psychology*, *6*, 23–31.

Welldon, E. (2015). Forensic psychotherapy. *Psychoanalytic Psychotherapy*, *29*, 211–227.

Willner, P. (2006). Readiness for cognitive therapy in people with intellectual disabilities. *Journal of Applied Research in Intellectual Disabilities*, *19*, 5–16.

10
SCHEMA THERAPY

Marije Keulen-de Vos and David P. Bernstein

Schema Therapy is a medium- to long-term form of psychotherapy primarily for patients[1] with personality disorders. It is usually delivered in an individual format, but it can be administered in groups or as a combination of individual and group therapy. In this chapter, we describe the underlying principles for Schema Therapy and its forensic adaptation, and illustrate the forensic model with a case example. Next, we present the current status of the evidence of Schema Therapy in forensic settings and make suggestions for future research on this topic.

Overview of the therapy

Theoretical model

Schema Therapy (ST; Young, Klosko, & Weishaar, 2003) combines different elements from various therapeutic approaches. For example, certain techniques or theoretical concepts are derived from cognitive-behavioural traditions, and other techniques and concepts are psychoanalytically oriented or originate from Gestalt and experiential therapies. The main concepts of the Schema Therapy approach are early maladaptive schemas, dysfunctional coping styles and schema modes. Early maladaptive schemas are cognitive structures that contain self-defeating themes about oneself, others and the environment (Rafaeli, Bernstein, & Young, 2011; Young et al., 2003). These schemas are similar to the schema concept of Beck's cognitive model (Beck, Freeman, & Davis, 2004). However, unlike cognitive therapy, ST places more emphasis on the origin of these schemas. According to ST, schemas originate from universal emotional needs, identification with significant others, experiences during childhood and adolescence, and early temperament. Moreover, children imitate and internalise significant others (Bandura, 1986). Schema Therapy

TABLE 10.1 Early maladaptive schemas, domains and corresponding universal needs

Early maladaptive schemas	Domains	Universal needs
Abandonment / instability / mistrust / abuse / emotional deprivation / defectiveness / shame / social isolation / alienation	Disconnection and rejection	Attachment and security
Dependence / incompetence/ vulnerability to harm or illness / enmeshment / undeveloped self / failure	Impaired autonomy and performance	Autonomy and dependence
Entitlement / grandiosity / insufficient self-control	Impaired limits	Limits and boundaries
Subjugation / self-sacrifice / approval or recognition seeking	Other directedness	Validation of needs and feelings
Negativity / pessimism / emotional inhibition / unrelenting standards / hyper criticalness / punitiveness	Over vigilance and inhibition	Spontaneity and play

Note: For a detailed description of each schema, see Keulen-de Vos, Bernstein, & Arntz, 2014.

distinguishes five universal emotional needs: the need for secure attachment; autonomy and independence; limits and boundaries; validation of needs and feelings; and spontaneity and play (Young et al., 2003). When these needs are profoundly unmet – for example in situations of trauma, abuse or neglect – or when there is a lack of balance between needs (i.e. too much/little of a good thing), a distorted blueprint about oneself and the world is likely to develop. Maladaptive cognitive patterns begin early in life and develop throughout the course of a lifetime. Over time, these schemas become more consistent and less susceptible to change. Young and colleagues (2003) defined 18 schemas that cover five domains that are consistent with the emotional needs (see Table 10.1).

Typically, the activation of maladaptive schemas elicits strong and painful emotions, such as fear, anger or shame. ST defines three broad, usually dysfunctional, coping styles that are often used to deal with these emotions: passively giving in to a schema (i.e. schema surrender); avoiding situations that trigger a certain schema (i.e. schema avoidance); and doing the opposite of a schema (i.e. schema overcompensation). Some people may have a predominant style of coping; for example, someone with a more narcissistic personality stance may tend to overcompensate, whereas someone with a borderline personality dynamic may tend to avoid. These coping styles are comparable to defence mechanisms in psychodynamic therapy, although in ST they are not based on instinctive sexual and aggressive desires.

The combination of particular maladaptive schemas and dysfunctional coping styles manifest themselves in certain emotional states which are labelled as schema modes. A schema mode is a state-like concept that represents someone's emotions as well as cognitions and behaviour at a particular time. So a schema mode depends on the schema that is activated, the emotional response that is elicited and how someone deals with it. Young and colleagues (2003) originally distinguished 11 schema modes; over time, others have proposed and reported evidence for additional modes (e.g. Bamelis, Renner, Heidkamp, & Arntz, 2011; Bernstein, Arntz, & de Vos, 2007; Lobbestael, van Vreeswijk, & Arntz, 2008). Typically, four dysfunctional schema mode domains are distinguished: child modes that refer to feeling, thinking and acting in a child-like manner; avoidant coping modes that involve attempts to protect oneself from pain by means of avoiding; parent modes that relate to self-directed criticism or demands that reflect internalised parent behaviour and emotional stance; and overcompensatory modes that refer to extreme attempts to overcompensate painful feelings (i.e. child modes). The healthy domain refers to expression of healthy, balanced self-reflection, and feelings of pleasure and joy. Table 10.2 (later) provides an overview of schema modes and their corresponding schema mode domains. Modes fluctuate from time to time; the extent to which someone has natural control over these fluctuations may also change. Healthy individuals are considered able to understand and regulate their emotional swings and are less prone to strong fluctuations, while individuals who suffer from psychopathology are less cognisant of when one mode changes into another. Moreover, not all schema modes are relevant for each individual. Schema Therapy is particularly developed for individuals with personality disorder (PD). According to ST theory, each personality disorder is characterised by a different combination of schema modes. Borderline Personality Disorder (BPD), for example, is characterised by the vulnerable child mode (feelings of abandonment), angry child mode (uncontrolled anger), punitive parent mode (self-mutilation) and detached protector mode (emotional detachment) (Young et al., 2003).

Assessment phase

Schema Therapy assumes that changes in dysfunctional modes will lead to change in personality disorder symptoms. The goal is to reduce early maladaptive schemas, process painful emotions and to moderate or eliminate dysfunctional schema modes in order to help the patient meet their basic emotional needs in a more healthy and successful manner. In the initial assessment phase, the therapist works together with the patient to assess the patient's early maladaptive schemas and dysfunctional coping responses (or in more severe PD patients, their schema modes), exploring the origins and links to the patient's presenting problems, such as addiction and criminal/aggressive behaviour. In forensic ST, the focus is on the patient's schema modes, because the mode concept facilitates working with extreme and fluctuating modes such as those seen in these patients (see *schema mode work*, described below). The therapist assesses schema modes from a variety of sources, including questionnaires (e.g. the Schema Mode Inventory;

Lobbestael, van Vreeswijk, Spinhoven, Schouten, & Arntz, 2010); observation of the patient's emotional states within and outside of the therapy session (for example, from observations of nursing staff in closed settings); information in the patient's clinical notes, such as descriptions of their crimes; and imagery techniques designed to trigger schemas for assessment purposes. An important feature of the assessment process is that the therapist explains the mode concept to the patient, and teaches them to use the 'language' of schema modes to describe their own emotional states. For example, the therapist might explore the origins and functions of the patient's Detached Protector mode, asking the patient to come up with a name that they can use to label this 'side' of them (e.g. 'the Wall'), thus facilitating communication. The mode concept and language is emotionally neutral and non-judgmental, making it possible for therapist and patient to discuss the patient's problematic behaviours constructively. The assessment phase culminates with a case conceptualisation, which the therapist shares with the patient in a simplified form. In less complex patients, the assessment process takes five to ten sessions. In more severe patients, the therapist may need to immediately address motivational issues and other challenging patient behaviours, which means that the assessment process may require more time to complete. The entire therapy in closed forensic settings usually requires three years, encompassing an attachment phase (roughly first year), a mode reprocessing phase (roughly second year) and a reintegration phase (roughly third year). Therapy is usually delivered twice per week in the first two years, with diminishing frequency in the third year until termination.

Limited reparenting and empathic confrontation

The cornerstone of Schema Therapy practice is the therapeutic relationship that is defined as *limited reparenting*. It parallels a healthy parenting style. A parent wants what's best for their child. This involves providing warmth, nurturance, playfulness, but also discipline and confrontation or setting appropriate limits in a firm and consequential but not overly punitive manner. The same applies to the therapist-patient relationship, although within the bounds of a professional relationship. The therapist provides for some of what the patient missed growing up in terms of his or her basic emotional needs (e.g. secure attachment, limit setting), within appropriate limits and boundaries.

Limited reparenting needs to be balanced by *empathic confrontation*, a technique in which the therapist confronts the patient with their maladaptive behaviour patterns, when they occur inside or outside of the therapy session. The therapist brings the patient's behaviour to their attention in a manner that is clarifying but also compassionate and non-judgmental. The therapist recognises that the patient engages in maladaptive behaviour because it is rooted in maladaptive schemas and dysfunctional coping responses, not because the patient is being 'bad' or is morally defective. The patient needs the therapist to point these patterns out to them repeatedly, whenever they occur, so that he can gain insight into them and begin to change them. It is the combination of limited reparenting and empathic confrontation that moves the therapy forward.

Cognitive, behavioural and experiential interventions

Schema Therapy has a large 'tool kit', combining techniques from cognitive, behavioural, psychodynamic, object relations and humanistic/experiential schools of therapy. *Cognitive techniques* (e.g. diaries) are used in order to increase a patient's insight of cognitions, feelings and behaviour that form the basis of a schema mode. They aim to challenge and restructure cognitive distortions. *Behavioural interventions* are targeted at dysfunctional behavioural patterns and practice of new, more adaptive coping. Furthermore, these interventions may encourage a patient's confidence in behavioural change (Rafaeli et al., 2011; Young et al., 2003).

Experiential techniques are used in order to overcome emotional distance and reprocess emotions, especially those arising from traumatic and other adverse experiences in childhood. Typical experiential techniques are role play, (guided) imagery and chair-work. Role play involves re-enactment of original situations from the past or the present or made-up situations. After the initial role play, role reversal and rescripting is initiated (Kellogg, 2004; Landy, 2000). During rescripting, the therapist alters painful elements in the scenes that are relived, so that associated thoughts, feelings and behaviours are modified and change is facilitated (Rush, Grunert, Mendelsohn, & Smucker, 2000; Smucker & Niederee, 1995). In chair-work, the patient switches between chairs and is invited to have dialogues between different parts or emotions of the self. These 'conversations' can also take place between the patient and, for example, a significant other (Kellogg, 2004; Paivio & Greenberg, 1995). Imagery is a technique in which the therapist asks the patient to visualise an upsetting childhood memory or traumatic image of their past. Patients are invited to explore their emotions and later on to intervene in the scene with new, healthier responses (Rafaeli et al., 2011; Smucker & Boos, 2005). Experiential techniques are supplemented with cognitive and behavioural techniques.

Schema mode work

In *schema mode work*, the therapist helps the patient to recognise, and change, their maladaptive schema modes, and to build up a strong healthy adult mode that can view situations in a balanced way and make healthy choices. They use the entire repertoire of ST techniques, which is fully integrated with schema mode work, to achieve this. Schema mode work is most suitable for patients with severe PDs, such as the forensic patients described in this chapter. These patients exhibit emotional states which are extreme, and often fluctuate from moment to moment, making it very difficult to make progress with more standard therapeutic approaches. Instead, the therapist's interventions need to be focused on the mode that is present at a particular moment in time. In most cases, the patient's maladaptive coping modes make it very difficult to reach a vulnerable side of the patient, in which emotions and emotional needs are accessible. Instead, the patient's modes keep the therapist at bay: for example, a Detached Protector mode that keeps the therapist at a distance, avoiding feelings or any meaningful contact; a Self-Aggrandiser mode that is superior and arrogant, demeaning and devaluing the therapist; a Bully and Attack mode, intimidating the therapist and keeping them off balance; or a Conning Manipulator mode that attempts to manipulate the therapist into fulfilling the patient's hidden agenda (e.g. gaining special favours), at the expense of any real insight or attempt to change.

The therapist responds to these maladaptive modes by using a variety of techniques to flip or switch the patient into more therapeutically productive emotional states, specifically states involving emotional vulnerability (e.g. Vulnerable Child mode), where the therapist can gain access to the patient's emotions and provide for some of their unfulfilled emotional needs; or the Healthy Adult mode, where the patient can self-reflect in a balanced and objective way on themselves and their situation. This process takes time and requires patience and persistence on the part of the therapist. In very severe patients, such as forensic patients with Cluster B PDs, it often takes a year before the patient develops sufficient trust in the therapist to start to 'bring the wall down', revealing more emotional vulnerability. Our clinical experiences, which are confirmed by the preliminary results of our randomised clinical trial, suggest that the therapist's efforts eventually pay off, as the patient develops an attachment relationship with the therapist, providing a secure base from which the therapist helps the patient to reprocess their early maladaptive schemas and schema modes, leading to more adaptive coping and lowering the risk of recidivism.

Adaptations for forensic settings

Forensic treatment focuses on psychopathology and the causes of crime; its primary target is to reduce recidivism risk to an acceptable level so that offenders can be rehabilitated. The aim of ST in forensic settings is to reduce recidivism risk by means of targeting schema modes that represent psychological risk and protective factors for violent behaviour. In effect, Schema Therapy promotes psychological change as a means to reduce the risk of reoffending. Although personality disorders are similarly prevalent in general and forensic settings, there are a number of differences in patient profiles. First of all, in forensic patients, reactive aggression is a more immediate, prominent issue compared to those in general psychiatric settings. Second, offenders may display more marked affective and interpersonal deficits, such as emotional coldness, manipulation and deception. Third, offender treatment is usually compulsory, whereas general psychiatric patients are generally treated on a voluntary basis. Involuntary treatment can affect motivation for and engagement in treatment. A related aspect is that involuntary treatment may set up a dynamic of irritable and defensive behaviour and evoke strong negative feelings and mistrust because the patient feels that their sense of autonomy is violated (Petrila, 2004; Sainsbury, Krishnan, & Evans, 2004). This may, in turn, affect the therapist's motivation for providing treatment and the way in which a therapeutic relationship is formed (Ross, Polaschek, & Ward, 2008). Finally, where Schema Therapy is applied in forensic hospitals it must be recognised that these are unique environments and in some respects very different from general psychiatric hospitals. In forensic hospitals, staff are not only responsible for treatment and a patient's well-being, but also for the safety of the patient and their environment (Gadon et al., 2006; McCann, Ball, & Ivanoff, 2000). This is also true for prison and community forensic contexts. This means that the relationship between patient and staff is more complex in forensic settings. Dependent on the type of forensic facility (i.e. outpatient, inpatient), the balance between care and treatment will vary. For these reasons, we found it essential to adapt Schema Therapy for forensic purposes (Bernstein et al., 2007). We developed an explanatory model for criminal behaviour in which we conceptualise particular schema modes as psychological risk or protective factors. Next, we expanded the list of schema modes by adding emotional states that are very prevalent in offenders, but seldom seen in general psychiatric settings (Bernstein & Nentjes, 2015).

According to Schema Therapy, criminal and violent behaviour can be explained in terms of sequences of schema modes. The events preceding the criminal/violent act are often initiated by painful emotional triggers (i.e. situation in which someone feels abandoned, lonely, hurt, etc.). Child modes are triggered and subsequently covered up, avoided or overcompensated. For example, a girlfriend breaks up with a person; he feels abandoned (vulnerable child) and angry (angry child). To numb the pain, he takes a lot of drugs which results in a lack of impulse control. This progresses towards stalking and threatening his ex-girlfriend (bully and attack). Often, criminal behaviour is mediated by substance abuse/dependency (detached self-soother). Child modes are not always the trigger for criminal behaviour. In some cases criminal behaviour stems from a sense of entitlement or revenge. For instance, someone feels sexually aroused and entitled to have sex. If a woman refuses to comply, he forces himself on to her while threatening her. In a way, schema modes can be considered as internal risk or protective factors for antisocial behaviour. Some modes are referred to as internalising (directed towards self, i.e. child, avoidant coping and parent modes) while others are externalising (directed towards others, i.e. overcompensatory modes). Healthy modes (healthy adult and playful child) serve as a buffer and promote healthy behaviour and an integrated sense of self. Development of antisocial behaviour does not solely originate from maladaptive schema modes. Antisocial behaviour is the result of a reciprocal relationship between positive childhood experiences (i.e. secure attachment), predisposing factors (i.e. temperament, trauma) and activated schemas. In addition, external risk and protective factors such as the presence/absence of a social support system and (un)employment play a role (see Figure 10.1) (Andrews & Bonta, 2010; Bernstein & Nentjes, 2015).

We have added five schema modes to Young's original schema mode model. Table 10.2 provides an overview of all schema modes and the corresponding mode domains. The five forensic modes are: angry protector; conning and manipulative; predator; the obsessive-compulsive overcontroller; and paranoid overcontroller. The *angry protector mode* refers to an emotional state in which someone shows their anger in an indirect and controlled fashion. In this mode, one typically comes across as hostile, withdrawn and bad-tempered. This behaviour is coupled with hostile facial expressions, voice and

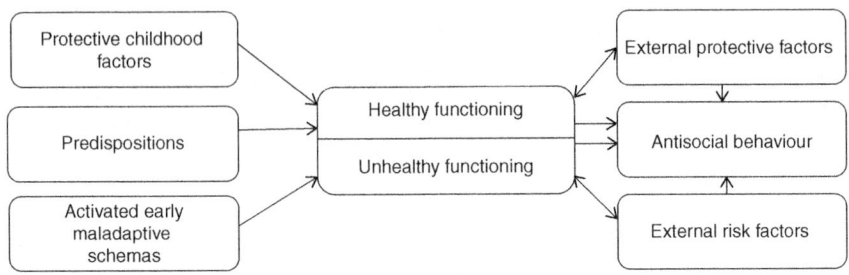

FIGURE 10.1: Explanatory ST model for antisocial and violent behaviour.
Source: Adapted from from Bernstein & Nentjes, 2015.

body language. The reason for this behaviour and attitude is to keep people at a safe distance. A patient is not likely to admit their anger; instead they may come across as cynical and devaluing. In therapy, the therapist is given little or no room to approach the patient directly. The *conning and manipulative mode* involves deceiving, lying and manipulating to get what you want. These methods are often displayed indirectly or discreetly. For example, the patient may claim to help someone, or express sympathy in order to get into favour with that person so that it is easier to exploit that individual. The *predator mode* is best described as a cold and callous emotional state. It refers to ruthless and instrumental aggression in order to get what you want without caring about the consequences. Other people are quickly labelled as a threat, obstacle or enemy that needs to be eliminated. Thus the purpose of the predator mode is to gain something, rather than to express anger. In this state, one may come across as empty and expressionless. This particular mode is added to the original model, because this type of behaviour/affect is often seen in criminal behaviour.

The *overcontroller modes* (paranoid and obsessive-compulsive) refer to attempts to protect oneself from threat, either real or imagined, by focusing attention, exercising control and ruminating. In the paranoid subtype, the individual constantly (mis)interprets social situations and the environment around them. They tend to focus on small details and continuously ruminate about the hidden meaning of these details. They are likely to come across as hyper-vigilant. In the obsessive-compulsive subtype, someone copes with (perceived) threats by performing certain routines repeatedly or by maintaining an excessive focus on details. The underlying emotion is anxiety (Bernstein et al., 2007; Keulen-de Vos, Bernstein, & Arntz, 2014).

Forensic PD patients pose specific challenges for their therapists. For example, these patients may be devaluing and hostile which makes it difficult for the therapists to stand their ground. Also, the restrictive nature of a forensic hospital may discourage a therapist's inclination to serve as a parent-like role model. As a result, therapists may be too distant towards the patient, or overly critical. Furthermore, their tendency to self-disclose (within appropriate limits) may be hindered. The forensic Schema Therapy model provides a valuable framework for therapists to understand and recognise challenging affective and behavioural states. Labelling personality pathology as fluctuating schema modes, in effect as different sides of a person, may promote a 'whole person' orientation.

TABLE 10.2 Schema modes and corresponding domains

Schema modes	Mode domains
Vulnerable Child Angry Child Impulsive Child Lonely Child	Child Modes
Detached Protector Detached Self-Soother Compliant Surrenderer Angry Protector* Complaining Protector	Avoidant Coping Modes
Punitive Parent Demanding Parent	Parent Modes
Self-Aggrandiser Bully and Attack Conning and Manipulating* Predator* Obsessive-compulsive Overcontroller* Paranoid Overcontroller*	Overcompensatory Modes
Healthy Adult Playful Child	Healthy Modes

Note:* = forensic modes.

Therapist training

Schema Therapy is a complex form of therapy that requires time, training and supervision to master. Because of the unique challenges of working with forensic patients, it is recommended that therapists seeking to learn ST have prior forensic experience and receive training and supervision from registered ST training programmes and supervisors who themselves have forensic specialisation in ST. The therapy is certified through the International Society for Schema Therapy (ISST), as well as national registries in ST. Therapists wanting to learn ST should have at least a basic psychologist's level of certification, or comparable certification for other related disciplines (e.g. psychiatry, social work, creative arts therapy), including two to three years of experience in giving therapy.

For example, Kersten and Bernstein have a training programme in the Netherlands that focuses on therapists working with forensic and addicted patients, and is certified by the Dutch ST registry as well as the Dutch association for cognitive-behavioural therapy. The programme consists of eight days of training spread over three to four months, including theory and technique, with a strong emphasis on experiential learning through in-class exercises (e.g. role playing various ST techniques) and practice with actual patients. The programme emphasises the schema mode model, including recognising and working with modes in clinical practice, and learning to work with one's own emotional reactions when patients' schema modes (e.g.

Self-Aggrandiser mode, Bully and Attack mode) 'push the therapist's buttons'. After the first two days of training, therapists begin working with one to two 'practise patients', that is, patients, typically from the institution where the therapist is working, selected to give the therapist the opportunity to learn ST. Much of the 'learning curve' in forensic ST comes from trying out the methods in practice and receiving feedback from qualified supervisors. In most forensic institutions, supervision is provided in groups of three to five therapists led by a supervisor with forensic ST experience. Supervision includes discussion of case material, role playing different scenarios to practise ST interventions, discussion of counter-transference reactions and watching videotape or listening to audiotape of therapy sessions, where possible. Typically, an external supervisor is hired to lead these groups until sufficient in-house expertise is developed so that a senior therapist from within the institution can take over the supervisor's role. The goal, ultimately, is to make each institution self-sufficient in maintaining high-quality ST through in-house supervision.

Mastery of ST is assessed by practical examinations, including producing a forensic ST case conceptualisation and case report, and demonstrating an ST technique in class using a classmate to play the patient. After participants have gained sufficient experience with their practice patients, they may submit therapy tapes for independent evaluation by qualified experts using the Schema Therapy Rating Scale. The entire process, including training and supervised experience with patients, typically requires about a year to two years before therapists demonstrate sufficient competency in ST to meet certification standards. It is highly recommended that therapists continue to participate in supervision or peer-supervision groups, even after achieving competence in ST, given the rigours of working with challenging forensic patients with personality disorders.

Client characteristics (indicators/contra-indicators)

Primary inclusion criteria for forensic Schema Therapy are Cluster B PD, PD Not-Otherwise-Specified with predominantly Cluster B traits, a high risk of reoffending and a history of aggressive behaviour. Exclusion criteria for the forensic adaptation of ST are serious neurological impairments, an autistic spectrum disorder, the presence of current psychotic symptoms or disorders, current drug or alcohol dependency (but not abuse) and current serious mood disorders. These mental states present too severe an impediment to successful treatment for personality disorders because of the effects on treatment outcome (e.g. Krampe et al., 2006). Some of these disorders (i.e. substance dependency and mood disorders) require specific stabilising treatment. If these mental states are in remission, Schema Therapy can still be considered. Patients with intellectual disabilities (ID) are excluded from regular forensic Schema Therapy, but are eligible for the adapted version of Schema Therapy for ID offenders (see Keulen-de Vos et al., 2016a). In the next paragraphs all exclusion criteria are briefly discussed. The decision algorithm is presented in Figure 10.2.

The forensic adaptation of Schema Therapy was originally developed for offenders with Cluster B PDs and PD-NOS because these disorders are associated with a high

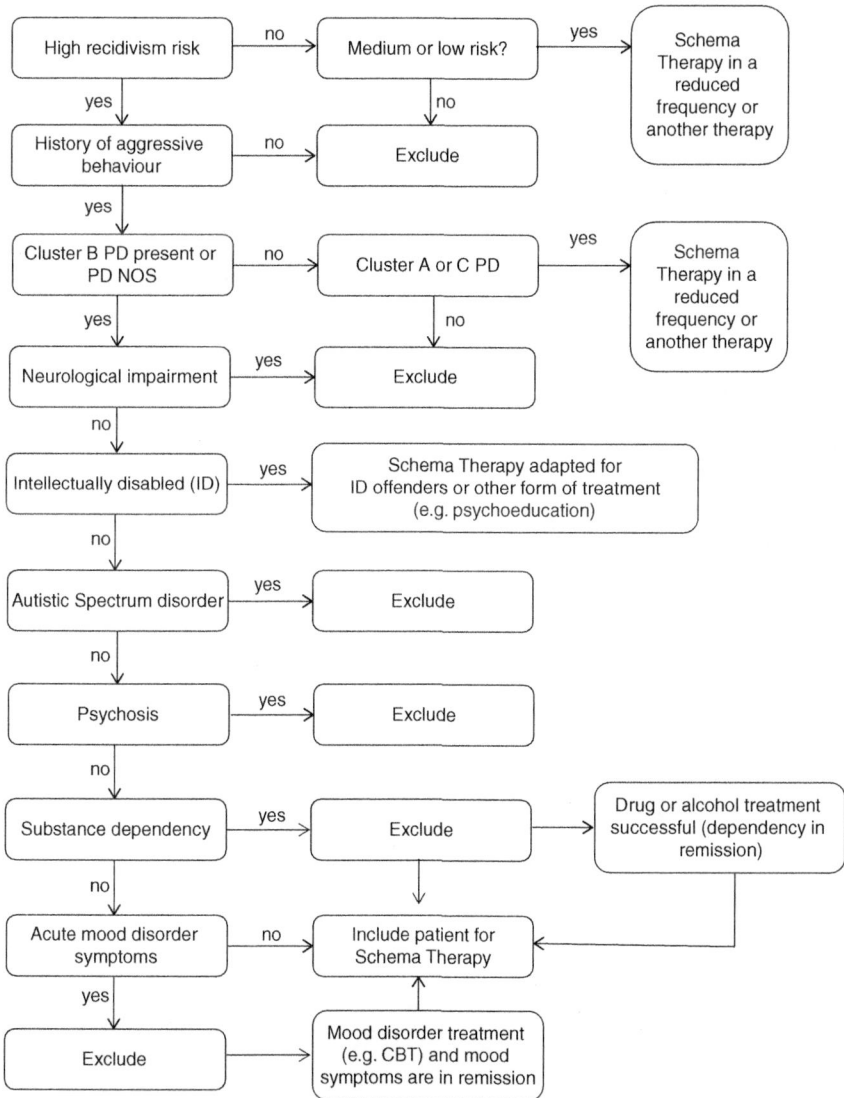

FIGURE 10.2: Decision algorithm for Schema Therapy in forensic settings.
Source: Adapted from Bernstein & Nentjes, 2015.

risk of reoffending (Coid, Hickey, & Yang, 2007; Leistico, Salekin, DeCoster, & Rogers, 2008). For example, the risk of recidivism in psychopathic offenders is considered 2–4 times greater than any other offenders (Hemphill, Hare, & Wong, 1998). Schema Therapy is deemed most cost effective for patients who are at moderate or high risk of reoffending (Bernstein et al., 2012), but ST is not contra-indicated for patients with medium or low risk. In those cases, a less intensive treatment plan is advised (e.g. therapy once instead of twice a week). Patients with Cluster A or C personality disorders are not necessarily excluded from ST, but there is no specific explanatory model with regard to criminal and violent behaviour in these patients. If ST is to be pursued for these PDs, it is advised to consult with experienced therapists who work with ST in Cluster B PD patients. In terms of history of aggressive behaviour, there are no restrictions with regard to type of aggressive behaviour (e.g. sexual violence, domestic violence, self-directed aggression). For every crime, or example of aggressive behaviour, a specific schema mode sequence is reconstructed.

Standard forensic Schema Therapy is excluded in case of serious neuropsychological impairments, such as dementia, Korsakoff's disease, and deficits in memory and reading function. These impairments coincide with problems with concentration and attention and therefore impede clinical outcome (Aharonovich, Nunes, & Hasin, 2003). For the same reason, offenders with an intellectual disability (ID), which is characterised by significant deficiencies in both intellectual capacities (IQ<80) and adaptive behaviour, such as reasoning, learning and problem-solving skills, are also excluded from regular forensic ST. However, many individuals with intellectual disabilities do show highly challenging or aggressive behaviour and are at high risk of reoffending. It was in this spirit that Keulen-de Vos and colleagues (2016a) initiated the adaptation of Schema Therapy for ID offenders (ST-ID). Differences between standard forensic ST and ST-ID are the addition of schema modes that reflect typical emotional states for ID patients (e.g. regressive child), a strong focus on psychoeducation and visual techniques (i.e. through arts therapy) instead of cognitive demands, and a systems approach (Keulen-de Vos et al., 2016a).

Patients with severe autistic spectrum disorders (ASD), such as Asperger and pervasive developmental disorders are excluded from regular forensic Schema Therapy because their deficits in theory of mind and emotional connectedness prevents them from forming a close therapeutic bond with their therapist. However, in the case of mild ASD disorders, certain aspects of ST may be beneficial for ASD offenders, for example explaining behaviour and (the absence) of emotional expressions in terms of schema modes.

Patients who suffer from current serious active psychotic episodes or psychotic syndromes (i.e. schizophrenia) are to be excluded from forensic Schema Therapy because ST may cause these patients to destabilise. In imagery techniques, for example, the therapist asks the patient to visualise an upsetting memory and invite the patient to explore their feelings and re-enact this memory. Those with active psychotic symptoms may find it difficult to distinguish reality from imagery, and therefore may readily decompensate. However, in individuals with diagnoses of schizophrenia who are stable with well-managed symptoms, Schema Therapy may be beneficial to target underlying personality pathology.

Schema Therapy is suitable for offenders with Cluster B PD who suffer from comorbid drug and alcohol abuse. In fact, ST defines this type of behaviour as an avoidant coping mode (detached self-soother mode). However, patients who suffer from acute substance dependency are excluded from ST because their frequent intoxicated state and related behaviours and their cognitive stance (i.e. telling lies, irresponsibility and manipulation) interferes with treatment. In order to benefit from therapy, addiction treatment is required first.

Finally, Schema Therapy is not indicated for PD offenders who have acute comorbid mood or anxiety disorders (i.e. bipolar disorders, PTSD) or a tendency to dissociate. ST is a long-term treatment, while patients with acute mood and anxiety disorders are in need of immediate relief of symptoms. If these symptoms are decreased, for example through the use of psychotropic medication and/or short-term cognitive-behavioural therapy, ST can be indicated to target underlying personality pathology.

Status of the evidence in forensic settings

Evidence supporting the schema mode model

A number of studies have supported the schema mode concept in PD patients. For example, research has shown that Borderline PD patients scored higher on vulnerable child, impulsive child, detached protector and punitive parent compared to Cluster C patients (Arntz, Klokman, & Sieswerda, 2005; Lobbestael, Arntz, & Sieswerda, 2005; Lobbestael, Vreeswijk, & Arntz, 2008). Others have provided empirical support for the schema mode model for Narcissistic PD patients by showing that they indeed rated higher on enraged child, self-aggrandiser and detached self-soother compared to Cluster C patients (Bamelis et al., 2011). Studies also show that switching between modes can be induced experimentally, for example, by showing patients short film segments depicting child abuse. For example, Lobbestael and colleagues (Lobbestael, Arntz, & Sieswerda, 2005) found that patients with Borderline and Antisocial PD exhibited different patterns of psychophysiological response – hyper-reactivity in the Borderline PD patients, and under-reactivity in the Antisocial PD patients – but the same implicit abuse-related associations. This study supports the theory that modes are triggered by environmental stimuli and involve both schema activation and patterns of physiological arousal that may be a function of different coping styles.

Evidence for the effectiveness of ST in non-forensic populations

There are also several studies that support Schema Therapy as evidence-based treatment for non-forensic patients with Borderline PD. A three-year multi-centre randomised clinical trial (RCT) plus one year follow-up by Giesen-Bloo and colleagues (2006) examined the effectiveness of ST versus transference focused therapy (TFT) in a sample of 86 predominantly female BPD outpatients. The treatment and follow-up results indicated that patients who received ST showed significantly more (sustained) improvement in a broad range of BPD symptoms, such as self-harm, emotional lability, identity disturbance and fears of abandonment, compared to patients who received TFT. The ST patients also reported better quality of life than the TFT patients, and ST also proved more cost effective than TFT (Giesen-Bloo et al., 2006). Similar findings were reported in the study by Nadort and colleagues (2009). In their study, 62 BPD outpatients were randomly assigned to two years of Schema Therapy with or without additional phone support. Results indicated that 42 per cent of the patients recovered from their Borderline PD symptoms. Phone support did not have added value.

A RCT by Farrell, Shaw and Webber (2009) examined the effectiveness of Schema Group Therapy in a sample of 32 female BPD outpatients. Patients were randomly allocated to either ST and Treatment as Usual (TAU), or to stand-alone TAU. The findings showed reduction in BPD symptoms in both treatment conditions, but significantly greater reductions in the ST-TAU condition (94 per cent compared to 16 per cent) (Farrell et al., 2009). Schema Group Therapy is now being investigated in an international, multi-centre randomised clinical trial of Borderline PD patients (Wetzelaer et al., 2014).

Bamelis and colleagues (Bamelis, Evers, Spinhoven, & Arntz, 2014) examined the effectiveness of Schema Therapy among 323 patients with Cluster C PDs, as well as paranoid, histrionic or narcissistic PDs. Patients were randomly assigned to ST, TAU or clarification-oriented psychotherapy. Significantly more patients in the ST condition recovered from their PD symptoms compared to TAU and clarification-oriented psychotherapy, regardless of their particular personality disorder. Schema Therapy was also superior with regard to drop-out rates. Gender differences have not been analysed (Bamelis et al., 2014). The effect sizes of these four studies vary between 0.86 and 3.13.

Effectiveness of ST techniques

There are several studies that support the evidence base of Schema Therapy techniques. For example, research has shown that visual representations of events (i.e. imagery) trigger more emotions than verbal representations do (Arntz & Weertman, 1999; Holmes, Arntz, & Smucker, 2007; Holmes, Mathews, Dalgleish, & Mackintosh, 2006; Holmes, Mathews, Mackintosh, & Dalgleish, 2008). This has proven to be particularly effective in patients with post-traumatic stress disorders (PTSD) (Arntz, Sofi, & van Breukelen, 2013; Arntz, Tiesema, & Kindt, 2007; Long et al., 2011).

As is apparent from this short review, there is an evidence base for the use of theoretical concepts (i.e. schemas and modes) and techniques (i.e. imagery) of Schema Therapy, as well as evidence for the effectiveness of Schema Therapy in general, especially for patients with Borderline Personality Disorder and Cluster B Personality Disorders. However, we need to know more about the usefulness of ST in other samples (i.e. other disorders, different settings) taking into account gender, age and culture.

Evidence for the ST theoretical model in forensic patients

Since its introduction in the forensic field (Bernstein et al., 2007), several attempts have been made to validate early maladaptive schemas and the schema mode concept in offenders. For example, a study by Keulen-de Vos and colleagues (2016b) examined whether schema modes are of explanatory value in understanding criminal behaviour. The criminal records of 95 male offenders with Cluster B PDs that contained information on the events leading up to the crime and the crime itself were assessed with an adapted version of the Mode Observation Scale (Bernstein, de Vos, & van den Broek, 2009). Results showed that criminal behaviour is often preceded by vulnerable feelings such as sadness, loss or shame (vulnerable child), loneliness (lonely child) and states of intoxication (detached self-soother). Criminal behaviour was characterised by impulsivity (impulsive child), anger (angry child), callous aggression (predator) and intimidation (bully and attack). Retrospective reports of modes from descriptions of patients' crimes also predicted future aggressive and other incidents in forensic hospitals, and were associated with facets of the PCL-R (Keulen-de Vos et al., 2016b). Other studies have supported the use of early maladaptive schemas in explaining impulsive lifestyle and antisocial behaviour features of psychopathy (Chakhssi, Bernstein, & de Ruiter, 2014), and offending behaviour in sex offenders who sexually assault children and adults (Chakhssi, de Ruiter, & Bernstein, 2013).

Evidence for the effectiveness of ST as a forensic treatment

A seven-year case study of a psychopathic patient (Chakhssi, Kersten, de Ruiter, & Bernstein, 2014) (PCL-R score = 29) treated with Schema Therapy for three years with a three-year follow-up found impressive evidence of reduced recidivism risk, reductions in early maladaptive schemas and improved social functioning. Three years post-therapy, the patient was living independently, working and had not recidivated.

A major randomised clinical trial of the effectiveness of Schema Therapy for forensic patients with mostly Cluster B PDs was recently completed at seven forensic hospitals ('TBS clinics') in the Netherlands (Bernstein et al., 2012). One hundred and three male patients with Antisocial, Borderline, Narcissistic or Paranoid PDs were randomly assigned to receive three years of either Schema Therapy (ST, $N = 54$) or usual forensic treatment (TAU, $N = 49$). Approximately 50 per cent of patients were psychopathic, based on a PCL-R score of 25 or higher, and about 20 per cent received PCL-R scores of 30 or higher. Patients were assessed repeatedly at six-month intervals on multiple measures including risks and strengths, personality disorder symptoms, early maladaptive schemas and schema modes, and progress into and through the resocialisation phase of treatment. A three-year post-treatment follow-up to assess actual recidivism is planned for 2018. Preliminary findings in the first 30 patients to complete the study suggested that Schema Therapy was outperforming usual treatment with regard to recidivism risk (as measured with the HCR-20), rehabilitation (i.e. supervised and unsupervised leave) and dropout, though differences were not yet statistically significant in this small sample. For example, ST patients received supervised and unsupervised leave more rapidly (a mean of 3.5 months earlier) than the TAU patients (Bernstein et al., 2012).

Preliminary analyses of a few key variables (e.g. rehabilitation) in a larger sample of patients who had completed the study (N=72, unpublished) showed that ST was continuing to outperform TAU, with some differences already being statistically significant. Analyses in the full sample are currently in progress. If ST significantly outperforms TAU, it would be the first demonstration of an effective treatment for this extremely challenging population.

Case study

Max is a 35-year-old man of Eastern European origin with a PCL-R score of 33 (i.e. psychopathic range) who was sentenced for treatment with an indefinite sentence in a high security forensic (TBS) hospital. As a young boy, he was seriously neglected by his mother. After moving to the Netherlands, he was physically abused by his father and stepmother, and sexually abused by an older cousin. He had exhibited serious behaviour problems from a young age. By the time he entered secondary school, he was involved in drugs and criminality, eventually becoming a powerful figure in the criminal underworld. One evening, after taking drugs and feeling that his life was 'out of control', he decided that someone 'had to die'. He met a woman in a bar, lured her outside and brutally murdered her. He was sentenced to forensic treatment, part of which included five years of twice per week Schema Therapy from a senior therapist along with once per week Art Therapy and later Drama Therapy as ancillary treatments.

In the initial phase of Schema Therapy (approximately the first year), Max showed suspiciousness and a pronounced need for control (Paranoid Overcontroller mode), as well as anger (Angry Child mode) and self-aggrandisement (Self-Aggrandiser mode). He filled the sessions with monologues detailing his complaints against the clinic (Complaining Protector mode). The therapist used empathic confrontation to interrupt these diatribes, creating moments when the patient could reflect on his emotional states and how they were triggered in specific situations ('Which side of you is this that won't let me get a word in edgewise?'). The therapist introduced the 'language' of schema modes, helping the patient to identify and label the different states that manifested themselves inside and outside of the sessions. Over time, the patient and therapist worked together to create a schema mode model depicting Max's schema modes in the form of a diagram (see Figure 10.3). In his Art Therapy sessions, he created paintings and sculptures of his modes, deepening his understanding of the modes by making tangible representations of them.

In his very first session, Max asked if the therapist was 'strong enough' to handle him. Out of his mistrust, he often asked why she did certain things, such as bringing a new pen to the session. The therapist adapted her limited reparenting stance to provide the safety, stability, predictability and secure limits that the patient had lacked as a child. For example, she gave clear and straightforward explanations, and was strong and authoritative, but also warm, interested and involved. As his trust slowly increased, his need for control decreased. He seemed calmer during the sessions, listened attentively when the therapist spoke and began to share significant

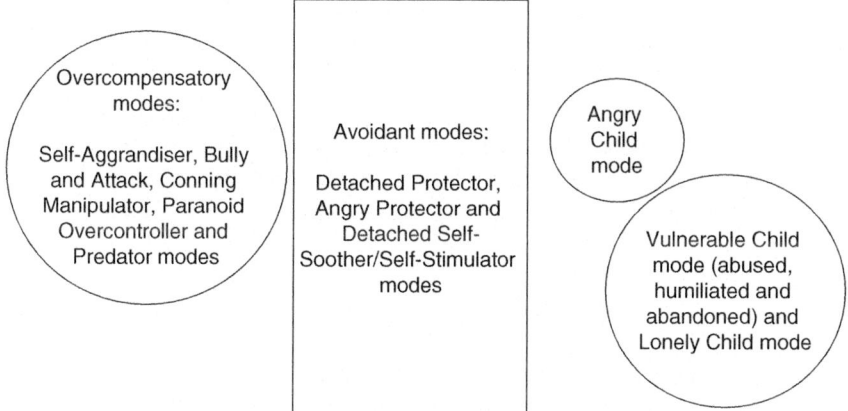

FIGURE 10.3: Schema mode model for 'Max'.

Note: Overcompensating modes on the left, avoidant coping modes in the middle (in the rectangle), and child modes on the right.

Source: Adapted from the work of Young, Klosko, and Weishaar, 2003.

information about his life. He had many psychosomatic complaints, which he shared with the therapist, turning to her for reassurance. An interesting feature of this case is that the patient had diagnoses of both Antisocial and Borderline Personality Disorder. He could switch modes rapidly from vulnerability, for example, becoming tearful when talking about his abuse history (Vulnerable Child mode); to outbursts of anger (Angry Child mode); to extreme detachment and coldness (Detached Protector and Predator modes). He seemed genuinely disturbed by his 'senseless' murder of a female stranger, unlike the contract murders he had carried out, which were 'just business'. He concluded that he must be unfit for life in normal society.

The second phase of therapy (approximately the second year) was characterised by 'two steps forward and one step back'. Max had frequent conflicts with ward personnel, where he questioned their motives and devalued their competence. His anger would escalate, leading him to isolate himself in his room to avoid further incidents. His therapist helped him to analyse these situations in terms of modes in himself and in the staff, which triggered each other, producing escalations. She also worked with ward personnel to recognise these patterns of modes-triggering-modes, and intervene more effectively. Sometimes his anger would increase in the therapy sessions to the point where his therapist had to set limits. Limit setting in Schema Therapy is done in a firm and consequential, but personal way, emphasising rights such as safety and respect: 'Your anger is leaving me feeling uncomfortable right now. You and I both have the right to feel safe. If you're having trouble controlling your anger now, then we need to take a break in the session.' In this same phase, the therapist introduced experiential techniques, using guided imagery to link present situations to painful childhood events involving abuse or neglect. By reprocessing these traumatic events, the therapist helped the patient to gain some relief from them, and reduced the intensity of his emotional responses to current conflictual situations.

In the third and final phase of therapy (approximately years three to five), Max showed fewer maladaptive modes and an increase in his capacity to self-reflect and handle problematic situations adaptively (Healthy Adult mode). His conflicts with ward staff decreased significantly and he developed greater patience and frustration tolerance. He applied for supervised leave, the beginning of the 'resocialisation' process of gradually reintegrating into the community. His leave was approved by the Ministry of Justice, which was not a foregone conclusion, given his very high PCL-R score and history of violent offences. However, at the last minute, he decided to put his leave on hold indefinitely, because of fears that members of his old criminal network might find and kill him. Eventually, however, he went on supervised leave, and then applied for and received unsupervised leave, proceeding through these phases without incident. During this period, he showed mostly Healthy Adult mode during his therapy sessions. The therapist had become a trusted, maternal figure, and sounding board whom he could turn to for advice and feedback. The sessions were reduced to once per week, and then made less frequent. Throughout the therapy, the therapist's genuineness and transparency, and her willingness to confront and set limits on him when needed, helped to overcome his mistrust and provided a secure attachment relationship from which he could progress. By the end of the therapy, his risk assessment scores on the HCR-20 indicated a reduction from high to moderate risk levels, with his moderate risk due mostly to past (i.e. Historical) risk items and not current, dynamic ones. At the time of this writing, approximately two years after his therapy ended, he had not recidivated.

Key directions for future research

In future studies, it would be useful to test whether different schema modes or mode combinations are related to different *(sub)types* of offenders (i.e. sex offenders e.g. child molesters, child pornography users, rapists, sexual sadists, violent offenders or offenders in general), and to investigate issues of *gender and culture*. Gender, and a patient's cultural and ethnic background, are important because it may influence how (personality) psychopathology is manifested (Salekin, Rogers, Ustad, & Sewell, 1998). For example, BPD symptoms in men are typically expressed via externalising behaviour (e.g. substance abuse, other-directed aggression), while females tend to exhibit internalising pathology (e.g. self-harming behaviour, depression) (McCormick et al., 2007; Tadić et al., 2009). Accordingly, gender-related expressions of psychopathology may refer to different schema modes. Also, cultural factors such as implicit norms and values, attitudes and beliefs may influence symptom or mode presentation and determine whether certain social behaviours, cognitions and (lack of) emotional expressions are considered appropriate or maladaptive (Kirmayer, Rousseau, & Lashley, 2007).

The overall aim of Schema Therapy is to heal underlying child modes so that dysfunctional overcompensatory or coping modes are no longer called for. ST claims that schema modes are fluctuating emotional states. Future research should examine whether child and overcompensatory schema modes indeed fluctuate over the course of forensic treatment, thus whether the nature of these schema modes progresses over time. Next, it would be helpful to know whether schema modes and mode switching could be outcome measures for treatment effectiveness. For example, it could be tested if successful treatment outcome is related to less extreme mode switching and associated physiological and behavioural expressions.

Taken as a whole, future research should focus on which Schema Therapy techniques and concepts are most effective for which problems in which offenders, and under which circumstances. For example, research is needed to compare the effectiveness of ST delivered as an individual therapy and ST as group therapy. One innovative form of group ST has been developed specifically for forensic patients at Rampton Hospital in the UK, and has been successfully implemented there and in a women's prison in Switzerland (Beckley & Gordon, 2009).

Creative Arts Therapies, such as drama, movement, music, and art therapies, have the potential to enrich ST practice, through their use of techniques that trigger and reprocess emotions. In a pilot study of ten male forensic patients (van den Broek et al., 2011), both Psychotherapy and Creative Arts Therapy variants of ST were more effective at eliciting vulnerable schema modes, compared to usual forensic treatment. Cross-fertilisation between ST and Arts Therapies may lead to more effective outcomes for forensic patients, in light of their difficulties in coping with emotions.

ST may also be more effective when delivered within the context of a multidisciplinary treatment team that has been trained to recognise and work with schema modes. Bernstein (2016) has developed a team-based form of ST, 'Safe Path', which has been implemented in several closed forensic settings, including adult and youth forensic settings in hospitals and prisons. In a preliminary study of high-risk forensic youth who were involuntarily committed to a special closed unit, ST appeared to have a beneficial effect on the treatment climate, an important factor in promoting positive therapeutic outcomes (Bernstein, Heynen, & van der Helm, 2015).

Finally, ST needs to be extended to other populations, such as youth and offenders with different types of offences (e.g. paedophilic sex offenders). In a pilot study, ST appeared to be effective in civilly committed youths with emerging Cluster B personality disorders and externalising behaviour problems. Providing ST before young people develop more entrenched maladaptive patterns may prove effective at reducing long-term criminal trajectories.

Note

1 The term patient refers to a generic relationship with a therapist and is not specifically used because of the forensic context.

Further reading

International Society for Schema Therapy (ISST). www.schematherapysociety.org
Rafaeli, E., Bernstein, D. P., & Young, J. (2011). *Schema Therapy: Distinctive Features*. New York: Routledge.
Van der Wijngaard, R., & Bernstein, D. (2011). *Schema Therapy: Working with Modes*. www.schematherapy.nl.

References

Aharonovich, E., Nunes, E., & Hasin, D. (2003). Cognitive impairment, retention and abstinence among cocaine abusers in cognitive-behavioral treatment. *Drug and Alcohol Dependence*, 71(2), 207–211.

Andrews, D. A., & Bonta, J. (2010). *The psychology of criminal conduct* (5th edn). New Providence, NJ: Anderson Publishing.

Arntz, A., Klokman, J., & Sieswerda, S. (2005). An empirical test of the schema mode model of borderline personality disorder. *Journal of Behavior Therapy and Experimental Psychiatry*, 36, 226–239.

Arntz, A., Sofi, D., & van Breukelen, G. (2013). Imagery rescripting as treatment for complicated PTSD in refugees: A multiple baseline case series study. *Behavior Research and Therapy*, 51, 274–283.

Arntz, A., Tiesema, M., & Kindt, M. (2007). Treatment of PTSD: A comparison of imaginal exposure with and without imagery rescripting. *Journal of Behavior Therapy and Experimental Psychiatry*, 38, 345–370.

Arntz, A., & Weertman, A. (1999). Treatment of childhood memories: Theory and practice. *Behavior Research and Therapy*, 37(8), 715–740.

Bamelis, L. L. M., Evers, S. M. A. A., Spinhoven, P., & Arntz, A. (2014). Results of a multicenter randomized controlled trial of the clinical effectiveness of schema therapy for personality disorders. *American Journal of Psychiatry*, 171, 305–322.

Bamelis, L. L. M., Renner, F., Heidkamp, D., & Arntz, A. (2011). Extended schema mode conceptualizations for specific personality disorders: An empirical study. *Journal of Personality Disorders*, 25(1), 41–58.

Bandura, A. (1986). *Social foundations of thought and action: A social cognitive theory*. Englewood Cliffs, NJ: Prentice-Hall.

Beck, A. T., Freeman, A. M., & Davis, D. D. (Eds) (2004). *Cognitive Therapy for personality disorders* (2nd edn). New York: The Guilford Press.

Beckley, K., & Gordon, N. (2009). *Schema Therapy Manual*. Nottingham Healthcare NHS Trust (UK): Unpublished.

Bernstein, D. P. (2016). *Safe Path: An integrated, team based approach for people with aggression, addiction, and antisocial behavior*. Unpublished manuscript.

Bernstein, D. P., Arntz, A., & de Vos, M. E. (2007). Schema-focused therapy in forensic settings: Theoretical model and recommendations for best clinical practice. *International Journal of Forensic Mental Health*, 6(2), 169–183.

Bernstein, D. P., Heynen, E., & van der Helm, P. (2015). *The Safe Path program: Working with high risk forensic youth and their treatment team in a closed treatment setting*. Paper presented at the annual schema therapy conference, Amsterdam, the Netherlands.

Bernstein, D. P., & Nentjes, L. (2015). *Schema Therapy for forensic patients with personality disorders*. Utrecht: Kwaliteit Forensische Zorg.

Bernstein, D. P., Nijman, H., Karos, K., Keulen-de Vos, M. E., de Vogel, V., & Lucker, T. (2012). Schema Therapy for forensic patients with personality disorders: Design and preliminary findings of a multicenter randomized clinical trial in the Netherlands. *International Journal of Forensic Mental Health, 11*(4), S312–S324.

Bernstein, D. P., de Vos, M. E., & van den Broek, E. P. A. (2009). *Mode Observation Scale (MOS)*. Unpublished manuscript.

Chakhssi, F., Bernstein, D. P., & de Ruiter, C. (2014). Early maladaptive schemas in relation to facets of psychopathy and institutional violence in offenders with personality disorders. *Legal and Criminal Psychology, 19*(2), 356–372.

Chakhssi, F., Kersten, T., de Ruiter, C., & Bernstein, D. (2014). Treating the untreatable: A single case study of a psychopathic patient treatment with psychotherapy. *Psychotherapy, 51*(3), 447–461.

Chakhssi, F., de Ruiter, C., & Bernstein, D. P. (2013). Early maladaptive cognitive schemas in child sexual offenders compared with sexual offenders against adults and nonsexual violent offenders: An exploratory study. *Journal of Sexual Medicine, 10*, 2201–2210.

Coid, J. W., Hickey, N., & Yang, M. (2007). Comparison of outcomes following after-care from forensic and general adult psychiatric services. *British Journal of Psychiatry, 190*, 509–514.

Farrell, J. M., Shaw, I. A., & Webber, M. A. (2009). A schema-focused approach to group psychotherapy for outpatients with borderline personality disorder: a randomized clinical trial. *Journal of Behavior Therapy and Experimental Psychiatry, 40*, 317–328.

Gadon, L., Johnstone, L., & Cooke, D. (2006). Situational variables and institutional violence: A systematic review of the literature. *Clinical Psychological Review, 26*(5), 515–534.

Giesen-Bloo, J., van Dyck, R., Spinhoven, P., van Tilburg, W., Dirksen, C., van Asselt, T., Kremers, I., Nadort, M., & Arntz, A. (2006). Outpatient psychotherapy for borderline personality disorder: A randomized clinical trial of schema focused therapy versus transference focused psychotherapy. *Archives of General Psychiatry, 63*, 649–658.

Hemphill, J., Hare, R., & Wong, S. (1998). Psychopathy and recidivism: A review. *Legal Criminology Psychology, 3*, 141–172.

Holmes, E. A., Arntz, A., & Smucker, M. R. (2007). Imagery rescripting in cognitive behavior therapy: Images, treatment techniques and outcome. *Journal of Behavior Therapy and Experimental Psychiatry, 38*, 297–305.

Holmes, E. A., Mathews, A., Dalgleish, T., & Mackintosh, B. (2006). Positive interpretation training: Effects of mental imagery versus verbal training on positive mood. *Behavior Therapy, 37*(3), 237–247.

Holmes, E. A., Mathews, A., Mackintosh, B., & Dalgleish, T. (2008). The causal effect of mental imagery on emotion assessed using picture-word cues. *Emotion, 8*(3), 395–409.

Kellogg, S. (2004). Dialogical encounters: contemporary perspectives on 'chair-work' in psychotherapy. *Psychotherapy: Theory, Research, Practice, Training, 41*(3), 310–320.

Keulen-de Vos, M. E., Bernstein, D. P., & Arntz, A. (2014). Schema Therapy for offenders with aggressive personality disorders. In R. C. Tafrate & D. Mitchell (Eds), *Forensic CBT: A Practioner's Guide* (pp. 66–83). Chichester: Wiley-Blackwell.

Keulen-de Vos, M. E., Frijters, K., Haga, T., Lansink, L., Strijbos, N., de Vries, E., & Wilms, W. (2016a). *Helpers en Helden: schemagerichte therapie voor forensische patiënten met een licht verstandelijke beperking.* [Schema therapy for offenders with intellectual disabilities]. Utrecht: Kwaliteit Forensische Zorg.

Keulen-de Vos, M. E., Bernstein, D. P., Vanstipelen, S., de Vogel, V., Lucker, T. P., Slaats, M., Hartkoorn, M., & Arntz, A. (2016b). Emotional states in criminal and violent behavior of forensic cluster B PD patients: A retrospective and prospective study. *Legal and Criminological Psychology, 21*, 56–76.

Kirmayer, L. J., Rousseau, C., & Lashley, M. (2007). The place of culture in forensic psychiatry. *Journal of the American Academy of Psychiatry and the Law, 35*, 98–102.

Krampe, H., Wagner, T., Stawicki, S., Bartels, C., Aust, C., Kroener-Herwig, B., Kuefner, H., & Ehrenneich, H. (2006). Personality disorders and chronicity of addiction as independent outcome predictors in alcoholism treatment. *Psychiatric Services*, 57, 708–712.

Landy, R. L. (2000). Role theory and the role method of drama therapy. In P. Lewis & D. Read Johnson (Eds), *Current approaches in drama therapy* (pp. 50–69). Springfield, IL: Charles C. Thomas.

Leistico, A. R., Salekin, R. T., DeCoster, J., & Rogers, R. (2008). A large-scale meta-analysis relating the Hare measures of psychopathy to antisocial conduct. *Law and Human Behavior*, 32, 28–45.

Lobbestael, J., Arntz, A., & Sieswerda, S. (2005). Schema modes and childhood abuse in borderline and antisocial personality disorders. *Journal of Behavior Therapy and Experimental Psychiatry*, 36, 240–253.

Lobbestael, J., van Vreeswijk, M. F., & Arntz, A. (2008). An empirical test of schema mode conceptualizations in personality disorders. *Behavior Research and Therapy*, 46, 854–860.

Lobbestael, J., van Vreeswijk, M. F., Spinhoven, P., Schouten, E., & Arntz, A. (2010). Reliability and validity of the short schema mode inventory. *Behavioral and Cognitive Psychotherapy*, 38, 437–458.

Long, M. E., Hammons, M. E., Davis, J. L., Frueh, B. C., Khan, M. M., Elhai, J. D., & Teng, E. J. (2011). Imagery rescripting and exposure group treatment of posttraumatic nightmares in veterans with PTSD. *Journal of Anxiety Disorders*, 25, 531–535.

McCann, R. A., Ball, E. M., & Ivanoff, A. (2000). DBT with an inpatient forensic population: The CMHIP Forensic Model. *Cognitive and Behavioral Practice*, 7, 447–456.

McCormick, B., Blum, N., Hansel, R., Franklin, J.A., St John, D., Pfohl, B., Allen, J., & Black, D.W. (2007). Relationship of sex to symptom severity, psychiatric comorbidity, and health care utilization in 163 subjects with borderline personality disorder. *Comprehensive Psychiatry*, 48, 406–412.

Nadort, M., Arntz, A., Smit, J. H., Giesen-Bloo, J., Eikelenboom, M., Spinhoven, P., van Asselt, T., Wensing M., & van Dyck, R. (2009). Implementation of outpatient schema therapy for borderline personality disorder with versus without crisis support by the therapist outside office hours: A randomized trial. *Behavior Research and Therapy*, 47, 961–973.

Paivio, S. C., & Greenberg, L. S. (1995). Resolving 'unfinished business': Efficacy of experiential therapy using empty-chair dialogue. *Journal of Consulting and Clinical Psychology*, 63(3), 419–425.

Petrila, J. (2004). Emerging issues in forensic mental health. *Psychiatric Quarterly*, 75(1), 3–19.

Rafaeli, E., Bernstein, D. P., & Young, J. (2011). *Schema Therapy: Distinctive Features*. New York: Routledge.

Ross, E. C., Polaschek, D. L. L., & Ward, T. (2008). The therapeutic alliance: A theoretical revision for offender rehabilitation. *Aggression and Violent Behavior*, 13, 462–480.

Rush, M. D., Grunert, B. K., Mendelsohn, R. A., & Smucker, M. R. (2000). Imagery rescripting for recurrent, distressing images. *Cognitive and Behavioral Practice*, 7, 173–182.

Sainsbury, L., Krishnan, G., & Evans, C. (2004). Motivating factors for male forensic patients with personality disorder. *Criminal Behavior and Mental Health*, 14(1), 29–38.

Salekin, R. T., Rogers, R., Ustad, K. L., & Sewell, K. W. (1998). Psychopathy and recidivism among female inmates. *Law and Human Behavior*, 22(1), 109–128.

Smucker, M. R., & Boos, A. (2005). Imagery rescripting and reprocessing therapy. In A. Freeman, M. Stone, & D. Martin (Eds), *Comparative treatments for borderline personality disorder* (pp. 215–237). New York: Springer Publishing.

Smucker, M. R., & Niederee, J. (1995). Treating incest-related PTSD and pathogenic schemas through imaginal exposure and rescripting. *Cognitive and Behavioral Practice*, 2, 63–93.

Tadić, A., Wagner, S., Hoch, J., Başkaya, O., von Cube, R., Skaletz, C., Lieb, K., & Dahmen, N. (2009). Gender differences in axis I and axis II comorbidity in patients with borderline personality disorder. *Psychopathology, 42,* 257–263.

van den Broek, E., Keulen-de Vos, M. E., & Bernstein, D. P. (2011). Arts therapies and schema focused therapy: A pilot study. *The Arts in Psychotherapy, 38,* 325–332.

Wetzelaer, P., Farrell, S., Evers, S. M. A. A., Jacob, G. A., Lee, C. W., Brand, O., van Breukelen, G., Fassbinder, E., Fretwell, H., Harper, R. P., Lavender, A., Lockwood, G., Malogiannis, I. A., Schweiger, U., Startup, H., Stevenson, T., Zarbock, G., & Arntz, A. (2014). Design of an international multicentre RCT on group schema therapy for borderline personality disorder. *BMC Psychiatry, 14,* 319.

Young, J. E., Klosko, J., & Weishaar, M. (2003). *Schema Therapy: A Practitioner's Guide.* New York: Guilford.

11
SENSORIMOTOR PSYCHOTHERAPY

Naomi Murphy

Experience of working with forensic clients highlights the need to address both trauma and attachment deficits in order to develop and improve capacity to tolerate strong negative affect and improve relational functioning. Drawing on affective neuroscience, sensorimotor theory emphasises the need for the left hemisphere to be kept engaged in the therapeutic process. This can be achieved by mindful study of the body's response to emotionally triggering situations and through developing awareness of how procedural learning in relation to attachment deficit is stored in the body.

Sensorimotor therapy, devised by Pat Ogden, incorporates a number of body-oriented techniques into psychotherapy. Clients are encouraged to notice the three-way relationship between belief, emotion and the body and become aware of when they are experiencing threat and identify how they cope with it. With forensic clients it becomes possible to identify the interpersonal 'threat' within apparently innocuous situations. These can lead to extreme acting out if left untreated. It is also possible to identify habitual patterns of relating which maximise the possibility of perceived 'threat' occurring. Emphasis in treatment is upon either encouraging the completion of defensive actions the body wanted to make when in danger in order to reduce post-traumatic symptoms or allowing for the body to be inhabited in ways that lead to improved social engagement.

Although affective neuroscience supports the theoretical principles that drive sensorimotor treatment, limited research into efficacy has been completed. Despite this, initial endeavours using this approach with a population high in psychopathy suggest this could be a promising way of working with forensic clients.

Overview of the therapy

Experience of working with forensic clients highlights the need for therapists to possess skills in addressing both trauma and deficits in early attachments. This leads to exploration of therapeutic modalities focusing primarily upon addressing these inter-related needs. The capacity to regulate emotions effectively develops as a direct consequence of how an individual is parented and reflects the attunement and sensitivity to which the individual is exposed (Schore, 2003). When attachment figures are abusive or neglectful or an individual is exposed to repeated interpersonal trauma, the nervous system and affect-regulating brain structure fail to develop adequately. Porges (2011) describes how, in these circumstances, individuals are more likely to develop either autonomic tendencies towards sympathetic hyperarousal leading to hypervigilance and being over-prepared for danger or autonomic parasympathetic hypoarousal leading to numbness, detachment and passivity. Hypervigilant, 'paranoid' interpretation of events can contribute to situations involving even mild insult or rejection being perceived as severely threatening, leading to an extreme response. Hypoarousal may also contribute to extreme detachment that may facilitate aggressive actions that would be unthinkable to most people.

Many therapeutic interventions consist of 'sharpening up' the higher parts of the brain, especially those in the left hemisphere, rational brain to reduce thinking errors and cognitive distortions. Such interventions derive from the belief that affective consciousness is a consequence of reflecting on physiological changes and concluding this is a response to emotion. By strengthening the capacity to reflect on the changes, and thus draw an alternative conclusion, one hopes to disrupt the individual's need to act out their distress behaviourally. Indeed, working cognitively is useful, in enabling the individual to analyse what went wrong and to identify situations which may make them vulnerable to offending. However, many people who commit violent crime aren't in a rational state of mind when offending. Instead they find themselves overwhelmed with strong affect that restricts their capacity to think logically, their ability to draw on the intellectual knowledge they may have about themselves and their functioning, or think rationally about the consequences of possible behaviours. Mainstream psychological therapies such as CBT or psychodynamic therapy pay scant attention to the pre-programmed physical response patterns that have evolved and are evoked in response to situations experienced as personally threatening for the individual.

Sensorimotor and somatic psychotherapies (SP) draw on a different theoretical understanding of affect. Affective neuroscientists (e.g. Panksepp, 1998) argue that affective consciousness does not require cognition and is independent of language. Instead, they contend that 'felt experience can be *anoetic* – unreflective, unthinking primary process kind of consciousness that precedes our cognitive understanding of the world' (Panksepp & Biven, 2012, p14). Emotion is not merely a learned response but reflects evolutionary development and is thus primarily located in the seat of the brain.

A proliferation of neuroimaging studies (e.g. Damasio, 2000; Hull, 2002; Lanius et al., 2001; Lindauer et al., 2004, Rauch et al., 2005) indicate that when patients with PTSD are exposed to cues to their trauma, parts of the brain are activated which support extreme emotion whilst parts of the brain that inhibit emotional arousal and enable expressive speech are deactivated. Van der Kolk (2006) summarises that 'they have trouble thinking and speaking' and notes 'the imprint of trauma doesn't 'sit' in the verbal, understanding part of the brain but in much deeper regions – amygdala, hippocampus, hypothalamus, brain stem – which are only marginally affected by thinking and cognition.' These and other neurobiological studies (Vasterling, Brailey, Constans, & Sutker, 1998; Clark et al., 2003) show that people process their trauma from the 'bottom up, body to mind – not top down' (Wylie, n.d.). They also show that individuals have problems with sustained attention and working memory which makes it difficult for them to remain focused in the present.

Van der Kolk writes (2006, p. 6) that 'trauma can be conceptualised as stemming from a failure of the natural physiological activation and hormonal secretions to organise an effective response to threat. Rather than producing a successful fight or flight response, the organism becomes immobilised' (or 'freezes'). He continues (p. 7), 'When people lack sources of support and sustenance … they are likely to learn to respond to abuse and threat with mechanistic compliance or resigned submission. Particularly if the brutalisation has been repetitive and unrelenting, they are vulnerable to continue to become physiologically dysregulated and go into states of extreme hypo- and hyperarousal accompanied by physical immobilisation.' With offenders it seems possible that the individual, sensing the threat to self through a change in their arousal, might take drastic action to 'fight back' and divert the threat before immobilisation occurs.

It is well established that threat activates the sympathetic and parasympathetic nervous systems and more prolonged exposure to threat is associated with the sympathetic nervous system being primed for mobilisation with decreased parasympathetic tone (Porges, 2011). Insecure attachment in childhood is also associated with poorer vagal tone (Diamond, Fagundes, & Butterworth, 2012). Van der Kolk states that for traumatised individuals to be successfully treated, they need to 'activate their mPFC [medial prefrontal cortex], insula and anterior cingulate by learning to tolerate orienting and focusing their attention on their internal experience, while interweaving and conjoining cognitive, emotional and sensorimotor elements of their traumatic experiences' (Van der Kolk, 2006, p. 12).

Informed by this research, SP interventions are aimed at working with the right hemisphere of the brain and, in particular, the more primitive, lower part of the brain, because of its role in implicit emotional processing. Ogden's sensorimotor psychotherapy (e.g. Ogden & Fisher, 2015; Ogden, Minton, & Pain, 2006) as with other psychotherapeutic approaches advocated by experts in trauma (such as van der Kolk, 2006; van der Hart, Nijenhuis, & Steele, 2006; Rothschild, 2000) or affect (Panksepp & Biven, 2012; Porges, 2011; Schore, 2003; Siegel, 2010) emphasises the 'dominance of non-verbal, body-based, implicit processes over verbal, linguistic, explicit processes …

not only interpreting and attending to the client's narrative and emotions but also as participating in and attending to the communications that occur beneath the words in a body tête-à-tête' (Ogden & Fisher, 2015, p. 25).

Sensorimotor psychotherapy arose from the efforts of Pat Ogden to incorporate body-oriented techniques derived from years of training in Rolfing[1] (Feitis, 1978) and the Hakomi method[2] (Kurtz, 1990) into psychotherapy. Attention to movement, breath and action tendencies is not unusual in healing traditions beyond Western culture such as yoga and tai chi. In the West, some attention has been focused on movement and sensation, e.g. Feldenkrais and Alexander techniques, but these haven't been embraced within mainstream psychological therapies that are specifically aimed at addressing trauma and neglect. Ogden recognised that the strength of body-oriented therapies is in understanding that current physiological states and action tendencies are influenced by past experience. Rather than assist clients in establishing a coherent narrative of their experiences as in most talking therapies (thus indicating to the client that the verbal account is of utmost interest), SP therapists facilitate self-awareness and self-regulation by encouraging the client to 'become a careful observer of the ebb and flow of internal experiences, mindfully noticing whatever thoughts, feelings, body sensations and impulses emerge' (van der Kolk, 2006, p. 12) and to thus become aware of the body's response to threat and trauma. Clients become more aware of their bodies and in particular the two-way relationship between belief and emotion and how the body is inhabited. For instance, understanding how the belief 'I can't let myself feel vulnerable' is manifest in posture, movement and physical sensation and how these aspects of the body impact upon emotion and belief. Through the use of SP, a more coherent narrative will often also emerge but unlike other forms of psychological therapy, this is not a primary goal of SP. Instead, within SP, the encoding of the event is addressed, the goal being 'reorganisation' rather than 're-experiencing' (Fischer, 2009).

SP initially involves psychoeducation about the effect of trauma or attachment failure on the body. Patients are supported in restoring the body to equilibrium whilst discussing affect-triggering experiences. 'Mindful study of how an event was once organised somatically and emotionally is the precursor to its potential reorganisation and encoding as an event that is finally 'over' rather than 'still happening' or 'never over"' (Fischer, 2009, p. 318). The emphasis upon dual awareness (mindful study of the body whilst speaking about a traumatic experience) enables the patient and therapist to notice the impact on bodily sensations, movement, perception, emotion and cognition and the therapist teaches the patient how to utilise somatic resources such as movement and posture to stay within a 'window of tolerance' (Ogden, 2009), recover from traumatic reminders, restore equilibrium and to experience a state of somatic safety. Davidson et al. (2003) note that the mindful observation prevents the individual from becoming emotionally overwhelmed. Fischer (2009) likens these experiments to mothers playing 'peek-a-boo' as a way of non-verbally developing skills that contribute to affectively tolerating separation.

Trauma-focused interventions in SP involve familiarising the client with their sensorimotor experiences when feeling under threat; in addition to *flight, fight* and *freeze*, SP makes use of *submit* and *attach* as responses to fear. For instance, in the case of attach, when feeling threatened, one might try and establish a rapport with the source of the threat to minimise risk. If it is not possible to evade a sexual assault or fight the perpetrator, one might submit to minimise the chance of the perpetrator using force. Animal studies (such as those described in Peter Levine's Nature's Lessons in Healing Trauma on YouTube) illustrate that when faced with inescapable threat, animals freeze and appear to feign death to evade predators who require the stimulation of activity to trigger their aggression. These studies also illustrate that once the threat has passed, animals discharge the pent-up energy they built up through movements they were prevented from completing by entering a phase of spasms. Post-traumatic stress is hypothesised (e.g. Levine, 2010) to occur because humans have developed the capacity to over-ride the body's innate need to discharge this energy. However, over-riding this need leaves the nervous system unable to move forward from the trauma and confused about where there may be an ongoing threat.

When working with trauma, the SP therapist attempts to reduce the individual's affective arousal to within a manageable range. Working with the client's physiological awareness through tracking arousal, the therapist is able to identify potential defensive actions that were ineffective or incomplete due to fear or risk of greater danger. For instance, a client discussing his father's beatings may slightly raise his hand as he talks about his father. Exploration of this gesture may lead to experimenting with pushing (i.e. the client wanted to push his father away but knew he would be overpowered). The therapist may then encourage the client to push against his or her hand or a cushion and to study the effect of this push on the body. Another client may present with restless legs whilst discussing his violent mother, perhaps symbolising the wish to flee; in this instance, the client might be encouraged to walk round the room and notice the effect on the body. It is not uncommon for clients to spasm or shake when completing these kind of exercises.

Character-focused interventions involve 'body-reading' to identify habitual patterns that have emerged in response to attachment failure and to build awareness of how these are stored within the body. For instance, someone who felt very frightened as a child might develop their body in order to ward off potential threat (for example the very visible upper body strength often seen in forensic clients). Often, habitual patterns lead to over-reliance on certain movements/postures placing a strain on the body over time. Character-focused interventions explore the impact of these habitual strategies and experiment with alternative responses in an attempt to provide the missing attachment experience. In this example, the client's fear might be acknowledged and validated and a more nurturing response provided. Character strategies ultimately restrict emotion (it's hard to feel pride in oneself if one has a tendency to adopt a posture associated with shame such as looking at the floor when talking to others; its hard to feel vulnerable with a stiff back and chest pushed forward) so interventions are aimed at encouraging the individual to experience deeper, broader affect. Examples of interventions include mindfully studying the response to core beliefs such as 'I'm unlovable' or 'I'm useless'. The therapist might make this statement about his or herself (the therapist) and ask the client to notice his own felt response to this; the client often experiences profound sadness and compassion when hearing a therapist say, 'I'm no good, I'm useless' which can enable him to recognise that he is also deserving of compassion. Alternatively, the therapist might encourage the client to work with a memory elicited when this belief is studied and then provide the response the parent ought to have provided. If the belief is manifest in body posture or movement, for instance keeping head down, averting gaze and shrinking into one's body, the client might be encouraged to mindfully study what happens when a different posture or movement is utilised that permits greater social engagement.

SP is a beneficial way of working with forensic clients because ultimately it assists the client in developing skills to remain within a window of emotional tolerance even when faced with emotionally triggering stimuli. Thus the client becomes less dependent on extreme behavioural acting out to cope with strong negative affect and is capable of experiencing a broader range of affect. Because the individual is able to remain in a state of emotional stability, he or she is more likely to retain the capacity to observe and reflect on cognitions and observe and desist from impulses to act out. SP also explicitly recognises and values adaptations the body utilised to cope with trauma and neglect and encourages the client to be curious about their bodily reactions rather than judgmental. This can be particularly valuable in working with people who have experienced high levels of shame in their lives as a consequence of what has happened to them and are also used to being shamed because of what they have done.

One of the most delicate tasks in working with forensic clients is enabling them to manage to stay in a state of emotional equilibrium when discussing their own actions in order to connect emotionally with what they have done and truly appreciate the enormity of their actions. Because SP is focused upon the client remaining within a window of tolerance, the work can enable the client to gain a much deeper appreciation of their actions and the triggers to these than would be achieved when the individual is compelled to emotionally disconnect to survive the discourse. Of particular interest is the focus on understanding the client's response to threat, either physical or psychological, which enables clear connections to be made between the client's own traumatic past and cues to threat within the antecedents to the offence. For instance, a client – Lemar – who murdered his partner after several years of verbally and physically abusing her, discovered through exploration of his bodily sensations, that he had unresolved fear of abandonment stemming from childhood and his belief that his mother voluntarily relinquished his care to the Local Authority. Addressing his own history enabled him to recognise cues to threat of abandonment. This enabled him to recognise the role that threat of abandonment played in his offending and work to diminish this.

Adaptations for forensic settings

In many ways, SP is extremely suitable for forensic clients since it is a treatment that can adequately cope with extremely disturbed and, at times, dissociated clients. However, there are a number of adaptations that may be necessary.

In addition to having an understanding of the client's presenting problem and developmental history, establishing an understanding of an individual's capacity to be curious about their body, posture, habitual movements and bodily sensations is useful for any SP practitioner. Within forensic practice, some understanding of how the body has been used in situations to ward off psychological or physical threat is also crucial. For instance, in working with a man who had killed a woman but had a long history of engaging in pub fights with men, we explored the foot tapping that occurred whenever he spoke of fighting. I had been curious about whether the foot tapping was precursory behaviour to 'kicking away' the threat and naively wondered whether pushing his foot into the ground might be a useful intervention. However, the individual had stamped on his victim's head so this suggestion caused alarm but allowed us to study the impulse to stamp and make links between a traumatic attack he experienced and his own attack on another. This study led to him lying on his back and pushing against the wall with his feet. This reduced him to tears but also brought relief from the nightmares he was experiencing. Such experience reinforces the need for therapist familiarity with the actual mechanics of a client's former violence (e.g. use of limbs, range of actions, sites of target, etc.) in order to be mindful of what actions may or may not be possible.

The culture and physical environment of forensic settings can pose a challenge to SP work although few are insurmountable. The greatest challenge is possibly posed by the lack of familiarity of staff with this approach. Forensic institutions are often characterised by a culture of fear and paranoid anxiety about anything unfamiliar. Education of the institution about the approach is essential and preparing any staff that might observe the intervention from outside the room about any behaviours that might deviate from customary talking therapy practice is important. For instance, my practice room is one of several supervised by a prison officer (from outside the room). If therapy leads us to conclude that standing up in the session will be useful, I advise the observing officer not to be alarmed if he glances through the window and observes we are not seated. Ordinarily, standing up in a session might indicate an elevated threat level and trigger a response on the part of the officer.

Physical touch is a significant part of standard SP practice due in part to the repair of missing attachment experience, e.g. offering asexual comfort such as laying a hand on a hand. Additionally, contact can facilitate the completion of defensive impulses, e.g. offering a hand to push against. However, touch is not essential. Physical touch is alarming within, and prohibited by, many forensic institutions as it triggers anxiety about the development of inappropriate relationships. Pushing against a wall or a firm cushion or gym ball can more than adequately substitute for pushing against a hand. However, this can also cause anxiety because of being 'out of the ordinary' and/or where the item might be relevant to an offence (e.g. a cushion might not be advisable if the client had smothered their victim). Words can communicate care and comfort and in some cases it might be possible to make use of some touch. For instance, where a client has their foot crossed over their knee, a rested hand on top of the client's uppermost shoe may be interpreted as more neutral contact than a touch to the arm.

Some work, for instance exploration of boundaries via physical proximity, may require a larger room than is ordinarily available for psychological therapy. There are also occasions when a session longer than 50 minutes may be helpful in resolving a traumatic episode although any deviations from normal practice should be planned and thus predictable for the client, therapist and the system.

Therapist training

There are some excellent texts on working with the body in therapy, which could be recommended as essential reading for any therapist wishing to enhance their skills and their ability to attend to non-verbal communication and impulses. These are listed at the end of the chapter. However, to successfully integrate sensorimotor knowledge into one's psychotherapeutic approach really does require the procedural learning that is facilitated by engaging in experiential training. Unlike some training courses where it is permissible for one to role play a service user in order to enable fellow trainees to develop therapeutic skills, sensorimotor training courses are genuinely experiential in that the individual is required to work with their own personal material in order to understand the experience of both receiving and delivering the intervention. Experiential learning is the most robust form of training in any modality but this is arguably more essential preparation for treatment in this modality than some other models where a cognitive understanding of the model may be sufficient to enable the therapist to adapt their practice.

There are training courses in therapeutic ways of working with the body such as Somatic Experiencing. However, these courses are primarily focused upon releasing trauma from the body. In contrast, sensorimotor psychotherapy is ultimately about integration of the physical impact upon the body with emotions and cognitions and is as efficient in dealing with attachment deficits as trauma.

Training courses in sensorimotor psychotherapy (or developmental somatic psychotherapy) are aimed at those who already have core mental health professional status. Training such as that offered by the Sensorimotor Psychotherapy Institute (SPI)[3] and the Center for Somatic Studies is relatively lengthy in that one attends a number of intensive training modules spread over many months and is expected to rehearse skills and complete independent study in the intervening period. SPI training is run with a degree of regularity within the UK and is organised into four distinct courses; Level I (six months) is aimed at resolution of specific traumatic episodes and Level II (15 months) is aimed at addressing character strategies that emerge as a consequence of repeated attachment failure in childhood.

Completion of Level I training would be adequate for the needs of many therapists working within adult mental health. However, when working with forensic patients, one is typically required to alternate between interventions aimed at specific traumatic episodes and those aimed at addressing character adaptations. For instance, when attempting to address the intrusive memory of a client recalling a severe beating (when he tried to disagree with his mother as a child) progress may be hampered by the client's subjugating interpersonal style that has evolved to avoid conflict with authority figures.

Level III training (18 months) enables practitioners to have their skills strengthened and validated via a process of certification and involves submission of videotaped material. It is possible to gain certification by videotaping skills practised on the course rather than having to navigate complex procedures to gain permission from forensic service users. It is also possible to complete Level IV training to become an accredited trainer.

The capacity to practise mindfulness and awareness of what is happening in one's own body are key skills for sensorimotor psychotherapists. Therefore, supplementing formal sensorimotor therapy training with skills training in mindfulness, meditation, breath control and physical exercise such as yoga that encourages conscious connection with the physical self can be helpful.

Client characteristics (indicators/contra-indicators)

SP is suitable for a broad range of clients and there are distinct aspects that make it particularly useful in forensic practice where clients typically display a fairly high level of disturbance. The primary goals of SP are to resolve trauma, repair attachment deficit and enable effective emotional regulation. Many forensic clients have been exposed to extreme and repetitive trauma from a very early age and most are unable to regulate their emotions effectively. Early trauma interferes with the hippocampus's ability to store and 'catalogue' events and traditional therapies rely on the client's ability to work with memories, a task made more difficult when the memories are fragmented. Exploring traumatic events can also lead to the client being re-traumatised by further exposure to the trauma. SP doesn't require a cognitive understanding of what happened since the focus is the body's response. The therapist observes, then works with the first evidence of the body being affected by the discourse. For instance, an individual with a violent father may start exhibiting bodily signs of strain (such as hand gestures akin to a push) when discussing his father coming home from work. Within this example, the therapist might encourage the client to explore the impulse exhibited in the hand rather than taking the client further into memory in search of a violent episode to be analysed. Whilst SP lends itself readily to efficient resolution of trauma, there are also clear protocols for addressing attachment deficits and neglect in childhood which are often also a feature of a forensic client's history.

Because SP is less dependent on elaborate discourse and focused instead upon bodily experiences, SP may be more accessible to clients who might struggle to articulate their experiences but be able to describe what is happening in the 'here and now' within themselves. In addition, SP's ability to work towards reducing hyperarousal and hypoarousal could mean that clients that are experienced as particularly difficult to treat, including more psychopathic individuals, are not denied treatment opportunities.

SP is most effective when working with clients who are either able or willing to be curious about their bodily sensations and experiences even if they seem unable to engage in conversations about their actual life experiences. Conversely, there are clients who may, at least initially, appear a 'better therapeutic bet' as they engage more easily in cognitive discussions about their life experiences but struggle to feel safe enough to be curious about their bodily sensations. Paradoxically, some forms of mindfulness encourage distance from the body and facilitate avoidance of recognition of sensory stimuli and clients who are comfortable with this avoidance may be too resistant to engaging in sensorimotor psychotherapy. Ultimately, the degree to which the sensorimotor sphere can be focused upon within treatment will depend on the client's ability to be curious about their body. However, practise will improve the capacity to listen to bodily communications. In most cases, SP treatment is possible if adaptations are made to accommodate the individual needs of each client and if the therapist is sensitive to previous use of the body in situations of threat and to threaten (both psychological and physical). SP theory also offers a helpful framework for all staff to understand and intervene in client psychopathology and acting out behaviour when understood within the context of perceived threat.

Status of the evidence in forensic settings

Unfortunately, there is virtually no research evaluating the efficacy of this treatment approach with any population. However, anecdotal evidence suggests a profound effect upon even the most disturbed clients and, perhaps for this reason, SP is endorsed by eminent practitioners in trauma and personality disturbance such as Bessel van der Kolk, Kathy Steele, Onno van der Hart and Daniel Siegel.

Whilst SP itself has not been subject to rigorous research, the principles underlying SP are well researched and there is some evidence that interventions aimed at sensory integration can be effective in treating traumatised individuals above and beyond their therapy as usual. Kaiser & Gillette (2010) found significant improvements following the use of Sensory Learning Program; Lazar et al.'s (2005) brain imagery study of those who meditate indicates learning to notice one's internal experience can enable individuals to cope more effectively with affect, and van der Kolk et al.'s (2014) research into yoga as an intervention for women who had treatment-resistant PTSD indicates that this intervention significantly reduced PTSD symptomatology with effect sizes comparable to well-researched psychotherapeutic and psychopharmacologic approaches. As discussed below, conducting systematic evaluation is a natural next step in the evolution of this approach.

Case study

Niall is serving a life sentence for several rapes and sexual assaults of women. Each woman was raped in her own home after Niall had established an initial social interaction and exchanged telephone numbers after meeting in a public place. Niall experienced each woman as 'flirtatious' but he wasn't in a sexual relationship with any of them. Sex was a pervasive theme in Niall's life. He was sexually abused (aged ten) and was also expected to have sex with the 'girlfriends' of older men who had 'befriended' him. He fathered his first child at fourteen and had worked as a 'pimp' (after being encouraged into this by his older cousin). He was extremely promiscuous before his imprisonment in his late twenties. His first act of rape (unconvicted) occurred under pressure from his older associates for their 'entertainment'. Niall has also used violence extensively against men he felt had disrespected him but these incidents had not been reported to the police. Niall had previously had several relationships with staff members and was routinely experienced as flirtatious in his interactions with staff. He identified himself as 'addicted' to sex.

Niall lived with his mother and father in one room of a large house inhabited by several members of the extended family. Niall's father was often away at sea. Niall's father used extreme violence to discipline him for perceived misdemeanours and would expect Niall to choose the implement to be used for punishment and then await punishment whilst he had a meal. Niall's mother worked long hours and was rarely available. She was harsh in her interactions with Niall and also used physical chastisement although this was rarely as extreme as her husband's. All three family members shared the same bed and Niall was often present when his parents had sex although would pretend to be asleep. At times, the sex was coercive. Niall also witnessed his father's violence towards his mother and perceived that all the men in the household were frightened of his father. Niall had previously completed a standard sex offender group treatment programme; bright and articulate, the facilitators concluded that whilst he had participated fully, he remained a risk because he had only been able to engage at a cognitive level and there were concerns that an intellectual understanding of his offending wouldn't prevent recidivism.

Initial sessions focused on familiarising Niall with sensorimotor theory and encouraging him to connect with his bodily sensations and experience and notice the sense of his body when feeling stable and competent. Niall was already practicing meditation and yoga so was familiar with the notion of studying his experience and managed this very easily. Because Niall was poorly equipped to maintain his own boundaries and regularly over-rode the boundaries of others, we studied the experience of being in physical proximity to one another. This exercise involves standing far apart initially, noticing inner experience and then gradually reducing the distance and eventually settling on the one that has optimum comfort for the client. I instructed Niall that he was to stand stationary, beckon me to move closer until there was a discernible reaction, pause, study and repeat, until he experienced me as being uncomfortably close. Niall was extremely anxious during this exercise and was visibly perspiring at the thought of reducing the distance although we had been working together and sitting much closer for 18 months. He was apparently unable to assert any control over my proximity as he was dysregulated to the point that he couldn't identify any changes in his inner state, nor was he able to instruct me to move or halt. As a result, I moved closer in increments which we studied each time in order that we might notice the impact. Of most interest, when I was one footstep away from him, much closer than ordinary personal space would allow and despite his huge discomfort with the whole exercise, Niall flirtatiously quipped that he was going to be disappointed that I wouldn't get closer. Flirtatious behaviour had never previously materialised in our sessions. It was important to study its emergence at this point and led to Niall becoming more aware of how he used sex to regulate his emotions when he felt frightened. This also led to further exercises studying his difficulties in recognising and upholding his own boundaries. Exploring the inefficacy of his own boundaries enabled Niall to realise the importance of strengthening these which impacted upon his ability to recognise those of others and his attitude towards them.

When the exercise was reversed and Niall approached me, he was unable to heed my initial cues to approach/halt (which led to further study and experiments regarding the boundaries of others). Responding to my firm requests to halt raised his awareness of his hypersensitivity to rejection which led to much greater understanding of his offending cycle and the appreciation that rejection has a major influence over his offending. This was something he had previously found difficult to acknowledge.

Subsequent work focused upon studying Niall's use of sex in response to threat. Studying his body when he was feeling sad and trying not to cry had already made him aware that sex was an important regulatory mechanism for other forms of distress. He experienced erections and intrusive thoughts of sex in sessions when feeling overwhelmed by sadness and loneliness. He identified that when his parents had consensual sex in bed, he had felt relieved that there was no physical threat. Over time, mindful study of sadness led to him being able to experience sadness in the absence of an erection. Niall associated crying with shame ('being a wanker') and when feeling sad would often hang his head in shame as he fought back tears. When working with a non-offender, supporting the client's head's weight at the neck and taking over that role for the body may have been experienced as supportive and freed the body's resources up to deal with other aspects of the sadness. In place of this, I suggested that Niall rested his head on the back of his chair instead. Tears streamed down his face as he no longer expended his energy on coping with the body's need to hide in shame.

Niall recognised there was a part of him that craved acceptance. His use of flirting was initially an attempt to belong and avoid rejection by making women like him (*attach*). He identified that he often found himself in situations where he felt he had to engage in sex (*submit*) to avoid emotional rejection or threat (if he hadn't 'delivered sex' following flirtatious interactions with women including staff, he anticipated a punitive, rejecting response). Additionally, having sexual relationships with female staff enabled him to *avoid* feeling vulnerable within these relationships as he undermined the power the women had over him. Niall also became aware of the significance that rejection played in his sexual offending. He felt humiliated and rejected when women he had been flirting with did not actually want to have sex with him and then used sex as an attack on the source of his shame (*fight*). He also used sex to distract (*mental flight*) and self-soothe when he was distressed via flirting, masturbation or consensual sex. Studying his relationships with women and, in particular, interactions which were flirtatious, in contrast to those that weren't, enabled him to have a much better understanding of his feelings in relation to women. When he allowed himself to engage with his vulnerability, Niall was quite shocked to realise how frequently he felt rejected. He also discovered that, for him, flirting wasn't a harmless behaviour as it has the potential to trigger him into his offending cycle. Subsequently, there was an improvement in his relationship with women as his relationships became less flirtatious which was in turn reinforcing.

Key directions for future research

SP as a therapy lacks an established evidence base to support its efficacy as a treatment. Whilst there is solid neuropsychological evidence to support the theory behind the intervention, and anecdotal evidence that the therapy has a profound effect on clients, this model would really benefit from being rigorously tested as a treatment. This may be particularly so with more disturbed individuals where there are signs it could be a promising intervention. Absence of any research base undermines its utility, particularly in areas and countries which only support or fund treatments with demonstrated effects. However, in forensic settings, evidence is often limited, therefore embedding outcome evaluation into practice may mitigate this to some extent.

Some of the difficulties in establishing an evidence base probably arise from the smaller number of therapists trained in what is a relatively young approach. The rising acceptability of single case studies (Davies, Howells, & Jones, 2007; Barkham, Hardy, & Mellor-Clark, 2010) could be utilised to provide a foundation to demonstrate the efficacy of this treatment. SP includes an emphasis upon distinct phases of treatment, particular stages and identifiable cycles of intervention which afford a degree of assurance of treatment fidelity and could thus lend itself to evaluation more easily than some approaches.

Establishing an evidence base for SP as an intervention would enable exploration of which kinds of client might stand to make most gains and which might be more appropriately offered another kind of treatment. It would also allow for analysis of whether interventions aimed at trauma and those aimed at attachment deficit are equally as effective. Analysis of these different strands of treatment might also contribute something to an understanding of the role that these differing aetiological factors may play in the development of offending. Evaluation of other components of treatment such as relational mindfulness and experiments may also be of interest.

SP theory dictates that greatest gains should be in the alleviation of PTSD symptomatology and the ability to tolerate negative emotion without becoming hyperaroused or hypoaroused. Using measures of physiological arousal in session or coding the client's account of their physiological state could enable the identification of improvement in emotional regulation during session as well as overall improvement in this domain. Within session coding of tracking might enable client self-report to be more accurate than it sometimes is. Client evaluation of anxiety in relation to others may also prove interesting, as might the impact of SP treatment on physical health complaints. However, the relatively simple questions of whether using SP principles enables clients to stay in therapy or reduces treatment duration would make a great starting point.

Forensic services represent a good starting point for evaluation of treatment since these services are full of 'hard to treat' service users who find it difficult to access or maintain commitment to treatment. Such individuals often have a narrow window of tolerance and thus find themselves excluded or ejected from treatment. SP offers an opportunity to enable these clients to stay in therapy and experience some alleviation from their distress and, as such, it seems important that SP potential is fully explored and evaluated.

Notes

1 Rolfing, also known as structural integration, is a technique of deep tissue manipulation aimed at the release and realignment of the body and the reduction of muscular and psychic tension.
2 The Hakomi method is a form of mindfulness-centred somatic psychotherapy developed by Ron Kurtz in the 1970s.
3 Sensorimotor Psychotherapy® Institute – 805 Burbank St, Broomfield, CO80020.

Further reading

Ogden, P., & Fisher, J. (2015). *Sensorimotor psychotherapy: Interventions for trauma and attachment*. New York: Norton.
Ogden, P., Minton, K., & Pain, C. (2006). *Trauma and the Body: A sensorimotor approach to psychotherapy*. New York: Norton.
Rothschild, B. (2000). *The Body Remembers: The psychophysiology of trauma and trauma treatment*. New York: Norton. www.sensorimotorpsychotherapy.org

References

Barkham, M., Hardy, G. E., & Mellor-Clark, J. (2010). *Developing and delivering practice-based evidence*. Wiley Online Library.
Clark, C. R., McFarlane, A. C., Morris, P., Weber, D. L., Sonkkilla, C., Shaw, M., Marcina, J., Tochon-Danguy, H. J., & Egan, G. F. (2003). Cerebral function in posttraumatic stress disorder during verbal working memory updating: a positron emission tomography study. *Biological Psychiatry, 53*, 474–481.
Damasio, A. (2000). *The feeling of what happens*. London: Vintage.
Davidson, R. J., Kabat-Zinn, J., Schumacher, J., Rosenkranz, M., Muller, D., Santorelli, S. F., et al. (2003). Alterations in brain and immune function produced by mindfulness meditations. *Psychosomatic Medicine, 65*, 564–570.
Davies, J., Howells, K., & Jones, L. (2007). Evaluating innovative treatments in forensic mental health: A role for single case methodology? *Journal of Forensic Psychiatry & Psychology, 18*(3), 353–367. doi: 10.1080/14789940701443173
Diamond, L. M., Fagundes, C. P., & Butterworth, M. R. (2012). Attachment style, vagal tone, and empathy during mother–adolescent interactions. *Journal of Research on Adolescence, 22*(1), 165–184.

Feitis, R. (1978). *Ida Rolf talks about Rolfing and physical reality.* New York: Harper & Row.
Fischer, J. (2009). *Sensorimotor Approaches to Trauma Treatment,* www.janinafisher.com/pdfs/trauma.pdf. Retrieved from URL on 16 August, 2016.
Hull, A. M. (2002). Neuroimaging findings in post-traumatic stress disorder. *The British Journal of Psychiatry, 181*(2), 102–110.
Kaiser, E. & Gillette, C. (2010). A controlled pilot-outcome study of sensory integration in the treatment of complex adaptation to traumatic stress. *Journal of Aggression, Maltreatment & Trauma, 19,* 699–720.
Kurtz, R. (1990). *Body centred psychotherapy: The Hakomi method.* Mendocino, CA: Life Rythmn.
Lanius, R. A., Williamson, P. C., Bluhm, R. L., Densmore, M., Boksman, K., Neufeld, R. W., Gati, J. S., & Menon, R. S. (2001). Functional connectivity of dissociative responses in posttraumatic stress disorder: A functional magnetic resonance imaging investigation. *American Journal of Psychiatry, 158,* 1920–1922.
Lazar, S., Kerr, C., Wasserman, R., Gray, J., Greve, D., Treadway, M., McGarvey, M., Quinn, B. Dusek, J, Benson, H., Raucha, S., Moore, C., & Fischl, B. (2005). Meditation experience is associated with increased cortical thickness. *Neuroreport, 16,* 1893–1897.
Levine, P. (2010). *In an Unspoken Voice: How the Body Releases Trauma and Restores.* Berkeley, CA: North Atlantic Books.
Lindauer, R. J. L., Booij, J., Habraken, J. B. A., Uylings, H. B. M., Olff, M., Carlier, I.V. E., Den Heeten, G., Van Eck-Smit, B. L. F., & Gersons, B. P. R. (2004). Cerebral blood flow changes during script-driven imagery in police officers with post-traumatic stress disorder. *Biological Psychiatry, 56,* 1920–22.
Ogden, P. (2009). Modulation, mindfulness, and movement in the treatment of trauma. In Kerman, M. (Ed.), *Clinical pearls of wisdom: 21 leading therapists offer their key insights* (pp. 1–13). London: WW Norton & Company.
Panksepp, J. (1998). *Affective neuroscience: The foundations of human and animal emotions.* New York: Oxford University Press.
Panksepp, J., & Biven L. (2012). *The archaeology of mind: Neuroevolutionary origins of human emotions.* New York: Norton.
Porges, S. (2011). *The Polyvagal Theory: Neurobiological foundations of emotions, attachment, communication and self-regulation.* New York: Norton.
Rauch, S. L., van der Kolk, B. A., Fisler, R. E., Alpert, N. M., Orr, S. P., Savage, C. R., Fischman, A. J., Jenike, M. A., & Pitman, R. K. (2005). A symptom provocation study of posttraumatic stress disorder using positron emission tomography and script-driven imagery. *Biological Psychiatry, 57*(8), 873–84.
Rothschild, B. (2000). *The body remembers: The psychophysiology of trauma and trauma treatment.* New York: Norton. www.sensorimotorpsychotherapy.org
Schore, A. (2003). *Affect dysregulation and disorders of the self.* New York: Norton.
Siegel, D. (2010). *The mindful therapist: The clinicians guide to mindfulness and neural integration.* New York: Norton.
Van der Hart, O., Nijenhuis, E. R. S., & Steele, K. (2006). *The Haunted Self.* New York: Norton.
Van der Kolk, B. (2006). Clinical implications of neuroscience research in PTSD. *Annals of New York Academy of Science, 1071,* 277–93.
Van der Kolk, B., Stone, L., West, J., Rhodes, A., Emerson, D., Suvak, M., & Spinazzola, J. (2014). Yoga as an adjunctive treatment for posttraumatic stress disorder: A randomized controlled trail. *Journal of Clinical Psychiatry, 75*(6), e559–e565.
Vasterling, J. J., Brailey, K., Constans, J. I., Sutker, P. B. (1998). Attention and memory dysfunction in posttraumatic stress disorder. *Neuropsychology, 12,* 21–133.
Wylie, M. S. (n.d.). The limits of talk: Bessel van der Kolk wants to transform the treatment of trauma at www.traumacenter.org/products/pdf_files/networker.pdf, accessed 26 May, 2016.

# PART II
Key issues associated with individual therapies

12
INDIVIDUAL PSYCHOLOGICAL THERAPY WITH ASSOCIATED GROUPWORK

Claire Nagi and Jason Davies

Within the field of offender rehabilitation, interventions have traditionally been based on manualised, groupwork treatment which adhere to the 'what works' literature (Aos, Miller, & Drake, 2006; McGuire, 1995). The Risk Need Responsivity (RNR, Bonta & Andrews, 2017) model purports that treatment which is matched to the offender's level of 'risk', focused on offence specific 'needs' whilst addressing 'responsivity' issues, are most effective at reducing reoffending behaviour. Indeed research has shown that Offender Behaviour Programmes (OBP), which promote the RNR principles, can reduce recidivism by up to 35 per cent (Bonta & Andrews, 2017). One of the main criticisms of group-based offender treatment programmes has been that that they neglect the individual (Hollin, 2002; Wilson, 1996). There is also an argument that they are limited to providing general interventions only, and cannot replace the need for (individual) therapeutic input (Day, Kozar, & Davey, 2013). As we have seen in the chapters of this book, there is evidence to support the use of individual therapy in a variety of forensic settings. Further, there may be instances where individual therapy is the modality of choice (see Davies, in press). Each modality is typically selected for a number of specific reasons, and some services and settings show a preference for one modality over the other. However, in this chapter we will explore the growing use of combining modalities when providing treatment.

The debate regarding the modality of offender treatment delivery is not new and has been considered previously (e.g. Hollin & Palmer, 2006). Traditionally, group and individual modalities have been seen as two distinct choices. This has been reflected in the literature which has tended to focus on comparing individual and group treatment delivery rather than their potential use together. For example, a recent review found comparable outcomes for group-based and individual treatment in forensic settings (O'Brien, Sullivan, & Daffern, 2016). This conclusion echoes a widely reported idea that group and individual modalities are '*at least equivalent*', are both better than no treatment at all and could be complementary to each other (Davies, in press). Whilst it is acknowledged that each treatment modality has its own advantages and disadvantages, the benefits of combining modalities (i.e. individual *and* group work) is being recognised. This represents a third option for treatment delivery within forensic settings. Although there are instances of individual work being added to groupwork to address specific needs, there are some examples whereby the intervention has been developed using a combined therapy structure. These include a treatment programme for anger (Jones & Hollin, 2004) and an intervention to develop/enhance cognitive skills (Rees-Jones, Gudjonsson, & Young, 2012). This chapter will explore the functions of each therapy modality, examine the evidence of a combined treatment approach and explore the impact on clinical outcomes within a forensic setting.

What could a combined treatment modality offer?

There are a number of core features and functions of individual and group-based treatment intervention. These can be broadly grouped into two areas, namely: clinical and practical/service (see Table 12.1: Key Functions of Offender Interventions). It can be argued that individual and group modalities address either different clinical issues or similar issues in different ways. In addition, group and individual treatment approaches raise different practical and service benefits and challenges. Together, these open the possibility that the selective use of individual and group treatment, either sequentially or in combination, could be beneficial.

A combined treatment model can offer a number of benefits, not only for the individual but also from a service perspective. In this section we will consider the information contained in Table 12.1 in more detail. Alongside the strengths and reasons for each modality being employed, dilemmas and difficulties posed due to competing demands and interests will also be outlined and discussed.

Clinical

Using a combined approach to offender intervention enables a task separation into group and individually based aspects of treatment. For example, the individual component can allow for a personalised approach to treatment (Maletzky, 1999), that aims to address specific criminogenic and responsivity factors unique to each offender, taking into account features such as learning style, personality difficulties and literacy (Hollin & Palmer, 2006). Individual sessions would thus be driven by a bespoke, individualised forensic case formulation (see Sturmey & McMurran, 2011). As with general case conceptualisation (see below), this should: 1) *provide problem definition*; 2) *contain sufficient information for explanatory breadth*; and 3) *enable the establishment of outcome goals* (Hart, Sturmey, Logan, & McMurran, 2011). An individualised case formulation can also consider Offence Paralleling Behaviours

TABLE 12.1 Key functions of offender interventions

Core Area	Core Functions	Group	Individual
Clinical	Assessment	• Pre-treatment • Standard battery of assessment (including psychometric assessment) based on common risk and need	• Pre-treatment and continuous re-evaluation during treatment • Individualised assessment (often including psychometric assessment) based on presenting risk and need
	Formulation	• Use of common factors case conceptualisation (limited or no individual formulation)	• Idiographic case formulation (Sturmey & McMurran, 2011), detailing risky/offending behaviours and offence paralleling behaviours (Hart et al., 2011/2013; Daffern et al., 2010)
	Goal	• Address typical criminogenic needs and responsivity factors associated with risk or need	• Idiosyncratic/personalised approach (Maletzky, 1999) to address specific criminogenic needs and responsivity factors unique to each offender, including learning style and literacy (Hollin & Palmer, 2006)
	Content	• Typically psychoeducational (Day et al., 2013) • Manual based • Low levels of flexibility (Gannon & Ward, 2014) and personalisation	• Psychotherapeutic (Day et al., 2013) • Tailored interventions • Higher levels of flexibility (Gannon, 2015; Mann & Fernandez, 2006) • High levels of personal attention • Case-specific offence analysis (O'Brien et al., 2016) and risk/offence cycle (Mann & Fernandez, 2006) • Focus on additional factors such as mental health (Abracen & Looman, 2016)
	Engagement and Motivation	• Group-based preparatory work for later group-based interventions	• Individual-based preparatory work for later group or individual intervention • Client likely to engage poorly with group programmes (Di Fazio, Abracen, & Looman, 2001)
	Process	• Group-group member alliance (i.e. other and self focus) • Promotes group cohesiveness and expressiveness (Beech & Hamilton-Giachritsis, 2005) • Peers as a method of treatment, e.g. peers challenging each other (Hollin & Palmer, 2006) • Supportive, e.g. sharing problems with others/peers (Abracen & Looman, 2016) • Explore interpersonal skills/deficits, develop new conflict resolution and communication skills (Ware et al., 2009)	• Individual-therapist alliance (i.e. self/self-therapist focus only) • Attends to interpersonal issues and/or therapy ruptures (Wilson & Tamatea, 2013)

TABLE 12.1 (cont.)

Core Area	Core Functions	Group	Individual
	Confidentiality	• Lower levels – shared with group	• Higher levels – shared with therapist (Gannon, 2015)
	Sequence	• May be used at any point (including alongside individual treatment) if client willing/motivated to engage in group-work	• May be used at any point (including alongside group treatment) • May be used to facilitate engagement in group-based intervention
	Client suitability	• Low to moderate risk and need offenders • In conjunction with individual therapy – high-risk, high-need offenders (O'Brien et al., 2016)	• In conjunction with group therapy – high-risk, high-need offenders • Individuals with significant responsivity characteristics (O'Brien et al., 2016) • Client unwilling to attend groups due to preference • Client has specific impairments or inability to cope in a group setting (Ware et al., 2009)
	Physical/ resource requirements	• Need appropriate rooms able to cater for group (including space for 'small group' work) • Rooms need to be easily accessed by all participants • Multiple staff needed for each session • Multiple clients needed for each session	• Room required for each treatment di-ad • Practical solution when too few clients for groupwork (Gannon, 2015) • One therapist – one client for each session
Practical and Service	Staff requirements	• Multiple staff trained in specific treatment being facilitated • Group-based supervision by trained supervisor	• Therapy-trained staff • Usually individual supervision by a trained supervisor
	Therapist skills and training	• Trained for use in treatment approach – often a specific single manualised approach such as SOTEP • Trained in group process	• Trained in individual therapy – typically extensive and requiring additional professional registration (see chapters throughout this book)
	Therapist supervision	• Supervisor trained in the groupwork treatment • Supervisor may be trained in supervision skills	• Supervisor usually a qualified therapist • Supervisor has additional general or 'therapy model-specific' supervision training
	Evaluation	• Group-based design/controlled trial	• Single case design/case study (e.g. Davies & Sheldon, 2012)

(OPB; Daffern, Jones, & Shine, 2007; Kadra, Daffern, & Campbell, 2014), which may show themselves in a range of ways within a forensic context. For example, physical violence that serves the function of maintaining the individual's status may be enacted through boundary pushing, verbal abuse and/or argumentative behaviours in a restricted setting. Alongside this idiographic focus, group treatment based on a general case conceptualisation, will provide a focus on those risk and needs factors shown in the evidence to be associated with the problem being addressed (e.g. offending behaviour). The group format allows the psychoeducational elements (e.g. skills development) to be delivered in a consistent way (treatment integrity). Used together, individual and group approaches can provide assessment, psychotherapeutic intervention, psychoeducation, skills development and outcome evaluation. Both individual and group interventions can be guided by a range of forensic frameworks including RNR (Andrews & Bonta, 2010), Good Lives (Ward & Maruna, 2007) and the protective factors associated with risk management (e.g. internal and motivational factors such as those identified through the *Structured Assessment of PROtective Factors for violence risk* – SAPROF; De Vogel, de Ruiter, Bouman, & de Vries Robbé, 2007).

An important yet easily overlooked function of individual treatment alongside group intervention is to allow offenders to 'catch up' on missed groupwork. It can also be used to ensure understanding and to minimise confusion or inappropriate inference being drawn from group material. Additionally, individual sessions can assist with troubleshooting issues or problems that arise in the group setting. Specifically, therapy time can be used to provide a more detailed focus on group process issues, such as interpersonal difficulties (e.g. disruptive behaviour or conflict with other group members) and/or potential or actual therapy ruptures (Wilson & Tamatea, 2013). Attention can also be given to 'therapy interfering behaviours' such as dominating group discussions or collusion with others' problematic thinking or behaviour. Individual sessions can be used to address motivational impediments for treatment by anticipating or resolving threats to engagement (Jones & Hollin, 2004). Further, some authors argue that a combination of individual and group work can actually promote treatment engagement and minimise programme drop-out (Hollin & Palmer, 2006), a factor known to be associated with higher levels of recidivism (McMurran & Theodosi, 2007; Olver, Stockdale, & Wormith, 2011). The use of individual therapy in these ways could help offenders to attend group sessions and thus increase the likelihood of treatment completion. They can also provide clients with the opportunity to explore concerns that require clinical attention which may be missed in a group setting (Murphy & Meis, 2008). This can ensure that key idiosyncratic risk or need factors are not overlooked or omitted. Although individual sessions may be collaborative or therapist led, they can be delivered in a more flexible and responsive way than comparable manualised group-based treatment (Gannon, 2015; Mann & Fernandez, 2006). Therefore, individual therapy, when used as part of a combined modality treatment, can have multiple functions: 1) *clarify and consolidate the content of group therapy sessions* (Wilson & Tamatea, 2013); 2) *provide assistance with homework completion and skills generalisation/*

coaching (Rees-Jones, Gudjonsson & Young, 2012); 3) *enable further detailed assessment* (i.e. case-specific offence analysis or risk/offence cycle) (O'Brien et al., 2016; Mann & Fernandez, 2006); and 4) *focus on additional factors (i.e. mental health)* (Abracen & Looman, 2016). Individual treatment can also provide a more confidential forum where highly unusual or specific aspects of the treatment target (e.g. offence, mental health problem) can be addressed (Gannon, 2015).

In combined treatment, the groupwork component, as well as providing a forum for psychoeducation, can provide a range of specific therapeutic benefits. For example, the therapeutic group process (interpersonal dynamics) has been highlighted as an essential feature to effective treatment, and is distinct from that achieved in individual treatment (Yalom, 1995). However, the functionality of the group in terms of the intergroup therapeutic alliance (which is associated with change; Ross, Polaschek, & Ward, 2008) is likely to be influenced by therapist characteristics (Marshall, Fernandez, & Serran, 2003; Marshall & Burton, 2010). Peers can be a primary method of treatment through: feedback mechanisms, i.e. peers challenging each other; peers providing new perspectives or alternative interpretations; opportunities for vicarious learning, i.e. learning knowledge and skills by observing others (Ware, Mann, & Wakeling, 2009); and peer support, i.e. sharing problems with others/peers (Abracen & Looman, 2016; Hollin & Palmer, 2006; Mann & Fernandez, 2006). In a group format, individuals have the opportunity to recognise and develop interpersonal strengths and deficits, including conflict resolution and communication skills (Ware et al., 2009). Together, these features can promote group cohesiveness and expressiveness which has been linked to positive outcomes within offender populations (Beech & Hamilton-Giachritsis, 2005; Beech & Fordham, 1997). As a result, group facilitators need to attend to the process of learning (i.e. 'deep learning') and delivering the programme manual (Day et al., 2013) as well as to the group process itself. However, whilst a combined treatment modality allows treatment providers to draw on the benefits of group and individual treatment there are practical and service factors, which also need to be considered.

Practical and service

Providing individual and/or group treatment requires differing resources and practical considerations, which could result in one or other modality being difficult to provide. Physical and organisational issues include the physical environment (e.g. availability of appropriately equipped and sized rooms), procedural factors (e.g. the ability to move participants and/or place them in the same room) and individual restrictions (e.g. an individual currently placed on a segregation or management unit) (O'Brien et al., 2016). Delivering a combined model will undoubtedly impact on service resource due to extra requirements such as the different room requirements for each modality and possible differences in staff training, and perhaps their supervision.

Financial reasons are often used as a rationale for choosing a particular type of intervention and/or therapy modality. Although the financial implications of providing treatment in a combined way have not been reported, individual therapy is considered to be more cost intensive when compared with groupwork (Hollin & Palmer, 2006). However, if forensic services want to maximise treatment impact/success, the cost of increased therapy input may be offset if combined modality treatment results in fewer people dropping out or better outcomes being achieved. In order to fully consider cost effectiveness, factors such as the resource implications for delivery; short- and long-term outcomes; the impact on overall treatment programme length; and the effect on attendance and 'cancelled time' need to be detailed. However, within the research, there has been no agreed set criterion for calculating treatment cost effectiveness. Rather, different and varied approaches have been implemented making any cost comparison between treatments and modalities difficult. Davies (in press) argues that producing a cost effectiveness calculation will comprise of a two-step process: 1) data collection around the clinical impact of each treatment – the overall effect of the treatment; the equivalence of/degree to which one modality outperforms the other; and any differences between who enters one treatment modality or the other; and 2) developing a standardised approach/metric, such as a 'cost per unit gain', when reporting the economics of an intervention. For offending risk, this will include the costs of the resources for delivery, staff training and staff supervision and the costs (economic and emotional) of future offences along with the 'savings' made if harms are reduced or removed. Cost effectiveness research within the forensic field is required if we are able to accurately determine the cost effectiveness of each modality and combined intervention, either generally or for specific client groups. In the meantime, practitioners and researchers should routinely provide information on the known costs in order to begin this process of economic modelling (see Davies, 2015; Nagi, Davies, & Shine, 2014, for examples of how basic information can be reported).

Although there are likely to be many ways to combine modalities, published examples typically involve employing highly skilled staff to provide the individual therapy. These staff may not be certified in a specific therapy approach (see other chapters in this book for examples of therapist training); however, they are likely to be highly trained in general therapy skills (see Chapter 15). Therefore, as with treatment involving only an individual approach, the individual component of combined therapy is likely to be undertaken by a qualified therapist, who has received lengthy therapy training, has current professional registration and engages in regular therapy model-specific supervision. In comparison, group interventions in forensic settings are often manualised and delivered by a broad range of persons trained in the specifics of that group programme. However, even in manualised group treatment, greater treatment effects are likely to be obtained when treatment staff have specialist skills (including staff ability to develop rapport with clients and use skilled communication), ability and knowledge (Dowden & Andrews, 2004). Indeed, there is a distinction between 'basic' (i.e. Socratic questioning; use of behavioural techniques; generalisation of alternative thinking) and 'advanced' (i.e. personal resilience; instilling hope; use of positive language; interpersonal skills; expert therapy skill) therapist competencies within forensic settings (Mann & Fernandez, 2006). All staff, delivering through both modalities will require supervision, to support treatment delivery, staff functioning and boundary maintenance (Davies, 2015). This will require the supervisor to have a breadth of skill in relation to core therapeutic skills, individual and group treatment, the specific intervention being offered and the forensic context in which the treatment is being delivered (see Davies, 2015; Davies & Nagi, this volume, Chapter 14).

Compulsory treatment and treatment motivation

Within forensic settings, treatment is usually compulsory, regardless of whether or not the individual is motivated to change. The issue around compulsory versus voluntary offender treatment raises its own dilemmas in respect of motivation and behaviour change (see McMurran, 2002a, for a comprehensive review). Despite compulsory treatment, offenders will have a choice – they can choose to comply or not with the legal system requirements or treatment goals (Viets, Walker, & Miller, 2002). To some degree this will be influenced by the different motivational factors for offender treatment that have been identified in the literature. These can be broadly grouped into 1) *internal* i.e. achievement of valued goal; avoidance or escape from aversive emotions, and 2) *external* i.e. gaining social acceptance; avoidance of sanctions and disapproval (McMurran, 2002b). In respect of treatment modality then, there may be differences between those offenders showing a preference or 'choosing' to enter treatment and whether or not they have a preference for one modality or another. This 'modality preference' might also be influenced by the differing interpersonal components of individual and group treatment. For example, group settings can help tackle the secrecy associated with offending (Ware et al., 2009). An individual may therefore wish to attend individual sessions as a way of avoiding this experience of 'exposure'. Conversely, individual sessions can place a focus on predicting, managing and resolving therapy ruptures. Consequently, an individual may want to be 'out of the spotlight' and prefer the self-other focus that a group format will provide. Each of these forms of avoidance can detract from the treatment goal and lead to a lack of behaviour change. Arguably, a combined intervention model may help overcome some of these motivational barriers for offender treatment.

Status of the evidence in forensic settings

There are currently few offender interventions which incorporate a combined treatment framework, although there does seem to have been a move in this direction over recent years. The UK Sex Offender Treatment Programme has changed over time, increasing the number and format of treatment programmes available, some of which include a combined therapy modality (e.g. Mann & Thornton, 1998). There are also a number of interventions that have been developed using a combined modality approach. These include Dialectical Behaviour Therapy (DBT, Linehan, 1993) and Chromis (Tew & Atkinson, 2013).

Within a forensic inpatient setting, Jones & Hollin (2004) conducted a preliminary evaluation of an anger management programme developed for violent mentally disordered offenders (MDOs) detained within a UK high security setting. The authors concluded that the individual focus within the combined treatment programme led to high levels of attendance and homework compliance, with no drop-outs reported. Rees-Jones, Gudjonsson, & Young (2012) described the utility of an adapted Reasoning and Rehabilitation programme for adult male mentally disordered offenders (R&R2 MHP; Young & Ross, 2007) within UK-based medium and low secure mental health settings. The R&R2 MHP programme provided group treatment coupled with guided individual mentoring. The results indicated a high retention/completion rate (78 per cent). Yip et al. (2013) conducted a further study of the R&R2 MHP programme using a non-randomised controlled trial in a UK high secure unit for adult male offenders. The results indicated a high completion rate (80 per cent). Additionally, in contrast to the control group, significant (medium–large) treatment effects were found on self-reported measures (i.e. violent attitudes, social problem-solving and coping processes) and for staff-rated behaviours on the ward. One of the variables the authors attributed to these findings related to the individual mentoring sessions, particularly in limiting treatment drop-out. Nagi et al. (2014) described the utility of the General Treatment and Recovery Programme (GTRP) within a UK low secure setting. The results indicated a high attendance rate for group sessions (over 80 per cent), with no treatment drop-outs, and that those with low self-reported knowledge at the start of the programme showed large improvements in terms of knowledge acquisition post-treatment. However, attendance at individual sessions was considerably lower, with more than a third of the available sessions not attended. Overall, these findings suggest that programmes can feasibly be delivered but that participants may need additional support. However, none of the studies outlined above used recidivism as an outcome measure.

Within a forensic community setting, Di Fazio, Abracen, & Looman (2001) found no significant differences between treatment modality efficacy when using the Regional Treatment Centre Ontario Sex Offender Program. They compared the full treatment programme (i.e. groupwork plus individual therapy) and individual therapy alone on reducing rates of sexual recidivism in a high-risk/high-need sexual offender sample. Despite the findings, the authors concluded that high-risk offender groups with additional needs (i.e. serious mental illness or cognitive impairment) may be better served by individual therapy, whereas those without should complete the full treatment programme. This finding has been replicated with mentally disordered offenders supervised in the community (Looman, Abracen, & Di Fazio, 2014; Abracen, Gallo, Looman, & Goodwill, 2015). Consequently, the authors concluded that individual treatment is more cost effective than group treatment for high-risk, high-need sexual offenders presenting with serious mental illness and that such a model could be applied to non-sexual violent offenders.

Willis, Ward, & Levenson (2014) reported the findings of a multi-site study, which explored how the Good Lives Model (GLM) had been operationalised in 13

North American Sex Offender Treatment Programmes including prison (six), community (five) and civil commitment centres (two). One of the key aspects of treatment evaluation was the development of individualised intervention plans within a structured treatment manual (Willis, Yates, Gannon, & Ward, 2012). However, they found only one programme used individualised treatment plans and that the degree to which treatment components were tailored to individual clients varied substantially. Notably, a lack of resource was identified as a barrier to adopting this combined treatment approach in practice (i.e. written treatment manuals and construction of extensive individual treatment plans).

O'Brien et al. (2016) conducted a review of outcomes of individual and group-based offender treatments in studies published between 1 January, 1990 and 31 August, 2014. They found limited high-quality studies using individual treatments (n = 13) and even fewer comparisons of individual versus group-based treatment (n = 2). The authors concluded that there were comparable outcomes for group and individual treatment, but noted that most studies reviewed utilised a combined treatment modality or incorporated individual sessions to augment group-based approaches for high-risk, high-need clients. As described later, they suggest using a combined approach with high-risk, high-need offenders.

Personality focused interventions

In addition to interventions focused on criminogenic issues, there have been a small number of combined therapy interventions delivered to address aspects of personality disorder within forensic settings. In these studies, the main treatment targets are personality difficulties, with risky/offending behaviour representing one component of intervention. Evershed et al. (2003) examined the effectiveness of an 18-month DBT-based treatment programme for adult male mentally disordered offenders, detained within a UK high secure setting. All patients met the criteria for borderline personality disorder (n=17). Eight patients received DBT whilst the comparison group (n=9) received Treatment As Usual (TUA). The results showed a decrease in frequency of violent-related behaviour for both groups, with no significant difference between groups in relation to this factor. However, the DBT programme group engaged in less serious incidents than the TUA group at each six monthly time point (i.e. pre-, mid- and post-treatment assessments), demonstrating a greater reduction in seriousness of violent-related behaviours (53 per cent vs. 22 per cent reduction). The DBT group showed improvements on self-reported measures of hostility, cognitive anger, disposition to anger, outward expression of anger and anger experience. Furthermore, there was a low attrition rate, with only one person leaving the DBT programme.

Low, Jones, Duggan, & Power (2001) evaluated a 12-month DBT programme for female mentally disordered offenders within a UK high security special hospital. The participants displayed self-harming behaviour and met criteria for borderline personality disorder (n= 10). Patients were assessed on self-harm frequency and psychological variables at four time points (pre-, during, post-therapy and six-month follow-up). The results indicated a significant reduction in deliberate self-harm (DSH) and positive change on all psychological variables assessed. The authors acknowledged the lack of control group but that the preliminary findings suggested that this combined modality treatment might be effective for severe self-harm in institutional settings. Promising findings were also reported in a pilot study in three UK female prison settings (Nee and Farman, 2005). Two standard one-year DBT treatment programmes, three short (16 week) format programmes and a waiting list control group were included in the study. Of the total sample (n=30), 16 completed the treatment programmes and five transferred or released, giving a voluntary attrition rate of 33 per cent. Of these, data was available for 14 treatment completers. Of the total waitinglist control group (n=8), five completed all measures. Results indicated statistically significant improvements in a number of areas as evidenced through psychometric test scores and behaviour. No significant overall change was reported in the control group (though improvements were seen). Case studies were also published in relation to both these studies (Low, Jones, Duggan, MacLeod, & Power, 2001; Nee & Farman, 2007).

A paper by Tew & Atkinson (2013) describes the development, design and implementation of the Chromis programme for psychopathic violent offenders. A systematic review of the 43 men who had participated in Chromis at that point was conducted. The findings indicated that all participants met the DSPD criteria, had time to complete the programme, presented with treatment needs in line with programme targets and evidenced psychopathic traits that would be likely to disrupt treatment engagement and capacity for change. Additionally, preliminary investigations of the Chromis database showed a completion rate of around 95 per cent for each Chromis component. A study by Tew, Dixon, Harkins, & Bennett (2012) examined case studies of Chromis completers. The results indicated a reduction in self-reported anger pre- and post-treatment, and in actual acts of physical and verbal aggression as individuals progressed through treatment. However, impact evaluation research on Chromis is still in progress.

In conclusion, there is some emerging evidence to support the use of combined modality treatment; however, this research is very limited and generally based on descriptive or small sample research.

Considerations and practice issues

Who, why and when?

Due to the limited research, it is difficult to develop robust guidance for best practice for a combined treatment modality within forensic settings. Research to date has distinguished the functions of each therapy modality; however, little is known about who might benefit most, the rationale for combined therapy and/ or at what point should this type of intervention be offered within an individual's treatment trajectory. However, there have been some recommendations made with respect to offender treatment more generally, which may serve as a useful starting point.

Polaschek (2013, 2011a) has argued that modality selection (group, individual or combined) should be guided by the individual's level of risk and need. Specifically, Polaschek (2011b) has proposed that offender programme theories be categorised into three levels: 1) *Basic Level* – for offenders with few treatment targets wherein a low intensity, highly manualised programme with a psychoeducation format and less therapy skill is required; 2) *Mid Level* – for offenders with a wider range of treatment needs but with some strengths wherein case-specific information informs intervention delivered by skilled therapists; or 3) *High Level* – for complex clients who are resistant to treatment. In this level, formulation drives intervention, which can be delivered by highly skilled facilitators using an individual, group or combined approach, with the programme embedded in a residential environment. More recently, O'Brien et al. (2016) have described a model for the trajectory of offender treatment, which integrates individual and group-based interventions, via three pathways: 1) *Pathway 1: Offence-specific Group Interventions*; 2) *Pathway 2: Responsivity Issues Identified*; and 3) *Alternative Pathways for Treatment*. In this framework, low to moderate risk and need offenders would follow Pathway 1 (i.e. group treatment only), high-risk, high-need offenders follow Pathway 2 (i.e. combined treatment), and those offenders with significant responsivity characteristics follow the Alternative Pathway (i.e. individual treatment only). Both frameworks propose that offenders presenting with a high level of responsivity issues would be better served by a combined therapy model and/or individual work, regardless of risk level, however, much more work is required to test and elucidate these frameworks. For example, research is essential in order to evaluate what works and for whom, since there might be specific groups where a combined model of treatment is best served. Studies will also need to examine the differences in who benefits when treatment is offered through a group, individual or combined format. In the absence of current research, a therapy modality selection guide (Davies, in press) could be adapted and used to guide modality choice.

Key directions for future research

To date, there is no high-quality research which examines the comparative treatment efficacy of individual, group and combined modalities within offender populations. Whilst it is entirely plausible that individual and group modalities might be complementary and suited to different aspects of offender need, research evidence is required. There are central questions that research must address around why we would choose one therapy modality over another. It is likely that any evaluation research will need to include both group-based and individual level study designs. Use of methods such as single case designs, along with practitioners routinely collecting group level outcome evidence, should be best practice (see Davies

& Sheldon, 2012). Davies (in press) also provides the following recommendations: 1) effect size should be reported when describing the degree of change observed to make it easy to compare and integrate information from studies; 2) researchers should adopt a common metric to enable the cost effectiveness of treatments to be compared; 3) researchers need to attend directly to the question of modality equivalence when designing treatment studies; and 4) implementing rigorous practice-based evidence approaches should be expected whenever treatment is delivered. Research will need to focus on whether a combined treatment model leads to more positive clinical outcomes, and whether this is a general finding or occurs for specific needs and/or under specific circumstances.

Conclusion

Evidence of therapy modality choice in forensic settings is limited and the question of whether a combined modality treatment approach should be favoured over group- and/or individual-based interventions remains unanswered. Until there is sufficient data, practitioners will need to determine for themselves which modality/ies to use. This may be guided by the information in this chapter or frameworks such as those of Polaschek. However, it is incumbent on all practitioners and researchers to develop the evidence base in this area. This will need to directly examine therapy modality equivalence, clinical outcomes and cost effectiveness to accurately inform future treatment delivery.

Further reading

Davies, J. (in press). An examination of individual versus group treatment in correctional settings. In Devon Polaschek, Andrew Day, & Clive Hollin (Eds), *Handbook of Psychology and Corrections*. Chichester: Wiley.

Hollin, C. R., & Palmer, E. J. (2006). Offending behaviour programmes: Controversies and resolutions. In C.R. Hollin & E.J. Palmer (Eds), *Offending Behaviour Programmes: Development, Application and Controversies* (pp. 247–278).

Polaschek, D. L. L. (2011b). Many sizes fit all: A preliminary framework for conceptualizing the development and provision of cognitive-behavioral rehabilitation programs for offenders. *Aggression and Violent Behaviour, 16*, 20–35. doi: 10.1016/jvab.2010.10.002

References

Abracen, J., & Looman, J. (2016). Social skills and individual therapy. In *Treatment of High-Risk Sexual Offenders* (pp. 126–153). Chichester: Wiley-Blackwell.

Abracen, J., Gallo, A., Looman, J., & Goodwill, A. (2015). Individual community-based treatment of offenders with mental illness: Relationship to recidivism. *Journal of Interpersonal Violence. 31*(10), 1842–1858. http://doi.org/10.1177/0886260515570745

Aos, S., Miller, M., & Drake, E. (2006). *Evidence-Based Adult Corrections Programs: What Works and What Does Not*. Olympia, WA: Washington State Institute for Public Policy.

Beech, A., & Fordham, A. S. (1997). Therapeutic climate of sexual offender treatment programs. *Sexual Abuse: A Journal of Research & Treatment, 9*, 219–237.

Beech, A. R., & Hamilton-Giachritsis, C. E. (2005). Relationship between therapeutic climate and treatment outcome in group-based sexual offender treatment programs. *Sexual Abuse: A Journal of Research and Treatment*, 17(2), 127140. doi: 10.1007/s11194-005-4600-3

Bonta, J., & Andrews, D. A. (2017). *The psychology of criminal conduct* (6th ed.). New York: Routledge.

Daffern, M., Jones, L., & Shine, J. (2007). *Offence paralleling behaviour: A case formulation approach to offender assessment and intervention.* Chichester: Wiley.

Davies, J. (2015). *Supervision for Forensic Practitioners.* London: Routledge.

Davies, J. (in press). An examination of individual versus group treatment in correctional settings. In Devon Polaschek, Andrew Day, & Clive Hollin (Eds), *Handbook of Psychology and Corrections.* Chichester: Wiley.

Davies, J., & Sheldon, K. (2012). Single case methodologies. In K. Sheldon, J. Davies, & K. Howells (Eds), *Research in Practice for Forensic Professionals.* London: Routledge.

Day, A., Kozar, C., & Davey, L. (2013). Treatment approaches and offending behavior programs: Some critical issues. *Aggression and Violent Behavior*, 18(6), 630–635. http://doi.org/10.1016/j.avb.2013.07.019

De Vogel, V., de Ruiter, C., Bouman, Y., & de Vries Robbé, M. (2007). *SAPROF manual. Structured assessment of protective factors for violence risk.* Version 1. Utrecht: Forum Educatief.

Di Fazio, R., Abracen, J., & Looman, J. (2001). Group versus individual treatment of sex offenders: A comparison. *Forum on Corrections Research*, 13(1), 56–59.

Dowden, C., & Andrews, D. A. (2004). The importance of staff practice in delivering effective correctional treatment: A meta-analytic review of core correctional practice. *International Journal of Offender Therapy and Comparative Criminology*, 48(2), 203–214. doi: 10.1177/0306624£03257765

Evershed, S., Tennant, A., Boomer, D., Rees, A., Barkham, M., & Watson, A. (2003). Practice-based outcomes of dialectical behaviour therapy (DBT) targeting anger and violence, with male forensic patients: A pragmatic and non-contemporaneous comparison. *Criminal Behaviour & Mental Health*, 13(3), 198–213.

Gannon, T., & Ward, T. (2014). Where has all the psychology gone? A critical review of evidence-based psychological practice in correctional settings. *Aggression and Violent Behavior*, 19, 435–436.

Gannon, T. A. (2015). Treatment of men who have sexually abused adults. In D. T. Wilcox, T. Garrett, & L. Harkins (Eds), *Sex offender treatment: A case study approach to issues and interventions* (pp. 85–104).

Hart, S., Sturmey, P., Logan, C., & McMurran, M. (2011). Forensic case formulation. *International Journal of Forensic Mental Health*, 10, 118–28.

Hollin, C. (2002). An overview of offender rehabilitation: Something old, something borrowed, something new. *Australian Psychologist*, 37(3), 159–164. doi: 10.1080/00050060210001706826

Hollin, C. R., & Palmer, E. J. (2006). Offending behaviour programmes: Controversies and resolutions. In C. R. Hollin & E. J. Palmer (Eds), *Offending Behaviour Programmes: Development, Application and Controversies* (pp. 247–278).

Jones, D., & Hollin, C. R. (2004). Managing problematic anger: The development of a treatment program for personality disordered patients in high security. *International Journal of Forensic Mental Health*, 3(2), 197–210. http://doi.org/10.1080/14999013.2004.10471207

Kadra, G., Daffern, M., & Campbell, C. (2014). Detecting offence paralleling behaviour in a medium secure psychiatric unit. *Legal & Criminological Psychology*, 19, 147–159.

Linehan, M. M. (1993). *Cognitive-behavioural treatment of borderline personality disorder.* New York: Guilford.

Looman, J., Abracen, J., & Di Fazio, R. (2014). Efficacy of group versus individual treatment of sexual offenders. *Sexual Abuse in Australia and New Zealand, 6*(1), 48–56.

Low, G., Jones, D., Duggan. C., & Power, M. (2001a). The treatment of deliberate self-harm in Borderline Personality Disorder using Dialectical Behaviour Therapy: A pilot study in a high security hospital. *Behavioural and Cognitive Psychotherapy, 29,* 85–92.

Low, G., Jones, D., Duggan, C., MacLeod, A., & Power, M. (2001b). Dialectical Behaviour Therapy as a treatment for deliberate self-harm: Case studies from a high security psychiatric hospital population. *Clinical Psychology and Psychotherapy, 8,* 288–300.

McGuire, J. (1995). *What works: Reducing reoffending: Guidelines from research and practice.* Chichester: Wiley.

McMurran, M. (2002a). *Motivating offenders to change: A guide to enhancing engagement in therapy.* Chichester: John Wiley & Sons.

McMurran, M. (2002b). Motivation to change: selection criterion or treatment need? In M. McMurran (Ed.), *Motivating offenders to change: A guide to enhancing engagement in therapy* (pp. 3–13). Chichester: John Wiley & Sons.

McMurran, M., & Theodosi, E. (2007). Is treatment non-completion associated with increased reconviction over no treatment? *Psychology, Crime & Law, 13*(4), 333–343.

Maletzky, B. M. (1999). Group of one. *Sexual Abuse: A Journal of Research and Treatment, 11*(3), 179–181. doi: 10.1177/107906329901100301

Mann, R. E., & Fernandez, Y. M. (2006). Sex offender programmes: Concept, theory and practice. *Offending Behaviour Programmes: Development, Application and Controversies,* 155–177.

Marshall, W. L., & Burton, D. L. (2010). The importance of group processes in offender treatment. *Aggression and Violent Behaviour, 15,* 141–149. doi: 10.1016/j.avb.2009.08.008

Marshall, W. L., Fernandez, Y. M., & Serran, G. A. (2003). Process variables in the treatment of sexual offenders: A review of the relevant literature. *Aggression and Violent Behavior, 8,* 205–234.

Nagi, C., Davies, J., & Shine, L. (2014). Group treatment in a male low secure mental health service: A treatment description and descriptive evaluation. *The Journal of Forensic Practice, 16*(2), 139–155. doi: 10.1108/JFP-01-2013-0006

Nee, C., & Farman, S. (2005). Female prisoners with borderline personality disorder: Some promising treatment developments. *Criminal Behaviour and Mental Health, 15*(1), 2–16. doi: 10.1002/cbm.33

Nee, C., & Farman, S. (2007). Dialectical behaviour therapy as a treatment for borderline personality disorder in prisons: Three illustrative case studies. *Journal of Forensic Psychiatry and Psychology, 18*(2), 160–180. doi: 10.1080/14789940601104792

O'Brien, K., Sullivan, D., & Daffern, M. (2016). Integrating individual and group-based offence-focussed psychological treatments: Towards a model for best practice, *Psychiatry, Psychology and Law,* 1–19, doi: 10.1080/13218719.2016.1150143

Olver, M. E., Stockdale, K. C., & Wormith, J. S. (2011). A meta-analysis of predictors of offender treatment attrition and its relationship to recidivism. *Journal of Consulting and Clinical Psychology, 79,* 6–21.

Polaschek, D. L. L. (2011a). An appraisal of the Risk-Need-Responsivity Model of Offender Rehabilitation and its application to correctional treatment. *Legal and Criminological Psychology, 17,* 1–17. doi: 10.1111/j.2044-8333.2011.02038

Polaschek, D. L. L. (2011b). Many sizes fit all: A preliminary framework for conceptualizing the development and provision of cognitive-behavioral rehabilitation programs for offenders. *Aggression and Violent Behaviour, 16,* 20–35. doi: 10.1016/jvab.2010.10.002

Polaschek, D. L. L. (2013). How to train your dragon: An introduction to the special issue on treatment programmes for high-risk offenders. *Psychology, Crime & Law, 19*(5–6), 409–414. doi: 10.1080/1068316X.2013.758963

Rees-Jones, A., Gudjonsson, G., Young, S. (2012). A multi-site controlled trial of a cognitive skills program for mentally disordered offenders. *BMC Psychiatry, 12,* 1–11. doi: 10.1186/1471-244X-12-1

Ross, E. C., Polaschek, D., & Ward, T. (2008). The therapeutic alliance: A theoretical revision for offender rehabilitation. *Aggression and Violent Behaviour, 13,* 462–480. doi: 10.1016/j.avb.2008.07.003

Sturmey, P., & McMurran, M. (2011). *Forensic case formulation.* Chichester: Wiley-Blackwell.

Tew, J., & Atkinson, R. (2013). The Chromis programme: From conception to evaluation. *Psychology, Crime & Law, 19,* 415–431. doi: 10.1080/1068316X.2013.758967

Tew, J., Dixon, L., Harkins, L., & Bennett, A. (2012). Investigating changes in anger and aggression in offenders with high levels of psychopathic traits attending the Chromis violence reduction programme. *Criminal Behaviour and Mental Health, 22*(3), 191–201. doi:10.1002/cbm.1832

Viets, V. P., Walker, D. D., & Miller, W. R. (2002). What is motivation to change? A Scientific analysis. In M. McMurran (Ed.), *Motivating offenders to change: A guide to enhancing engagement in therapy* (pp. 15–30). Chichester: John Wiley & Sons.

Ward, T., & Maruna, S. (2007). *Rehabilitation: Beyond the risk paradigm.* London: Routledge.

Ware, J., Mann, R. E., & Wakeling, H. C. (2009). Group versus individual treatment: what is the best modality for treating sexual offenders? *Sexual Abuse in Australia and New Zealand, 1*(2), 70–78.

Willis, G. M., Ward, T., & Levenson, J. S. (2014). The Good Lives Model (GLM): An evaluation of GLM operationalization in North American treatment. *Sexual Abuse: A Journal of Research and Treatment, 26*(1), 58–81.

Willis, G. M., Yates, P. M., Gannon, T. A., & Ward, T. (2012). How to integrate the Good Lives Model into treatment programs for sexual offending: An introduction and overview. *Sexual Abuse: A Journal of Research and Treatment, 25*(2), 123–142.

Wilson, G. T. (1996). The manual-based treatments: The clinical application of research findings. *Behaviour, Research & Therapy, 34,* 295–314.

Wilson, N. J., & Tamatea, A. (2013). Challenging the 'urban myth' of psychopathy untreatability: The high-risk personality programme. *Psychology, Crime & Law, 19*(5–6), 493–510. doi:10.1080/1068316x.2013.758994

Yalom, I. D. (1995). *The theory and practice of group psychotherapy* (4th edn). New York: Basic Books.

Yip, V. C-Y., Gudjonsson, G. H., Perkins, D., Doidge, A., Hopkin, G., & Young, S. (2013). A non-randomised controlled trial of the R&R2MHP cognitive skills program in high risk male offenders with severe mental illness. *BMC Psychiatry, 13,* 267–278.

Young, S., & Ross, R. R. (2007). *Reasoning and rehabilitation 2 for youths and adults with mental health problems: A prosocial competence program.* Ottawa: Cognitive Centre of Canada. Available from www.cognitivecentre.ca.

13
ETHICAL ISSUES IN THE TREATMENT OF OFFENDERS

Tony Ward

Ethical challenges in the forensic and correctional domains are frequently formulated in terms of specific obligations such as consent to treatment, confidentiality or a duty to warn potential victims. Unfortunately, such an approach fails to provide practitioners with a broad enough understanding to identify and respond to the ethical flashpoints that accompany this type of work. In this chapter I explore four clusters of ethical problems and dilemmas that frequently arise in the context of offender assessment and treatment: human rights; punishment; moral repair; and the dual relationship problem. It is anticipated that familiarity with these overarching ethical themes will provide practitioners with a greater appreciation of normative issues in their day-to-day work and as a consequence of this enhanced understanding, become better ethical decision makers.

Introduction

Ethical issues arising from forensic and correctional practice are typically discussed in rather narrow terms such as consent, competency and the limits of confidentiality (e.g. Bonner & Vandecreek, 2006; Haag, 2006; IACFP, 2010). The point of such ethical analyses is to identify challenges that occur in the front line of practice and to help clinicians to decide how best to respond to these concrete problems. At one level this makes perfect sense; why burden busy practitioners with the task of deep engagement with complex normative questions? Better to equip them with a code of ethics containing a set of principles and standards of practice to guide them in their decision making. There are two worries with this strategy. First, it can create inflexibility because clinicians look to standards contained in the code to resolve every ethical concern they experience. There may not be enough tools in the ethical toolbox to deal with all the difficulties that occur in clinical contexts.

The second worry is that it may lead to *ethical blindness*. Because of their derivation from clinical experience, ethical codes often do not have anything meaningful to say about practice matters that are outside the normal moral experience of practitioners. You do not know what you do not know. In my opinion, a more useful way to think about ethical challenges within the forensic and correctional practice context is by conceptualising them in ways that directly point to the nature of the problem at hand; for example, in terms of human rights, punishment or restorative justice.

In this chapter I adopt this approach and explore four clusters of ethical problems and dilemmas that frequently arise in the context of offender assessment and treatment. First, I discuss the concepts of *moral and human rights* and examine their relevance for offender risk assessment and treatment outlined. Second, I address ethical issues that directly arise from the moral concept of *punishment* for practitioners, a frequently overlooked normative problem. Third, ethical problems created by offenders' dual status as both victims of crime and as offenders are explored; this is what has been referred to as the issue of *moral repair*. Finally, a related ethical topic, the *dual relationship problem*, is analysed and its impact on forensic practice overviewed.

Human and moral rights

Individuals' moral rights spell out their legitimate ethical claims against other people, and the corresponding duties others have to them. The claims in question arise from peoples' moral status and are typically based on attributes such as autonomy (i.e. the capacity to be self-governing), liberty (i.e. freedom from undue interference from others) and welfare (i.e. the degree to which a person's well-being related needs have been met). For example, each member of the community is entitled to basic respect from others and can reasonably anticipate that their view on important issues will be taken into account when decisions concerning community services and goods are made. Individuals can justifiably claim that other persons should listen to what they have to say, consider it as much as they do their own opinions, and when making decisions give everyone's interests equal weighting. If legitimate claims are disregarded then those responsible have failed to live up to their obligations. From a welfare perspective, individuals' essential needs for medical care, nutrition, education, bodily integrity, and accommodation ought to be met if they are able to function as self-governing agents.

Moral rights and their respective claims can be viewed as the ethical canvass against which members of the community seek to live their lives and work cooperatively to advance their own and others' interests. Moral rights are wide-ranging and concerned with issues that go beyond the protection of core interests or basic human needs. Entitlements to fair consideration in work-related matters, the right to be loved and to love in return, and the right to be treated with respect all involve moral rights in some form or another. What is needed in moral decision making, in addition to moral rights, are rights that protect the empowerment and well-being requirements that comprise dignity. The notion of human dignity is a fundamental moral concept that signifies the intrinsic value and universal moral equality of human beings. Due to their inherent dignity, all human beings are presumed to have the same degree of moral standing when it comes to considering the social and political arrangements that directly affect their core interests and subsequent well-being. Rights that seek to protect dignity will guarantee each person access to services and goods that enable them to function as purposeful agents able to pursue their own conception of a good life without unjustified interference from others. Such rights are what have been termed *human rights* (Gewirth, 1981; Griffin, 2008; Nickel, 2007).

The concept of human rights is a moral (and legal) one that can fulfil this role by virtue of its ability to safeguard the provision of the social, economic, environmental and psychological goods necessary for a dignified human life. They can be viewed as a moral foundation or bedrock without which no life that could be considered human could be lived. In this respect, human rights are *one way* of instantiating fundamental human values, or standards of what is worthwhile, good or right, within a community. The relationship between values and human rights is well captured by Freeden (1991):

> a human right is a conceptual device, expressed in linguistic form, that assigns priority to certain human or social attributes regarded as essential to the adequate functioning of a human being; that is intended to serve as a protective capsule for those attributes; and that appeal for deliberate action to ensure such protection. (p. 7)

Human rights are typically cast in a universal form, and it is assumed that they apply to all human beings by virtue of their underlying common needs based on the fact of embodiment, environmental conditions and related interests (Gewirth, 1981; Griffin, 2008; Orend, 2002; Tasioulas, 2012). In his classic text, Nickel (2007) identifies a number of key human rights features. According to Nickel, human rights:

- are universal and extend to all peoples of the world;
- are moral norms that provide strong reasons for granting individual significant benefits;
- have normative force through both national and international institutions;
- are evident in both specific lists of rights and at the level of abstract values;
- and set minimum standards of living rather than depicting an ideal.

From a human rights perspective, offenders are simultaneously *rights-holders* (with a right to non-interference in personal affairs unless they infringe upon the rights of others), *duty-bearers* (in that they are able to pursue personal goals as long as they do not infringe upon the rights of others) and *rights-violators* (when they infringe upon the rights of others through offending behaviour) (see Ward & Birgden, 2007; Ward, Gannon, & Birgden, 2007). Treatment approaches based on a human rights model would treat offenders as rights-holders (addressing histories of neglect, abuse and inadequate socialisation that require support to achieve goals in socially acceptable ways) as well as duty-bearers (providing learning experiences and resources to develop due regard for the rights of others through increasing empathy skills, problem-solving capacity, supportive social networks, and intimacy skills or appropriate alternatives). The threat to offenders' moral and human rights as a consequence of assessment and treatment revolves around the way this assessment is undertaken, and the implications for their future release plans and management.

I now comment on three implications of the human rights perspective for offender treatment within the correctional and forensic domains. The major implications are as follows: 1) importance of avoiding unjustified discrimination; 2) dealing with the inevitable pressures toward paternalism and working collaboratively wherever possible; and 3) working with offenders to promote good or better lives, rather than adopting a simple risk reduction and management intervention model.

Discrimination

According to human rights ideas and their associated norms, it is wrong to discriminate against individuals on the basis of ethically irrelevant factors when allocating goods and services. The exact nature of the discriminatory factors depends on the issue at hand in the context of offending and rehabilitation. Obviously, variables such as offenders' ethnicity, religious beliefs, sexual orientation, occupation and gender are irrelevant, and it would be wrong to exclude such individuals from treatment purely upon the basis of their presence. Additional, and often overlooked, factors are those associated with the type and severity of the offence and offenders' assessed level of risk. It is common for sex offenders to be placed in protection wings due to the threat and frequency of assaults on them by other prisoners. The difficulty is that the additional levels of security needed to ensure their continued safety may mean they have less access to goods such as joint leisure, vocational training and educational resources (Ward & Birgden, 2007). Though there may be good reasons for this, it is a concern that sometimes such access is denied because it is easier for correctional staff rather than being a necessary consequence of limited resources. This is ethically unacceptable and may well be a violation of a human right to effective rehabilitation (ICCPR, 1966). Additionally, the fact that an offender may have committed a serious crime that warrants a long sentence and moral condemnation does not on its own mean that he or she should be denied the opportunity to actively participate in a reform process or that legitimate claims to essential psychological and social resources be denied. Unfortunately, the attitude that high-risk offenders are not 'people like us' and therefore their needs and interests are of little ethical importance is widespread and (arguably) partially responsible for overly harsh and restrictive punishment and correctional practices (Laws & Ward, 2011; Ward & Laws, 2010).

Practitioners have a responsibility to look carefully at their work with offenders and ask themselves the following two questions: 1) are offenders being subject to unnecessarily restrictive and harsh living conditions, and 2) are they being denied legitimate access to treatment resources because of what they have done and their characteristics? For example, psychopathy has been prematurely regarded by researchers to be virtually untreatable and, as a consequence of this viewpoint, there has been little sustained research into the development and evaluation of suitable interventions for individuals diagnosed as psychopathic. If the answer is yes to either of these questions, I suggest there is a danger of a human rights violation occurring.

Paternalism

The issue of paternalism has been surprisingly overlooked in ethical analyses of offender rehabilitation and, if present, may pose a strong threat to human rights (Glaser, 2003). Paternalism has been defined by Beauchamp and Childress (2009) as 'The intentional overriding of one person's preferences or actions by another person, where the person who overrides justifies this action by appeal to the goal of benefitting or of preventing or mitigating harm to the person whose preferences or actions are overridden' (p. 208). In a standard risk-oriented rehabilitation programme, risk is typically construed as risk to the community and the offender, and it is offenders' preferences or goals that are overridden. From this perspective, when offenders' well-being is thought to depend on their staying out of prison and having their deviant characteristics eliminated or modified, paternalism may be evoked as a justification. Thus, mandated assessment and treatment, geographical restrictions and civil commitment can all be viewed as being partly in the offenders' interests. Glaser (2011) recently argued that strength-based rehabilitation models are also at least weakly paternalistic because they are based on practitioners' assumptions about what is in an offender's best interests rather than what offenders actually express. The ethical problem with paternalism is that it conflicts with individuals' autonomy and therefore threatens their dignity as rational, self-determining individuals. In this type of situation, someone else decides what a person should do and ignores what it is he or she wants. The degree to which current rehabilitation initiatives for offenders are paternalistic is contestable, but Glaser does make a strong and useful point. If paternalism is unjustified on any particular occasion, it violates the autonomy or freedom requirement of human rights and therefore is ethically unacceptable. One of the problems with adopting a risk management approach to treatment is that offenders are viewed primarily as potential threats to society, risks to be identified and contained. This can quickly lead to a failure to take into account their needs and personal goals and a tendency to assume that therapists have an obligation, and in fact are best positioned, to decide on the details of treatment and rehabilitation plans.

Good Lives Plans

I suggest that all offender rehabilitation initiatives should be founded upon strength-based intervention plans that incorporate their core commitments and also address the need to protect the public. A strength-based rehabilitation model aims to help offenders acquire the competencies and social opportunities and supports necessary to realise reflectively endorsed personal goals. These goals will be derived from core human needs, personal abilities and interests, and cultural resources, and reflect individuals' self-conceptions (Ward & Maruna, 2007). I will not go into detail here, but note that in a number of previous papers and books, I have systematically described how the Good Lives Model of offender rehabilitation can provide clinicians with a framework to assist in the construction of these plans with their constituent intermediate and intrinsic goals (e.g. Laws & Ward, 2011; Ward & Laws, 2010; Ward & Maruna, 2007; Ward & Stewart, 2003). The key point is that a strength-based intervention plan will have a strong desistance focus and have at its heart a clear description of offenders' core values and their associated identities. For example, an indigenous individual who weights cultural identity and knowledge acquisition most heavily might have an intervention plan that involves going to university to learn about African-American history and language and meeting with others like him/herself who are attempting to turn their lives around. Risk management and reduction are sought through the fashioning of better lives, and the personal commitments of individuals are carefully factored in their plans in ways that are deeply responsive to their agency and dignity as human beings. The aim is to enhance a person's functioning (i.e. address entitlements and needs) and to reduce individuals' risk of reoffending (i.e. meet their obligations to others).

There are two ways risk reduction can occur within strength-oriented treatments. First is the establishment of the internal and external resources needed to implement a good life plan in socially acceptable and personally fulfilling ways, that can directly alter criminogenic needs/risk-relevant factors. For example, learning the skills necessary to become a carpenter or welder will make it easier for an offender to develop the skills for concentration and emotional regulation, thereby reducing impulsivity, a criminogenic need. Second, the reduction of risk can occur indirectly when an offender is strongly motivated to engage in treatment because of his involvement in projects that are personally engaging. For example, an individual might work hard at overcoming substance abuse problems because of a wish to attend a mechanic training course. In actual practice, having a good life plan both directly and indirectly impacts one's dynamic risk factors. Thus, the advantage of strength-based perspectives is that they are founded on human rights ideas and norms and explicitly balance the interests and entitlements of offenders with those of members of the public.

Punishment – the moral status of offenders

An important set of ethical issues that are indirectly related to assessment and treatment concerns the moral status of offenders. Offenders by virtue of being members of the moral community (and hence justifiably punished) possess equal moral status to non-offenders (Ward & Salmon, 2009). This equal standing gives each person the authority to make certain claims of members of the moral community, and in turn to acknowledge his or her own obligations to respect the legitimate claims of other people. Preventative schemes such as civil detention restrict the liberty of serious offenders who *may* reoffend in the future and, as a consequence, subjects them to coerced treatment and management. Restricting liberty on the basis of what an individual may do undermines legal principles and core rights such as the presumption of innocence, finality of sentencing, the principle of proportionality, and the principle against double punishment (Doyle, Ogloff, & Thomas, 2011). However, perhaps the greatest threat to the human rights of offenders springs from the problem of punishment.

The problem of punishment arises from the need to ethically justify intentionally harming another human being, when normally such actions are deemed as unacceptable. It is not enough to state that criminal actions are deserved, or that punishment is likely to result in a reduction in crime or the reformation of an offender's character. What are also required are reasons for permitting the infliction of harm on others. Thus, it is necessary to provide an argument to justify the state acting in ways that impose harms on those who break the law. In addition to the suffering experienced by offenders and their families, there is the question of the financial cost to the state of building and running prisons rather than putting resources to alternative uses such as creating better healthcare services or providing free high-quality education and vocational training for everyone.

State-inflicted punishment in the criminal justice system involves the intentional imposition of pain (sanction, burden) on an individual following his or her violation of important social norms that are intended to protect significant common interests of members of the political community (Bennett, 2008). A common view among philosophers and theorists of law is that the criminal justice institution of punishment has at least six essential elements to it (Boonin, 2008). In essence, the actions constituting legitimate punishment should: follow an offence against legal rules; be imposed and implemented by individuals authorised by the state; be intentional (directed toward a particular end or action outcome); be reprobative (express disapproval or censure); be retributive (follow an actual wrongful act committed by the offender); and be harmful (result in suffering, a burden or deprivation to the offender).

There are at least three theories of the justification of punishment evident in the literature: retributive, consequential and communicative/restorative (Boonin, 2008; Ward & Salmon, 2009). According to the *retributive theory*, the primary aim of punishment is to hold offenders accountable for crimes by inflicting burdens that are roughly equal in harm to those inflicted on their victims. It is a question of restoring moral balance. *Consequential* theorists assert that punishment is more likely than other types of crime reduction practices to produce an overall aggregate effect of crime reduction and that this is what justifies them. The claim is that punishment functions to deter, incapacitate or reform offenders and that these effects in turn reduce the overall crime rate. Finally, for *communicative/restorative* theorists, the aim of punishment is to repair or restore offenders' relationships with victims (if possible), and the broader community. For example, Duff (2001) argues that there are three aims integral to the institution of punishment: secular repentance, reform, and reconciliation through the imposition of sanctions.

Ward and Salmon (2009) argue that retributive and communicative theories of punishment explicitly endorse the *equal status* of all members of the moral community, while the consequential theory is more ambivalent, stressing as it does the overriding importance of the *consequences* of punishment. Thus, if the overall good of the community is served by the imposition of severe restrictions on offenders' freedom and access to social goods, then it is ethically justifiable. I do not have the space to examine the cogency of the three theories of punishment and their implications for correctional practitioners in detail (see Ward & Salmon, 2009). However, because of its conceptual links with utilitarianism, the consequential theory of punishment has an uneasy relationship with the concept of human rights, and, arguably, struggles to find space for this important moral concept.

The relationship between punishment theories and risk assessment is complex but significant. Ward and Salmon (2009) state that:

> the types of interventions logically implied by consequential theories of punishment resembles those promoted by the current treatment paradigm dominating correctional jurisdictions throughout the western world, the Risk–Need–Responsivity model. (p. 242)

The Risk-Need-Responsivity model of offender rehabilitation is closely aligned with the current emphasis of offender practitioners on risk assessment and risk management, and, in this respect, the latter inherits the ethical challenges facing consequentialist models. The concern is that offenders are treated as a means to the ends of other people (i.e. goals, needs) and are not treated as ends in themselves (i.e. as persons of equal value and dignity). Offenders' interests, commitments and wishes may be too easily overridden in the perceived interests of community protection. While I appreciate the social and clinical need to identify potentially dangerous individuals and to take reasonable steps to prevent them from harming other people, it is important to take a balanced perspective when making decisions that are likely to curtail someone's rights. What is being suggested is that one of the background ethical assumptions inherent in risk management approaches to offender treatment is the endorsement of a consequentialist theory of punishment. It is not that punishment is necessarily treatment (see Glaser, 2003) but, rather, because offenders are typically undergoing or face the possibility of punishment, practitioners should confront the ethical issues that arise from this consequence. More specifically, they ought to critically examine the practices they are engaged in themselves and note any ethically problematic features of their practice or the institutions for which they work. There is a danger that risk assessment and treatment can be underpinned by a consequential defence of punishment, and thus makes it easy for practitioners to justify the interests of the community more than those of the offender. That is, there could be a lack of moral balance. For example, there may be a failure to consider the possibility of potential harm to the offenders when creating risk management treatment plans (following a risk assessment) through the imposition of unnecessarily severe restrictions, and depriving them of the opportunity to make important life decisions for themselves. In addition, the weakening of core relationships and social connection to other people may cause significant damage to an offender, frustrating, as it does, basic human needs for connectedness and intimacy. Of course, it may be that a consequential justification will satisfy practitioners but given its perceived lack of alignment with human rights norms, it makes sense to be cautious. I encourage practitioners to use the human rights distinction between entitlements and duties when formulating risk assessment reports and plans. Keeping offenders' entitlements to services and goods firmly in mind, alongside the need to protect the public from further harm, will hopefully culminate in plans that attempt to enhance offenders' functioning while also reducing their reoffending risk (Ward & Maruna, 2007).

Another potential ethical problem to keep in mind is that some components of what have been considered to be treatment, may more resemble punishment (Ward & Salmon, 2009). For example, cognitive restructuring in sex offender treatment in part consists of getting offenders to accept responsibility for what they have done. This aim is often accompanied by therapist attempts to induce guilt and remorse in the belief that offenders will then be more motivated to engage in the behaviour change component of treatment. In my eyes, this looks suspiciously like punishment (see also victim empathy – Ward & Salmon, 2009).

Moral repair

An ethical issue to do with offenders' moral status and its implication for assessment and treatment revolves around the concept of *moral repair*. The key ethical concern from a moral repair viewpoint is to determine to what degree, if any, an offender's own past experience of victimisation ought to be taken into account in the treatment process (Ward & Moreton, 2008). There is some overlap with the moral concepts of rights, punishment (see above) and dual relationships (below), all of which in some way revolve around attempts to balance the interests of offenders, victims and the community.

Walker (2006) states that moral repair is 'restoring or creating trust and hope in a shared sense of value and responsibility' (p. 28) following the experience of intentional and unjustified harm at the hands of another person or persons. Offenders who have been physically, emotionally or sexually abused in the past have rights to be treated in ways that reflect this acknowledgement of harm. According to Walker, there are six core tasks encompassed by moral repair: (1) placing responsibility on the offender; (2) acknowledging and addressing the harm suffered by the victim; (3) asserting the authority of the norms violated by the offender and the community's commitment to them; (4) restoring or creating trust among the victims in the relevant norms and the practices that express them; (5) creating hope that the norms and the individuals responsible for supporting them are worthy of trust; and (6) re-establishing or establishing adequate moral relationships between victims, wrongdoers and the community. It is clear that a core task is acknowledging the harm experienced by the person concerned and responding appropriately to this fact.

What are the ethical implications for practitioners engaged in offender assessment and treatment? Offenders who have been victimised possess a dual status from a moral repair viewpoint: they are legitimately subject to censure *and* also have a right to an acknowledgement of the harm they have experienced and to be recipients of genuine efforts to repair the damage inflicted on them. A concern is that practitioners who are engaged in a risk informed assessment and subsequent treatment of offenders who have been victims of violence in the past might overlook their entitlements to some type of restoration. Rather, they could concentrate on the task of identifying risk levels and associated dynamic risk factors, and designing an intervention plan intended to reduce or eliminate them (Douglas, Blanchard, & Hendry, 2013). The concept of human rights can help practitioners to avoid this ethical mistake by virtue of its stress on offenders' entitlements to a range of services and goods, *and* their obligations to others. The subsequent formulation of a risk management and treatment plan should reflect this dual awareness and arguably seek to ensure that any subsequent interventions enhance their capabilities (and hence repair the damage inflicted) alongside reducing their risk of recidivism. A reliance on a simple risk reduction model without a strong human rights lens may result in an overly narrow and ethically problematic set of recommendations. Ward and Moreton (2008, p. 320) capture the need to address both offenders' own victimisation issues alongside delivering treatment that decreases their chances of reoffending well:

> The normative position we have sketched in this article can achieve the aim of developing an integrated approach to the two ethical issues (offender as victim and wrongdoer) by basing treatment on the provision of the core conditions for offender agency within a human rights framework. The focus on agency promotes the provision of capabilities and skills required to effectively pursue offenders' own goals and interests while appreciating that other people also have legitimate claims to the same thing. In addition, the vindication of offenders' own abuse concerns and the validation of the norms that were violated in their abuse help to attune them to the universality of such norms and, therefore, to the legitimate claims of their own victims. Strength-based treatment strategies seek to build competencies in a way that respects offenders' particular preferences and basic needs; they also help to repair the damage caused by their own experience of abuse.

Dual relationship problem

The dual relationship problem in the correctional and forensic domains emerges from the overlap and subsequent experience of role conflict between two sets of ethical norms: those associated with community protection and justice versus norms related to individual well-being and autonomy (Ward, 2013). The problem occurs because many forensic practitioners have their professional roots in mental health or social disciplines such as psychiatry, clinical psychology, social work or law, and, as such, may struggle to ethically justify aspects of forensic and/or correctional work. The value conflict is between norms that seek to increase the well-being of the individuals that practitioners work with via the enhancement of well-being and reduction of suffering. The specific ethical codes formulated to guide practice in the domains of forensic/correctional and mental health have been designed to accomplish distinct aims and inevitably conflict in certain arenas of performance. A good example of this occurs in risk assessment, where the aim to arrive at a likelihood that the offender will commit another offence often results in virtually no attention being paid to what is in his or her best interests. Further, there may be no thought about how best to balance offenders' interests in living 'good' lives against the desires of members of the community to feel safe, and to experience reduced rates of predation. The conflict between the two sets of codes or norm clusters may make it difficult for practitioners to decide on a course of action when assessing or treating offenders; and once this has been accomplished, make it harder to justify their intended actions. According to Ward (2013):

> the problem of dual relationships is a manifestation of the wider underlying ethical issue of *value pluralism*. Value pluralism occurs when a number of distinct ethical codes (or if you prefer, sets of norms) exist within a society or community, none of which can be established as ethically superior by a rational, impartial observer ... The clash between the various ethical codes may be a *horizontal* one between codes at the same level of abstraction (e.g., a professional ethical code versus a criminal justice employee code) or *vertical*, where professional norms conflicts with more abstract principles (e.g., human rights norms might clash with those regulating staff conduct at a high security prison). (p. 94)

Ward (2013) concludes that all of the attempted solutions to the dual relationship problem fail because of its source in value pluralism. He argues for the application of a procedural approach based on the concept of moral acquaintances, where individuals experiencing role or value conflict (within themselves or with other) attempt to create treatment plans based on shared moral commitments and beliefs. In order to have a chance at creating mutually agreed-on plans that respect individuals' varying values and beliefs, it is necessary to engage in dialogues that are open and intent on incorporating varying viewpoints. In other words, ethical focus should be on the quality of relationships as well as principles and norms such as rights and duties.

In risk assessment (and subsequent risk-oriented treatment) the priority is to estimate the potential of individuals to harm others rather than to identify each individual's needs, rights and obligations. This can create problems of balance and partialism. The ethical risks arising from the dual relationship problem for practitioners are that they will: (a) fail to acknowledge there is a problem, or (b) dismiss its significance. The former possibility means that practitioners will suffer from *ethical blindness* where real and pressing moral issues are simply not noticed because of a lack of knowledge and/or normative sensitivity. Human rights theory with its insistence on the equal value of all members of the moral community, and requirement that everyone's core interest should be attended to, can help to overcome this limitation. Because there is an explicit effort to actively factor in everyone's interests and viewpoints, there is a reduced danger of privileging some group or persons at the expense of others. The latter possibility arises from failure to accept that there are multiple and at times conflicting values in play during an assessment process (and subsequent risk management), which can not be easily rationally resolved. Thus all persons implicated in the assessment and treatment process should have their perspectives and personal priorities noted and taken into consideration. They should be seen as moral acquaintances rather than moral strangers.

M*oral acquaintances* have some overlapping norms relating to the problem in question; they are not total strangers and can arrive at similar decisions about how best to act (Hanson, 2009). These overlapping norms may be based on a shared understanding of human nature (e.g. needs for material goods, relatedness, autonomy, safety) and conditions or be oriented around a specific issue, for example the need to protect the community from crime, or the rights of offenders to receive educational or vocational training. Moral acquaintances look for common, or overlapping, norms relating to a particular issue. They view any actions proceeding from these common norms (and associated principles) as justified if they are embedded within a coherent normative system, and are internally consistent (or, at least, not blatantly contradictory). They may agree on what to do but have different reasons for doing so. The only requirement is that the reasons presented should be rationally derived from a coherent (i.e. non-contradictory and mutually supportive) set of norms and principles. For example, one forensic practitioner might justify the implementation of a treatment with an offender because of the anticipated beneficial effect on reoffending rates while another forensic practitioner might argue that the offender ought to receive treatment because of pressing psychological needs. However, despite working from distinct – and equally coherent – normative systems, the two forensic practitioners might share a common belief that if a certain course of action can reduce human suffering without resulting in unjustified pain to others it ought to be undertaken. The two forensic practitioners are moral acquaintances – rather than strangers – by virtue of the fact that they share some norms that are directly linked to the issue in question: whether or not to resource treatment for offenders. They accept that each other's decision to provide treatment is based on good reasons, within a coherent normative system, although they do not subscribe to each other's particular viewpoint.

Conclusion

In this chapter I have identified a number of general ethical issues that are directly or indirectly associated with offender assessment and treatment: human rights, punishment, moral repair and the dual relationship problem. All of these forensic and correctional ethical problems are conceptually linked by a desire to achieve morally balanced decisions concerning the right ways to act in specific contexts. How should the core interests and priorities of offenders be taken into account when engaging in a risk assessment or when formulating and delivering a treatment plan? Is the aim of correctional treatment to reform individuals or to restore the ruptures within community relationships (i.e. between victims, offenders and the members of the community)? Again and again, it comes down to looking for a way to balance competing, possibly incommensurable, values and their associated norms.

In my view, the concepts of moral rights and human rights can be helpful in avoiding some of the ethical pitfalls that are pervasive in the field. Ultimately, there are no easy solutions because at the very heart of risk assessment and risk-oriented treatment is the problem of value pluralism and the incommensurability of values such as community protection and offender freedom and well-being. It is possible to reach an agreement between the parties involved in the particular situation in question or at least to make a genuine effort to do so. One of the advantages of adopting a human rights framework when working with offenders is that practitioners learn to automatically think about the overall balance of interests at stake in specific situations, and to take note of each person's obligations and entitlements. Reflecting on rights in a risk assessment, management and treatment context is likely to create greater knowledge of the ethical complexities of practice with offenders and ultimately will increase ethical responsiveness and sensitivity.

Particular ethical challenges noted in the literature such as confidentiality, consent, competency, compulsory treatment, civil commitment and so on all have their source within the four classes of ethical concerns discussed in this chapter. There are no decision-making algorithms available to grind out the 'correct' answer to complex clinical ethical problems. Certainly codes of ethics and their constituent principles and standards are valuable resources, but that is all they are. Practitioners need to develop ethical sensitivity and responsiveness so that they are able to identify ethical hotspots as they are forming. It is important to work on the development of professional virtues such as flexibility, compassion, humility, respect, empathy, problem-solving and mediation skills, and the ability to tolerate uncertainty and intense emotional climates. Finally, practitioners would do well to remind themselves that there is no bright line between professional competency and ethical maturity; they are two sides of the same coin. A competent clinician will be an ethical one. In the end, apparent dichotomies such as values and knowledge, and emotional and cognitive capacities, are interwoven. Understanding the interlinked nature of these factors will help practitioners working in the forensic and correctional domains to do *good* work, in every sense of that word.

Further reading

Beauchamp, T. L., & Childress, J. F. (2009). *Principles of Biomedical Ethics* (6th edn). New York: Oxford University Press.

Ward, T. (2013). Addressing the dual relationship problem in forensic and correctional practice. *Aggression and Violent Behavior*, *18*, 92–100. doi: 10.1016/j.avb.2012.10.006

Ward, T., & Birgden, A. (2007). Human rights and clinical correctional practice. *Aggression and Violent Behavior*, *12*, 628–643. doi: 10.1016/j.avb.2007.05.001

References

Bennett, C. (2008). *The apology ritual: A philosophical theory of punishment*. Cambridge: Cambridge University Press.

Beauchamp, T. L., & Childress, J. F. (2009). *Principles of Biomedical Ethics* (6th edn). New York: Oxford University Press.

Bonner, R., & Vandecreek, L. D. (2006). Ethical decision making for correction mental health providers. *Criminal Justice and Behavior*, *33*, 542–564. doi: 10.1177/0093854806287352

Boonin, D. (2008). *The problem of punishment*. New York: Cambridge University Press.

Douglas, K. S., Blanchard, A. J. E., & Hendry, M. C. (2013). Violence risk assessment and management: Putting structured professional judgment into practice. In C. Logan & L. Johnstone (Eds), *Managing clinical risk: A guide to effective practice* (pp. 29–55). Abingdon: Routledge.

Doyle, D. J., Ogloff, J., & Thomas, S. (2011). Designated as dangerous: Characteristics of sex offenders subject to post-sentence orders in Australia. *Australian Psychologist*, *46*, 41–48. doi: 10.1111/j.1742-9544.2010.00006.x

Duff, R. A. (2001). *Punishment, communication, and community*. New York: Oxford University Press.

Freeden, M. (1991). *Rights*. Minneapolis, MN: University of Minnesota Press.

Gewirth, A. (1981). *Reason and morality*. Chicago, IL: The University of Chicago Press.

Glaser, B. (2003). Therapeutic jurisprudence: An ethical paradigm for therapists in sex offender treatment programs. *Western Criminology Review*, *4*, 143–154.

Glaser, B. (2011). Paternalism in the rehabilitation of sex offenders. *Sexual Abuse: A Journal of Research and Treatment*, *23*, 329–345. doi: 10.1177/1079063210382044

Griffin, J. (2008). *On human rights*. Oxford: Oxford University Press.

Haag, A. M. (2006). Ethical dilemmas faced by correctional psychologists in Canada. *Criminal Justice and Behavior*, *33*, 93–109. doi: 10.1177/0093854805282319

Hanson, S. S. (2009). *Moral acquaintances and moral decisions: Resolving conflicts in medical ethics*. New York: Springer.

IACFP (2010). Standards for psychology services in jails, prisons, correctional facilities, and agencies (3rd edn). *Criminal Justice and Behavior*, *37*, 449–808. doi: 10.1177/0093854810368253

Laws, D. R. & Ward, T. (2011). *Desistance from sexual offending: Alternatives to throwing away the keys*. New York: Guilford Press.

Nickel, J. W. (2007). *Making sense of human rights* (2nd edn). Oxford: Blackwell Publishing.

Orend, B. (2002). *Human rights: Concept and context*. Ontario: Broadview Press.

Tasioulas, J. (2012). Towards a philosophy of human rights. *Current Legal Problems*, *65*, 1–30. doi: 10.1093/clp/cus019

Walker, M. U. (2006). *Moral repair: Reconstructing moral relations after wrongdoings*. New York: Cambridge University Press.

Ward, T. (2013). Addressing the dual relationship problem in forensic and correctional practice. *Aggression and Violent Behavior*, *18*, 92–100. doi: 10.1016/j.avb.2012.10.006

Ward, T., & Birgden, A. (2007). Human rights and clinical correctional practice. *Aggression and Violent Behavior*, *12*, 628–643. doi:10.1016/j.avb.2007.05.001

Ward, T., Gannon, T. E., & Birgden, A. (2007). Human rights and the treatment of sex offenders. *Sexual Abuse: A Journal of Research and Treatment, 19*, 195–204. doi: 10.1007/s11194-007-9053-4

Ward, T., & Laws, D. R. (2010). Desistance from sexual offending: Motivating change, enriching practice. *International Journal of Forensic Mental Health, 9*, 11–23. doi: 10.1080/14999011003791598

Ward, T., & Maruna, S. (2007). *Rehabilitation: Beyond the risk paradigm*. London: Routledge.

Ward, T., & Moreton, G. (2008). Moral repair with offenders: Ethical issues arising from victimization experiences. *Sexual Abuse: A Journal of Research and Treatment, 20*, 305–322. doi: 10.1177/1079063208322423

Ward, T., & Salmon, K. (2009). The ethics of punishment: Correctional practice implications. *Aggression and Violent Behavior, 14*, 239–247. doi: 10.1177/1079063210382049

Ward, T., & Stewart, C. A. (2003). Criminogenic needs and human needs: A theoretical model. *Psychology, Crime, & Law, 9*, 125–143.

14
SUPERVISING THE THERAPISTS

Jason Davies and Claire Nagi

Providing psychological therapy in forensic settings is challenging and demanding, requiring a broad range of skills and knowledge. For many therapy approaches, there is a requirement for therapists to receive specific supervision of their practice from an accredited person; this is generally incorporated into their practice requirements. Such supervision needs to provide protected time in which the practitioner can consider and review their practice, consult with others and explore options to difficulties. In addition, supervision provides a mechanism through which the therapist can demonstrate ongoing proficiency in the therapeutic approach being used. This chapter considers the common components of supervision for those providing individual therapy regardless of the therapeutic approach being employed.

An overview of supervision

Supervision grew up alongside the development of therapies, providing the forum for teaching, modelling, shaping and correcting practice. There are now a very large number of accessible general texts on clinical supervision such as *Supervision in Clinical Practice* (Scaife, 2013), *Essentials in Clinical Supervision* (Campbell, 2011), *Fundamental Themes in Clinical Supervision* (Cutcliffe, Butterworth, & Proctor, 2005), *Fundamentals of Clinical Supervision* (Bernard & Goodyear, 2014) and profession-specific texts such as *Supervision and Clinical Psychology* (Fleming & Steen, 2004), *Supervision in Social Work* (Kadushin, 1992) and *Skills of Clinical Supervision for Nurses* (Bond & Holland, 2011). These sit alongside more specific texts such as the *Handbook of Psychotherapy Supervision* (Watkins, 1997). Although almost 20 years old, this text remains a useful resource covering issues in training supervisors, with chapters on undertaking supervision research and chapters on supervision for a number of specific psychotherapy approaches. The more recent

The Wiley International Handbook of Clinical Supervision (Watkins & Milne, 2014) acts to some degree as a successor, although it follows a more general format of covering material relevant to clinical supervision in a broader sense, with a small number of chapters on supervision as practiced within a small number of psychotherapies. Additionally, the new *American Psychological Association – Clinical Supervision Essentials Book Series*, already includes texts on supervision for a number of specific therapies including Cognitive-Behavioural Therapy (CBT), Psychodynamic approaches and Humanistic approaches.

Many of the forms of therapy described in the preceding chapters require those delivering them to engage in supervision with a more experienced (and often specially qualified) practitioner of that therapeutic model. The explicit purposes of such specialist supervision include ongoing education in the therapeutic model and its associated competencies, and ensuring practitioner adherence to the model of therapy being practiced. Over time, multiple functions of supervision have been recognised, the components of which are now commonly summarised under the three headings described by Proctor (1986), namely: *formative* – the educational and competence development function; *normative* – the ethical practice and standards checking function; and *restorative* – the emotional processing and well-being function. The formative aspect of supervision has been described as containing three factors: 1) tasks and skills; 2) decision making and accountability; and 3) learning from experience – reflective practice (Fowler, 1996). The normative element includes factors such as quality, safety and ethics whilst the restorative component is associated with providing emotional support, building confidence and exploring practice anxieties (Ayer, Knight, Joyce, & Nightingale, 1997). The interpersonal relationship between the supervisor and supervisee, the supervision working alliance (Mor Barak, Travis, Pyun, & Xie, 2009), sets the context within which supervision can occur. This is also said to contain three elements necessary for a functional alliance – bond (the relationship between the supervisor and supervisee), supervisee goals (what is wanted/needed from supervision) and tasks (how to meet the goals) (Bordin, 1983). In forensic settings, it could be argued that a *contextualising* function could be added to Proctor's three. Contextualising emphasises the importance of supervision for such things as considering the impact of the setting, understanding offending behaviour, examining risk and managing boundaries. Whilst this could be seen to be contained within the normative function, this addition emphasises the need for supervision in forensic settings to provide a regular and explicit focus on safety and risk, and as a way to explore the impact of the forensic context on the thinking and actions of the therapist.

There are many definitions of supervision in the literature; however, for the purposes of this chapter, we will draw from the definition provided in a recent book on the topic – *Supervision for Forensic Practitioners* – by Davies (2015) which describes supervision as: 'A formalised relationship (one to one or group) in which regular, protected time is allocated in which a trained supervisor supports, develops and evaluates the practice of the supervisee through the use of a range of methods and techniques … supervision is focused on competence, ethical practice, quality and the emotional impact on the practitioner' (pp. 3–4). Davies notes that the outcome of supervision is an impact 'on the actions of the supervisee and thus the positive effect on the client or task' (p. 4). The importance of this definition for therapists in forensic settings is its broad nature and recognition of functions, thus avoiding the possible narrowing of supervision to a focus solely on the therapy being provided.

Supervision in forensic settings needs to address a range of domains including the technical proficiency associated with providing therapy. Day (2012) and Davies (2015) have both drawn on the work of Lizzio & Wilson (2002) to show how practitioner competencies can be described within the forensic context. The spectrum of skills and knowledge required means that supervisors need to be aware of a range of other work and a range of complex issues, in addition to the therapeutic activity. This introduces two very important questions for the supervisor to address before contracting to provide supervision to a therapist in forensic settings: 1) what is the role (e.g. responsibilities, tasks) of this therapist in this setting; and 2) what is the nature and purpose of the supervision I am being asked to provide (e.g. am I supervising work other than therapy, does this therapist have other supervision and, if so, what arrangements are there for communication between supervisors and this therapist)? Even where the supervisor is only providing input to the therapy provided by the supervisee, they will need to have awareness of a broad range of factors and ensure any non-therapy work is appropriately supervised. This requirement is heightened if the therapist's 'therapy model specific' supervisor is their only supervisory avenue within the forensic setting.

Throughout this chapter we will use the term therapist to denote the therapist receiving supervision (i.e. the supervisee) and supervisor to denote the more experienced (therapy-trained) supervisor. We will also focus on individually delivered supervision to reflect the focus of the book. However, it is worth noting that there are many variations in supervision delivery such as peer, professional and various forms of group-based delivery (see Davies, 2015). Frequently, practitioners will engage in more than one supervisory relationship at any given time. This also needs to be managed within an overall framework of supervision to minimise the potential for conflict, omission and unnecessary duplication.

Using supervision models

Supervision models provide coherent ways to conceptualise the tasks and practice of supervision. In addition to the supervision competencies required by the therapy model being used, and accepting the three broad functions of supervision described by Proctor, there are a number of models and frameworks developed for supervision that are worthy of consideration because of the usefulness they might have.

As with any area of competence, skill and knowledge develop over time, moving the therapist from novice to experienced. As a result, the nature and type of supervision needed by the therapist will change over time. One widely used framework for understanding the changing needs within supervision is the Integrated Developmental Model proposed by Stoltenberg & McNeill (2010). In this framework it is argued that the supervisee's needs change as they gain experience, knowledge, competence and skill and that one key task for the supervisor is to match their style and technique to the needs of the supervisee (Scaife, 2013). This may show itself in the differing roles taken by the supervisor, such as that of coach, mentor, teacher and administrator (Morgan & Sprenkle, 2007); each being adopted according to the needs of the therapist and the situation. In many ways, this model parallels the 'stages of learning' described by Benner (1982). In this, the worker is viewed as moving through defined stages from 'novice' to 'expert' with different performance, learning needs and approaches associated with each stage. Rolfe (1997) adds 'reflexive practitioner' as the endpoint after expert; arguing that the most proficient workers have the ability to 'reflect in action' on their practice. Although such approaches describe a linear process, it is likely that development is complex and involves revisiting and revising competencies over time. It is also likely that individuals will have differing levels of competence/be at different stages of development for various aspects of their role. Importantly for the supervisor, these developmental frameworks not only provide a way to broadly conceptualise the therapist's needs, likely strengths, anxieties and their 'within therapy' focus, but also guides the supervisor on how to best deliver supervision to ensure learning is provided and that quality can be assured. For example, Stoltenberg & McNeill (2010) suggest that the level 1 therapist (novice) is likely to be motivated yet anxious, focused on building their skills and dependent on the supervisor for structure, instruction and direction. It is essential that the supervisor engage in direct observations of the level 1 therapist's work. With these in mind the supervisor is likely to act as a role model, provide reinforcement and conceptualisation. At the other end, the experienced therapist will be self-directed and able to reflect on their practice in real time and so will tend to use supervision in a consultative way, sometimes to address blocks within a therapeutic relationship.

Supervisors may also make use of models in order to guide other aspects of the supervision task. For example, the supervision hour outlined by Davies (2015) and based on O'Donoghue (2014) and Wosket and Page (1994) provides a structure for the management of the time available for supervision. This model identifies five tasks that need to occur within each supervision session (starting, planning, space, bridge and review) and the preparation and action that needs to occur outside supervision. With times allocated for each of these tasks, this model helps ensure that the tasks of supervision can be achieved in the hour typically allocated to the task.

Distinct from the previous models, the seven-eyed supervision model (Hawkins & Shohet, 2006) provides a framework through which the process of supervision can be conceptualised. This model identifies seven areas of focus within supervision, each providing different information and opportunities to inform both supervision and the practice of the therapist. The seven areas are:

- Focus on the client (e.g. their needs and presentation).
- Focus on the techniques and interventions being used.

- Focus on the therapeutic alliance (the relationship between client and therapist).
- Focus on the therapist/supervisee themself (including transference and counter-transference).
- Focus on the supervisory alliance (the relationship between the supervisor and supervisee).
- Focus on the supervisor's processes (e.g. supervisor experiences and responses to the supervision session/material).
- Focus on the setting and wider context (including organisational factors and other interventions).

Hawkins & Shohet (2006) argue that 'good supervision of in-depth work with clients must involve all seven processes, although not necessarily in every session' (p. 98). Further, they suggest that supervisors often use some processes more frequently than others or not use some at all.

In a slightly different vein, Milne (2009) provides a set of principles he suggests form the foundation for delivering Evidence-Based Clinical Supervision. The principles cover a range of within and outside supervision factors:

1. Take account of the context.
2. Adopt a problem-solving approach.
3. Critically use what is known.
4. Specify the model of practice.
5. Integrate theory and practice.
6. Verify any assumptions.
7. Critically engage with information.
8. Attend to the supervisory alliance.
9. Use the supervision cycle (as outlined in the supervision hour above).
10. Be collaborative.
11. Ensure the supervisor is supported.
12. Evaluate supervision.

These therapy-neutral supervision frameworks provide structures and mechanisms with which to manage and monitor the supervision task. Those interested in models and frameworks might also wish to consult the text by Holloway (1995) in which she details a comprehensive framework for supervision. Where the role of the supervisor is to support the therapy offered by the therapist, specific supervision tasks and processes drawn from the therapy model can be used alongside to ensure supervision is appropriately tailored, consistent and functional. With this in mind, it is likely that a mental or actual checklist of these models and processes could be helpful to review the quality of supervision as it takes place. This might include therapy-specific checklists – such as the CBT Supervision: Adherence and Guidance Evaluation; SAGE (Milne, Reiser, Cliffe, & Raine, 2011) – and checklists of supervision quality – such as the Manchester Clinical Supervision Scale (Winstanley & White, 2011). Alternatively, supervisors and therapists can use approaches that allow therapy characteristics and progress to be monitored on a routine (session by session) basis – such as the Global Review Form: Supervision Version (Davies, 2015).

Some key ideas in supervision

Supervisor qualities

Research suggests that effective supervision is impacted by supervisor factors (e.g. skills and competencies); supervisee factors (e.g. engagement and openness to learning); and setting factors (e.g. prioritising supervision) at the very least. Supervision has traditionally been therapy specific; however, as with many forms of therapy, there are some common components that skilled supervisors from any theoretical orientation are likely to utilise. As shown in Figure 14.1, there are a range of general factors that contribute to effective supervision along with two sets of specific supervision competencies: 1) those relating to the context or setting (in this case, the specialist nature of the forensic setting); and 2) those task-specific skills and knowledge (for our purposes those that relate to the specific therapy). In order to examine some of these in more detail, we will explore some of the factors associated with the supervisor. Interested readers may wish to refer to Davies (2015) for more discussion of supervisee, supervisor and setting factors.

Researchers have identified many supervisor attributes as important. For example, Nelson, Barnes, Evans, and Triggiano (2008) highlight the importance of supervisor qualities such as being flexible and adaptable, along with the ability to set (and manage) boundaries and being skilled at providing difficult feedback. In addition, Falender and colleagues (Falender, 2014; Falender et al., 2004), in considering the supervision of psychologists, have provided a detailed description of the supervisor competencies which they group under the headings of skills, knowledge, values and social context. Further, Hall-Lord, Theander, and Athlin (2013) emphasise the

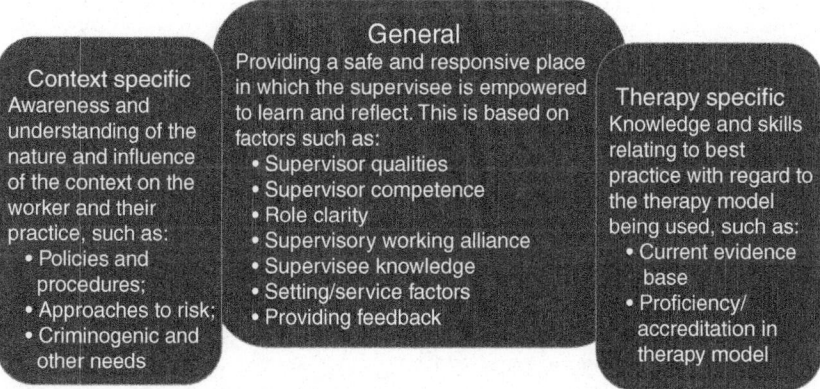

FIGURE 14.1: General and specialist areas of competence for therapy supervisors in forensic settings.

importance of the supervisor having role clarity, i.e. being clear of their role(s) and responsibility towards the supervisee (and the client and service).

The forensic setting

The forensic setting influences therapy and supervision through the limits and requirements the environment asserts on practice. This might include daily routines restricting the times and places in which therapy can be delivered; policies and procedures which determine reporting and sharing of certain information; overt power differentials indicated by staff having keys which can engender a 'them and us' stance, and the creation of 'clusters of clients' (e.g. men with specific types of offending history) living together. Each setting will bring with it a raft of influences on therapy. For example, in a prison setting, security may set restrictions on what can be done where and when, and might also influence what those accessing therapy are willing or able to engage in outside the therapy session (e.g. what activities or tasks they feel safe to engage in within their cell). Individuals may also feel the 'need' to maintain a 'hard' exterior in order to reduce vulnerability; and to complete work for 'external' reasons such as parole hearings. Other settings such as child custody, inpatient forensic mental health and probation are discussed by Davies (2015). A helpful question for supervisors to ask to examine the impact of the setting on the therapy (and supervision) is 'if this therapy/supervision was taking place in another setting what would be different?'. The supervisor and supervisee could experiment with identifying different settings and with targeting the question to specific tasks (e.g. what out of session work might you suggest, what behavioural experiments might be undertaken, who might you suggest they speak with?).

The supervisor needs to know what is taking/has taken place

As the focus of supervision is on the tasks and experience of the therapist, there needs to be a way for relevant 'raw' material to be brought to supervision. One method is for the therapist to report their recollections, observations and notes from the encounter(s). Whilst this is widely used in supervision, a range of factors such as the recall, awareness and potential biases of the therapist intrinsically limit this approach. Careful questioning and exploration on the part of the supervisor and/or gathering information from other sources (e.g. colleagues) can mitigate these to some degree. In addition, many forms of therapy supervision have a case reporting structure designed to aid the therapist in collating information to take to supervision. Where such a structure does not exist, supervisors may wish to develop their own from available generic ones (e.g. Appendix A from Stoltenberg & McNeill (2010), and Bernard & Goodyear (2014, p. 157)).

However, live supervision and therapy recording provide more robust mechanisms. Live supervision describes 'real time' observation on the part of the supervisor either by sitting in the session and observing the client-therapist interaction or doing this through a one-way screen. However, more common is the use of audio or video recordings of actual sessions. Direct observation is particularly important for those undergoing training in a specific therapy model. Stoltenberg and McNeill (2010) argue that for inexperienced therapists 'observation of their clinical work is imperative ... [as they] are not able to perceive accurately what they are doing in the session, let alone what is going on with the client' (pp. 70–71). This is likely to be compounded by the inexperienced therapist's focus on their technique and own reactions. The need for observation could also extend to the experienced therapist who is a novice within a forensic context. Clearly, augmenting the therapist's recall and view with direct information from the session offers an opportunity to consider what was done rather than what the therapist thought was done. As such, it is likely that these methods increase the reliability of ratings of competencies made by supervisors. In addition to using recordings to examine what has taken place, it is possible to use these to probe the experience and decision making of the therapist. For example, Interpersonal Process Recall (IPR; Clarke, 1997; Kagan & Kagan, 1997) is a structured approach in which the supervisor takes the role of 'enquirer' whose task is to stop the recording at various points and use questions and prompts to aid the therapist in recalling supplementary information (about their own thinking and affect). The recording is used as source material to enable the therapist to both 'remember the session detail' but also to see themselves from a distance. Despite the potential usefulness of such methods, there may be physical and procedural obstacles to making recordings in forensic environments. Therefore, the supervisor will need to develop ways to facilitate this that are specific to each forensic context.

The supervisor needs to draw on learning theories to guide the learning process

The formative function of supervision requires that the supervisor is able to support therapist learning and development. To this end, there are a range of learning processes and methods that have been described in relation to adult learning which are easily applied to individual therapist supervision. A broad framework of assessment (i.e. of knowledge, skill, learning style, etc.), competence development and progress evaluation can be used as a guide within which specific learning theory can be applied. Indeed, James, Milne, Marie-Blackburn, and Armstrong (2006) have described a five-step approach for supervising CBT therapists that integrates the three elements of this broad framework with learning models and techniques.

Theories of adult learning tend to foster a distinction with child education which is most explicit in the work of Knowles, Holton, and Swanson (1998) who use the term andragogy to emphasise this difference. Their model is underpinned by a number of guiding principles such as adults learn best when taking an active role and when drawing on experience. These factors can help shape the ways in which supervision is provided. Additionally, learning within supervision can be informed by approaches that seek to describe specific attributes or behaviours which may impact on learning. For example, Pratt (1988) details the ways in which the supervisee's need for direction and/or support should elicit different actions and approaches by the supervisor.

The application of the Zone of Proximal Development (ZPD; Vygotsky, 1978) to supervision has been described by several authors (e.g. James et al., 2006; Wilson & Lizzio, 2009). This approach describes a four-stage process of assisted learning in which the learner extends their competencies through support rather than by simplifying or breaking the task into small components. Specifically, tasks that the learner could achieve with assistance are said to be in their ZPD. The learner first achieves the task with assistance from others; then through assistance from self (such as self-talk), following which performance becomes automated and thus no new learning takes place. However, the fourth stage requires the learner to become consciously aware of their performance in order to allow new learning (such as refinements, adjustments and modifications) to be achieved through review and revision. Applied to supervision, ZPD requires that the supervisor can help the supervisee identify what might be in their ZPD and then tailor their assistance to maximise learning.

Clearly, for each therapy there will be a great deal of therapy-specific knowledge and skill that the therapist will need to master and remain competent to apply. For those therapists who are more experienced, experiential learning models such as the experiential learning cycle described by Kolb (1984) can be helpful. In this model, experience acts as the starting point for examining practice through: 1) reflection, then 2) conceptualisation, and finally 3) experimentation. Thus an exchange between the client and the therapist (experience) is examined and reviewed (reflection) leading to new ideas or theories (conceptualisation) which form the basis for action (experimentation).

Adaptations for forensic settings

Those supervising therapists in forensic settings are likely to need a range of additional competencies due to the need for specialist knowledge and skills in the areas of criminogenic and risk issues, as well as understanding the setting and services in which they work. This is likely to include the need for competence in relation to the legal system, court processes, specialist assessments, risk and systems understanding (Day, 2012). For therapy supervisors, it is likely that familiarity with offence-specific frameworks along with broader offending behaviour treatment principles such as those of Risk, Need and Responsivity (e.g. Andrews & Bonta, 2010) and the Good Lives Model (e.g. Ward & Maruna, 2007) are important. In addition, understanding risk – such as that posed by and to the client – will be essential to safe practice and the well-being of the therapist. The challenge of therapists engaging in positive risk taking (e.g. Titterton, 2010) in forensic settings necessitates careful balancing of what might be useful and what is possible.

Day (2012) in his paper on supervising psychologists in forensic settings, identifies a range of problems that can arise within four broad areas of forensic practice: 'professional competence', 'identity and role', 'integrity' and 'responsive stance'. Most, if not all of these, could be directly applied to therapists working in forensic settings even where individual therapy is the worker's only role. However, as Day notes, whilst there are generally clear guidelines for supervising those in training, there has been much less attention paid to supervising those who are trained.

Attending to boundaries in supervision

Boundaries represent the edge or limit of appropriate behaviour (Gutheil & Gabbard, 1998) and within forensic settings special attention needs to be given to at least two areas: the boundaries between the supervisor and the therapist, and those between the therapist and the client. For our purposes we will concentrate on therapist/client boundaries. Research has been conducted relating to boundary problems in therapeutic settings (e.g. Gutheil & Gabbard, 1998; Peternelj-Taylor & Yonge, 2003) and the role supervision can play in managing these (e.g. Walker & Clark, 1999). However, within forensic settings the consequences of boundary problems can be much more significant for the therapist and the client.

A number of different levels of boundary difficulty have been identified. Love & Heber (2001) describe boundary inattention (paying insufficient attention to the forensic context); boundary crossing (engaging in minor lapses in boundaries) and boundary violation (engaging in behaviour that is outside service or professional policy/ethics) with examples of each in a forensic context. Although there is no detailed information on the rates of therapist/client boundary violations in forensic settings, examples have been documented. More broadly, a study of boundary violations between prison employees and inmates in a US prison setting revealed rates of 2.5% – the majority of which were described as dual relationships (forming friendships but no sexual contact) (Marquart, Barnhill, & Balshaw-Biddle, 2001). In her small study in a forensic hospital setting, Evershed (2010) reported boundary violations were most common amongst unqualified female staff. Most importantly, however, she noted that boundary problems may be subtle and may have benign intent.

Davies (2015) details the three elements necessary for boundary violations to take place: namely, practitioner factors, client factors and contextual factors. Supervisors' attention to such factors, along with an understanding of the 'triangle of boundary maintenance', highlights the importance of procedural, physical and relational factors in the healthy maintenance of boundaries. Supervisors play an important role in 'boundary watch', helping to examine the decisions and practice of the therapist to help identify early signs of boundary inattention. One simple method for conceptualising boundary extremes is the boundary see-saw described by Hamilton (2010). She proposes that either end of the see-saw is associated with boundary violations – at one end the 'security guard' is likely to be under-involved and risks becoming abusive and controlling; at the other extreme the 'super carer' is likely to be over-involved and risks becoming abusive through the development of dual relationships. In many ways this overlaps with the concepts of the Drama Triangle (Karpman, 1968) in which the extremes of rescuer, persecutor and victim can be played out. Such metaphors can be extremely helpful in discussing issues within therapy and how these might support or undermine the development and maintenance of safe boundaries.

Supervisor training

As with any set of competencies, supervisors need to be trained and supported to take on this task. However, as far as we are aware, there is no specialist training for supervisors working in a forensic setting nor of any specific therapy approach in a forensic context. Despite this, there are a small number of generic supervisor training programmes and many therapy approaches that have their own supervisor training programme leading to therapy-specific supervisor accreditation. It is therefore incumbent on the supervisor to combine their training in therapy supervision with developing skills in supervision in forensic settings through their own means such as reading and their own supervision. In addition, we would suggest that therapists may also benefit from training focused on how to maximise their use of supervision. Therapists and supervisors should consult the therapy accreditation body to find details of supervision requirements and accredited supervisors.

Status of the evidence in forensic settings

Researching supervision provided to therapy staff working with forensic clients is in its infancy. Within the broader supervision literature, studies have found that supervision can have a positive impact on outcome and, further, that the absence of supervision can be detrimental (e.g. Bradshaw, Butterworth, & Mairs, 2007; Harkness & Hensley, 1991; Kilminster & Jolly, 2000). Studies have also reported that workers can provide descriptive evidence of the ways in which supervision has had an impact (e.g. Cheater & Hale, 2001; Manthorpe, Moriarty, Hussein, Stevens, & Sharpe, 2013). Perhaps the most robust study to date by Bambling and colleagues showed that supervision could positively impact on the working alliance and treatment outcomes (Bambling, King, Raue, Schweitzer, & Lambert, 2006). Studies have also reported positive effects for supervision on staff (e.g. Butterworth, Bell, Jackson, & Pajnkihar, 2008; Magnuson, Wilcoxon, & Norem, 2000) including within forensic settings (Long, Harding, Payne, & Collins, 2013). Specifically, studies have shown impacts on well-being (Bégat, Ellefsen, & Severinsson, 2005), lower burnout (Edwards et al., 2006; Hyrkäs, Appelqvist-Schmidlechner, & Haataja, 2006) and less emotional exhaustion (Knudsen, Roman, & Abraham, 2013). The absence of supervision in forensic settings has also been recognised. For example, a newspaper reported a damages settlement for a member of staff providing sex offender treatment who argued they had been psychologically harmed and that an absence of supervision was, at least in part, a contributory factor (Johnston, 2003). In addition, Clarke (2012) argues that supervision is a critical factor in maintaining resilience in forensic practitioners. However, the general evidence base for the impact of supervision is limited and negatively affected by problems with the research design as described by Ellis, Ladany, Krengel and Schult (1996) and Freitas (2002). It is therefore critical that research and systematic evaluation is undertaken to critically examine the impact of supervision on clients and therapists in forensic settings.

Conclusion

Therapist supervision is generally viewed as an essential element of safe and effective practice. Effective supervision is founded upon a functional working alliance that provides support and learning whilst upholding standards and maintaining a focus on the forensic context. As well as competence in supervision, approaches to learning and development, and the therapy model itself, those supervising therapists in forensic settings require additional context-specific competencies. This is likely to mean that those providing therapy supervision will need to access specialised training and supervision themselves in order to meet this challenge. Alongside this, there is enormous opportunity for undertaking research into the impact of supervision given that the evidence base for (therapy) supervision in forensic settings is yet to be established.

Further reading

Bernard, J. M., & Goodyear, R. K. (2014). *Fundamentals of Clinical Supervision* (5th edn). International Edition: Pearson.
This text provides a wealth of information and a wide range of specific tools such as a Self-Reflection Activity to aid with therapy dilemmas (p. 169) and a suit of resources contained within The Supervisor's Toolbox, pp. 304–357.
Campbell, J. M. (2011). *Essentials of clinical supervision* (Vol. 28). Chichester: John Wiley & Sons.
A useful paperback containing prompts, tips and exercises.
Davies, J. (2015). *Supervision for Forensic Practitioners*. London: Routledge.
This text focuses upon supervision provided within forensic contexts including prisons, probation and forensic mental health settings. It addresses a broad range of topics and is designed as a resource for supervisors, supervisees, researchers and service providers.

References

Andrews, D. A., & Bonta, J. (2010). *The psychology of criminal conduct* (5th edn). LexisNexis.
Ayer, S., Knight, S., Joyce, L., & Nightingale, V. (1997). Practice-led education and development project: developing styles in clinical supervision. *Nurse Education Today*, 17(5), 347–358.
Bambling, M., King, R., Raue, P., Schweitzer, R., & Lambert, W. (2006). Clinical supervision: Its influence on client-rated working alliance and client symptom reduction in the brief treatment of major depression. *Psychotherapy Research*, 16(3), 317–331. http://doi.org/10.1080/10503300500268524

Bégat, I., Ellefsen, B., & Severinsson, E. (2005). Nurses' satisfaction with their work environment and the outcomes of clinical nursing supervision on nurses' experiences of well-being – a Norwegian study. *Journal of Nursing Management, 13*(3), 221–230.

Benner, P. (1982). From novice to expert. *AJN The American Journal of Nursing, 82*(3), 402–407.

Bernard, J. M., & Goodyear, R. K. (2014). *Fundamentals of Clinical Supervision* (5th edn). International Edition: Pearson.

Bond, M., & Holland, S. (2011). *Skills of clinical supervision for nurses: A practical guide for supervisees, clinical supervisors and managers.* Maidenhead: Open University Press.

Bordin, E. S. (1983). A Working Alliance Based Model of Supervision. *The Counseling Psychologist, 11*(1), 35–42. http://doi.org/10.1177/0011000083111007

Bradshaw, T., Butterworth, A., & Mairs, H. (2007). Does structured clinical supervision during psychosocial intervention education enhance outcome for mental health nurses and the service users they work with? *Journal of Psychiatric and Mental Health Nursing, 14*(1), 4–12.

Butterworth, T., Bell, L., Jackson, C., & Pajnkihar, M. (2008). Wicked spell or magic bullet? A review of the clinical supervision literature 2001–2007. *Nurse Education Today, 28*(3), 264–272. http://doi.org/10.1016/j.nedt.2007.05.004

Campbell, J. M. (2011). *Essentials of clinical supervision,* Vol. 28. Chichester: John Wiley & Sons.

Cheater, F. M., & Hale, C. (2001). An evaluation of a local clinical supervision scheme for practice nurses. *Journal of Clinical Nursing, 10*(1), 119–131.

Clarke, J. (2012). The resilient practitioner. In J. Clarke & P. Wilson (Eds), *Forensic Psychology in Practice: A Practitioner's Handbook* (pp. 220–239). Basingstoke: Palgrave Macmillan.

Clarke, P. (1997). Interpersonal process recall in supervision. In G. Shipton (Ed.), *Supervision of psychotherapy and counselling: Making a place to think* (pp. 93–104). Maidenhead: Open University Press.

Cutcliffe, J. R., Butterworth, T., & Proctor, B. (Eds) (2005). *Fundamental themes in clinical supervision.* London: Routledge.

Davies, J. (2015). *Supervision for forensic practitioners.* London: Routledge.

Day, A. (2012). The nature of supervision in forensic psychology: Some observations and recommendations. *The British Journal of Forensic Practice, 14*(2), 116–123. http://doi.org/10.1108/14636641211223675

Edwards, D., Burnard, P., Hannigan, B., Cooper, L., Adams, J., Juggessur, T., et al. (2006). Clinical supervision and burnout: the influence of clinical supervision for community mental health nurses. *Journal of Clinical Nursing, 15*(8), 1007–1015. http://doi.org/10.1111/j.1365-2702.2006.01370.x

Ellis, M. V., Ladany, N., Krengel, M., & Schult, D. (1996). Clinical supervision research from 1981 to 1993: A methodological critique. *Journal of Counseling Psychology, 43*(1), 35.

Evershed, S. (2010). The grey areas of boundary issues when working with forensic patients who have a personality disorder. In P. Willmot & N. Gordon (Eds), *Working Positively with Personality Disorder in Secure Settings* (pp. 127–145). Chichester: John Wiley & Sons.

Falender, C. A. (2014). Clinical supervision in a competency-based era. *South African Journal of Psychology, 44*(1), 6–17. http://doi.org/10.1177/0081246313516260

Falender, C. A., Cornish, J. A. E., Goodyear, R., Hatcher, R., Kaslow, N. J., Leventhal, G., et al. (2004). Defining competencies in psychology supervision: A consensus statement. *Journal of Clinical Psychology, 60*(7), 771–785. http://doi.org/10.1002/jclp.20013

Fleming, I., & Steen, L. (Eds) (2004). *Supervision and clinical psychology: Theory, practice and perspectives.* Hove: Brunner-Routledge.

Fowler, J. (1996). Clinical supervision: What do you do after saying hello? *British Journal of Nursing, 5*(6), 382–385.

Freitas, G. J. (2002). The impact of psychotherapy supervision on client outcome: A critical examination of two decades of research. *Psychotherapy: Theory, research, practice, training, 39*(4), 354–367. http://doi.org/10.1037/0033-3204.39.4.354

Gutheil, T. G., & Gabbard, G. O. (1998). Misuses and misunderstandings of boundary theory in clinical and regulatory settings. *American Journal of Psychiatry*, *155*(3), 409–414.

Hall-Lord, M. L., Theander, K., & Athlin, E. (2013). A clinical supervision model in bachelor nursing education – Purpose, content and evaluation. *Nurse Education in Practice*, *13*(6), 506–511. http://doi.org/10.1016/j.nepr.2013.02.006

Hamilton, L. (2010). The boundary seesaw model: Good fences make for good neighbours. In A. Tennant & K. Howells (Eds), *Using Time Not Doing Time*. Chichester: Wiley-Blackwell.

Harkness, D., & Hensley, H. (1991). Changing the focus of social work supervision: Effects on client satisfaction and generalized contentment. *Social Work*, *36*(6), 506–512.

Hawkins, P., & Shohet, R. (2006). *Supervision in the helping professions* (3rd edn). Maidenhead: Open University Press.

Holloway, E. L. (1995). *Clinical supervision*. Thousand Oaks, CA: Sage Publications.

Hyrkäs, K., Appelqvist-Schmidlechner, K., & Haataja, R. (2006). Efficacy of clinical supervision: Influence on job satisfaction, burnout and quality of care. *Journal of Advanced Nursing*, *55*(4), 521–535. http://doi.org/10.1111/j.1365-2648.2006.03936.x

James, I. A., Milne, D., Marie-Blackburn, I., & Armstrong, P. (2006). Conducting successful supervision: Novel elements towards an integrative approach. *Behavioural and Cognitive Psychotherapy*, *35*(2), 191. http://doi.org/10.1017/S1352465806003407

Johnston, P. (2003). £150,000 award for prison officer on sex wing. 1 April, 2014. URL retrieved on 17 April, 2014, from www.telegraph.co.uk/news/uknews/1426270/150000-award-for-prison-officer-on-sex-wing.html

Kadushin, A. (1992). *Supervision in Social Work* (3rd edn). New York: Columbia University Press.

Kagan, H., & Kagan, N. I. (1997). Interpersonal process recall: Influencing human interaction. In C. E. Watkins (Ed.), *Handbook of Psychotherapy Supervision* (pp. 296–309). New York: John Wiley & Sons.

Karpman, S. (1968). Fairy tales and script drama analysis. *Transactional Analysis Bulletin*, 7, 26–30.

Kilminster, S. M., & Jolly, B. C. (2000). Effective supervision in clinical practice settings: a literature review. *Medical Education*, *34*(10), 827–840.

Knowles, M. S., Holton, E. F., III, & Swanson, R. A. (1998). *The Adult Learner* (5th edn). Woburn: Butterworth-Heinemann.

Knudsen, H. K., Roman, P. M., & Abraham, A. J. (2013). Quality of clinical supervision and counselor emotional exhaustion: The potential mediating roles of organizational and occupational commitment. *Journal of Substance Abuse Treatment*, *44*(5), 528–533. http://doi.org/10.1016/j.jsat.2012.12.003

Kolb, D. A. (2014). Experiential learning: Experience as the source of learning and development. Upper Saddle River, NJ: Prentice Hall Inc.

Lizzio, A. J., & Wilson, K. L. (2002). The domain of learning goals in professional supervision. In M. Patton & W. McMahon (Eds), *Supervision in the helping professions: A practical approach* (pp. 27–41). Frenchs Forest, NSW: Pearson Education Australia.

Long, C. G., Harding, S., Payne, K., & Collins, L. (2013). Nursing and health-care assistant experience of supervision in a medium secure psychiatric service for women: implications for service development. *Journal of Psychiatric and Mental Health Nursing*, *21*(2), 154–162. http://doi.org/10.1111/jpm.12066

Love, C. C., & Heber, S. A. (2001). Staff-patient erotic boundary violations: Part 3 – Environmental Factors. *On the Edge*, *8*(1), 1–1, 12–16.

Magnuson, S., Wilcoxon, S. A., & Norem, K. (2000). A profile of lousy supervision: Experienced counselors' perspectives. *Counselor Education and Supervision*, *39*(3), 189–202.

Manthorpe, J., Moriarty, J., Hussein, S., Stevens, M., & Sharpe, E. (2013). Content and purpose of supervision in social work practice in England: Views of newly qualified social workers, managers and directors. *British Journal of Social Work*. http://doi.org/10.1093/bjsw/bct102

Marquart, J. W., Barnhill, M. B., & Balshaw-Biddle, K. (2001). Fatal attraction: An analysis of employee boundary violations in a southern prison system, 1995–1998. *Justice Quarterly*, *18*(4), 877–910. http://doi.org/10.1080/07418820100095121

Milne, D. L. (2009). *Evidence-Based Clinical Supervision*. Chichester: John Wiley & Sons.

Milne, D. L., Reiser, R. P., Cliffe, T., & Raine, R. (2011). SAGE: preliminary evaluation of an instrument for observing competence in CBT supervision. *The Cognitive Behaviour Therapist*, *4*(4), 123–138. http://doi.org/10.1017/S1754470X11000079

Mor Barak, M. E., Travis, D. J., Pyun, H., & Xie, B. (2009). The impact of supervision on worker outcomes: A meta-analysis. *Social Service Review*, *83*(1), 3–32. http://doi.org/10.1086/599028

Morgan, M. M., & Sprenkle, D. H. (2007). Toward a common-factors approach to supervision. *Journal of Marital and Family Therapy*, *33*(1), 1–17.

Nelson, M. L., Barnes, K. L., Evans, A. L., & Triggiano, P. J. (2008). Working with conflict in clinical supervision: Wise supervisors' perspectives. *Journal of Counseling Psychology*, *55*(2), 172–184. http://doi.org/10.1037/0022-0167.55.2.172

O'Donoghue, K. B. (2014). Towards an interactional map of the supervision session: An exploration of supervisees and supervisors experiences. *Practice*, *26*(1), 53–70. http://doi.org/10.1080/09503153.2013.869581

Peternelj-Taylor, C. A., & Yonge, O. (2003). Exploring boundaries in the nurse-client relationship: Professional roles and responsibilities. *Perspectives in Psychiatric Care*, *39*(2), 55–66.

Pratt, D. D. (1988). Andragogy as a relational construct. *Adult Education Quarterly*, *38*(3), 160–172. http://doi.org/10.1177/0001848188038003004

Proctor, B. (1986). Supervision: A co-operative exercise in accountability. In M. Marken & M. Payne (Eds), *Enabling and Ensuring*. Leicester: National Youth Bureau for Education in Youth and Community Work.

Rolfe, G. (1997). Beyond expertise: Theory, practice and the reflexive practitioner. *Journal of Clinical Nursing*, *6*(2), 93–97.

Scaife, J. (2013). *Supervision in clinical practice*. London: Routledge.

Stoltenberg, C. D., & McNeill, B. W. (2010). *IDM Supervision* (3rd edn). London: Routledge.

Titterton, M. (2010). Positive risk taking. HALE. URL retrieved on 27 May, 2014, from www.haletrust.com/system/files/Positive+Risk+Taking.pdf

Vygotsky, L. S. (1978). *Mind in society: The development of higher psychological processes*. Cambridge, MA: Harvard University.

Walker, R., & Clark, J. J. (1999). Heading off boundary problems: Clinical supervision as risk management. *Psychiatric Services*, *50*(11), 1435–1439.

Ward, T., & Maruna, S. (2007). *Rehabilitation*. London: Routledge.

Watkins, C. E. (1997). *Handbook of psychotherapy supervision*. New York: John Wiley & Sons.

Watkins, C. E., Jr, & Milne, D. L. (2014). *The Wiley international handbook of clinical supervision*. Chichester: John Wiley & Sons.

Wilson, K. L., & Lizzio, A. J. (2009). Processes and interventions to facilitate supervisees' learning. In N. Pelling, J. Barletta, & P. Armstrong (Eds), *The practice of clinical supervision* (pp. 138–164). Bowen Hills, Queensland: Australian Academic Press.

Winstanley, J., & White, E. (2011). The MCSS-26©: Revision of the Manchester Clinical Supervision Scale© Using the Rasch Measurement Model. *Journal of Nursing Measurement*, *19*(3), 160–178. http://doi.org/10.1891/1061-3749.19.3.160

Wosket, V., & Page, S. (1994). *The Cyclical Model of Supervision*. London: Routledge.

15

SELECTING THERAPIES AND THERAPISTS

Jason Davies and Claire Nagi

One of the major challenges facing those providing psychological therapies within forensic settings is to decide which approach to adopt. As we have seen in the chapters presented throughout this book, a wide range of therapies exist that can be delivered to individuals. Although the nature of the evidence for each intervention differs, generally the authors have shown that these treatments can be effective. In this chapter we consider ways to make decisions regarding therapy choice and approaches to therapist accreditation and selection.

Introduction

As has been demonstrated throughout the chapters of this book, a range of individual therapy approaches are being used in forensic settings. Although not an exhaustive list of treatments, these chapters provide a platform from which we can consider methods for selecting therapies, or therapists, for particular needs or clients. What is clear from the evidence provided by the various authors is that a number of individually delivered treatment approaches work, for a range of needs, for an array of individuals and in different forensic settings. Whilst some approaches may be more suited to a small number of treatment needs, others can be applied to a wider range of needs. In addition to targeting risk and criminogenic factors, it is evident that there are common additional areas of need that frequently present themselves in the forensic population. These include issues relating to trauma, emotional difficulties, interpersonal difficulties and mental health needs. Importantly, such factors may be directly linked to offending behaviour, or may 'sit alongside' as distinct needs in their own right. Collectively, the treatments described have targeted a spectrum of criminogenic and mental health issues drawing on a variety of theoretical models to underpin the assumed mechanisms of change. Importantly, there are few global exclusion criteria, limited perhaps to the presence of active psychosis.

An initial idea for this chapter was to develop a 'therapy selection flowchart' using the evidence base, and the indications and contra-indications for each intervention as a starting point. Indeed, bodies such as the American Psychological Association have developed an approach to examining therapies that uses an assessment of the available evidence, to indicate whether or not there is sufficient support for the use of a specific therapy and/or whether the approach could prove harmful. Through this process, a list of Evidence Supported Therapies (ESTs) has been established by Division 12 (Society of Clinical Psychology) of the American Psychological Association (see www.div12.org/psychological-treatments/treatments/, accessed 10 April, 2016). However, such an approach to creating an 'endorsed' therapy list has been criticised on a number of levels. This includes questioning the fundamental assumption underpinning such an approach – i.e. that the 'treatment approach' is the primary agent of change (Blatt & Zuroff, 2005). Whilst this challenge might be strongly contested by those advocating particular models of therapy, the apparent outcome equivalence of treatments (discussed below) would suggest that the treatment model may not be the primary agent of change. Another challenge is the assumption that a narrow focus on symptom change (typically used as the index of change) is the best outcome indicator (Blatt & Zuroff, 2005) and that if a broad range of outcomes was used more sophisticated patterns of 'what works' might emerge. Indeed, outcomes have been shown to be very dependent on the measures used (Huppert et al., 2001). 'Philosophical challenges' such as the implicit medicalisation and compartmentalisation of people and difficulties underpinning the concept of 'this treatment works for this condition' have also been made, with critics indicating that such an approach treats people and 'difficulties' as discrete, independent and homogeneous. Finally, a more general criticism has been voiced – that such an approach fosters 'brand endorsement' (Rosen & Davison, 2003) and the promotion of a plethora of therapies each with their own training and structures.

The puzzle of treatment equivalence

What has emerged from the chapters, and is noted from the wider psychotherapy literature, is that as well as many interventions being better than nothing, many approaches work for the same areas of need and have similar reported levels of effectiveness. The phenomenon of therapy equivalence, often referred to as the 'Dodo bird effect' (Luborsky et al., 2002; Rosenzweig, 1936), raises a number of possibilities:

1. There are differences but we don't detect them.
2. Different people gain from different interventions.
3. There are common underlying factors.

It is therefore important to consider these possibilities in order to determine the ways in which therapy and therapist selection could be made.

The failure to detect differences between therapies

The ability to detect differences between a group of people receiving an intervention against another group receiving no treatment or a different treatment, will be affected by research design factors and researcher allegiance effects. Research design factors include a group of related issues which interact with one another, such as the scale of the difference between the groups, the nature of the comparison group and the number of participants who took part (both initially and who remained to the end of the study). Thus the more extreme the difference in outcome between the groups (effect size), the fewer people you will need to make a confident judgment that a difference exists between the groups. We might think of treatment versus no treatment as a design in which more extreme differences are likely to be found. In contrast, when comparing two or more active interventions (e.g. an intervention that works to 'some degree' with another that works to a large degree) much larger groups of people will be required. Grissom (1996) has argued just this – that apparent therapy equivalence may be an artefact of underpowered studies. Therefore, insufficient participant numbers and extrapolating from treatment versus no treatment studies may lead us to wrongly conclude that there is no (statistically *and* clinically) significant difference between treatment approaches. To complicate this further, it has also been noted that where active treatment is compared to a no treatment group, the comparison group is often less well matched with the treatment group than when two active treatments are compared (Luborsky et al., 2002). The issues of small numbers and heterogeneous groups are common in forensic settings; obtaining sufficient numbers of people who can be matched according to key characteristics is difficult and thus our ability to determine differences between active treatments will be compromised. In the other direction, very large samples (as often found in group treatment programme research) can also be problematic as small differences between groups can be statistically significant even though the level of clinical significance might be negligible. In order to compensate for these difficulties, at least to some degree, other ways of presenting findings are increasingly being used. For example, within the broader psychotherapy literature, metrics such as effect size are being used to describe treatment impact. This indicates how 'big' the treatment effect is; however, other forms of clinical significance should also be used (see Jacobson & Truax, 1991; Ogles, Lunnen, & Bonesteel, 2001 for a further discussion). Furthermore, Grissom (1996) suggests extending the ways in which data are analysed and reported (e.g. including the use of metrics such as the 'probability of superiority estimate').

Researcher allegiance effects are being increasingly recognised as an important issue in psychotherapy impact research (e.g. see Dragioti, Dimoliatis, & Evangelou, 2015; Luborsky et al., 1999). This effect describes the impact of the expectations and model preferences of researchers on the results and reported findings. For example,

Luborsky et al. (1999) argue that much of the difference found between treatments can be accounted for by researcher allegiance and suggests a range of mechanisms through which this might occur, and ways to try to moderate it. Despite this, Dragioti et al. (2015) found that routine reporting of allegiance or explicitly adopting methods to address this are rarely used. Until design and allegiance factors are adequately reported and addressed, we cannot conclude with certainty that treatment equivalence is present across therapies. However, this does not prevent us from accepting the current position of treatment equivalence until proven otherwise.

Different people benefit from different treatments

Although group level changes may suggest treatment equivalence, this does not provide us with clear information about what works at the level of the individual. Based on the descriptions contained within the chapters of this book, it could be reasonable to suggest that different treatments work in different ways or that they act on different aspects of the person or the issue at hand. This would mean that different people might gain from each of the treatments to a greater or lesser degree. Whilst it is commonplace to assume that because the same *proportion* of individuals appear to benefit from different treatments that it is the same *people* who benefit from each of the treatments it has been recognised that 'sub-groups of patients might do better or worse with a specific treatment' (Luborsky et al., 2002; p. 9). However, this issue has not been (and is not easy to) examine in forensic settings. In order to be able to consider this fully, authors such as Blatt and Zuroff (2005) have argued that broader evaluations of treatment impact are needed – that outcomes should go beyond specific symptom reduction alone. Further, they state that 'treatment research needs to address more complex questions like what kinds of treatments are effective, for what kinds of patients, in what kinds of ways, and through what kinds of mechanisms or processes of therapeutic change' (Blatt & Zuroff, 2005; p. 480). It is possible that some people are helped by some treatments and not others (whom we might call 'specific responders') whilst other people are helped by a range of treatments (those we might term 'general responders').

One component affecting treatment response may be the degree of 'buy-in' shown by both client and therapist (we might term these client allegiance and therapist allegiance respectively; c.f. researcher allegiance above). Whereas researcher allegiance might be seen as a problem in that it can influence reported outcomes, client and therapist allegiance could be seen as important conditions for successful therapy. Black (1996) has argued that treatments based on active participation (as psychological treatments generally are) will be sensitive to, and influenced by, patient and staff beliefs and preferences. One tangible element of this could be the 'theory of change' shared by the therapist and client. For example, Ilardi & Craighead (1994) noted that effective therapy was underpinned by the therapist sharing a therapeutic rationale with the client. This explanation acts as a basis for understanding the person's difficulties and provides an approach to managing, addressing, resolving or overcoming them. The need to articulate a model of change and maximise 'buy-in' might provide the foundation to argue that therapists should be encouraged to train in an approach they believe in so that they can deliver this with fidelity and confidence (maximising therapist allegiance). Secondly, this would demand that clients have the opportunity to express their views and wishes regarding the treatment that they are to receive in order to promote client allegiance.

There is still a great deal more to understand about 'who might benefit from what'. However, in order to examine if different people benefit from different treatments, it may be possible to make use of single case experimental designs (e.g. AB-based approaches; Bloom, Fischer, & Orme, 2006; Davies & Sheldon, 2012) to examine the impact of different therapies and/or therapeutic 'strategies' on the same person.

There are common factors which account for treatment impact

Whilst treatment differences might be missed, and different people might gain from each treatment, it is also possible that treatment equivalence can be explained by the presence of common factors across treatment models. These common factors can be thought of as 'those dimensions of the treatment setting (therapist, therapy, client) that are not specific to any particular technique' (Lambert, 2005; p. 856). Although 'placebo treatments' may contain a range of important elements (e.g. attention and warmth from the therapist), Lambert (2005) notes that the degree of change in placebo conditions is less than is found in an active therapy.

Early responses, i.e. treatment change noted before specific therapy techniques have been applied, provide interesting evidence of possible common factors (e.g. Blatt & Zuroff, 2005; Ilardi & Craighead, 1994; Lambert, 2005). Most typically, common factors have been associated with the quality of the therapeutic relationship (especially in the early stages of therapy) and the pre-treatment characteristics of the patient (Blatt & Zuroff, 2005) such as readiness to change. For example, those who might be considered early responders to treatment, appear to engage in therapy in a particular way as shown by factors such as moving to new problems in each session rather than returning to the same one (Lambert, 2005). Authors have also suggested that there are common factors, ingredients or 'principles of change' which lead to therapeutic change. Based on this, it should follow that therapists would need to be skilled at providing those 'common factors' associated with the basic principles of change (Messer & Wampold, 2002; Rosen & Davison, 2003) rather than a specific form of therapy per se. These would include a range of alliance and allegiance factors as well as skills and competencies.

The therapist matters

Regardless of the reason for apparent equivalence or the possibility of the 'hidden superiority' of one approach over another, studies have shown that the person providing the treatment has a sizeable effect on outcome. Whilst the mechanism(s) of therapist impact is/are debated, the evidence of this effect has been shown in a range of studies in medical as well as psychological settings. For example, a study of medication treatment for depression, reported large differences between the treating psychiatrists (McKay, Imel, & Wampold, 2006). Strikingly, the 'best psychiatrists' were associated with greater improvement in their placebo condition than the poorest psychiatrists in their treatment condition! This suggests that the therapist effect might be greater than the medication effect alone (although of course it may be that the poor psychiatrists in this study failed to provide adequate information about medication compliance for a 'therapeutic dose' of treatment to be reached). Within the psychological therapy field, several studies have shown that therapists vary greatly in their outcomes (e.g. Brown, Lambert, Jones, & Minami, 2005) even when comparing therapists who have 'positive outcomes' (Huppert et al., 2001). However, this picture is further complicated by findings suggesting that different therapists may have different outcomes on different measures (i.e. those scoring highly in one area of change did not necessarily score highly in others) (Huppert et al., 2001). Despite this, significant therapist contributions to outcome have been found in highly structured therapy where the scope for variation in the treatment approach is restricted (Huppert et al., 2001). There are several other interesting conclusions drawn by Huppert and colleagues. They found that the most and least effective therapists had similar drop-out rates (although we must remember that most therapists in their study were effective in part) and that certain features and qualities of the therapist (e.g. experience) appeared to be related to some aspects of outcome whilst other features such as theoretical orientation, gender and age did not appear to be. A final, and important observation, especially for examining outcomes, is that the therapist may impact on whether data is completed by those receiving therapy (Brown et al., 2005). There may be many reasons for this. However, one way to address this would be to make outcome evaluation 'everyone's business' by embedding routine measurement into interventions.

Iatrogenic effects: warning – therapies and therapists may cause harm

There is a growing awareness that along with benefits, therapists need to be alert to the possibility of causing harm. Within forensic settings, the idea that treatment might cause harm to those receiving it has largely been limited to debates about psychopathy. This stems from research by Rice and colleagues who concluded that treatment doesn't work for this group and more importantly that it can increase problems, risk and offending (Rice, Harris, & Cormier, 1992). However, careful consideration of both the intervention used and the study design, reveals that drawing a generalised conclusion that 'treatment doesn't work' for this group cannot be supported. In their review of the literature, D'Silva, Duggan, & McCarthy (2004) suggested that whilst 'psychopaths tended to have worse outcomes ... we do not have the evidence to conclude that high-scoring psychopaths have a negative response to treatment' (pp. 173–4). Perhaps more important for our considerations within this book is the possibility of iatrogenic effects amongst those who would not meet the criteria for psychopathy. Although this has been acknowledged by some, notably Lawrence Jones, who has detailed ways in which treatments in forensic settings may have harmful effects (e.g. Jones, 2007), it is necessary to look outside the forensic field to consider this proposition more fully.

At the level of the treatment approach, Lilienfeld (2007) argues for the importance of identifying 'potentially harmful therapies (PHTs)', i.e. treatments for which there are demonstrated harmful effects that endure and have been replicated. He discusses a number of treatments that fulfil the criteria, and argues that a focus on PHTs might be more important than focusing on evidence supported therapies. However, therapists may fail to report 'negative therapy outcomes' or attribute the deterioration to other factors. This may be complicated by the fact that harm can be a complex concept that may show itself in a variety of ways (Lilienfeld, 2007) such as:

- Improvement in some areas and deterioration in others;
- harm experienced by others (e.g. reduction in symptoms in the client but increased distress in a spouse);
- drop-out from (harmful) treatment;
- different short- and long-term outcomes (e.g. increased symptom experience in the short term but gains in the longer term or vice versa);
- and effective therapies being harmful if delivered improperly; or harmful for some clients but beneficial to others.

Such problems may be counteracted by actively acknowledging that harmful responses can occur, and planning possible reactions to these in advance. Whilst it is unethical to replicate iatrogenic effects in a systematic way, mechanisms for better reporting of practice outcomes would help (Lilienfeld, 2007). To detect harm requires ongoing individual monitoring, whilst responding to it is best achieved through careful consideration and review of the intervention – ideally with an external person (e.g. clinical supervision or a local clinical review panel).

At the level of the individual, research from the wider psychotherapy literature has shown harmful effects in relation to a number of specific psychological treatments (Lilienfeld, 2007), with a percentage (often reported as between three and ten per cent) appearing worse after therapy. However, such effects have all too often remained hidden; outcomes typically concentrate on whether the treatment works in general rather than for specific individuals. Thus, even in treatments that might be beneficial, when group average treatment gains are reported, as well as winners, some people may have deteriorated because of treatment. A simple way to combat this bias would be for the number of people showing improvement and deterioration to be routinely reported along with the consequences of deterioration for the individual or society. This would help determine the overall impact and cost effectiveness of interventions. Ethical issues and models for understanding the process of change are equally complex in relation to possible harms. For example, treatment is sometimes continued even when harm (e.g. distress) is reported. Some models of the process of change (e.g. the Assimilation Model; Stiles, 2006) would anticipate the possibility of deterioration prior to an eventual improvement beyond the baseline position for some individuals. However, when deterioration during therapy is observed, what may not be readily apparent is whether the deterioration is part of a process of change or is because the intervention is not working and is causing harm. Individual case prediction of what might happen during the treatment course, based on a formulation, could be helpful in distinguishing these possibilities. Case formulation itself raises many challenges and issues (Davies, Black, Bentley, & Nagi, 2013) however, this is beyond the scope of our consideration here. Thus whether or not to continue at points of deterioration and also determining the endpoint of therapy require careful and detailed decision making supported by peer examination and supervision (Davies, 2015).

Unless the possibility of harm resulting from treatment is recognised and monitored, potential harm/s caused to some by widely accepted treatments will be overlooked. One possibility for furthering our understanding of what works (and how), and raising alerts when deterioration is noticed, would be the creation of a database such as ALERT (Brown et al., 2005) which would collect routine data and provide feedback to treating clinicians. Clearly, such an approach would require international collaboration and funding; however the benefits could be significant.

Therapist standards and selection

Therapist accreditation

As we have seen in previous chapters, there are already established routes for training and registration in many of the specific therapy approaches. These typically require the therapist to engage with a programme of therapy-specific learning during which they demonstrate their adherence to delivering a specific model. Together these training routes have fostered the development of therapist standards and have led to detailed work to articulate and assess competencies associated with each of the approaches. Within each therapy, integrity is often defined using 'adherence checklists' which require evidence of particular aspects of the model in action (and sometimes in a particular sequence). A traditional assumption has been that effective therapy rests upon model adherence and treatment integrity. Indeed, the assumption in treatment trials, and to some degree amongst those providing interventions, is that there is standardisation across those providing a specific treatment. However, given the observation that trained therapists vary, it seems reasonable to ask 'do all those who are accredited to provide a specific therapy deliver the same intervention and if not, in which way(s) might it vary?' Additionally, the evidence concerning possible therapy equivalence and the scope for further improvements in the impact of therapies, make it important to explore what is standardised (e.g. the treatment sequence, particular treatment components) and how similar are features such as formulations from multiple practitioners concerning the same client. These issues are beyond the scope of this chapter; however, they require investigation.

They provide grounds for suggesting that it may be possible to also accredit individuals who do not practice a specific therapy yet can a) evidence effectiveness and b) demonstrate that they attend to and utilise evidence-based therapeutic approaches and strategies.

The Evidence Directed Therapist (EDT)

Certifying those providing a recognised (evidence-based) therapy is clearly one mechanism for therapist accreditation. However, as noted above, although therapy training courses lead to the individual being accredited it seems that each person delivering a treatment will do so in their own way. An additional approach, based on the notion of common factors and principles of change, would be to accredit those who use an effective but 'non-branded' approach, based on those factors for which there is an evidence base. Such an approach would mean that therapists would be required, amongst other things, to be able to:

1) Articulate the model of change being applied to the individual case (so that this can be communicated to the client to promote engagement in a common endeavour of therapy).
2) Demonstrate competence in common factors.
3) Demonstrate the impact of their work through routine evaluation.

In order for this approach to be viable, further work is needed to detail the common factors linked to positive therapeutic outcomes. Inevitably, these will concentrate on therapist factors including fostering a therapeutic alliance (e.g. Marshall, Fernandez, & Serran, 2003; Marshall et al., 2002; Ross, Polaschek, & Ward, 2008), principles of change such as a shared theory of the change process, a way to determine the focus of the treatment sessions (e.g. priorities, what to attend to) and specific skills (which might include skills in assessing those client characteristics associated with positive outcomes and drop-out; knowledge and skills in evaluating individual change and skills associated with processes such as engagement and problem solving). From this it would be possible to develop a checklist of those factors that therapists would need to demonstrate. Developing a profile of competencies and descriptions of common principles could be achieved, in part, from a systematic review of the therapy-specific 'checklists' available. Work on this has already been undertaken by researchers at University College London, although their approach has been to specify competencies for different therapies and for working with different 'clinical groups and contexts' (see https://www.ucl.ac.uk/pals/research/cehp/research-groups/core/competence-frameworks, accessed 10 April, 2016).

Developing a method of accreditation for and recognition of Evidence Directed Therapists (in addition to specific therapy-trained individuals), along with methods for recording and sharing data across all forms of therapy, could be a significant step forward for therapy practice and research in forensic settings. Such a move beyond only providing set models of treatment could enable increased responsivity to be introduced into therapy and allow more focus to be given to identifying those common therapy principles and components associated with change to be demonstrated. However, this would also force an acceptance that therapy isn't standardised although the underlying principles may be. Such an approach would result in treatment governed by core questions such as:

- What does the literature say might work?
  - General and specific skills and competencies
  - Principles derived from offender treatment models (e.g. RNR; GLM)
  - Approaches that have been shown to be effective
- What do other sources of data suggest might work? (e.g. own past experience; supervision)
- What are my therapeutic biases and what model/framework can I give my allegiance to?
- What is the client telling me that they engage with/what can they give their allegiance to?
- What would be the most prudent intervention? (cheapest, quickest, least demanding – for greatest possible gain)
- What methods of evaluation can be adopted?
- How will the treatment fit with other interventions being provided?

Selecting a therapist

Within forensic settings, consideration of and research relating to client choice of therapy is a rarity. However, within the wider psychotherapy literature it has been suggested that 'clients should seek the most competent therapist possible … whose theoretical orientation is compatible with their own' (Messer & Wampold, 2002; p. 24). This would suggest a move from a 'one size fits all' approach in forensic settings to a 'horses for courses' approach with flexibility and responsiveness as key features. What such a shift must not signal is any drift from the evidence of 'what works' and the principles underlying risk reduction. In fact, such an approach might increase the attention to those factors as therapists are required to deliver their intervention in an individually tailored, responsive, carefully planned and considered way. Routine outcome evaluation would also enable therapists to detail their effectiveness with each individual and be clear about any differential effects observed across areas of need or with different responsivity issues. As suggested earlier, it may be that there are 'general responders' who can engage with a wide range of therapists and therapeutic models; however, for 'specific responders' their allegiance to the therapist and the therapy approach could be pivotal to a successful outcome. These factors should be weighed together with emerging principles designed to support decision making about individual and group-based interventions in forensic services (e.g. O'Brien, Sullivan, & Daffern, 2016; Polaschek, 2011). A further extension would be for therapists to use regular feedback from clients to inform the nature of the intervention (e.g. Green & Latchford, 2012) – even those in forensic settings whose feedback and views are often questioned because of possible motivations for providing information. Fostering client decision making about therapy will demand highly skilled therapists who are able to help shape the emerging evidence base relating to therapy in forensic settings. It also will place much more onus on the individual therapist to have awareness of their own competencies and limitations as well as on the use of supportive, developmental and governance structures such as those present in effective supervision.

Routine practice evaluation

In order to demonstrate outcomes and progress our understanding of individual therapy in forensic settings, the need for routine practice evaluation has never been more important. It remains the case that most treatments offered in forensic settings can be seen as innovative and should be evaluated using detailed analysis of individuals (Davies, Howells, & Jones, 2007; Davies, Jones, & Howells, 2010). However, there is a need to develop, in parallel, evaluation based on frequently collected clinician and client data (e.g. Bentley et al., in press). There is also a case for an international collaboration to develop a system of evaluation based on common measures across people and places. We advocate that all therapists should therefore take an active role in evaluating the impact of the interventions they provide. At minimum this would be a first step to ensuring effective treatment is provided and that possible harms are detected early. However, it would also enable more sophisticated questions to be examined and a more refined understanding of 'what works' and 'how it works' to be developed over time.

Conclusion

Although many psychological therapies may be better than 'treatment as usual' or no treatment, the evidence suggests that there is still a great deal of scope for enhancing outcomes. Whilst therapies appear to have reached an effectiveness ceiling, the 'puzzle' of apparent therapy equivalence raises the possibility that the time may have come to give more consideration to common therapy factors and the development of evidence directed therapists who are trained, supervised and who routinely assess change and outcome. It also requires that we examine how therapy and therapist selection takes place with each client and how treatment impact can be enhanced. Recent 'must read' texts, such as *Maximising the benefits of psychotherapy* by David Green and Gary Latchford, provide a robust challenge to practitioners and researchers to critically consider 'what works' and the ways to build evidence of treatment outcomes. It may be that selecting the therapist is as, if not more, important than the therapy choice (when harmful or ineffective therapies are discounted); ensuring that the therapist is highly skilled (e.g. through training and accreditation) and appropriately supported (e.g. through supervision) is a necessary foundation for this. However, allegiance/'buy-in' by both therapist and client appears to be an often overlooked yet highly important area for much more detailed examination.

Acknowledgement

Thanks to Lawrence Jones for discussions relating to 'non-therapy specific' therapist accreditation.

Further reading

Green, D., & Latchford, G. (2012). *Maximising the benefits of psychotherapy: A practice-based evidence approach*. Chichester: John Wiley & Sons.
Lambert, M. J. (2005). Early response in psychotherapy: Further evidence for the importance of common factors rather than 'placebo effects.' *Journal of Clinical Psychology*, 61(7), 855–869. http://doi.org/10.1002/jclp.20130
Lilienfeld, S. O. (2007). Psychological treatments that cause harm. *Perspectives on Psychological Science*, 2(1), 53–70.
Luborsky, L., Rosenthal, R., Diguer, L., Andrusyna, T., Berman, J., Levitt, J., et al. (2002). The Dodo Bird verdict is alive and well – mostly. *Clinical Psychology: Science and Practice*, 9, 2–12.

References

Bentley, N., Davies, J., Sellen, J., & Maggs, R. (in press). An initial evaluation of the Global Review Form as an approach to measuring individual change. *Journal of Forensic Psychiatry and Psychology*.
Black, N. (1996). Why we need observational studies to evaluate the effectiveness of health care. *BMJ: British Medical Journal*, 312(7040), 1215.
Blatt, S. J., & Zuroff, D. C. (2005). Empirical evaluation of the assumptions in identifying evidence based treatments in mental health. *Clinical Psychology Review*, 25(4), 459–486. http://doi.org/10.1016/j.cpr.2005.03.001
Bloom, M., Fischer, J., & Orme, J. G. (2006). *Evaluating practice: Guidelines for the accountable professional* (5th edn). Boston: Allyn and Bacon.
Brown, G. S., Lambert, M. J., Jones, E. R., & Minami, T. (2005). Identifying highly effective psychotherapists in a managed care environment. *American Journal of Managed Care*, 11(8), 513–520.
D'Silva, K., Duggan, C., & McCarthy, L. (2004). Does treatment really make psychopaths worse? A review of the evidence. *Journal of Personality Disorders*, 18(2), 163–177.
Davies, J. (2015). *Supervision for Forensic Practitioners*. London: Routledge.
Davies, J., & Sheldon, K. (2012). Single case methodologies. In K. Sheldon, J. Davies, & K. Howells (Eds), *Research in Practice for Forensic Professionals*. London: Routledge.
Davies, J., Black, S., Bentley, N., & Nagi, C. (2013). Forensic case formulation: Theoretical, ethical and practical issues. *Criminal Behaviour and Mental Health*, 23(4), 304–314. http://doi.org/10.1002/cbm.1882
Davies, J., Howells, K., & Jones, L. (2007). Evaluating innovative treatments in forensic mental health: A role for single case methodology? *Journal of Forensic Psychiatry & Psychology*, 18(3), 353–367. http://doi.org/10.1080/14789940701443173
Davies, J., Jones, L., & Howells, K. (2010). Evaluating individual change. In M. Daffern, L. Jones, & J. Shine (Eds.), *Offence paralleling behaviour: A case formulation approach to offender assessment and intervention*. Chichester: Wiley & Sons.
Dragioti, E., Dimoliatis, I., & Evangelou, E. (2015). Disclosure of researcher allegiance in meta-analyses and randomised controlled trials of psychotherapy: A systematic appraisal. *BMJ Open*. http://doi.org/10.1136/bmjopen-2014-007206

Green, D., & Latchford, G. (2012). *Maximising the benefits of psychotherapy: A practice-based evidence approach*. Chichester: John Wiley & Sons.

Grissom, R. J. (1996). The magical number .7± .2: Meta-meta-analysis of the probability of superior outcome in comparisons involving therapy, placebo, and control. *Journal of Consulting and Clinical Psychology*, 64(5), 973–982.

Huppert, J. D., Bufka, L. F., Barlow, D. H., Gorman, J. M., Shear, M. K., & Woods, S. W. (2001). Therapists, therapist variables, and cognitive-behavioral therapy outcome in a multicenter trial for panic disorder. *Journal of Consulting and Clinical Psychology*, 69(5), 747–755.

Ilardi, S. S., & Craighead, W. E. (1994). The role of nonspecific factors in cognitive-behavior therapy for depression. *Clinical Psychology: Science and Practice*, 1(2), 138–155.

Jacobson, N. S., & Truax, P. (1991). Clinical significance: A statistical approach to defining meaningful change in psychotherapy research. *Journal of Consulting and Clinical Psychology*, 59(1), 12.

Jones, L. F. (2007). Iatrogenic interventions with personality disordered offenders. *Psychology, Crime & Law*, 13(1), 69–79. http://doi.org/10.1080/10683160600869809

Lambert, M. J. (2005). Early response in psychotherapy: Further evidence for the importance of common factors rather than 'placebo effects'. *Journal of Clinical Psychology*, 61(7), 855–869. http://doi.org/10.1002/jclp.20130

Lilienfeld, S. O. (2007). Psychological treatments that cause harm. *Perspectives on Psychological Science*, 2(1), 53–70.

Luborsky, L., Diguer, L., Seligman, D. A., Rosenthal, R., Krause, E. D., Johnson, S., et al. (1999). The researcher's own therapy allegiances: A 'wild card' in comparisons of treatment efficacy. *Clinical Psychology: Science and Practice*, 6, 95–106.

Luborsky, L., Rosenthal, R., Diguer, L., Andrusyna, T., Berman, J., Levitt, J., et al. (2002). The Dodo Bird verdict is alive and well – mostly. *Clinical Psychology: Science and Practice*, 9, 2–12.

Marshall, W. L., Fernandez, Y. M., & Serran, G. A. (2003). Process variables in the treatment of sexual offenders: A review of the relevant literature. *Aggression and Violent Behavior*, 8, 205–234.

Marshall, W. L., Serran, G., Moulden, H., Mulloy, R., Fernandez, Y. M., Mann, R., & Thornton, D. (2002). Therapist features in sexual offender treatment: Their reliable identification and influence on behaviour change. *Clinical Psychology & Psychotherapy*, 9(6), 395–405. http://doi.org/10.1002/cpp.335

McKay, K. M., Imel, Z. E., & Wampold, B. E. (2006). Psychiatrist effects in the psychopharmacological treatment of depression. *Journal of Affective Disorders*, 92(2–3), 287–290. http://doi.org/10.1016/j.jad.2006.01.020

Messer, S., & Wampold, B. (2002). Let's face facts: Common factors are more potent than specific therapy ingredients. *Clinical Psychology: Science and Practice*, 9, 21–25.

O'Brien, K., Sullivan, D., & Daffern, M. (2016). Integrating individual and group-based offence-focussed psychological treatments: Towards a model for best practice. *Psychiatry, Psychology and Law*. http://doi.org/10.1080/13218719.2016.1150143

Ogles, B. M., Lunnen, K. M., & Bonesteel, K. (2001). Clinical significance: History, application, and current practice. *Clinical Psychology Review*, 21(3), 421–446.

Polaschek, D. L. L. (2011). Many sizes fit all: A preliminary framework for conceptualizing the development and provision of cognitive–behavioral rehabilitation programs for offenders. *Aggression and Violent Behavior*, 16(1), 20–35. http://doi.org/10.1016/j.avb.2010.10.002

Rice, M. E., Harris, G. T., & Cormier, C. A. (1992). An evaluation of a maximum security therapeutic community for psychopaths and other mentally disordered offenders. *Law and Human Behavior*, 16(4), 1–14.

Rosen, G. M., & Davison, G. C. (2003). Psychology should list empirically supported principles of change (ESPs) and not credential trademarked therapies or other treatment packages. *Behavior Modification, 27*(3), 300–312. http://doi.org/10.1177/0145445503253829

Rosenzweig, S. (1936). Some implicit common factors in diverse methods of psychotherapy. *American Journal of Orthopsychiatry*, 412–415.

Ross, E. C., Polaschek, D. L. L., & Ward, T. (2008). The therapeutic alliance: A theoretical revision for offender rehabilitation. *Aggression and Violent Behavior, 13*(6), 462–480. http://doi.org/10.1016/j.avb.2008.07.003

Stiles, W. B. (2006). Assimilation and the process of outcome: Introduction to a special section. *Psychotherapy Research, 16*(4), 389–392. http://doi.org/10.1080/10503300600735497

16
CONCLUSIONS AND FUTURE DIRECTIONS

Jason Davies and Claire Nagi

We have clearly come a long way since the arguments of 'nothing works' in the 1970s; however, we are now at a point where another surge of research and innovation is required. In this chapter we will consider some of what can already be evidenced in relation to individual therapies and present some of the issues which face those providing psychologically based therapies in forensic settings. One essential task is to extend the limited evidence base through practitioners and researchers combining forces to develop our knowledge and understanding of what works, who it works for, why it works and how effects can be maximised.

The use of psychological therapies as part of a rehabilitation agenda within forensic settings has been shown to be valid and useful. This has been reflected in both an expanding 'what works' literature (e.g. Craig, Dixon, & Gannon, 2013) and in the funding allocated to such treatments by governments around the world. However, whilst there has been a great deal of focus on group-based treatment, the application of individually tailored and delivered psychological interventions has been largely overlooked. This is despite the current emphasis on idiographic formulation as the foundation for treatment (e.g. Sturmey & McMurran, 2011). As we have seen in this volume, there are many types of individual intervention that might be provided in forensic settings and many important reasons why an individualised approach might be selected over that of a group. Whilst the evidence provided by the authors shows some efficacy in forensic settings, attention to evidencing the impact of individual treatment on risk and other needs has been largely neglected. However, there is a wealth of research into treatment efficacy that has been undertaken in non-forensic settings. Together the evidence points towards a possible phenomenon of 'treatment equivalence' as discussed in Chapter 15. However, this may present us with a new version of Martinson's 'nothing works' – many therapies work, at least to some degree, but maybe not for the reasons we think they do. We are therefore faced with an important set of challenges – how do we maximise positive outcomes and develop our understanding of what works, why it works, what features of treatment are most important for whom, and how treatment harms can be recognised and minimised when they arise?

The chapters in Part I provide us with treatment options relating to clearly articulated theories and models of understanding and change. Each of these has a set of principles, and knowledge and skill competencies that help to define the therapy and the practice of the therapist using that approach. Together with the evidence already gathered and research being undertaken or yet to come, these therapies provide an optimistic foundation for advancing treatment in order to reduce risk, develop prosocial options for living and address common needs such as past trauma, attachment/relationship problems, social exclusion, and symptoms associated with mental health problems commonly experienced by those in forensic services. In this chapter we will consider a number of 'hot topics' that we believe need to be attended to in order to progress our understanding of psychological therapies within forensic settings, and to identify ways to maximise the gains that can be made. Whilst many of these are general issues, they will be considered from an individual treatment standpoint.

Selecting the approach to and modality of treatment

Decisions about the modality of delivery (typically group *or* individual), and the therapeutic model to be employed have often been governed by practical choices and service needs rather than a detailed understanding of what is likely to be most effective for a given individual. In many ways this is a reflection of the status of the current evidence and the availability of resources. For example, in many services the treatment available will be predetermined by the number, training and experience of the staff employed to deliver therapies. This has a significant impact on our ability to drive forward the evidence base as most services will not be able to make simple choices such as the gender of the therapist, let alone have options as to which (if any) treatment models to employ. A strength of this has been that many services (and the people working within them) have become expert in specific therapy models and in adapting the model (and even the therapist's approach) to meet need, provide interventions for criminogenic factors and address responsivity issues. With CBT-informed group approaches, for example, this has evidently led to an increase in rehabilitation and delivered outcomes such as a reduction in recidivism *for some*. However, this has also meant that there has been limited flexibility to meet need or to 'think strategically' about questions such as what might be the most effective and efficient approach for each individual in order to maximise gains. Selecting which treatment to employ may not be of primary importance if the major factors determining treatment outcome are therapy-neutral common factors and the qualities and competencies of the therapist themselves. However, as Part I lays testament to, many believe that there are features of different treatment approaches that are responsible for individual change and it may be that our approaches to research are not sufficient to detect differential outcomes. A similar issue presents itself when we consider the modality of treatment. Many of the treatments in this book can be offered in an individual or group format; however, it is only recently that several authors have begun to provide some examination of, and guidance for, making decisions about individual and group treatment. As we have seen in Chapter 12, there is a growing use of group and individual treatment – combined modality treatment – the argument being that each modality may be particularly suited to certain functions. Davies (in press) has examined the uses of each modality whilst O'Brien, Sullivan, & Daffern (2016) and Polaschek (2011) have begun to develop decision heuristics for selecting the modality. What is clear from these authors is that individually delivered interventions are likely to have a key role, perhaps with the most complex individuals. However, knowing when to make use of each treatment modality is a critical issue, and work is needed to develop and test the decision-making heuristics described. If nothing else, different therapists and modalities might be important to maximise client allegiance to the change process (see Chapter 15).

Examine fundamental therapy factors and assumptions

In reviewing the literature it appears that there is a current ceiling effect with respect to treatment change as measured at a cohort or group level. This is shown in the proportion of people who benefit from an intervention or more commonly in the percentage reduction in reconviction rates attributed to the intervention. In addition, there appears to be a treatment equivalence effect (as discussed in Chapter 15) in which active effective treatments appear to produce similar overall levels of change. Whilst this may be an artefact of extraneous factors such as an individual not having choice over the treatment (thus not maximising client allegiance) this may also reflect a lack of attention to subtle yet significant responsivity and personalisation factors. Individually tailored treatment has now entered mainstream thinking, in part because of the increased focus on personalised medicine in fields such as cancer treatment.

There are many central features of individual therapy delivery that have become the norm through 'custom and practice' rather than through evidence that they maximise treatment gains. These include the treatment setting, session length, between-session influences and support, and treatment sequencing. We will consider two examples – who delivers the therapy and the dose of therapy.

Determining who delivers therapy

Individual therapies are generally provided by staff with high levels of training and a specialist (therapy-specific) qualification. This contrasts with many of the established group interventions which have moved from delivery by therapists to delivery by 'facilitators', echoing a move from psycho-therapy to psycho-education programmes. This has been, at least in part, a consequence of the level of resources needed to meet the scale of the need. However, the associated manualisation of treatment can negatively impact on treatment delivery and hamper outcomes (see Marshall, 2009). As a way to provide at least partial tailoring (and to maximise engagement) there has been an increased use of combined (group and individual) modality approaches. Yet this may not be the most effective solution, and may continue to limit treatment efficacy, for example if therapist factors (e.g. Luborsky, McLellan, & Diguer, 1997; Marshall et al., 2002) play an important role in therapy outcomes. Allied to this, there are a range of inputs provided to the therapist/treatment facilitator (e.g. training and supervision) because of their expected effect on client outcomes. Though, as reported by Davies (2015) there is limited evidence concerning the impact of therapist supervision on staff and the 'client'. Thus research to determine the impact the therapist factors (e.g. style, training, model, supervision) have on treatment gains need to be undertaken.

Treatment dose

The Risk – Needs – Responsivity (RNR) framework (Andrews & Bonta, 2010) would indicate that those with the highest risk require the highest dose of therapy. However, how might we understand dose in this context? In most cases, dose has been viewed as the total number of sessions or hours of treatment provided (and attended). However, how the 'dose' is delivered, i.e. the frequency of the sessions – something that might be thought of as treatment intensity – might be equally important. Typically, interventions are delivered once or twice weekly; however, research on treatment dose and intensity is sparse. For example, it may be that a few hours in a single block of time each week is insufficient to maximise internalisation and application and that the same number of sessions provided in a more intense way e.g. daily for fewer weeks/months would be advantageous. Further, it may be that some individuals would benefit from a higher treatment intensity than others and that dose and intensity factors vary in different modalities of treatment.

Through these two examples it is clear to see that there are many therapy factors that have not been tested in a systematic way. There is a need to attend to such factors as well as the more 'obvious factors' such as the treatment model, if we are to maximise outcomes in forensic settings.

Investigating how therapies work

An ultimate question is the mechanism through which therapies lead to change. As the chapters in Part I attest to, there are many theories relating to possible mechanisms of change that underpin interventions. This can be seen in the approach to formulation (and the theoretical component of formulation) within the models. In addition, there are more global theories of change such as the Good Lives Model (Ward & Maruna, 2007) and Cognitive Self Change (Bush, Harris, & Parker, 2016). Of course it may be that there are meta-mechanisms that account for change – such as forming a positive relationship – which all therapies will contain. In order to undertake research in this area we need a clear understanding of what each therapy indicates should (and should not) change during the course of therapy, if it works as expected. From this it would be possible to investigate the mechanisms of change, i.e. what is changing and *why*, and to determine whether all elements of the treatment thought to be useful are indeed equal in their impact, are sequential (e.g. one aspect forming a foundation for a later element) or are redundant. An alternative would be to take a therapy-neutral stance and examine evidence-based principles of change examining common factors. Such studies would help determine how treatment effects can be maximised.

Do only what is necessary and consider ways in which psychotherapy may be ineffective/harmful

As we have seen in Part I, there is regularly a need to provide therapy for other issues faced by those in forensic services (such as trauma and mental health needs) in addition to addressing criminogenic factors. However, deciding what to provide treatment for and in which setting (for example in custody or the community) has been the focus of very little research. As well as knowing what to treat and where to deliver it, we also need to know how much of something to provide and when to stop. However, decisions about when to 'stop' are frequently governed by fixed or even arbitrary points (e.g. when a set course of intervention or number of sessions have been delivered). What if one more or one fewer sessions was required to maximise the desired outcomes? In some ways, such outcome questions are also ethical issues that require a considered response (see Chapter 13). In line with many other parts of the world, the Welsh Assembly Government has promoted the notion of prudent healthcare (www.prudenthealthcare.org.uk/, accessed 23 August, 2016). In this framework it is argued that inputs should be sufficient to bring about change but that the least expensive method for achieving this should be attempted first (stepped care). This approach also requires that resources be allocated to the greatest need (c.f. the RNR approach; Andrews & Bonta, 2010) and that evidence be used to reduce variation (e.g. to limit services providing different interventions without evidencing their impact). In addition, co-production is highlighted within the prudent healthcare model. Within forensic contexts it is likely that co-production would need to include a range of voices including victims and perpetrators of crime; however, this under-explored area is probably the topic for a separate text!

It is now more widely accepted that therapies may cause harm (Chapter 15) something that has generally been overlooked. However, there is a possibly less toxic, but equally wasteful, version of causing harm – doing things that are not necessary. Some of the implications of such thinking may raise ethical issues (Chapter 13) and may require engagement with policy makers and those with a vested interest in service provision (e.g. victims and offenders). In addition, refined approaches to health economics may be necessary in order to determine the cost effectiveness of treatments. This will need to include costs for direct and indirect resources in order to avoid developing overly simplistic solutions (see Davies, in press; Wolff, Helminiak, & Tebes, 1997). Focusing on any of these requires detailed consideration of what needs to change and how to assess that change (see below).

The idea of doing only what is needed and ending treatment when change has been achieved requires clear articulation of the treatment components and phases. This also requires that any consolidation and generalisation phases are detailed beforehand. Doing what is necessary may also require us to look beyond individual or group therapy to wider skills and domains of life (e.g. Barnao, Robertson, & Ward, 2010).

Outcome evaluation – everybody's business

Forensic services have generally been poor at scrutinising and reporting treatment outcomes other than for large-scale implementations of complex and lengthy group treatment packages. This is despite there being external bodies such as parole boards and mental health review tribunals who are very focused on what risks and needs an individual presents, and for whom idiographic evidence would be very welcome.

There are many reasons why understanding and quantifying the impact of treatment in forensic settings can be difficult. Typically, the treatments offered are lengthy, with 18–24 months or more of treatment not uncommon. This requires large cohorts and results in very long 'lead-in times' before the whole treatment can be evaluated, especially when using group comparisons. Second, treatments often occur in closed environments where individuals are removed from the contexts, relationships and perhaps opportunities to offend. This may mean that it is a long time after treatment before individuals are able to evidence the impact of treatment in a real world setting. Psychometric testing and important developments such as Offence Paralleling Behaviour (see Daffern, Jones, & Shine, 2010, for an overview, and Davies, Jones, & Howells, 2010, for ways to use this for outcome assessment) can aid in estimating the impact of treatment on offending behaviour or other need even before the individual has returned to the community. However, these are proxy measures and the 'gold standard' remains prosocial improvement and reduced recidivism in real world contexts. It is also important to recognise that offending behaviours are generally low frequency yet high consequence acts meaning even longer may be needed before it is possible to judge if an intervention has made a difference (perhaps five or even ten years). Finally, it is not uncommon for individuals to be subject to multiple 'interventions'. This may include psychological treatments, medications, education, social and occupational interventions as well as the change made to the context/environment when someone is incarcerated. Further, it may be that the sequence in which the interventions are provided is as important as the inputs. Evidently, the more (co-occurring) factors there are, the more difficult it will be to determine which of them have contributed to the change.

In medicine there is an increasing move for surgeons to report their own outcomes (including survival rates) for the work that they do. This has led some specialties adopting criteria that must be met for some interventions to be delivered at a particular centre. It is accepted that there are significant challenges and differences between a discrete medical intervention and a complex and perhaps long-term psychological treatment; however, it would be naïve to argue that assessing the outcomes of each therapist are impossible. This would seem to be a key challenge for the next stage of work in the treatment field. Approaches to individual change evaluation using systematic approaches have been around for a long time and have been outlined for use in forensic settings (e.g. Davies & Sheldon, 2012; Davies, Howells, & Jones, 2007). However, it is also unlikely that any one service would have sufficient resources to provide a vast array of options to enable research to take place to identify what might work best for whom. Given that services typically have different approaches it would be possible to build a research collaboration that would support research across settings in order to enable these critical questions to be more meaningfully considered. Such an international venture would overcome the difficulty of trying to introduce variation in a single service. This would also help address concerns about researcher allegiance biasing outcomes, as it is likely that such a collaboration would naturally include staff with a range of views about treatment, effectiveness and outcomes. Dedicating resources to single case, small scale and international research would allow decisions about approach and modality to be evidence-based.

Conclusion

This book has provided a range of evidence for approaches to individual therapy within forensic contexts. This includes a number of innovations in theory and practice drawn from outside the mainstream of forensic services. In addition, we have considered ideas about when and where individual therapy might be placed within a treatment spectrum or individual pathway as well as a host of ways in which research and practice can develop in this area. Given the progress that has been made in the 40 years since Martinson's conclusions (Martinson, 1974), there is much to be hopeful about regarding how treatments may further develop in the forensic field over the next 40 years.

References

Andrews, D. A., & Bonta, J. (2010). *The psychology of criminal conduct* (5th edn). LexisNexis.

Barnao, M., Robertson, P., & Ward, T. (2010). Good Lives Model Applied to a Forensic Population. *Psychiatry, Psychology and Law, 17*(2), 202–217. http://doi.org/10.1080/13218710903421274

Bush, J., Harris, D., & Parker, R. (2016). *Cognitive Self Change: How offenders experience the world and what we can do about it*. Chichester: John Wiley & Sons.

Craig, L. A., Dixon, L., & Gannon, T. A. (Eds) (2013). *What works in offender rehabilitation: An evidence-based approach to assessment and treatment*. Chichester: Wiley-Blackwell.

Daffern, M., Jones, L., & Shine, J. (Eds) (2010). *Offence paralleling behaviour: A case formulation approach to offender assessment and intervention*. Chichester: Wiley & Sons.

Davies, J. (in press). An examination of individual versus group treatment in correctional settings. In Devon Polaschek, Andrew Day, & Clive Hollin (Eds), *Handbook of psychology and corrections*. Chichester: Wiley.

Davies, J. (2015). *Supervision for forensic practitioners*. London: Routledge.

Davies, J., & Sheldon, K. (2012). Single case methodologies. In K. Sheldon, J. Davies, & K. Howells (Eds), *Research in Practice for Forensic Professionals*. London: Routledge.

Davies, J., Howells, K., & Jones, L. (2007). Evaluating innovative treatments in forensic mental health: A role for single case methodology? *Journal of Forensic Psychiatry & Psychology*, *18*(3), 353–367. http://doi.org/10.1080/14789940701443173

Davies, J., Jones, L., & Howells, K. (2010). Evaluating individual change. In M. Daffern, L. Jones, & J. Shine (Eds) *Offence paralleling behaviour: A case formulation approach to offender assessment and intervention*. Chichester: Wiley & Sons.

Luborsky, L., McLellan, A. T., & Diguer, L. (1997). The psychotherapist matters: Comparison of outcomes across twenty-two therapists and seven patient samples. *Clinical Psychology: Science and Practice*, *4*(1), 53–65.

Marshall, W. L. (2009). Manualization: A blessing or a curse? *Journal of Sexual Aggression*, *15*(2), 109–120. http://doi.org/10.1080/13552600902907320

Marshall, W. L., Serran, G., Moulden, H., Mulloy, R., Fernandez, Y. M., Mann, R., & Thornton, D. (2002). Therapist features in sexual offender treatment: their reliable identification and influence on behaviour change. *Clinical Psychology & Psychotherapy*, *9*(6), 395–405. http://doi.org/10.1002/cpp.335

Martinson, R. (1974). What works? Questions and answers about prison reform. *The Public Interest*, *35*, 22–54.

O'Brien, K., Sullivan, D., & Daffern, M. (2016). Integrating individual and group-based offence-focussed psychological treatments: Towards a model for best practice. *Psychiatry, Psychology and Law*. http://doi.org/10.1080/13218719.2016.1150143

Polaschek, D. L. L. (2011). Many sizes fit all: A preliminary framework for conceptualizing the development and provision of cognitive–behavioral rehabilitation programs for offenders. *Aggression and Violent Behavior*, *16*(1), 20–35. http://doi.org/10.1016/j.avb.2010.10.002

Sturmey, P., & McMurran, M. (2011). *Forensic case formulation*. Chichester: John Wiley & Sons.

Ward, T., & Maruna, S. (2007). *Rehabilitation*. London: Routledge.

Wolff, N., Helminiak, T. W., & Tebes, J. K. (1997). Getting the cost right in cost-effectiveness analyses. *American Journal of Psychiatry*, *154*(6), 736–743.

SUBJECT INDEX

Note: figures are denoted by *italics*, tables by **bold** font and notes by the suffix 'n'

9/11 terrorist attacks 92

ACAT (Association for Cognitive Analytic Therapy) 49, 50
ACT (Acceptance and Commitment Therapy) 4, 11–27
activity theory 41
Adaptive Information Processing model (AIP) 85, 89, 91, 93
adolescents 21, 51, 52, 53, 92, 93, 157
Adverse Childhood Experiences study 96
affective mentalising 103, 104, 110–11, 113, 114
affiliative: behaviour 73, 80; emotions 59, 60, *75*; relationships 65, 68, 75
ALERT database 250
American Psychological Association (APA) 21, 62, 92, 229, 244
Angry Child mode 159, 163, **165**, 169, 171, 172, 173, *173*
Angry Protector mode 163–4, **165**, *173*
Anna Freud website 116
arousal: hypo/hyperarousal 181, 182, 189, 192–3; physiological 31, 101, 102, 104, 106, 109, 110, 111, 113, 169, 182, 184, 193
art therapy 17, 110, 111–12, 168, 172, 175

ASPD (Antisocial Personality Disorder) 22, 169, 171, 173; MBT and 100, 102, 104, 105–8, 110–11, 112, 114, 115
Assimilation Model 152, 250
Association for Contextual Behavioural Science (ACBS) 18, 19
attachment system 59, 68, 75, 78, 89, 101, 146, 182; ASPD and 105, 163; BPD and 104, 108; MBT and 102, 104, 109, 110–11, 112, 113; Schema Therapy and 158, **158**, 160, 162, 174; Sensorimotor psychotherapy and 180, 181, 182, 183, 184, 185, 187, 188, 192
autism spectrum disorders (ASD) 148, 166, *167*, 168; Asperger syndrome 71, 79, 168
automatic-controlled (implicit-explicit) mentalising 103, 104, 111–12
automatic thoughts 29, 30, **30**, **31**
avoidance strategies 12, 13, 14–15, 16–17, 19, 20, 23, 36, 72, 73, 153
avoidant coping modes domain 159, 163, **165**, 168, *173*

behavioural interventions 161
beliefs 29–30, **30**, **31**, 36–7, 46; core (implicit) 29–30, **30**, 37, 86, 88, 89, 94, 95, 131, 185; EMDR and 85, 86, 88, 93,

266 Subject Index

94, 95; Sensorimotor psychotherapy and 180, 183, 185
Bible 63
blocks to compassion 78–9, 80
BLS (bilateral stimulation) 87, 90–1, 94–5
boundaries 158, **158**, 201; in supervision 229, 233, 237–8; in therapy 16, 30, 44, 45, 48, 102, 160, 187, 190–1, 201, 204, 233
BPD (Borderline Personality Disorder) 5, 53, 55, 56, 100–17, 206–7; Schema Therapy and 158, 159, 169–70, 171, 173, 174
brain 61, 64, 65, 69, 73–4, 77, 78, 89, 96; injuries 21, 60, 79; Sensorimotor psychotherapy and 180, 181–2, 188, 189
British Association for Behavioural and Cognitive Psychotherapies (BABCP) 33
British Psychological Society 152
Buddhism 60, 67, 70
Bully and Attack mode 162, 163, 165–6, **165**, 171, *173*
Bully personality type 20

callousness 22, **30**, 36, 37, 65, 67, 72, 114, 135, 164
care-giving 66, 67–8, *68*, 69, 70
CAT (Cognitive Analytic Therapy) 4–5, 28, 41–58, *53*
CBT (Cognitive Behavioural Therapy) 2, 4, 11, 15, 28–40, **30**, **31**, 150, 154, 181, 229, 235, 258; ACT and 4, 21, 22, 25; EMDR and 92; IDD and 150; PTSD and 93; recidivism 11, 34, 258; Schema Therapy and *167*, 169; sex offenders and 85–6
CBT Supervision: Adherence and Guidance Evaluation (SAGE) 232
Center for Somatic Studies 187
Centre for Workforce Intelligence (CfWI) 50
CFT (Compassion Focused Therapy) 5, 59–84, *68*, *75*
character-focused interventions 184–5, 188
characteristics of clients 19–21, 33–4, 50–1, 91, 130, 149–51, 166–9, *167*, 188–9
childhood experiences, adverse 22, 62, 96, 104; CAT and 42, 44, 48, 51, 52, *53*; CBT and 35, 36, 37; CFT and 60, 62, 63, 66, 68, 72, 77; MBT and 101, 104, 112; psychodynamic psychotherapy and 146, 147; Schema Therapy and 157, 161, 163, 172, *173*; Sensorimotor psychotherapy and 181, 182, 184, 185, 187; sex offenders and 85, 86; sexual abuse 88, 89, 90–1, 92, 93, 94–5, 132, 135, 172, 190; *see also* attachment system
child modes domain 159, 163, **165**, *173*, 175
Chromis programme 204, 207
clarification-oriented psychotherapy 170
clean pain 13, 14, 16
Clinical Supervision Essentials Book Series 229
Cochrane: Library 151; Review 93
cognitive mentalising 104, 111, 113–14
cognitive techniques 161
combined modality approaches 6, 197–212, **199–200**, 260
compassion *see* CFT (Compassion Focused Therapy)
competencies, care-focussed 66, 67, 68–9, *68*, 70, 71, 72, 74, 75, 77, 80
Complaining Protector mode **165**, 172
Compliant Surrenderer mode **165**
'concrete thinking' 102
Conning Manipulator mode 162, 163, 164, **165**, *173*
constructivism 28
Constructivist and Existential College of the UK Council for Psychotherapy 130
Contact with the Present Moment 12, 13, 15, 16, 20, 23
contextualising function of supervision 229
Continuous Professional Development (CPD) 33
coping strategies 11, 14, 15, 16, 42, 54, 59, 88, 145, 157, 158–9, 160, 161–2, 169, 175; avoidant coping modes 159, 163, **165**, 168, *173*
core (implicit) beliefs 29–30, **30**, 37, 86, 88, 89, 94, 95, 131, 185
core pain 42, *53*, 54, 55
counter-transference 44, 144, 146, 166
Court Diversion Service 151–2
cruelty 61–4; *see also* callousness
CSA (childhood sexual abuse) 36, 72, 88, 89, 90–1, 92, 93, 94–5, 132, 135, 190

dangerous world **30**, 37, 88, 89
DBT (Dialectical Behaviour Therapy) 206–7

Subject Index

Defusion 12–13, 15, 17, 20, 23–4
The De-Identification Standard of Disclosures of Protected Health Information 22
Demanding Parent mode **165**
Detached Protector mode 159, 160, 162, **165**, 169, 173, *173*
Detached Self-Soother mode **165**, 168, 169, 171, *173*
Dialectical Behaviour Therapy (DBT) 107, 204
dilemmas 42, 43, *53*, 54, 55
dirty pain 13, 14
domains, mode (schema therapy) 158, **158**, 159, 163, 164, *164*, **165**
Drama: Therapy 172, 175; Triangle 238
drop-out rates 51, 170, 201, 205, 206, 207, 248, 249
dual relationships 213, 214, 221, 222–5

EDTs (Evidence Directed Therapists) 251–2
ego 144–5, 146, 147, 149
Ego Psychology School 145
EMDR (Eye Movement Densensitisation and Reprocessing) 5, 85–99
emotional needs 157–9, **158**, 160, 161–2
emotional pain 47, 54, 55, 105, 158, 159, 161, 163, 173
emotions: affiliative 59, 60, *75*; regulating 74–7, *75*, 79, 218; *see also* feelings
empathic confrontation 160–1, 172
empathy 93, 102, 144; ASPD and 104, 106–7, 111; CFT and 59–60, 63, 65, 67, *68*, 69, 71–2, 73, 74, 76–7, 78, 79; of therapist 45, 143, 153; for victims 22, 55, 93, 105–6, 135, 154, 221
Enhanced Thinking Skills 112, 114
Entitled personality type 20
entitlement 29, **30**, 36, 37, 88, **158**, 163, 218
Epictetus 28–9
Essentials in Clinical Supervision 228
ethical issues 6, 213–27, 229, 249–50, 261
Evershed, S. 206, 237
Evidence Based Clinical Supervision 232
evidence, status of 21–2, 33–4, 51, 91, 114–16, 130–2, 151, 169–72, 189, 204–5, 238–9, 257, 259
Evidence Supported Therapies (ESTs) 244
evolutionary approach 59–84, *68*, *75*

experiential: avoidance 15, 16, 19, 23; learning 91, 165, 187, 236; techniques 37, 157, 161, 173
explicit-implicit mentalising *see* automatic-controlled mentalising
external/internal mentalising 103, 104, 105, 106, 110–11, 113, 163
Eye Movement Densensitisation and Reprocessing International Association (EMDRIA) 91

feelings 11, 12, 13, 15, 16, 17; ACT and 19, 20, 24; ASPD and 105–6, 111; CAT and 42–3, 44, 47, 48, 54, 55, 56, 61; CBT and 28, 35, 36, 37; CFT and *68*, 69, 70, 71, 73, 78, 79–80; EMDR and 94, 95; hidden 144, 145, *145*, 147, 153; IDD 148–9, 152, 153, 154; MBT and 100, 102–3, 108, 109, 113; PCT and 132, 135; psychodynamic psychotherapy and 143, 144, 145, *145*, 146, 147, 152, 153, 154; Schema Therapy and 158, **158**, 159, 161, 162, 168, 171, 173; Sensorimotor psychotherapy and 183–4, 191–2; unconscious 143, 144, 145, *145*, 147, 153; *see also* emotions; TFPs (Thoughts, Feelings, People)
Fixed Role Therapy 121, 126, 129
flexibility, psychological: ACT and 12, 13, 15–16, 20, 21, 23; CBT and 32; modeling 15, 16, 20, 22
forensic modes 163–4, **165**
Fundamentals of Clinical Supervision 228
Fundamental Themes in Clinical Supervision 228

genetic dispositions 59, 64, 65, 67, 76, 77, 79, 105
Good Lives Model (GLM) 14, 46, 49, 60, 129, 137, 201, 205–6, 218, 236, 260
group-based therapy 2, 6, 14–16, 32, 107, 111, 112, 115, 136, 151, 157, 175, 197–212, **199–200**, 257, 258, 259
GTRP (General Treatment and Recovery Programme) 205
guilt 68, 69, 70, 72–4, 80, 221

Handbook of Psychotherapy Supervision 228
Hands of Control 18, 24
Healthy Adult mode 161, 162, 163, **165**, 174

268   Subject Index

healthy lifestyle 15, 17
Healthy Modes 163, **165**
Hertfordshire, University of 129
humanistic therapy 2, 161, 229
human rights 6, 213, 214–16, 217, 218, 219, 220, 221, 222, 223, 224–5
hypo/hyperarousal 181, 182, 189, 192–3

IAPT (Improving Access to Psychological Therapies) 50
id 144
IDD (Intellectual and Developmental Disability) 3, 5, 92, 142, 146, 147–56, 166, *167*, 168
implicit (core) beliefs 29–30, **30**, 37, 86, 88, 89, 94, 95, 131, 185
implicit-explicit (automatic-controlled) mentalising 103, 104, 111–12
Impulsive Child mode **165**, 169, 171
Institute for Psychotherapy and Disability 149
Institutional Adjustment 15, 18
Integrated Developmental Model 231
intermediate beliefs 29, **30**
internal/external mentalising 103, 104, 105, 106, 110–11, 113, 163
International Centre for Prison Studies 11
International Journal of Applied Psychoanalytic Studies 151
International Society for Schema Therapy (ISST) 165
Interpersonal Process Recall (IPR) 235
IQ 148, 150

justice: communicative/restorative 219; consequential 219, 220–1; restorative 73; retributive 73, 219, 220

laddering 121, 127–8
Lessons From an Iceberg 20
limited reparenting 160, 172
Lonely Child mode **165**, 171, *173*

maladaptive schemas, early 157, 158–9, **158**, 161–2, 163, 171
Manchester Clinical Supervision Scale 232
manipulative behaviour 16, *53*, 111, 114; *see also* Conning Manipulator mode
MBT (Mentalisation Based Therapy) 5, 100–20

mental health 3, 4, 14, 64, 77, 79, 92, 146, **199**, 202, 261; ACT and 18, 21; CAT and 41, 45; CBT and 31; CFT and 59, 60; EMDR and 92, 93; PCT and 127, 130
mindfulness 32, 60, 69, 76, 77–8, 183, 188, 189; ACT and 4, 11, 12, 14, 15, 17, 18, 19, 22, 23
mode domains (schema therapy) 158, **158**, 159, 163, 164, *164*, **165**
Mode Observation Scale 171
modes, forensic 163–4, **165**
Mollification (PICTS) 29
mood checks 31, 143–4
mood disorders 166, *167*, 169
moral: acquaintances 223, 224; repair 213, 214, 221–2, 224–5; rights 214–16; status 218–19
morality 71–2, 79, 80
motivation 2, 102, 122, 160, **199**, **200**, 221; ACT and 14, 16, 17, 19; CBT and 29, 32, 33–4; compassion as 59, 60, 64, 65–70, *68*, 71, 73, 76, 77, 78, 79, 80; EMDR and 85, 90, 93; psychodynamic psychotherapy and 149, 150; for treatment 44, 45, 90, 93, 149, 150, 162, 201, 204, 218
multimodal therapy 28
Multiple Self-States Model (MSSM) 43, 45, 53

narcissism 20, 52, 53, 54, 64, 106, 114, 158, 169, 170, 171
National Association for the Dually Diagnosed 149
National Library of Medicine (NLM) 21
National Offender Management Service (NOMS) 114
National Probation Service 115
Netherlands 165, 171, 172
New Harbingers Publications 19
NHS (National Health Service) 5, 114, 115, 131, 142
NICE (National Institute for Health and Clinical Excellence) 107
non-judgement 69
Northern Kentucky University 93

object relations 41, 49, 146, 161
Obsessive-Compulsive Overcontroller 163, 164, **165**
offence drivers 85, 88, 89, 91, 94

Offence Paralleling Behaviours (OPB) 48, 198–201, 262
Offender Behaviour Programmes (OBP) 197
OPD (Offender Personality Disorder) pathway 56, 114–16
other/self mentalisation 103, 106, 110, 111, 113, 114
other-self patterns of relating 42, 53–4
outcome evaluation 6, 201, 244–5, 246, 248, 262–3
overcompensatory modes domain 159, 163, 164, **165**, *173*, 175
overcontroller modes 163, 164, **165**
Overt Aggression Scale-Modified (OAS-M) 115

paedophilia 17, 63, 88, 175
pain 13, 14, 16, 21, 42, *53*, 54, 55, 68, 69, 71, 74, 219; emotional 47, 54, 55, 105, 158, 159, 161, 163, 173
Paranoid Overcontroller mode 163, 164, **165**, 172, *173*
parasympathetic nervous system 68, 78–9, 80, 181, 182
Parent Modes domain 159, 163, **165**
paternalism 216, 217
Pathways Model 85, 86, 88–9, 95–6
PCL-R (Psychopathy Checklist-Revised) 114, 171
PCT (Personal Construct Theory) 4, 5, 41, 121–41
Personal Construct: Gateway 130; Psychology Association 130
Personal, Interpersonal, and Community Reinforcement (PIC-R) 29
personality disorders (PDs) 5, 51, 107, 130, 131; case study 52–6, *53*; cluster A *167*, 168; cluster B 162, 166–7, *167*, 168, 170, 171–2, 175; cluster C *167*, 168, 169, 170; combined modality approaches 206–7
personality types 19–20
perspective-taking 12, 69, 71–2, 104, 129
phenotypes 59, 60–1, 62, 64–5, 66–7, 68, 71, 77
PICTS (*Psychological Inventory of Criminal Thinking*) 29
Playful Child mode 163, **165**
Portman and Tavistock NHS Trust 115
Predator mode 163, 164, **165**, 171, 173, *173*

prementalistic modes of thinking 102, 106, 109, 111, 114
Present Moment, Contact with 12, 13, 15, 16, 20, 23
pretend mode 102–3, 105, 106
primary beliefs 29
prosocial behaviour 59–84, 85, 129; ACT and 1, 13, 14, 15, 17, 19, 20, 23
psychic equivalence 102, 104–5, 106, 113, 114
psychodynamic psychotherapy 2, 3, 5, 142–56, *145*, 181
psychoeducation 77–8, 112, 168, 183, **199**, 201, 202, 208, 259
psychopathology 47–8, 49, 64, 70, 71, 109, 167, 217, 248–9; ACT and 19, 20, 21; CAT and 48, 49; CFT and 70, 71; group-based therapy 207; MBT and 174; personality disorders and 107–8, 114; recidivism 167; Schema Therapy and 159, 162, 171, 172, 174; Sensorimotor psychotherapy and 180, 189
psychosis 19, 21, 51, 60, 92; exclusion from therapy 50, 150, 166, *167*, 168, 244
PTSD (post-traumatic stress disorder) 19, 60, 62, 65, 77, 169, 170; Sensorimotor psychotherapy and 182, 184, 189, 192–3
punishment 213, 214, 218–21, 224–5
Punitive Parent mode **165**, 169
purposeful living 4, 12, 13, 24

R&R2 (Reasoning and Rehabilitation program) 205
rational-emotive behaviour therapy 28
Readiness for Dissemination ratings 14
recidivism 262; CBT and 11, 34, 258; combined modality approaches 201, 205; ethical issues and 218, 221, 222, 224; IDD and 150, 151, 152, 154; personality disorders and 166–7; psychodynamic psychotherapy and 151, 154; psychopathology and 167; reducing 85, 88, 143, 162, 171, 197; Schema Therapy and 162, *167*, 171, 174; Sensorimotor psychotherapy and 190; sex offenders and 85–6, 93
Regional Treatment Centre Ontario Sex Offender Program 205
rehabilitation 1, 29, 162, 171, 172, 216, 217–18, 257, 258

Subject Index

relational patterns 41, 42, 43, 44, 45, 46–7, 48, 49, 53–4, *53*, 55, 66–7, 180
repertory grids 55, 121, 125–6, 128, 130–1, 132–6, **133**, *134*
research, future 24–5, 38, 56, 95–6, 116–17, 136–7, 154, 174–5, 192–3, 208–9
restorative function of supervision 229
RFT (Relational Frame Therapy) 12
risk management 5, 17, 32, 33, 127, 218, 229, *233*, 236; CAT and 46, 47, 48, 49; combined modalities 201; ethical issues and 217, 218, 220–1, 222, 223–4; IDD and 152; psychodynamic psychotherapy and 150
Risk, Needs, Responsivity (RNR) 1, 14, 49, 86, 136–7, 197, **199**, 201, 207, 220, 236, 260, 261
role play 161, 165, 166
role relationships 65–6; *see also* RRs (Reciprocal roles)
RP (Relapse Prevention) 85, 86; *see also* recidivism
RRPs (reciprocal role procedures) 42, 43, 46, 47, 51, 53, 54, 55
RRs (reciprocal roles) 42, 43, 44, 45, 46, 47, 48, 49, 54
rupture repair model 46

SAMHSA (Substance Abuse and Mental Health Services Administration) 14, 21, 92, 93
Sand Ridge Secure Treatment Center 96
SAPROF (*Structured Assessment of PROtective Factors for violence risk*) 201
schema mode domains 158, **158**, 159, 163, **165**
schema modes 158–9, 160, 161–2, 163, **165**, 171, 172, 173, 174
schemas, maladaptive 157, 158–9, **158**, 161–2, 163
Schema Therapy (ST) 5, 28, 37, 157–79, *164*, **165**, *167*
SCM (structured clinical management) 115
SDO (social dominance orientation) 64
SDRs (sequential diagrammatic reformulations) 43, 48, 53–4, *53*, 55
secondary beliefs 29, 37
Self-Aggrandiser mode 162, 165–6, **165**, 169, 172, *173*
Self-as-Context (SAC) 12, 13, 15, 16, 23

self-esteem 108, 111, 143
self-focus 61, 64, 66, 67, 72, 74, 110, **199**
self-harm 42, 102, 105, 108, 112, 132, 169, 174, 206–7
self/other mentalisation 103, 106, 110, 111, 113, 114
self-other patterns of relating 42, 53–4
Self-righteous personality type 20
self-self patterns of relating 42, 53–4, 66
self, sense of 43, 53, 55, 61, 72, 73, 78, 105, 106, 125, 131, 163
self-states 43, 48, 52, 53, *53*, 54, 55, 135
Sensorimotor psychotherapy (SP) 5, 180–94
Sensory Learning Program 189
Serenity Prayer 11, 12
sex offenders 33, 63; ACT and 13–14, 17, 20, 22–4; case studies 22–4, 94–5, 132–6, **133**, *134*, 151–4, 190–2; CAT and 51; CBT and 28, 85–6; childhood experiences 85, 86, 89, 90–1, 93, 94–5, 105, 132, 135, 172, 190, 221; combined modality approaches 204, 205–6; EMDR and 85–99; ethical issues 216, 221; IDD and 146, 147; Pathways Model 85, 86, 88–9, 95–6; PCT and 121, 131, 132–6, **133**, *134*, 137; psychodynamic psychotherapy and 149, 151–4; Schema Therapy and 163, 168, 171, 174, 175; Sensorimotor psychotherapy and 190–2; supervision for therapists 238; *see also* paedophilia
shame 5, 14, 77, 79, 94; CFT and 59, 60, 61, 68, 72–4, 77, 78; MBT and 105, 106, 111; PCT and **133**, 135; Schema Therapy and 158, **158**, 171; Sensorimotor psychotherapy and 184, 185, 191, 192
Sheep personality type 20
Skills of Clinical Supervision for Nurses 228
S.M.A.R.T. (Specific, Measurable, Attainable, Realistic, and Timely) goals 14, 17, 19
snags 42–3, *53*, 55
social mentalities 65–70
SDO (social dominance orientation) 64
Socratic method 30, 203
Somatic Experiencing 187
SOTEP (Sex Offender Treatment Evaluation Project) 85–6, 93, **199**, 204
SPI (Sensorimotor Psychotherapy Institute) 187

Subject Index

substance abuse 79, 108, 114, 125, 147, 150, 218; ACT and 15, 16–18, 19, 21, 22; case studies 21–2, 35, 36, 52, *53*, 54, 132; Schema Therapy and 159, 163, 166, *167*, 168–9; as 'trap' 42, *53*, 54
SUDS (Subjective Units of Distress Scale) 87, 88, 94
super-ego 144, 145, 146
supervising therapists 6, 228–42, *233*, 260
Supervision and Clinical Psychology 228
Supervision for Forensic Practitioners 229
Supervision in Clinical Practice 228
Supervision in Social Work 228
sympathetic nervous system 68, 181, 182

target memories 90, 91, 94, 95
teleological mode 102, 105, 106, 111
TFPs (Thoughts, Feelings, People) 12, 13, 14, 16, 17, 18, 19, 22, 23, 24
therapeutic alliance 16, 41, 44, 45–6, 47, 51, 55, 90, 127, **199**, 202, 232, 251
therapies, selecting 258–9
therapists, selecting 243–53, 259–60
therapists, training 18–19, 32–3, 49–50, 56, 91, 116, 129–30, 149, 165–6, 187–8, 250–1
therapy equivalence 6, 203, 209, 244–8, 250, 253, 257, 259
thinking, prementalistic modes of 102, 106, 109, 111, 114
TPPs (target problem procedures) 43, 47, 48, 55
TPs (target problems) 43, 47, 55
transference 44, 55, 144, 147, 149, 153
transference focused therapy (TFT) 169–70
traps 42, 43, *53*, 54, 55
trauma 21, 35, 243, 258, 261; CAT and 42, 55; CFT and 60, 70, 72, 77, 79; EMDR and 5, 85, 86, 87, 89, 90, 92, 93, 96; MBT and 101–2, 104, 108, 114, 116; psychodynamic psychotherapy and 146, 149; Schema Therapy and 158, 161, 163, 173–4; Sensorimotor psychotherapy and 5, 180, 181, 182, 183–4, 188, 192; *see also* PTSD
treatment equivalence 244–8, 257, 259

United States 24, 33, 62, 93, 107, 149, 205–6
University College London 251

valued living 11, 12, 13, 14, 15, 16, 17, 19, 24
victims 34, 73, 131, 135; (lack of) empathy for 22, 55, 93, 105–6, 135, 154, 221; blaming **30**, 37, 89, 91, 132; offenders as 35, 48, 90, **133**, *134*, 135, 214, 221–2
violent offenders 34, 63, 181; ASPD and 105, 106, 115; case studies 35–8, 112–13, 132–6, **133**, *134*, 172–4, *173*, 190–2; CAT and 47, 54; CBT and 35–6; combined modalities 201, 205, 206, 207; MBT and 108, 112–13, 115; PCT and 132–6, **133**, *134*; pychodynamic psychotherapy and 146, 149; Schema Therapy and 162, 163, *164*, 168, 174; Sensorimotor psychotherapy and 186, 188, 190–2
Virginia Center for Behavioural Rehabilitation 96
VOC (Validity of Cognition) scale 87, 88
Vulnerable Child mode 159, 162, 163, **165**, 169, 171, 173, *173*

Welsh Assembly Government 261
WHO (World Health Organization) 63, 93
The Wiley International Handbook of Clinical Supervision 229
WOMBATs (Ways Of Me Behaving And Thinking) 121, 129
women 21, 22, 24, 35, 63–4, 92, 189, 206–7; female staff 191–2, 237; implicit beliefs about 88, 132; personality disorders 107, 108, 111–12, 114, 169, 170, 206; Schema Therapy and 169, 170, 174, 175

young (juvenile) offenders 33, 34, 127, 137, 148, 175

ZPD (Zone Proximal Development) 44–5, 47, 48, 236

AUTHOR INDEX

Abracen, J. 205
Ainsworth, M. 101
Alvarez, A. 148, 149
Andrews, D. A. 1, 29
Armstrong, P. 235
Athlin, E. 233–4
Atkinson, R. 207
Austin, M. A. 78

Bakhtin, M. M. 41
Bambling, M. 238
Bamelis, L. L. M. 170
Barbaree, H. E. 89
Barnes, K. L. *233*
Baron-Cohen, S. 107
Bartels, A. A. J. 71
Bateman, A. W. 102, 104, 105
Beail, N. 5, 142–56
Beauchamp, T. L. 217
Beck, A. T. 28, 31, 157
Beck, J. 31
Benner, P. 231
Bennett, A. 207
Bennett, D. 46
Bernard, J. M. 234
Bernstein, D. 5, 157–79
Black, L. 33–4
Black, N. 246
Blagys, M. D. 143
Blair, J. 71
Blair, K. 71

Blatt, S. J. 246
Bloom, M. 247
Bolz, M. 76
Bonta, J. 1
Bowlby, J. 101, 146, 150–1
Brillhart, D. 4, 11–27

Carich, M. S. 86
Carpenter, J. 71
Cathell, K. 86
Cernkovich, S. A. 129
Childress, J. F. 217
Clarke, J. 239
Clarke, S. 15
Clayton, C. 5, 85–99
Collier, J. 112
Colwick, R. 86
Cowell, J. M. 71–2
Craighead, W. E. 246
Curren, R. 151

Daffern, M. 259
Danesh, J. 107
Datta, P. C. 93
Davey, L. 32
Davidson, R. J. 183
Davies, J. 1–8, 203, 209, 228–42, 243–56, 257–64
Day, A. 4, 28–40, 230, 236–7
Decety, K. 71–2
den Boer, J. A. 71

Di Fazio, R. 205
DiGiuseppe, R. 29–30
Dixon, L. 207
Donnellan, M. B. 61
D'Orazio, D. M. 86
Doty, J. 76
Dowden, C. 29
Dragioti, E. 246
D'Silva, K. 248
Duff, R. A. 219–20
Duggan, C. 206–7, 248

Eddins, R. 15
Ellis, A. 28
Ellis, M. V. 239
Evans, A. L. *233*

Falender, C. A. 233
Farrell, J. M. 170
Fazel, S. 107
Fernández, P. 22
Finlay, P. 93
Fischer, J. 183, 247
Fonagy, P. 102, 104, 105, 115
forensic modes 163–4, 165
Fransella, F. 131
Freeden, M. 215
Freeman, A. 29–30
Freitas, G. J. 239
Freud, A. 146, 150
Freud, S. 142, 144, 145

Galinsky, A. D. 71
Gannon, T. A. 38, 88
Garcia-Moreno, C. 63
García, P. 21
Gazzola, V. 71
Giesen-Bloo, J. 169
Gilbert, P. 5, 59–84
Gilin, D. 71
Gillette, C. 189
Gillie, B. L., 78
Gilligan, J. 111
Giordano, P. C. 129, 131
Glaser, B. 217
González-Menéndez, A. 21, 22
Goodyear, R. K. 234
Graham-Howard, M. L. 51
Green, David 253
Greenwald, R. 86

Grissom, R. J. 245
Gudjonsson, G. 205

Hall-Lord, M. L. 233–4
Hamilton, L. 237–8
Hanson, R. K. 46
Harkins, L. 207
Hawkins, P. 232
Hayes, S. 15–16, 21
Heber, S. A. 233
Hensley, B. 93
Hermanto, N. 70
Hilsenroth, M. J. 143
Hollin, C. R. 205
Holloway, E. L. 232
Holton, E. F., III 235
Howells, K. 32
Huppert, J. D. 248

Ilardi, S. S. 246

Jackson, T. 147, 151
James, C. W. 151
James, I. A. 235
Jones, D. 205, 206–7
Jones, L. 4, 121–41, 249
Jung, K. 145

Kaiser, E. 189
Keenan, T. 88
Kelly, G. A. 4, 126, 129
Kersten, T. 165
Keulen-de Vos, M. 5, 157–79
Keysers, C. 71
Klein, M. 5, 145, 146, 150
Knabb, J. J. 51
Knowles, M. S. 235
Kolb, D. A. 236
Korenini, B. 128
Kozar, C. 32
Krengel, M. 239
Kroner, D. 15

Ladany, N. 239
Lambert, M. J. 247
Lamelas, F. 21
Landenberger, N. A. 34
Lanza, P. 21
Latchford, G. 253
Laws, D. R. 46

Lazar, S. 189
Lazarus, A. 28
Levenson, J. S. 205–6
Levine, P. 184
Levin, M. 21
Lilienfeld, S. O. 249
Lindsay, W. R. 150
Lipsey, M. W. 33, 34
Lizzio, A. J. 230
Lobbestael, J. 169
Looman, J. 205
Love, C. C. 233
Low, G. 206–7
Luborsky, L. 246
Luoma, J. 15–16
Luyten, P. 103

Maddux, W. W. 71
Mahoney, M. J. 28
Malan, D. H. 144, 145, *145*, 147
Marie-Blackburn, I. 235
Marshall, L. E. 28, 32, 33
Marshall, W. L. 28, 89
Martinson, R. 1, 263
McCarthy, L. 248
McDonald, M. M. 61
McGauley, G. 5, 100–20
McGuire, J. 3
McMurran, M. 45
McNeill, B. W. 231, 234, 235
Meffert, H. 71
Meichenbaum, D. 28
Mills, J. 15
Milne, D. 232, 235
Mischel, W. 128
Mitchell, D. 29–30, 71
Mitzman, S. F. 43
Mooney, K. A. 28
Moore, M. E. 86
Moreton, G. 222
Morgan, R. 15
Murphy, N. 5, 180–94

Nadort, M. 170
Nagi, Claire 1–8, 205, 228–42, 243–56, 257–64
Navarrete, C. D. 61
Needs, A. 4, 121–41
Nelson, M. L. *233*
Nickels, J. W. 215

Norris, M. 127
Novaco, R. W. 33–4

O'Brien, K. 206, 208, 259
O'Donoghue, K. B. 231
Ogden, P. 180, 182, 183
Orme, J. G. 247

Padesky, C. A. 28
Page, S. 231
Parry, G. 46
Peters, R. 20
Pistorello, J. 21
Polaschek, D. L. L. 34, 88, 122, 208, 209, 259
Pollock, Philip 5, 51
Porges, S. W. 78, 181
Power, M. 206–7
Pratt, D. D. 236
Proctor, B. 229

Ramm, M. 33–4
Rees-Jones, A. 205
Renwick, S. J. 33–4
Ricci, R. 5, 85–99
Rice, M. E. 248
Riniolo, T. C. 78
Rodríguez, F. 22
Rolfe, G. 231
Rudolph, J. L. 129
Ryle, A. 28, 41, 46

Salmon, K. 220
Sappla, E. 76
Schult, D. 239
Seeler, L. 29–30
Shannon, K. 5
Shaw, I. A. 170
Sheldon, K. 247
Shohet, R. 232
Siegel, D. 189
Siegert, R. J. 85–6
Singer, T. 76
Stacey, J. M. 151
Steele, K. 189
Stoltenberg, C. D. 231, 234, 235
Sullivan, D. 259
Swanson, R. A. 235

Tafrate, R. C. 29
Tang-Smith, E. 73

Tew, J. 207
Thayer, J. F. 78
Theander, K. 233–4
Triggiano, P. J. *233*

van der Hart, O. 189
van der Kolk, B. 182, 189
Villagrá, P. 22
Vygotsky, L. S. 41, 45

Walker, M. U. 221
Wallace, J. 93
Ward, T. 5, 15–16, 38, 45, 46, 85–6, 88, 205–6, 213–27
Watson, S. , 131

Webber, M. A. 170
Willis, G. M. 205–6
Wilson, K. L. 230
Winnicott, D. 149, 150–1
Winter, D. 129, 131
Wosket, V. 231

Yakeley, J. 115
Yip, Y. V-C. 205
Young, J. 5, 28, 158, 159, 163
Young, S. 205

Zaki, J. 71
Zuroff, D. C. 246

Taylor & Francis eBooks

Helping you to choose the right eBooks for your Library

Add Routledge titles to your library's digital collection today. Taylor and Francis ebooks contains over 50,000 titles in the Humanities, Social Sciences, Behavioural Sciences, Built Environment and Law.

Choose from a range of subject packages or create your own!

Benefits for you
- » Free MARC records
- » COUNTER-compliant usage statistics
- » Flexible purchase and pricing options
- » All titles DRM-free.

REQUEST YOUR FREE INSTITUTIONAL TRIAL TODAY
Free Trials Available
We offer free trials to qualifying academic, corporate and government customers.

Benefits for your user
- » Off-site, anytime access via Athens or referring URL
- » Print or copy pages or chapters
- » Full content search
- » Bookmark, highlight and annotate text
- » Access to thousands of pages of quality research at the click of a button.

eCollections – Choose from over 30 subject eCollections, including:

Archaeology	Language Learning
Architecture	Law
Asian Studies	Literature
Business & Management	Media & Communication
Classical Studies	Middle East Studies
Construction	Music
Creative & Media Arts	Philosophy
Criminology & Criminal Justice	Planning
Economics	Politics
Education	Psychology & Mental Health
Energy	Religion
Engineering	Security
English Language & Linguistics	Social Work
Environment & Sustainability	Sociology
Geography	Sport
Health Studies	Theatre & Performance
History	Tourism, Hospitality & Events

For more information, pricing enquiries or to order a free trial, please contact your local sales team:
www.tandfebooks.com/page/sales

 **The home of Routledge books**

www.tandfebooks.com

Printed in Great Britain
by Amazon